The

IBM

S...

The
IBM LAN Server
Sourcebook

How to Connect Your Business at Warp Speed

Pat Scherer

Charlie Brown

John Wiley & Sons, Inc.

New York ■ Chichester ■ Brisbane ■ Toronto ■ Singapore

Publisher: Katherine Schowalter
Editor: Theresa Hudson
Managing Editor: Robert Aronds
Text Design: Tenenbaum Design
Composition: Impressions, a division of Edwards Brothers, Inc.

Designations used by companies to distinguish their products are often claimed as trademarks. In all instances where John Wiley & Sons, Inc. is aware of a claim, the product names appear in initial capital or all capital letters. Readers, however, should contact the appropriate companies for more complete information regarding trademarks and registration.

This text is printed on acid-free paper.

This publication is designed to provide accurate and authoritative information in regard to the subject matter covered. It is sold with the understanding that the publisher is not engaged in rendering legal, accounting, or other professional service. If legal advice or other expert assistance is required, the services of a competent professional person should be sought.

The authors and publishers of this book have applied their best efforts in creating this book; however, we make no warranty of any kind, expressed or implied, with regard to the documentation contained herein. The authors and publishers shall not be liable in any event for incidental or consequential damages in connection with, or arising out of, the use of the information in this book.

The product descriptions are based on the best information available at the time of publication. Product prices vary with supplier and are subject to change without notice. Contact the product suppliers for the latest pricing and product information.

All views expressed in this book are solely the authors' and should not be attributed to IBM or any other IBM employee.

Some of the figures used in this book incorporate clip art from Lotus Corporation's Freelance Graphics library.

Trademarks

Apple Computer, Inc.: Apple, AppleTalk, Macintosh, System 7
Artisoft, Inc.: LANtastic
Banyan Systems, Inc.: Banyan, Banyan Vines
Client Server Networking: Checkit, Watchit
Intel Corp.: Intel, Pentium
IBM Corp.: Anynet/2, AIX, AS/400, Communication Manager/2, Database Manager/2, High Performance File System, IBM, LAN Distance, LAN Netview, LAN Network Manager, LAN Requester, LAN Server, MVS, Netview for OS/2, NTS/2, OS/2, OS/2 Named Pipes, Netview, OS/400, PowerPC, Presentation Manager, PS/2, Risc System/6000, RS/6000, SNA, System Performance Manager/2, Ultimedia, VM, Warp, Warp Connect, WinOS2, Workplace Shell, Workplace OS
Lotus Development Corp.: cc:Mail, Lotus, Lotus Notes, Smartsuite
Massachusetts Institute of Technology: Kerberos
Micropolis, Inc.: Raidware
Microsoft Corp.: LAN Manager, Microsoft, Windows, Windows for Workgroups, Windows NT, Windows NT Advanced
Novell, Inc.: IPX, NetWare, NetWare Loadable Module, Novell
Open Software Foundation, Inc.: DCE, OSF
Radion, Inc.: OASAS
UNIX Systems Laboratories, Inc.: UNIX
WATCOM, Inc.: REXX

Library of Congress Cataloging-in-Publication Data:

0471-13170-9

Printed in the United States of America

10 9 8 7 6 5 4 3 2 1

Dedication

This book is dedicated to my husband, Vic, and to my family, friends, and coworkers, who encouraged me throughout this very long year.

Pat Scherer

I dedicate this book to the past and present LAN Server development team at IBM Austin. I'm proud to be associated with them—they made LAN Server the successful product it is today.

Charlie Brown

Contents

About the Book

> *Some books are to be tasted, others to be swallowed,*
> *and some few to be chewed and digested.*
>
> —*Sir Francis Bacon,* Essays or Counsels Civil and Moral

Whether you are thinking about installing a LAN, or simply need to know a little more about the LAN you currently have, this book is a good place to start. The goal of this book is to provide all of the information you need to evaluate, install, and use a small- to medium-size local area network using IBM OS/2 LAN Server.

LAN Server is currently celebrating its ninth year as the second most widely installed network operating system in the world. LAN Server offers a number of advantages in the areas of reliability, usability, scalability, and investment protection, which have long been exploited by large businesses and are just now being discovered by small network users. For smaller networks, there is no need to hire a full-time system administrator. Numerous options exist for doing all or part of the installation and maintenance yourself.

This is not a book for *dummies,* nor is it a book that attempts to educate you in every facet of networking. The goal is to aid you in completing your immediate task of setting up a network, while providing enough supporting information to help you make informed decisions and plan strategically. Plenty of references for your use in bringing your network online will be included.

To help you quickly locate the most relevant information, portions of the book will be marked with the following graphic symbols in the margin:

 Aids and quick references

 Time and money-saving tips

 Caution, important

 Cross references

A well-designed network will be customized to the needs of your business and provide adequate flexibility for future changes and growth. Whether you decide to install your own hardware or contract a service to do the work, the first four chapters will provide information to help you evaluate which LAN configuration will be best for your organization. Chapters 5 through 11 guide you through installing and using LAN Server. You will find the quick references and hands-on exercises valuable for quickly familiarizing yourself and other users with the network. The rest of the book describes enhancements to the network, what to do when something goes wrong, and where to get additional information.

There is quite a bit to accomplish, but it need not be a painful or boring journey. As you read through this book, try to think creatively about how you can use the network to improve your business or workplace. If you come up with a really great or unique idea, we would like to encourage you to share it with others through the BBS (a list of BBSs is provided in Appendix B). It is due to the ideas and encouragement of LAN Server users like yourself that this book was written.

The
IBM LAN Server
Sourcebook

CHAPTER 1

Why Install a LAN?

Look at every path closely and deliberately. Try it as many times as you think necessary. Then ask yourself, and yourself alone, one question . . . Does this path have heart? If it does, the path is good; if it doesn't, it is of no use.

—*Carlos Castaneda,* The Teachings of Don Juan

Perhaps you are considering installing a local area network but have not totally made up your mind. You may be concerned that installing and maintaining a LAN will be a complex undertaking, and wonder if it will be worth doing just to share some files or a printer. These concerns will be addressed by describing some ways in which your business may benefit from use of a LAN, and by giving you some perspective on changes in LAN technology over the last few years.

Having progressed far beyond simple file and print sharing, today's networks are considerably cheaper, more reliable, and easier to use than their predecessors of a few years ago. When LANs first appeared as a high-performance means of file and print sharing between computers in the 1970s, many factors prevented them from immediately finding their way into small businesses.

The first LANs were expensive, requiring special wiring. They were unreliable; something as simple as a loose adapter cable could disrupt the entire network. They were difficult to manage because network administrative and problem determination tools were almost nonexistent. The truth is that LANs in those days were a bane to many system administrators, but they were so useful that companies installed them, anyway.

LAN installation often began, as it does today, as a local departmental effort to share file and printer resources. In larger companies, these small departmental LANs eventually were interconnected to each other and to large system hosts. The growth in network size and complexity has brought about improvements in LAN design and cost. The result is the recent *down-sizing* and *rightsizing* movements in large corporations, and a proliferation of LANs in small businesses.

Today, the networking trend continues as we see a popularizing of terms such as *global networking, cybernet,* and *information highway.* Advances that have made LANs particularly attractive for use in small and medium-size businesses include:

- Significant cost reductions in wiring and components
- Reliability enhancements through use of concentrators and intelligent hubs
- Functional software enhancements for information and network management, fault tolerance, and efficient client/server computing
- Software licensing as a cheaper alternative to purchasing individual software packages

In upcoming chapters, a closer look will be taken at these topics as they are applied to creating a cost-effective and robust network. Probably the most difficult part of installing and using a LAN is selecting the configuration that will best meet the needs of your business. An ideal configuration will not only take into account your current needs, but also protect your investment by providing adequate flexibility and support for future growth. To assist you in determining the functions that will be of most use to your business, a look at network configurations and the ways in which networks are being employed in businesses today will be taken.

Network Configurations

Two network configurations are in common use today: client/server and peer networks (Figure 1.1). The client/server configuration is organized around one or more networked computers, designated as *servers,* which provide access to locally shared resources. *Resource* is a convenient term in networking used to describe anything that can be accessed via the network. The resources may be

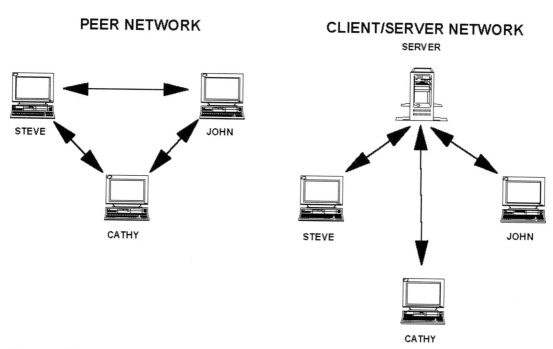

Figure 1.1 **Client/server and peer networks.**

a printer, a plotter, a CD-ROM, another serial device, such as a modem; or any directory, subdirectory, or file stored on a server's hard disk. The workstations that access these resources are called *clients* or *requesters.*

Servers provide numerous tools for managing access to shared resources and maintaining file integrity. For example, one job of the server's file system is to control write-access to a file so that two people cannot change a file simultaneously and interfere with each other's work. The software packages that provide these tools and tie your network together are called *network operating systems* (NOSs). Examples of NOSs are IBM's LAN Server products, Novell's Netware products, and Microsoft's NT Server.

There is another related group of products called *peer networks,* in which workstations on a network share files and printers and directly access one another's resources. These products were originally designed to provide local resource sharing on a network that does not include a server. Surveys are showing, however, that peer networks are often arranged in a manner similar to a client/server configuration: Files and printers are being set up on a dedicated server rather than being distributed throughout the network. This trend is understandable when you consider the performance implications of someone on the network running a long program or file transfer via your local DOS PC, or worse yet, running an unprotected application and accidentally crashing your system.

This situation is considerably improved by using OS/2 as the base operating system. The preemptive multitasking capabilities of OS/2 allow multiple users to access the shared resources on your workstation without negatively impacting local performance. OS/2's memory protection scheme ensures that a crashed program will not affect any sessions other than the one that crashed.

Peer networking products do not provide as high a level of functionality and performance as is provided by full-fledged servers. They are, however, less expensive than server products and can be good candidates for businesses starting out with a small two-to-eight-workstation network. Paired with higher-performance servers on larger networks, peer workstations can provide access to additional printers, as well as direct two-way communication and file sharing between individual workstations on the network.

Table 1.1 **Network Operating System and Peer Comparison**

Peer Product Characteristics	**Server-Based NOS Characteristics**
Low cost	Higher Cost
Basic file and print sharing	File and print sharing plus file and print management, public application support, security, administration, fault tolerance, auditing, statistical logging
Supports small networks—1 to 6 concurrent users, 3 to 20 users in network	Scalable to very large networks—up to 1,000 users per server and multiple servers per network
Easy to install	Easy basic Install/More Options
Easy to use	Requires setup for ease of use
Resources distributed; users control access	Resources centralized; administrator controls access
Moderate performance	High performance and capacity
Moderate reliability	High reliability

Examples of peer networking products include IBM's OS/2 and DOS Peers, Novell's Netware Lite, Microsoft's Windows for Workgroups, and Artisoft's LANtastic.

 Table 1.1 provides a comparison of peer versus server-based network operating system characteristics. Chapter 12 provides more information on using peer services. For a comparison of specific products, see Appendix A.

Benefits of Using a LAN

Most of this book will be focusing on the server configuration; more specifically, OS/2 LAN Server Releases 3.0, 3.01, 4.0, and the LAN Requester 4.0 component of Warp Connect. IBM provides two versions of OS/2 LAN Server: Entry and Advanced. The difference between the two versions is primarily file system performance. The Advanced version can handle roughly three times the number of users concurrently accessing files on a server as can be handled by the Entry version (up to 1,000 users versus around 300). The Advanced version also offers some administrative capabilities not offered by the Entry version. A more complete description of the features
 offered in each LAN Server version and release can be found in Chapter 3.

This chapter deals with common elements supported by most leading network operating systems, although packaging and implementation of these functions vary between products. As you read this chapter, note the functions that would be most beneficial to your business. You can then use your notes to select the packaging options that will best suit your requirements. It is also a good idea to note the areas in which you are most likely to grow or change, and to look for options that include enough flexibility to accommodate these changes.

The following hierarchy provides a convenient way to categorize the potential benefits of a network:

- Protecting assets
- Saving money
- Saving time
- Improving quality

It is interesting to note that the most fundamental benefit is the one we are least likely to consider when selecting a LAN: protecting assets. Protecting assets gains importance, however, when you consider the consequences of losing the information that your business requires for its day-to-day operations.

Protecting Your Assets

How long has it been since you last backed up important information on your workstation? What would be the consequences if you went into work tomorrow morning and found that your hard disk was irretrievably damaged? A catastrophic loss of data can occur in other ways as well: Power outages or system crashes before information can be saved; computer viruses; any disaster resulting in destruction of your computer or storage media. You could lose data by something as simple as leaving your diskettes in the car on a hot day. Far more data is lost through user error than by hardware failures, power surges, and natural disasters combined. Do you really think about the consequences of your actions before executing a **Delete** *.*? The fact that OS/2 and DOS make you type a **Y** before deleting the files only adds insult to injury when you unconsciously type a routine sequence of commands and a moment later watch your work disappear.

Networks incorporate a number of features that provide a relatively secure environment as compared to the stand-alone workstation. A network server is often used as a centralized repository for databases and other important files. Files on a server can be protected from being inadvertently altered or deleted by assigning *privilege levels* for users accessing the file. An advantage of keeping important files in a central location is that this arrangement makes it easy to regularly back up the information to media, such as tape. Backups need to be run at a time when the file server is not in use. They can easily be set up to run automatically at a regularly scheduled time, such as nightly or on weekends.

Power outages can be handled through a battery backup and software feature called an *uninterruptable power supply*. When a power outage occurs, the server switches over to use the battery and, depending on the sophistication of the hardware, sends a message alerting the person managing the network that the power has been disrupted. If power is not restored by the time the battery runs low, the server will send another alert before it closes files and performs an orderly shutdown. The second alert gives users an opportunity to save their work and access any critical files needed before the server shuts down. All this assumes that the power outage is limited to the server. Of course, if the power outage is widespread, the person administering the network will probably already be aware of the outage. In either case, all open files will be closed and all data will saved to disk before the server shuts down.

Another facet of asset protection involves maintaining access to resources and information. Many businesses are dependent on the availability of particular information, such as accounts, pricing, inventories, or schedules. Most of us have experienced situations in which we could not get a prescription filled, make a reservation, or use a credit card because the "system was down." If information availability is critical to your business, fault-tolerant techniques can be used to create a second set of duplicate files that are updated simultaneously with changes made to the original set. The duplicate files can be located on a second drive that may use the same or a separate disk controller (Figure 1.2). A disk controller is the hardware that controls movement of the disk when files are being accessed. The use of two drives that use a single disk controller is called *mirroring*. The use of separate disk controllers is called *duplexing*. The key to fault tolerance is to minimize the probability that a failure at any one point will bring down the network or result in a permanent loss of data. Therefore, while mirroring would protect against a failure of the disk drive, it would not provide uninterrupted service if the disk controller failed. Protection of this type requires duplexing.

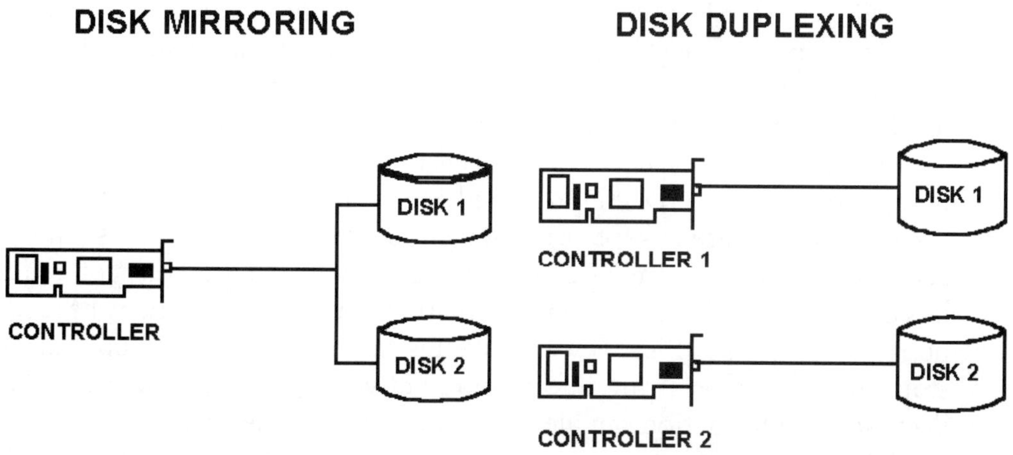

DISK MIRRORING   **DISK DUPLEXING**

Figure 1.2 **Disk mirroring and duplexing.**

Fault tolerance can be taken to almost any level. For example, how do you protect against a major disaster, such as a fire or flood? You might choose to duplex to a system in a different building and keep all your backup tapes in a waterproof and fireproof vault. The important thing is to provide adequate protection to insure that any likely mishap does not result in shutting down your business.

Saving Money

Historically, the first use of LANs was for file and printer sharing. Instead of supplying a printer for each stand-alone system, a smaller number of printers could be shared by everyone on the network. Particularly for businesses requiring high-quality printer support, a LAN provides an efficient mechanism for sending print jobs to the printer directly from the your PC. That means you no longer have to copy a file to a diskette, walk over to the print server, and wait around for the file to print. LAN Server uses a method called *spooling* to queue the print instructions it receives from you and your coworkers. The spooled jobs can then be printed in the order received, or they can be reprioritized to run in a different order, such as small jobs first. The status of your print job can be checked without leaving your desk, so there are no wasted trips.

Printers are not the only devices that can be shared on the network. Users can also share plotters, faxes, modems, scanners, and CD-ROMs. New networked hardware is being introduced daily. The hardware can be grouped into pools to efficiently handle more volume than could be accommodated by a single resource. For example, printers can be pooled so that a job can be routed to second printer when the first one is in use.

Another way that a network can save money is by decreasing the amount of disk storage space (DASD) required across the network. A single copy of each file or database is kept at the server, rather than many copies scattered across individual systems or diskettes. The overall result is that you require less disk storage to access server information than you would have needed to house the duplicate files. Fewer diskettes are needed for backup and data storage, or for transferring information between you and your coworkers, because the information can all be accessed over the network.

Additional disk space is saved through sharing applications stored on the server. Some applications may be run directly on the server, or portions of the application may be copied to your local system. In the first case, little or no disk space would be required on your system to run the application. In the second case, you would still save disk space because you would rarely need to copy all portions of the application to effectively use it. For example, many applications include online documentation, extra fonts, or sample programs that you may not regularly need. You can store only the portions of the application that are regularly used and access a single copy on the server if less frequently used portions of the application are needed. An added bonus with this arrangement is that many software companies provide licensing for multiple copies of an application installed via a server at a lower price than would be paid for the same number of off-the-shelf software packages. Software licensing is a good deal for all concerned, because savings are passed on from elimination of paper and packaging that would otherwise take up space on shelves and in landfills.

Installing applications from a server is much faster and easier than installing them from diskette. You do not have to feed diskettes into your system, and file copies execute faster over the network. Some software is enabled for an IBM utility, called Configuration, Installation, and Distribution (CID), which lets a person administering the server create a script that answers the questions that are normally required during an install (you know, those trick questions that you answer to prove you *really want* to install the software). The script can be used to reduce the number of questions you have to answer for what is called a *lightly attended* install, or it may be used to answer all the questions for an *unattended install.* A single bootable diskette can be prepared, which allows a network-attached workstation to connect to the server to install the operating system and the OS/2 LAN Server client code. More will be described about CID in Chapter 13.

Another advantage of distributing applications from a server is that software upgrades and maintenance can be more easily applied to the network. It is easier to insure that the latest version of an application is installed on a server than to keep track of various versions that may be installed on individual workstations (Figure 1.3). A utility may be purchased to automatically apply upgrades of CID-enabled software across the network, or a message can be sent to notify users to initiate the install at their convenience. A LAN Server audit feature will even keep track of who has accessed the new resource.

Years ago, LAN Server introduced support for public applications. These are normal applications, such as editors, spreadsheets, and graphics software, that reside on the server and are configured by the administrator to be shared

Figure 1.3 **Servers make software maintenance easier.**

with the network. Depending on how they are configured, public applications invoked by a network client will actually run on the server or a combination of the client and server. This is in contrast with standard applications, which may be shipped across the network as files and are run on the client workstation. With an OS/2 or Windows client on LAN Server 4.0, icons for public applications appear in a public application folder immediately after logging on. These applications can then be executed in the same way as local applications: with a click of the mouse button.

 ## Saving Time

I have already mentioned a few ways in which a network can save you time, such as installing applications and printing. Time is also saved in transferring files, particularly if the file or set of files is too large to fit on a single diskette. Since users can directly access files on the server, there is less need for transferring copies between individuals. When private copies of files, applications, or directories are desired, you use the same familiar DOS commands (COPY and XCOPY) to copy these resources between the server and your workstation as you would use to copy files between local hard drives. This is how it works: When you want to use a resource, you assign a drive letter to it. One way to do this is by entering the following command:

```
NET USE S: \\IRVING\NEWNEWS
```

The preceding example assigns the drive letter S: to a resource called NEWNEWS located on a server named *IRVING*. You could then view the directory of NEWNEWS by typing **DIR S:**.

Copying a file, WHOS.1ST, from NEWNEWS to a directory called NEW-STUFF on your PC would be done as follows:

```
COPY S:\WHOS.1ST C:\NEWSTUFF\WHOS.1ST
```

Since the server resource is treated like another disk drive on your local system, you can change directories, view a file, print a file, and do many other tasks in the same way you would with files on your local workstation. Depending on the operating system you use, there are even easier ways to view and use network resources. These will be explored in upcoming chapters.

 # Another Way to Save Time— Network Communication

Networks are very efficient ways to communicate, share, and transfer information. This is particularly true if you regularly communicate with people who work at different times of the day or week, or who work outside your immediate area. Imagine, for example, that you have some information to share with five other people and you do not want to take the time to set up a meeting to discuss it. You speak with Jim and then go see Doug. While repeating the information to Doug, he has an idea that you want to check out with the rest of the group. By the time you finish speaking to everyone, you may wish you had called the meeting.

Networks do not replace face-to-face meetings for every instance of communication, but they are great ways to provide information to many people simultaneously. Time management and other professionals are beginning to address the question of what modes of communication are most useful for a given situation. Networks provide a number of options, as shown in Table 1.2. Some of these options will be discussed, and instances in which they can best be applied will then be reviewed.

One common form of network communication is messaging. Messages are short notes that can be sent to one or more users' screens. The user must be logged on to the network at the time the message is sent to receive it. Messaging is best used for important information that may require immediate action. An example of such a message might be, A cloud raining golf ball sized hail is heading for the parking lot. (In Texas, this message is more effective in emptying the office faster than Fire!) Messages get displayed as a pop-up on everyone's screen, so be careful what you type! In my workplace, an indicator that a new person just got introduced to the network is a message like Hello there! or Testing, which gets propagated to every screen in the building. You know a broadcast message is coming well before you see it on the screen by a wave of *beeps* echoing down the corridor like an invasion of cartoon roadrunners. It seems that every new person must try this once (yes,

Table 1.2 **What's the Best Way to Communicate?**

Criterion	Method	Example
Immediate importance to network users	Message	Server Shutdown
Private correspondence	E-Mail	Recommendations . . . what do you think?
Information directed to one	E-Mail	Account status
Information directed to many	E-Mail or Bulletin	Schedule change
Record-keeping	E-Mail or Forum	Auditable process
General information	Bulletin or Read Only Database	Cafeteria menu
Interactive General Information	Forum or Shared Database	Tips, How-to's, Q&A
Communication of an emotional or controversial nature or where lots of questions are anticipated	Meetings	Contract negotiation

Janet, it really works). Luckily, the resulting embarrassment and peer pressure generally take care of any potential long-term annoyance.

Another way to communicate is via electronic mail (e-mail). Electronic mail can be addressed to one or more individuals. The notes are generally held at a mail server, or *post office,* until they can be received. The post office allows you to receive mail even if you are not logged on to the network at the time the mail is sent. E-mail is not a built-in feature on most network operating systems, including OS/2 LAN Server, but it is a popular add-on.

E-mail packages, such as Lotus Corporation's cc:Mail, consist of a post office component for routing and storing mail, and a user interface for composing and viewing mail. If you are logged on, some e-mail applications send you a message or include a status field that indicates you have mail to view. This is analogous to getting a notification from the postman that you have a package waiting at the post office. Other less sophisticated applications require you to periodically check for any new notes or files received.

E-mail is useful for communicating private information to people who are not readily available for spontaneous face-to-face meetings. This includes large or geographically dispersed organizations, people who work multiple shifts, or people whose work requires sustained concentration. E-mail is used frequently by software developers, even when the addressee is across the hall, because it is less disruptive than phoning or popping into someone's office. I also use e-mail as a to-do list by keeping the notes on items requiring action in my in basket, and deleting or filing them only when the actions are complete. The filed notes serve as an excellent history of procedures and information gathered when performing earlier tasks.

A third way to communicate over the network is by setting up a shared area of the server to be used as a forum or bulletin board. This option is not for private notes to individuals but for information or discussions of general interest. Users may be allowed to view the information only on what is commonly called a *bulletin board,* or they may be able to append questions and additional information within a *forum.* Common uses for bulletin boards are for posting news items and procedures. Forums are conversational and open in nature; anyone can *listen* or join in, but no one (except a forum owner) can erase or alter existing information. Forums may be used by businesses to communicate on projects, address questions or topics of general interest, or provide an excellent interactive suggestion box.

Any shared file provides yet another form of network communication. An example is the inventory and price databases commonly seen in retail stores. Each transaction provides an update to the database, which can subsequently be viewed by other database users. If a retail store manager, for example, adds additional inventory at a changed price, everyone in the store will be aware of the changes the next time they access that particular item. No announcement is necessary.

Saving Time Through Teamwork and Parallel Processing

One of the best things about a network is that it facilitates working together. Time is saved by enabling people to share information, to work more efficiently in teams, and to pool resources. What began years ago as simple file and print sharing has evolved into the sophisticated file management techniques used in today's servers. Just as multiple people can simultaneously work on the same files and projects, networks allow multiple processors and other hardware to more efficiently distribute workload. The next steps in this evolution are *network-aware* and multiprocessor-oriented operating systems and applications that will allow programs to more easily utilize the combined processing capabilities of the network. Taken to its logical potential, these capabilities may in the not-too-distant future enable a network to emulate the massively parallel architecture of present-day supercomputers.

Improving Quality Through Information Access and Management

It is 8:00 P.M. and your stomach is growling. No one else is in the office and you wouldn't be there either except that you have a really important piece of work that must be completed by early tomorrow morning. As you start putting together all of the information you gathered during the day, you realize there are some important pieces missing. Unfortunately, the person who has the information you need is not in the office. You begin to regret not having gotten an earlier start and decide to try calling the person at home. You feel a twinge of guilt dialing the number that you have memorized from countless other times you have found yourself in a similar fix. Terrific; no answer! In desperation, you start rummaging through desk drawers and are rewarded by not one but three different versions of the information. There are enough inconsistencies that it is obvious that at least two of the documents are either old or wrong, but which is the right one? Or, for that matter, are any of them right?

Does this scenario seem familiar? Improved information access and information management combine to make LAN Server a valuable tool for reducing the confusion and mistakes that occur when multiple people are contributing to and sharing information.

The subject of information access was touched upon when describing network communication, but the advantages go far beyond efficiency. By providing a shared resource, such as a file directory, you can ensure that the most current version of any file or application is available to anyone who needs it, when they need it. LAN Server allows multiple users to simultaneously view a file, but guards against users inadvertently creating conflicting versions of a file by a mechanism known as *locking.* When a user wishes to write to a shared file, the file is first locked so that no other users can write to it. When the user has completed the changes, the file is unlocked, allowing another user to then gain write access.

By providing shared resources, you can stop being a middleman for people needing these resources. Once they are granted access to a resource, they can access it directly without your assistance. This brings up an important subject regarding network operating system flexibility. Resources that are on a server are not necessarily free for everyone to view. Any resource can be set up to be private or shared. For example, a private subdirectory can be set up for each individual user, and would function just like an extension of the user's own system; no other users could access files that were stored there.

At the other extreme, access to a shared resource can be left totally open, meaning that anyone (and everyone) can use the resource just as if it were their own (including altering or deleting files). A more conservative approach is for a subset of access privileges, such as read-only and execute, to be granted to any user of a specific resource. Users with only read and execute privileges, for example, can use and view the resources, but not change, create, or delete files. This arrangement protects against such problems as a user accidentally overwriting or reformatting a shared subdirectory.

But what if you want to let some users change, create, and delete files, while limiting other users to read only (perhaps you have a user with a bad history of reformatting your shared drive)? LAN Server provides the flexibility to specify different access privileges for individual users or groups of users. The person controlling access to the files, the designated administrator, can control access to as fine a level as individual files within a subdirectory. LAN Server provides mechanisms to selectively apply a set of access control specifications created for one resource to other resources. Options for managing access to resources will be covered in greater detail, along with administrative tasks, in Chapter 7.

How Other Businesses Are Using Their Networks

As mentioned earlier in this chapter, the use of networks, which began with large businesses, has been rapidly expanding into smaller businesses. This trend is expected to continue as networking products continue to improve in price and ease of use. Two other factors that may speed the introduction of networking to small businesses are the use of online services, such as CompuServe, Internet, and Prodigy for e-mail; marketing and information retrieval; and the introduction of highly functional Remote LAN Access products to enable users to access network resources over phone lines.

The use of Remote LAN Access products is analogous to the way users access the host resources of online services today. The difference is that Remote LAN Access products utilize the same PC-based applications as the LAN to provide a consistent, flexible, and scalable environment for remote users. It can, for example, allow a person to access network applications and information from home, or from another location or customer site. Remote LAN access, its uses, and a remote LAN access product called LAN Distance will be described more in Chapter 13.

Statistics gathered from recent surveys indicate that the most popular uses of the network continue to be shared printers, databases, and e-mail. The most common shared databases are pricing information, inventories, and financial/accounting data. Other common uses are shared information and document repositories. Newer and fast growing areas include application, imaging, and multimedia servers.

From a personal perspective, I and the coauthor are both developers and avid users of LAN Server and LAN Distance. We use LAN Server and OS/2 requesters in our offices at IBM to access shared files, applications, and printers. We use TCP/IP and its utilities for accessing the wide area network, as well as host and RISC System/6000-based development tools. We use Lotus Notes for e-mail and Lotus Smartsuite for developing documents and presentations. In writing this book, we set up shared access to a single master copy kept on a LAN Server 4.0 file server. We then set up our home computers with Warp for OS/2 3.0, the OS/2 requester from LAN Server 4.0 Advanced, TCP/IP file transfer and host emulation utilities, and LAN Distance.

Before setting up this environment, I never seemed to have the information I needed in the right place at the right time. I was constantly carrying manuals between my home and the office, and was seriously considering making duplicate copies of everything so that I could have them on hand. I was also afraid to make changes to the book without immediately communicating the changes to avoid conflicting versions. With the use of these tools, we can now readily access and share information, and be assured we are always working on the latest versions of the text.

Hopefully, you now have some ideas for how to apply networking to your business. If you are new to networking, the next chapter will give you some concepts and vocabulary to help you evaluate alternatives and begin planning how to put your network together.

CHAPTER 2

Just Enough LAN Concepts and Terminology

A motorcycle functions entirely in accordance with the laws of reason, and a study of the art of motorcycle maintenance is really a miniature study of the art of rationality itself.

—*Robert M. Pirsig,* Zen and the Art of Motorcycle Maintenance

As you focus on the concepts necessary to get your network up and running, please realize that there is much more to networking than what is covered in this chapter. For a more in-depth understanding of the subject, Appendix B provides suggestions for further reading. Another excellent source of information is the many networking forums and conferences listed there.

What You See is the Physical Network

The hardware that makes up a network consists of two or more workstations; an electronic medium (usually some form of cable); a wiring hub, where one end of the cable is plugged; and adapters called *network interface cards* (NICs) through which the other end of the cable is connected to the workstations (Figure 2.1). The two most common forms of networks today are Ethernet and Token Ring. In the early days of networks, Ethernet and Token Ring required totally different cabling. Token Ring, as the name implies, used to be laid out in a ring, with each workstation joined to the next

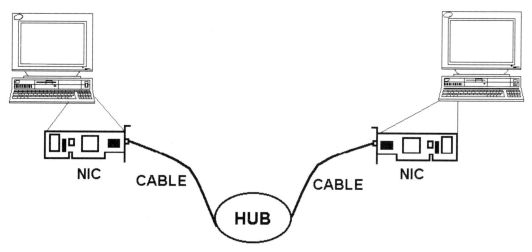

Figure 2.1 **The Physical Network.**

one by a shielded twisted-pair cable. Ethernet utilized a bus (or branched tree) configuration in which sections of coaxial cable were joined with repeaters.

Today, most Ethernet and Token Ring networks utilize a star configuration and may use shielded twisted pair, unshielded twisted pair, or fiber optic cabling. The type of cabling needed depends on the size of the LAN—a factor of distance and number of users. A hub forms the center of the star configuration and provides detection and the ability to bypass sections of the network that are malfunctioning. This provides better network reliability; a broken connection or similar problem will not bring down the entire network. Hubs also make it easier to locate a problem; one needs only to trace the connection that has shut down. Before the use of hubs, the entire network segment had to be methodically tested to locate the problem and reestablish network services. So, today Ethernet and Token Ring cabling and topologies have converged on a form that offers considerable advantages over earlier ones. The differences that still exist between Ethernet and Token Ring are contained within the NIC and low-level communication protocols. In Chapter 3, the differences between Token Ring and Ethernet as factors influencing hardware selection will be described.

Network Roles

The last chapter introduced the concepts of servers, clients, and peers. Most small networks employ a single multipurpose server. Larger networks have multiple servers that may each provide a specialized function, such as sharing a bank of printers, providing interactive services for a shared database, or running public applications. It is highly recommended for a network that has outgrown a single server to look at splitting servers by function, rather than duplicating resources on multiple servers. The reason for splitting function is that a specialized server can often take more advantage of performance tuning and the server architecture than can a general purpose server. This is analogous to completing tasks on an assembly line. For example, a worker can process more widgets in a given amount of time if each widget is the same and requires the same task to be performed. Different widgets or different tasks would require the worker to identify each widget and determine the task to be completed, locate different tools and parts, and so on. Likewise, hardware and software architecture often take advantage of a principle known as *locality of reference,* which basically means that as long as the computer is doing the same thing, it will keep all the right *tools* in memory, possibly combine requests going to the same destination, and minimize context switches. Using specialized servers makes particular sense when compared to the suboptimal arrangement of duplicating databases or applications across multiple servers.

Today, there is lots of hype concerning support for symmetrical multiprocessing, or the ability for operating systems and applications to distribute work between two or more processors on a single high-end computer. If your application has outgrown a single processor, carefully compare the overall capacity gained through use of this high-end equipment versus simply adding a second server. In the published benchmarks I have examined, including the October 1994 NOS benchmarks published by LANQuest and a December 1994 review of NOSs published by PC Magazine, the use of symmetrical multiprocessing resulted in a maximum throughput far below the 2× improvement one might anticipate. In the preceding references, for example, NT running on two processors underperformed Netware and LAN Server running on a single processor. This is not to say that symmetrical multiprocessing does not offer the potential to be more efficient than two separate computers, all design theories indicate that this potential exists. Unfortunately, many changes must be made in the operating systems and application software before the full benefits of symmetrical multiprocessing will be realized.

LAN Server was initially designed with very large networks in mind. For example, LAN Server has always provided users with the ability to simultaneously access resources from multiple servers. Another example of LAN Server's large network view is its division of network servers into logical groupings called *domains* (Figure 2.2). Domains are a collection of servers that interoperate to provide resources for a group of people in a *transparent* way, which means that the people using the servers would not need to know whether they were using resources from one server or many servers. Domains improve performance over large networks by distributing users across network resources. They also filter the complexity of the larger network from the user by initially presenting only the resources the user requires most often. It is an important task of the network planner/adminis-

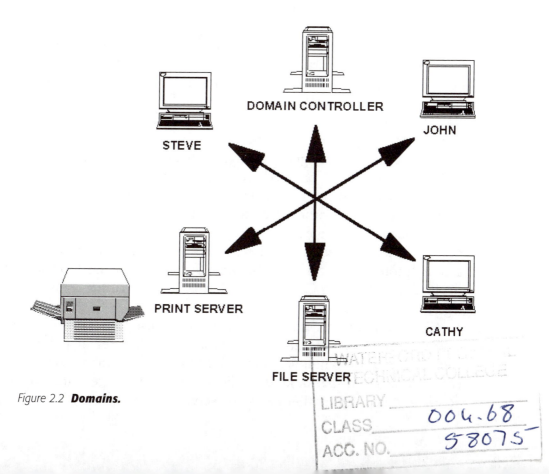

Figure 2.2 **Domains.**

trator to ensure domains are arranged into clusters of resources that are frequently accessed by each set of users. If you are on a very big network and want to browse a set of available resources, you should see only the subset of resources that you normally use. This saves time in locating resources and helps balance resource usage across the network.

But what if the resource you need is on a domain other than the one you normally use? No problem. Just specify the domain or server name of the resource you want to access. Cross-domain access is not quite as transparent as using resources within your own domain, but the process is no more difficult than the normal process of accessing resources using network operating systems that do not organize resources into domains. There are some tips to make cross-domain access more transparent, which will be discussed later.

Every LAN Server network is composed of at least one domain. Each domain has a unique domain name and one server designated as a *Domain Controller,* or *Primary Server.* Every workstation is a member of one of the domains. There can be an unlimited number of domains on a network; however, a network with fewer than ten servers and a few hundred users might need only a single domain and Domain Controller.

The Domain Controller keeps a master copy of all user accounts and access information contained on every server in the domain. This information is called the *Domain Control Database* and is central to providing the illusion of transparency within a multiserver network. The Domain Controller may also provide a central point for validating users' identifications and passwords when they log on to the network. If your domain contains additional servers, they may be assigned as *Backup Domain Controllers* or *Member Servers.* A Backup Domain Controller receives copies of the Domain Control Database at regular intervals from the Domain Controller. If the Domain Controller is busy or otherwise unavailable, the Backup Domain Controller can provide uninterrupted support by authenticating users logging on to the network. Member Servers share resources and have their own copy of user account profiles for local users. Member Servers can be used to take some of the load off a Domain Controller by locally authenticating users when they log on.

Clients are the workstations that you and I use to interact with servers. Client workstations are also called *Requesters.* LAN Server provides client support for DOS, Windows, and OS/2-based workstations. As mentioned earlier, a peer is a special kind of client that can share resources as well as access resources from other peers and servers.

How Clients and Servers Communicate

For workstations to communicate, two things must happen: A workstation must successfully initiate an information exchange with another workstation, and the two workstations must agree on a common set of semantics (Figure 2.3). In computer parlance, the initial exchange is called a *handshake,* and the semantics is called a *protocol.* It is important to provide you with at least a basic understanding of the protocols that LAN Server uses so that you can properly configure your network. Protocols also play an important part in determining which communication hardware and software products will interoperate and which will not. If you plan to integrate your LAN into a larger environment with, for example, wide area network (WAN) capability or multiplatform hardware support, understanding how protocols fit together will be more crucial than if you are putting together a small self-contained network.

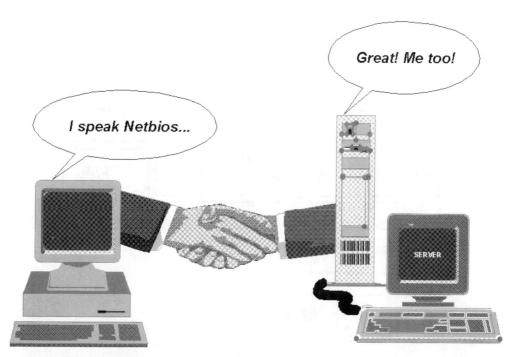

Figure 2.3 **Handshake and Protocol Exchange.**

LAN Server uses a protocol, called NetBIOS, which supplies a set of commands for communicating over networks, including several variations of Send and Receive commands. NetBIOS Send and Receive commands contain a data field that LAN Server utilizes to send specially formatted data called a *Server Message Block* (SMB). SMBs provide instructions for print and resource sharing across the network. Within LAN Server 3.0 and 3.01, NetBIOS interfaces directly to a protocol layer called a *Network Driver Interface Specification* (NDIS). NDIS is one of two common interfaces (the other one is ODI) that are used to support communication adapters.

LAN Server 4.0 adds another layer above NDIS as an extension, called the *Multiprotocol Transport Support* (MPTS). MPTS provides highly efficient function and address translation to allow protocols such as NetBIOS to be layered over other widely supported protocols (Figure 2.4). NDIS and MPTS together provide unequaled flexibility for integrating LAN Server with other commu-

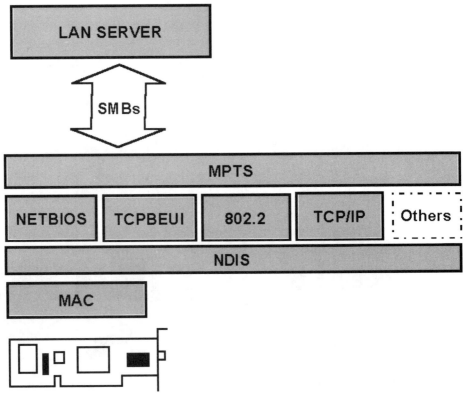

Figure 2.4 **LAN Server 4.0 Protocol Support.**

nication products and hardware platforms on large heterogeneous networks. Some examples of this flexibility are:

- LAN Server can coexist with numerous other network operating systems and communication products, such as Netware, Communication Manager, and Windows NT Server.
- One LAN Server can support multiple network applications using a single NIC, or dynamically assign sessions across multiple NICs for exceptional capacity and performance.
- LAN Server's NetBIOS can be layered over other protocols, such as TCP/IP.

Why would you care about TCP/IP? TCP/IP is a popular protocol for communicating across wide area networks, whereas NetBIOS is primarily used only on local area networks. The background behind this preference is that TCP/IP utilizes a series of directions embedded in its addresses that tell routers exactly where to send a frame. For this reason, TCP/IP is said to be a *routable* protocol. NetBIOS initially sends a broadcast message, called a *discovery frame,* across a network to find the route to a specific destination. The NetBIOS implemented by LAN Server keeps routes to its most recent destinations in a buffer to reduce broadcast traffic on the network; however, this refinement is not commonly included in standard NetBIOS implementations. For this reason, NetBIOS has gotten bad publicity for being an unroutable protocol that creates excessive broadcast traffic over the network. Since wide area networks may run anywhere from 4 to 8,000 times slower than local area networks, it is particularly important for WANs to guard their bandwidth against excessive broadcast traffic. Thus, for a growing number of users, TCP/IP has become the protocol of choice.

To summarize LAN Server's support for TCP/IP wide area networking, LAN Server 4.0 includes TCP/IP support via its MPTS extension. LAN Server 3.0 and 3.01 can also run over a TCP/IP network but require a separate product, called *NetBIOS for TCP/IP,* to provide the TCP/IP support.

The subject of addresses was briefly covered when describing NetBIOS versus TCP/IP routing; let us now go back to this important topic. Just as addresses allow mail to be delivered to your home, each network adapter on a workstation is identified by a unique number that allows it to be identified on the network. Some NICs, notably Token Ring adapters, have an address burned into the card, known as a *Universal Address.* This address is guaranteed to be unique as long as all other cards on the network are also using a Universal Address. The alternative is to assign your own unique address when you configure the workstation.

What happens if the address you use is not unique? Luckily, the code included with LAN Server is designed to catch this problem. A duplicate address check is run whenever a workstation is booted prior to the address being registered onto the network. If a duplicate is found, an error is logged, indicating you must change your address and reboot before using the network. If duplicate address checking was not done, a duplicate could be introduced. A problem would occur, because data meant to be received by one of the duplicate addresses would be intercepted by whichever duplicate workstation happened to encounter the data first. You can imagine the chaos this can introduce to a network; misrouted data can be a particularly difficult problem to debug!

A Resource by Any Other Name . . .

You are going to be asked to supply lots of names when you configure your network: a name for your domain, a name for each workstation, alias names for your shared resources, and names for each user or group of users. Jerry Pournelle, a regular feature writer for *Byte* Magazine, once wrote that he gives his computers names as soon as they come out of the box. He often refers to his computers by name in his articles. While this may seem odd, as Pournelle pointed out, "you are going to have to name them anyway." Workstation names are mapped to the address of the workstation's NIC. Routes are recorded as a series of addresses indicating the correct path to the destination. So, while it may seem somewhat confusing to have to generate and keep track of all those names, it's considerably easier than keeping track of NIC #400052756567, which can be reached by hanging a left at router #400065342598!

Network operating systems and network-aware programs use addresses to route information and workstation names as a friendlier means of referencing the workstations on which these adapters reside. Once on the workstation, network programs find their way to a particular resource by use of a path statement, such as C:\NETPATH\MYSTUFF. To avoid confusion between resources on the server and resources on your local machine, LAN

Server uses the server name at the beginning of the path statement. The server name is indicated by two backslashes (i.e., \\OZZY\MYSTUFF). This path sequence is an example of what is called the *Universal Naming Convention* (UNC). As mentioned in Chapter 1, LAN Server will also let you assign a drive letter to the resource located on the Server to make it handier to access. So, for example, you may assign to drive M MYSTUFF located on a server named OZZY by typing the following command:

NET USE M: \\OZZY\MYSTUFF

The preceding command is called a *Deviced Resource Assignment* and does not change the actual location of the resource on the Server, but simply allows you to access the resource in a more intuitive way. If, for example, you wanted to view the directory called MYSTUFF, you now only need to type **DIR M:**. Likewise, you can assign a remote printer to LPT2 (or any other available LPT):

COPY MYFILE.TXT LPT2

or use it directly via its UNC path:

NET COPY MYFILE.TXT \\FARPRINT\PRINTQ

Aliases are special names given to LAN Server shared resources, which allow the resources to be more easily accessed and maintained. Aliases are mapped to, and can replace, the more lengthy server and path specification to allow users to access resources without needing to know where they are located. For example, if you create an alias called STUFF for the subdirectory on OZZY, you could then access STUFF without having to include the server name:

NET USE M: STUFF

This device assignment is equivalent to the one shown earlier. The real value of aliases is that they vastly simplify administration. If, for example, you decided to move STUFF to a different server, you would not need to make any changes on the client workstations or inform anyone of the move. You only need to re-create the alias on the new server and delete it from the old one.

Logons, Shares, and Uses

An overview of network concepts and terminology would not be complete without describing the process of logging on to a network, and sharing and accessing resources. One of the first things you will do after installing LAN Server will be to log on to the network. You may do this by selecting a logon icon at the graphical user interface or using the command line interface to type **LOGON**.

After entering this command, you will be prompted to type a *user ID* and *password*. The first thing that happens when you log on is that LAN Server registers your user ID and password to associate you with the workstation you are using to log on. Next, LAN Server associates the names of your workstation, domain, and messaging queues with your NetBIOS session. Then, LAN Server will reestablish logon assignments and public applications that you have set up beforehand. Last, LAN Server will register your user ID and password with a utility called *User Profile Management* (UPM). This process is summarized in Figure 2.5.

LOGON...

✓ *Register user with workstation*
✓ *Check if user already logged on*
✓ *Add names to Netbios session*

✓ *Get logon assignments*
✓ *Register ID and password with UPM*

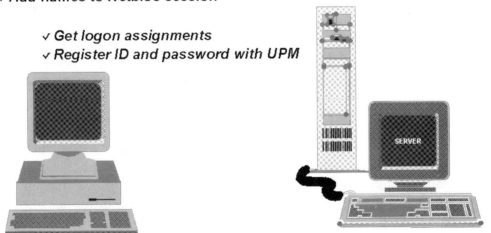

Figure 2.5 **The process of logging on.**

Logon assignments and public applications are server resources that have been set up to be accessed automatically when you log on. Their usage creates a single system image in which applications, files, printers, and other resources are available for use without having to issue a NET USE command. The resources appear just as if they existed locally on your workstation. Before any resource can be accessed, however, it must be defined and shared by creating a name for the resource, specifying the path to locate the resource, specifying who can access the resource, and, last, defining when the resource is to be shared (Figure 2.6). A resource, for example, may be shared whenever the server is running, or it may be shared at the time a client requests it, or only when an administrator manually invokes the share.

Many people get confused between the concepts of logging on to a network and accessing resources on a server. Logging on gives a user access to the network, but does not give the user access to resources. To access a resource, a user must have a preconfigured logon assignment, select the resource using the graphical user interface, or issue a NET USE command at

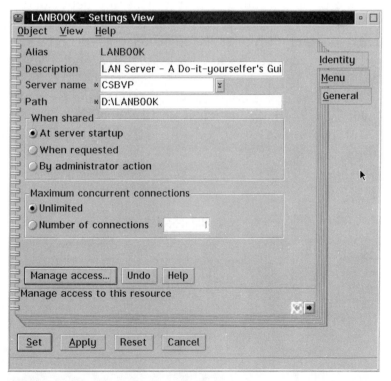

Figure 2.6 **Defining a resource with LAN Server 4.0.**

the command-line interface. The server then checks to see if the user has the appropriate level of privilege when the user attempts to use the resource. The user is allowed to use the resource only if the privilege level associated with the user ID matches what the user is attempting to do with the resource. The privilege levels recognized by LAN Server are the following:

NONE	No access is allowed.
READ	Users can read files and execute them.
WRITE	Users can modify files.
CREATE	Users can create a file, print job, or other resource.
EXECUTE	Users can execute EXE or COM files (OS/2 only).
DELETE	Users can delete subdirectories or files.
ATTRIBUTES	Users can change file attributes.
PERMISSIONS	Gives users limited administrative authority over the resource.

The reason for emphasizing the distinction between logging on to a network and using a resource is that it helps you better understand how LAN Server works in a multiserver environment. When you log on to a server on the network and wish to access resources on a second server, it is not necessary to log off the network and log on to the second server. You need to issue only a NET USE.

 This concludes the crash course in networking concepts. The next chapter will focus on the latest releases of LAN Server. Chapter 4 will continue with information on other hardware and software you will need to put your network together.

CHAPTER 3

About LAN Server

Doing more things faster is no substitute for doing the right things.

—*Stephen Covey,* First Things First

While LAN Server may not be a household word, it currently has a world-wide install base among leading network operating systems second only to Novell Netware. LAN Server's greatest concentration is in large government, financial, insurance, manufacturing, and retail accounts. Most likely, your bank or insurance company uses LAN Server today. LAN Server recently provided the communications support for the Indianapolis 500 and for a number of years has provided networking services for the Summer and Winter Olympics. One reason that LAN Server has not been more publicized is that, like other IBM products, LAN Server has been traditionally sold through direct channels rather than through retail outlets. IBM sales personnel either sold LAN Server as part of a contract to large corporate customers, or cus-tomers called in their orders through an 800 number (see Appendix B).

In recent years, IBM has been diversifying its businesses and sales channels. There is an active program now of training and certification for network consultants and computer software retailers to provide broader availability while maintaining a high standard of customer support. If your computer store does not carry LAN Server or other products you want, request them. This helps your store know which products are in demand, and is one way to ensure the products will be available in the future.

Another reason LAN Server is not better known is that it has often been confused with the discontinued Microsoft product called LAN Manager. This is understandable, since LAN Server and LAN Manager began as a joint effort between IBM and Microsoft in 1985. LAN Server and LAN Manager were the first industrial strength, PC-based network operating systems that could run on nondedicated hardware using a general-purpose operating system, the then newly developed OS/2. The LAN Server 1.0, 1.1, 1.2, and 1.3 releases were showcases for the power and versatility of OS/2. The OS/2 LAN Requester was included with OS/2 Extended Edition. OS/2 LAN Server was sold separately. Microsoft was, during this same period, developing and marketing new releases of LAN Manager. Customers, noticing subtle differences between the two products, were requesting that the products be merged. Soon after the release of LAN Server 1.3, IBM and Microsoft broke off their joint development effort. LAN Server Version 2.0 was released in 1990. Microsoft discontinued support for LAN Manager in early 1994 thus forcing customers to migrate to Microsoft's newly developed NT and Windows for Workgroups products, or look to other network operating systems for continued support.

While it bears little resemblance to the jointly developed products of the 1980s, LAN Server 4.0 retains the ability to interoperate with Microsoft products, including Windows for Workgroups and NT. For current LAN Manager users interested in sticking with the proven performance and reliability of an OS/2-based server, IBM has an easy-to-follow migration path. Instructions can be obtained by calling (800)IBM-4FAX. Other publications, called *Redbooks*, which cover network interoperability and migration topics and include tools for LAN Manager and Netware migrations to LAN Server, have been published by IBM's International Technical Support Center (ITSC). For more information, see References in Appendix B.

LAN Server Version 4.0 is IBM's seventh release of LAN Server for OS/2. IBM, meanwhile, has expanded its LAN Server offerings to include products for OS/400, AIX, VM, and MVS-based networks. The supported client base includes OS/2, DOS, DOS with Windows, and Macintosh. An exciting new offering in 1995, OS/2 Warp Connect provides the client components of LAN Server 4.0, LAN Distance, and numerous other client/server products bundled with the latest version of OS/2 Warp. These bundles are being offered far below the price of its individual component packages, so Warp Connect is well worth investigating if you plan to install two or more of these products. Development has also begun on products that will enable LAN Server to run on the newly developed Power PC. IBM's commitment to the LAN Server product line is evident in LAN Server's continued product enhancement, support, expansion of its retail markets, and broadening of its product offerings. Highly scalable LAN Server products are currently being developed for three markets ranging from small peer installations to large heterogeneous enterprise networks (Figure 3.1).

As mentioned earlier, LAN Server introduced the concepts of domains, aliases, and public application support as means of providing scalable configuration options for administrators and transparent network access for users. Other factors that account for LAN Server's growing popularity are IBM's policies for investment protection, reliability, and performance. While LAN Server has steadily increased its functionality, every release of LAN Server from 1.1 to 4.0 can interoperate within the same network. LAN Server even provides a migration utility to migrate LAN Server 1.0 into this environment. LAN Server also provides a common platform for coexistence with Novell, Microsoft, DEC, Artisoft, Lotus, and Banyan products.

With current offerings on AS/400, mainframe and RISC System/6000 platforms, and future integration of the open Distributed Computing Environment (DCE), LAN Server is rapidly expanding its interoperability with an almost limitless variety of hardware and software. This is a challenging environment for ensuring reliability. LAN Server's quality record is partly due

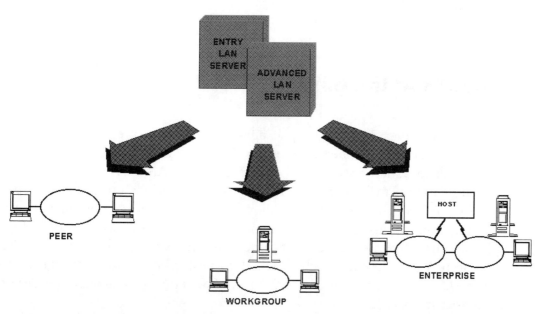

Figure 3.1 **LAN Server product expansion.**

to a quality improvement program that includes week-long, around-the-clock stress testing, extensive compatibility testing, the Ready for LAN Server product certification program for independent software vendors, customer participation in beta test, and causal analysis of reported defects.

A report released in October 1994 by the independent network tester, LANQuest Labs, showed that "LAN Server has the best performance at every load point from 200 to 800 equivalent users." The benchmarks, composed of a suite of nine popular business applications, were run against LAN Server version 4.0 Advanced, Windows NT Server version 3.5, and Netware version 4.02. At this time, LAN Server running on a single CPU was shown to outperform NT running on two. Other measurements comparing the Entry and Advanced versions of LAN Server show that the Entry version of LAN Server "provides very good performance for the small to medium network (20 to 80 users)," while the Advanced version of LAN Server is recommended for greater than 80 users.

Earlier measurements conducted on LAN Server 3.0 by LANQuest (September 1993), the National Software Test Lab (October 1993), and *PC Magazine* (October 26, 1993) show that LAN Server has had a long-term focus on performance, which has consistently kept it at the forefront. The latest reports on LAN Server performance can be obtained by dialing (800)IBM-4FAX.

What's in the Box?

The LAN Server 3.0 and 4.0 packages include the server (either Entry or Advanced), one copy of each requester (OS/2 and DOS Windows), the transport code, productivity aids, and documentation. LAN Server 3.0 provides its documentation in hard-copy form; online publications are available separately. LAN Server 4.0 provides online publications with the product. These online publications are searchable and can be printed in sections or in full. While the requester code is included in the package, legal use of the requesters requires that each installed requester be licensed through IBM. The U.S. list prices (year end 1994) for LAN Server and separate requester licenses are as follows:

LAN Server Entry Version (diskettes or CD-ROM) $795
LAN Server Advanced Version (diskettes or CD-ROM) $2,295
LAN Server Requester Licenses $50/user

As mentioned earlier, the LAN Server 4.0 OS/2 Requester is also packaged with Warp Connect. Warp Connect includes Warp (without WinOS2) or Warp Fullpack (with WinOS2), the OS/2 LAN Requester from LAN Server 4.0, OS/2 Peer, the LAN Distance Remote Client, TCP/IP 3.0, Lotus Notes Express Client, the Enhanced Internet Access Kit with Web Explorer, and Netware Requester 2.11 for OS/2. The US list prices for Warp Connect are as follows:

Warp Connect with WinOS2 (CD-ROM) $299
Warp Connect with WinOS2 (additional licenses) $289
Warp Connect without WinOS2 (CD-ROM) $229
Warp Connect without WinOS2 (additional licenses) $219

Use Warp Connect *with* WinOS2 if you *do not* have the latest version of Microsoft Windows on your workstation. Use Warp Connect *without* WinOS2 if you *do* have the latest version of Microsoft Windows installed. The list prices given are all nondiscounted, so you may want to check with your retailer and shop around for the best price. Table 3.1 provides a summary of the key features contained in LAN Server Versions 3.0, 3.01, and 4.0. The next few sections will describe these features in detail.

OS/2 LAN Server Version 3.0

OS/2 LAN Server Version 2.0, released in early 1992, first introduced the Advanced version of the product featuring a new installable file system called High-Performance File System 386 (HPFS386). HPFS386 continues to be a key feature of the Advanced Server in LAN Server versions 3.0 and 4.0. HPFS386 replaces the OS/2-supplied HPFS to provide a more efficient interface between the file system and the other LAN Server network components. As mentioned earlier, the Entry version provides comparable performance to the Advanced version with fewer than 80 users. The performance of the printer support between Entry and Advanced are also comparable. The

Table 3.1 **Key Features of LAN Server Versions 3.0, 3.01, and 4.0**

Feature Description	Version 3.0/3.01 Entry	Version 3.0/3.01 Advanced	Version 4.0 Entry	Version 4.0 Advanced
Public Application Support	X	X	Enhanced	Enhanced
Full Screen Interface	X	X		
Graphical User Interface			X	X
Command Line Interface	X	X	Enhanced	Enhanced
REXX Procedural Language Support			X	X
Application Programming Interface	X	X	X	X
Support for DOS, Windows, and OS/2 Requesters	X	X	Enhanced	Enhanced
Remote Administration	X	X	Enhanced	Enhanced
Security (Password Encryption, User Accounts, Event Audit)	X	X	X	X
OS/2 Peer Support	X	X	Enhanced	Enhanced
DOS and DOS/Windows Peer Support			X	X
802.2 and NetBIOS Protocol Support	X	X	X	X
TCP/IP Protocol Support			X	X
Cross-Domain Access	X	X	Enhanced	Enhanced
Single Logon	X	X	X	X

Advanced Server is designed to be a superhigh-performance file server for large networks. In fact, it will provide three to four times the capacity and performance of the Entry version on networks greater than 200 users. The Advanced Server also includes some additional functions that are made possible by the tight coupling of access control with files within the HPFS386: local security and disk fault tolerance.

Most companies that are concerned with controlling network access keep their servers in a locked room, but there are many cases in which it may not be practical or desirable to keep the server locked away. A common example is a multipurpose server in a manufacturing area or office that is used locally for

Table 3.1 **(continued)**

Feature Description	Version 3.0/3.01 Entry	Version 3.0/3.01 Advanced	Version 4.0 Entry	Version 4.0 Advanced
Configuration/Installation/Distribution (CID)Utility	X	X	Enhanced	Enhanced
Productivity Aids for Usability and Administration	X	X	Enhanced	Enhanced
Extensive Online Helps	X	X	Enhanced	Enhanced
Publications and References	X	X	Enhanced	Enhanced
Alert Service	X	X	X	X
File Replication Service	X	X	X	X
Support for Diskless Workstations (RIPL)	X	X	Enhanced	Enhanced
Support for Uninterruptible Power Supply	X	X	X	X
Support for Sharing/Pooling of NICs	X	X	Enhanced	Enhanced
Disk Space Limits Notification	X	X		
Disk Space Limits Enforced				X
Supports 4 NICs on a One LAN Segment		X		X
Disk Fault Tolerance		X		Enhanced
High-Performance File Server		X		X
Local Security for Server		X		X

routine tasks, such as checking printer or machine status. Local security provides a means to allow users to run these routine tasks locally on the server without compromising the security of other server and network resources. This is done by a bit of magic, called the *secured shell,* that ensures that a logon screen is displayed whenever the system is booted. Even using a DOS diskette to reboot the system will not circumvent the local security mechanism.

A person with administrator privilege can specify programs that can be used locally by users without logging on. For example, you in the role of administrator may choose to give users access to a text editor so that they can make corrections to documents locally at a print server without logging on to the network. If the users attempt to browse directories or access any program not specified by you, they will receive a request to log on. Once they log on, the screen and access privileges work the same as they would if the user logged on from a requester workstation. Users will see only the directories on the local server for which they have been granted read permission, and will be presented with the public applications to which they have been granted access.

Fault tolerance is another Advanced Server feature. While a book could easily be written on this topic alone, the idea, in a nutshell, is to write duplicate data to two locations to provide protection against data loss. While regularly backing up important data will limit data loss to the period between backups, the fault tolerant techniques of duplexing and mirroring help ensure that a complete copy of the data will always be available in the event of a disk failure. As described in Chapter 1, duplexing involves writing a duplicate copy of data updates to a second disk drive installed with a separate disk controller, while mirroring writes to a second disk that shares the same disk controller as the first. This level of fault tolerance is defined as Level 1 of the Redundant Array of Inexpensive Disks (RAID). RAID levels are a set of definitions that can be used to compare the degree of fault tolerance provided by hardware and software products. RAID Level 0 means there are no provisions for fault tolerance. RAID Levels 3 through 5 provide progressively higher levels of fault tolerance using such techniques as *striping* and *skewed parity*. Striping spreads data across an array of disk drives. The smaller the amount of information spread to each location, the greater the chance that information lost during a disk failure can be rebuilt. Skewed parity, used at RAID Level 5, spreads parity information used to detect and correct errors across an array of disk drives as well. Level 5 fault tolerance can be implemented on LAN Server using third-party products, such as Micropolis's Raidware or Radion's Open Architecture Scalable Array Subsystem (OASAS).

The remaining features described in this section are provided on both the Entry and the Advanced versions of LAN Server 3.0. LAN Server provides replication services for data files and its domain control database (DCDB). File and DCDB replication are provided by two different services but are closely related in the way they function. The DCDB, you may recall, is the central repository of all information regarding user accounts, logon assignments, public applications, and aliases for the domain. The DCDB resides on the domain controller but can be replicated to other servers for use in providing backup domain support, and in restoring function back to the domain controller in the event of a failure. The replication services allow you to designate a server as an *exporter* or an *importer* of information. It also lets you specify how often you want the data to be exported, the conditions that will trigger export of the data (such as changes to a file), and the extent of what will be exported (such as whether to export just the changed file or include all associated files).

LAN Server 3.0, like its previous versions, provides three different interfaces: the full-screen interface, the command-line interface, and the application-programming interface. It also makes use of a fourth, OS/2-supplied utility called User Profile Management (UPM); see Figure 3.2. If you are using LAN Server 3.0, you will most likely use all but the application programming interface in the course of sharing resources, creating user accounts, and using the system, because certain functions require use of a specific interface. Creating a user account within LAN Server 3.0, for example, must be done using UPM though modifying the account, which can be done from either UPM or the full-screen interface. The command-line interface is required to modify certain parts of the logon policy for a given user. In LAN Server 4.0, usability has been greatly strengthened by standardizing the level of function across all interfaces; this way, users have a choice of interfaces without needing to be proficient in all of them.

The full-screen interface provides a set of menus through which options can be selected for using, configuring, and administering the network. This interface contains most of the functions needed to use and administer the network, with the two exceptions already noted: user account creation and user logon policy modifications.

 After becoming familiar with LAN Server 3.0, you find the command-line interface to be the most convenient. Among other things, it enables you to

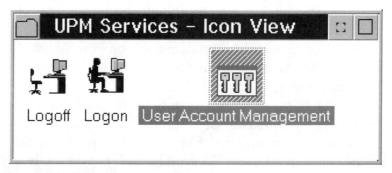

Figure 3.2 **The User Profile Management utility.**

create a command file to execute routine tasks. A command file is OS/2's name for a batch file; command files all use the extension .CMD. I have, for instance, a command file called SETUPLS.CMD for setting up a small 30-to-50 workstation network at conferences for teaching LAN Server User and Administrative Hands-On Workshops. The command file cleans up changes made in previous workshops. It then re-creates the shared resources and aliases I use: files, directories, print queues, and public applications. Next, it creates a user and administrator account for every workstation, and associates the accounts with the shared resources that were just created. During the User Hands-On Workshop, we go over use of the different interfaces and techniques users can implement to customize and automate their networking environments. During the Administrative Hands-On Workshop, we walk through the common administrator tasks and tools. In Chapters 7 and 11, you will have an opportunity to walk through the same processes that are taught during these hands-on workshops.

A series of NET USE commands in a batch or command file is an easy way to access resources on servers that you do not access on a daily basis. For example, if once a month you access accounting and marketing data on servers outside your domain, you could have a command file called MONTHLY that would access the servers and display the correct directories. As noted earlier, use of the command-line interface is mandatory for Operators who do not have access to the full-screen interface. It is also useful for users and administrators who may need to work from different workstations using both DOS and OS/2 requesters, because the command-line interface is fairly consistent across platforms.

The application-programming interface is for writing C language programs that interact with LAN Server. Programmers may utilize the full suite of OS/2 operating system calls in addition to the extensive LAN Server application programming interface (API). Programs can be written, compiled, and tested on the same workstation. Another advantage is that clients and servers utilize the same interface, so common code can be used to speed program development. Administrators in many large corporations have used the application-programming interface to customize their networks to provide simple screens for selecting network resources. Others have written utilities for more easily managing large complex networks.

As mentioned earlier, UPM is a utility provided by OS/2 to manage logons between different IBM products. It provides a graphical interface for users to log on, log off, and change passwords. In LAN Server 3.0, it is required by an administrator to create new user accounts. The most important use of UPM is that it uses the logon and password supplied to respond to logon challenges when you attempt to use resources outside your domain. As long as your user ID and password are consistent between domains and other supported services, you will not need to log on more than once to access resources anywhere on the network. This is a very important point if you plan to administer more than one domain: an account for a given user must be set up for each domain a user will access; however, *a user may access resources on any domain on which the user has an existing account without having to log off the current domain and onto the new one.*

You can administer the server locally or work remotely from any server or requester on the network. You must be logged on and have administrative authority on the domain that you are administering. You can also delegate routine administrative responsibilities, such as maintaining printers, resources, or accounts, by utilizing a special user type called *Operator* to give selected users the necessary access privileges.

LAN Server allows up to nine printers to be managed from a single server. Support includes print spooling and automatic routing to the first available printer. Administrators and printer operators can reorder, reprioritize, and cancel print jobs; and users can view their status in the print queue. OS/2 clients can utilize OS/2's workplace shell to set up printers from network print objects. To print a file, they need only to drag the file icon and drop it onto the printer object. LAN Server 4.0 adds bidirectional support for printers, which allows users to receive job status and maintenance messages directly from the printer.

LAN Server 3.0 includes numerous utilities and productivity aids for backup, migration, and problem determination. A utility that comes with the transport, called Configuration, Installation, and Distribution (CID), allows you to distribute code for LAN Server, OS/2, and other CID-supported applications from your server to LAN-attached workstations. The workstations do not require any existing code; they can be booted from two diskettes. A script can be created that supplies answers to configuration questions to allow the workstations to be configured automatically after they have been booted. Workstations can be installed and configured over the network in a fraction of the time it takes installing from diskettes.

The LAN Server OS/2 transport, called LAN Application and Protocol Support (LAPS), provides NetBIOS and 802.2 support (Figure 3.3). LAPS allows multiple applications to share a single NIC. It also allows one or more

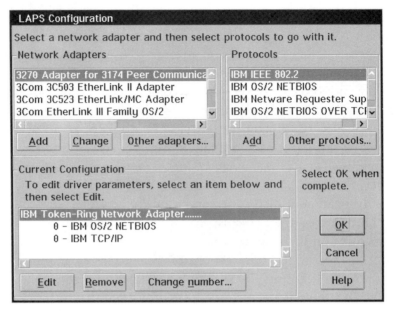

Figure 3.3 ***LAPS configuration.***

applications to be distributed across as many as two Ethernet or four Token Ring NICs for greater capacity and performance. The DOS transport is called LAN Support Program (LSP). It does not support adapter sharing or pooling. DOS applications running on an OS/2 workstation or server, however, can take advantage of the OS/2 transport and do not need LSP or a separate NIC installed.

LAN Server 3.0 uses information stored on the domain controller to map alias names to server locations, and users to public applications and other logon assignments. Aliases, you may recall, allow users to use a simple name, such as APPS, to indicate a resource stored on a particular server. The advantage of aliases is that the user does not need to know the location of a resource to access it, and that resources can be moved around freely without having to update locations on client workstations. Public applications are shared applications that are configured to execute in a client/server environment. When the users log on to OS/2 requesters, they see the icons of the shared programs appear in a public application folder on their OS/2 desktops. DOS public applications are accessible but somewhat more difficult to set up. Improvements made in LAN Server 4.0 made the setup and execution of DOS public applications more consistent with OS/2.

LAN Server 3.0 provides an OS/2 Peer Service, enabling OS/2 requesters to share files, printers, and modems. Sharing is limited to one remote user at a time. The OS/2 Peer-to-Peer product included with Warp Connect provides support for multiple users; this product is also sold separately.

Support for security and problem determination are extensive. LAN Server currently utilizes the Data Encryption Standard for providing password encryption. Several options exist for controlling security policies for groups and individuals on the network. These include password expirations, and disallowing duplication of previous passwords. Access to the network and to resources on the network can be controlled down to the level of individual files. Access can also be controlled for groups or individual users via LAN Server's Access Control Profiles. Failed attempts to enter a correct password invokes a waiting period designed to foil repeated attempts to breach the network, known as a *dictionary attack.*

Alerts, error messages, and auditing are fully configurable. An administrator, for example, can monitor every logon and resource access or a subset that meets specific conditions, such as failed logon attempts. LAN Server supports two types of alerts. The first type, called simply the *Alert Service,* uses the native LAN Server System Message Block (SMB) format for sending alert messages to all administrators and other designated personnel. The second type, called the *General Alert Service,* uses the 802.2 protocol to route alerts to LAN management programs, such as LAN Netview and LAN Network Manager.

LAN Server supports uninterruptible power supply (UPS), which you may recall protects the server from power outages. The UPS hardware switches over to battery power when an outage is detected to allow the server to keep running. A notification to LAN Server allows it to alert the administrator of the problem. If the power is not restored by the time the battery power runs low, another alert is sent to users, and the server begins a controlled shutdown to guard against any data loss.

LAN Server provides remote IPL support for OS/2 on medialess workstations. These are workstations that, for security or cost reasons, do not have disk drives or hard disk support. LAN Server allows these systems to be booted using profiles accessed from the server. Many different profiles can be created to provide a customized environment for each workstation.

Online Help is readily accessible from every interface. These Help panels guide you through installation and explain the meaning of every configurable parameter used by LAN Server. Task-level Help guides you through the common tasks of administering and using LAN Server. Typing **NET HELP** at a command line provides you with a list of LAN Server commands. NET HELP followed by the name of a specific command or utility gives you information on how the utility is used. Add the **/O** (for Options) parameter to the previous entry to get an explanation of the syntax and options used with that command.

An extensive set of hard-copy publications are available with the product. Additional copies and online documentation can be ordered separately (full names of references are listed in Appendix B). The documentation includes:

- The LAN Server Network Administrator's References
  —Volume 1—Planning, Installation, and Configuration
  —Volume 2—Performance Tuning
  —Volume 3—Network Administrator Tasks
- OS/2 LAN Requester User's Guide
- DOS LAN Requester and Windows User's Guide
- LAN Server Commands and Utilities
- LAN Server Problem Determination Guide

The product and documentation are provided in numerous languages, including English, French, German, Spanish, Italian, Swedish, Japanese, and Korean.

OS/2 LAN Server Version 3.01 (Version 3.0 Refresh)

LAN Server 3.01 updated LAN Server's support for operating systems and device drivers that came out after the release of LAN Server 3.0; it also added symmetrical multiprocessing support for the Advanced version running on a multiprocessor system supported by OS/2 SMP.

OS/2 LAN Server Version 4.0

LAN Server 4.0 took a major step forward in usability by replacing the full-screen interface of previous releases with a new graphical user interface

(GUI) for OS/2, Windows, and DOS workstations (Figure 3.4). The stream-lined administrative function available through the new GUI provides the ability to clone user accounts and resource definitions from existing objects and LAN Server-supplied templates. The OS/2 GUI used with the LAN Server and OS/2 requesters is object-oriented, which allows a user or administrator to associate objects through use of *drag-and-drop* techniques. For example, you can make a user a member of a group account simply by selecting the user's account icon, holding down the mouse button to drag the icon to the icon representing the group account, and dropping the user account onto the group account by releasing the mouse button. You can print a document on a network printer by dragging the document icon and dropping it onto the printer icon.

The GUI supplied by the DOS and Windows requesters is consistent with the Windows format, which features selectable pull-down lists rather than objects for files and other resources. Functions that were previously

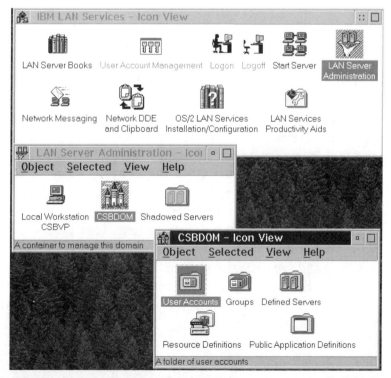

Figure 3.4 **LAN Server 4.0's new graphical user interface.**

spread between UPM, the full-screen interface, and the command-line interface have been consolidated within the GUI. The GUI is very user friendly and tends to be the interface of choice for users and for administrators administering small to medium-size networks.

The command-line interface has been enhanced to include all of the functions supported by the GUI. This includes the ability to create new user accounts and to propagate (or apply) a set of access control permissions to resource subdirectories. The improved command-line interface allows you to run a broader selection of tasks via batch or command files. Previous to LAN Server 4.0, only OS/2 workstations supported remote administration; and many administrative tasks, such as the ones previously mentioned, could be run automatically only via a user-supplied C Language program written to the LAN Server application programming interface.

For those of you who do not have the time or inclination to program but still want the flexibility that programming offers, a new set of REXX commands provides a front end to the application-programming interface. REXX is a set of simple but powerful macros that allow you to automate and customize the LAN Server environment without having to compile a program. To get you started in using REXX, the LAN Server 4.0 productivity aids provide several useful macros for LAN Server administration.

Performance, already excellent on LAN Server 3.0, was further improved by adding client-side caching. Additional improvements were made for logging on to the network and for using network print services.

LAN Server 4.0 vastly improved its support for DOS and Windows-based requesters. Previous LAN Server versions required users to choose between minimizing their memory requirements on their DOS workstations or optimizing performance. DOS LAN Requester provided the best performance and allowed adapters to be shared between multiple applications, but required 20 to 30KB more base memory than was required by the LAN Support Program. The total requirement was typically between 110 and 220KB, depending on the version of DOS (DOS 5.0 uses less memory than DOS 3.3) and whether the system was configured to use high memory. Base memory is the lower 640KB of memory required to load DOS device drivers.

In today's environment of complex applications, this is not much room to work. To conserve base memory, LAN Server and most other applications allow you to load the nondevice driver portion of the program into high memory, which is memory above the 1MB address space. You should take advantage of the high memory options whenever you have more than 1MB of memory available in your DOS workstations; the chapter on installing and configuring the Requesters will describe how. In LAN Server 4.0, the DOS LAN Requester was completely rewritten. The new version, called DOS LAN Services (DLS), gives you the best of both worlds: superb performance and functionality using less than 40KB of low memory.

Other enhancements for DOS and Windows-based requesters include:

- DOS peer services
- Public application support consistent with OS/2
- Remote administration from a DOS or Windows workstation
- Remote IPL
- Network DDE and Clipboard for both OS/2 and Windows requesters

The new Network Dynamic Data Exchange (DDE) and Clipboard allows users on OS/2 and Windows requesters to simultaneously view and update shared information on their desktops. You can, for example, use DDE to automatically update a copy of a spreadsheet located on another user's workstation whenever changes are made to your master copy. You can also use DDE as a videoconferencing tool to display a common clipboard at two workstations. Changes made to either clipboard will be displayed on both.

As described earlier, LAN Server 3.0 and 3.01 include a set of transports that provide NetBIOS and 802.2 protocol support. Customers using these products who also require support for TCP/IP need to purchase a separate package called NetBIOS for TCP/IP. LAN Server 4.0 provides Multiprotocol Transport Support (MPTS), also known as Anynet/2. MPTS is a superset of previously supplied transports, which provides, along with NetBIOS and 802.2, high-performance support for NetBIOS running over TCP/IP (called TCPBEUI) and native TCP/IP socket support. Support for NICs has also been greatly expanded over what was provided with LAN Server 3.x. LAN Server 4.0 now supports more than 70 percent of the Ethernet and Token Ring NICs currently available.

LAN Server 4.0 vastly streamlined its installation and configuration process. LAN Server 3.0 and 3.01 are installed and configured in four steps:

1. Install transport and reboot
2. Install LAN Server
3. Configure LAN Server and reboot
4. Tune performance and reboot

A free spreadsheet utility, available on several electronic bulletin boards, called CONFGLS, was a popular tool for completing step 4. CONFGLS takes user-supplied answers to such questions as How many clients and applications you are supporting, and outputs recommended configuration files that have been tuned to your network. LAN Server 4.0 includes a later generation of this utility, called the Performance Tuning Assistant (Figure 3.5), as part of the install process. LAN Server installation is further streamlined by the integration of the transport and the LAN Server installation and removal of the reboot requirement between steps 1, 2, 3, and 4. Code was added to the transport to identify NICs present during install. This eliminates the need for users to identify the hardware present in their workstations and simplifies CID installs. The installation process was also divided into an Easy basic install, appropriate for most users, and a customizable Tailored install. The

 two install options will be covered in detail in Chapter 6.

LAN Server 4.0 adds several new productivity aids for managing the network, migrating applications, and performing other routine maintenance. A complete description of utilities and productivity aids for LAN Server 3.0,

 3.01, and 4.0 is found in Chapter 12.

LAN Server provides a complete set of online helps to guide you through installation, configuration, and use of the network. Help for specific items is

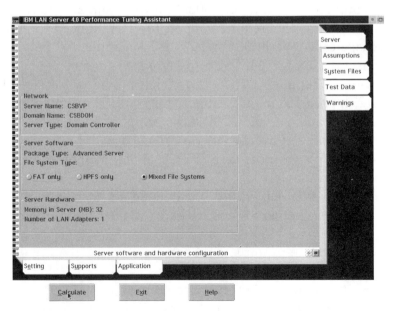

Figure 3.5 **The Performance Tuning Assistant.**

accessed by selecting a Help key that is present on every panel. The search functions and hypertext format allow users to freely locate and browse related topics. In addition to the Help, LAN Server 4.0 supplies all publications online. To facilitate locating the information you need quickly and easily, every word is searchable. Or, if you prefer, all or portions of the documentation can be printed. Utilizing customer feedback and an independent testing organization, the LAN Server Publications team reorganized and rewrote the publications with the intention to set a new standard for network usability. The *LAN Server 4.0 Up and Running* publication, for example, was written and tested with the goal of answering 90 percent of the questions a new administrator might ask within the first month of receiving the product. Early feedback obtained during beta testing indicated that reviewers were *pleased* with the ease with which they were able to install the product and perform various administrative tasks using the publication. Respondents ranked themselves from novices to advanced users of the network, indicating that publications were able to address the needs of users over a wide range of experience.

Finally, the Advanced version of LAN Server 4.0 added the capability for administrators to set and enforce hard disk limits for users. With prior releases and the Entry version of LAN Server, the administrator could set limits for a user account. When a user exceeded the limit, an alert was sent to the user and administrator informing them of the problem. With LAN Server 4.0 Advanced, the user receives an error message and is not allowed to exceed the limit set. The administrator can also set limits by directory and configure threshold alerts to be sent to warn users when they are approaching their set hard disk limits. A user could receive a warning, for instance, that only 20 percent of allocated disk space remains.

Complementary Products

LAN Server is IBM's strategic platform for LAN support. The following is a partial list of products that complement the functionality of OS/2 LAN Server:

- Additional Hardware Platforms
  —LAN Server for Macintosh

- —LAN Server for AIX
- —LAN Server for OS/400
- —LAN Server for VM and MVS
- ■ Remote LAN Access
  - —LAN Distance
  - —Distributed Console Access Facility (Decaf)
- ■ Host and WAN Communications
  - —Communication Manager/2
  - —TCP/IP for OS/2
  - —TCP/IP for DOS
- ■ Networked Multimedia
  - —LAN Server Ultimedia
- ■ Fault Tolerance
  - —OASAS 1
  - —Micropolis Raidware
  - —EZ-Raid
- ■ Network Management
  - —Netview for OS/2
  - —LAN Network Manager
  - —System Performance Manager/2
- ■ E-Mail
  - —Lotus Notes
  - —Lotus cc:Mail
- ■ Other Client/Server Applications
  - —Database Manager/2
  - —Lotus Smartsuite

LAN Server Ultimedia allows up to 40 full-motion video and sound sessions to be supported from a single server. Applications include education, information kiosks, and advertising.

Future Directions

IBM would like LAN Server to lead the way in connecting heterogeneous networks using nonproprietary Open Systems architectures. A design is in

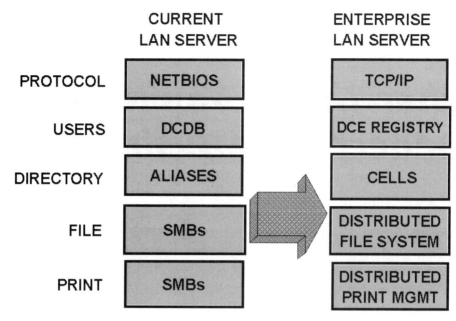

Figure 3.6 **Mapping LAN Server support into DCE.**

place for a future version of LAN Server to provide a gateway for existing clients to participate in the Open Systems Foundation's Distributed Computing Environment (DCE). DCE is an architecture for an integrated set of services that allow a workstation to access resources wherever they reside on a distributed network. DCE overcomes the obstacles of dissimilar hardware, operating systems, and protocols that otherwise limit or block interoperability. DCE-integrated services include security, directory, file access, interprocess control, device sharing, fault tolerance, and time synchronization. Figure 3.6 shows how the current LAN Server support will map into DCE. One of the most fundamental improvements DCE will offer administrators of large LAN Server networks will be the ability to administer several domains from a single point; there will no longer be a need to provide separate user accounts at each individual domain.

IBM will also be expanding LAN Server's offerings to include additional hardware platforms, beginning with the newly developed PowerPC. New technologies for distributed object programming will complement the services provided by DCE to enable IBM to focus on powerful platforms for interoperability in the upcoming years.

CHAPTER 4

Other Things You Need to Connect Your Business

*Things which matter most must never be
at the mercy of things which matter least.*

—*Goethe*

Discussions of NOS design often include the pros and cons of using a general-purpose versus a specialized operating system as a basis for the network. Logic suggests that an operating system specialized for networks will provide the most efficient environment for a server. The cost for this efficiency is often a loss in flexibility; an operating system specialized for resource management is generally not designed to run standard applications, such as your favorite spreadsheet or editor. This limits the degree of network application support that can be provided, as well as eliminates the ability for a user's workstation to be shared as a server. Applications can be sent as files to a client workstation to be run exclusively on the client, but there is no flexibility to run a portion or all of the application on the server without modifying the application to work with the server's specialized interface.

Reasons why you might want to run all or a portion of your applications on a server are to save disk space and memory on your client workstations and, in some cases, to get better performance. The extreme case of saving disk space is running all applications on the server and having medialess client workstations. Medialess workstations have no disk drives or hard drives and are totally dependent on a host or server to provide all the software the workstations will use, including the operating system. The service that provides all this code to a medialess workstation is called *remote initial program load* (RIPL). Many companies use medialess workstations as a security measure in addition to cost savings; if a workstation does not have a disk drive, it is extremely difficult for someone to copy information and remove it from the workplace.

If the CPU of the server has plenty of capacity and is faster than that of the client, sharing the application from a server will actually be faster than running the same application locally on the client. Another example of improving performance by running the application on the server is when the application is very large or requires lots of data that must be supplied by the server. A classic example of something that runs best on a server is a database engine that must access and manipulate a large amount of shared data. Putting the database engine on the client means that all the data being manipulated must be locked and shipped across the network.

Today's distributed databases use a query language to enable users to send requests to a database engine that does the work (data sorting and selecting) on the requester's behalf. The only information that has to flow over the network is the request and the final answer. Other applications that may benefit from being run at the server or a combination of server and client include: spreadsheets, graphics, desktop publications, project management and tracking tools, and computer-aided design. The positive effects of reducing network traffic are multiplied if the application is being run over a slow or highly congested network.

While OS/2 is a general-purpose operating system, LAN Server benefits from the fact that both were created with the other in mind. While the performance documented for LAN Server indicates that no sacrifices have been made in capacity or speed, most general-purpose DOS, Windows, and OS/2 applications can be configured to run in the server, the client, or both. General-purpose applications can also happily coexist with network services on the same server, making it possible for a user to utilize it as a shared, nondedicated system.

Which Operating System?

Today, you have lots of freedom in selecting an operating system and hardware platform on which to run LAN Server and LAN Server clients (Figure

4.1). The choices you make might include consideration of hardware you currently have on hand, as well as the operating systems and environments with which your organization is already familiar. Creating an inventory of your current hardware and installed software will prove invaluable if you do not have one already. The operating system used for the servers will depend on the hardware platform you choose:

- OS/2 2.1 or higher for an Intel 386 compatible or higher personal computer
- AIX/6000 for a RISC System/6000
- OS/400 for an AS/400
- VM or MVS for IBM mainframes

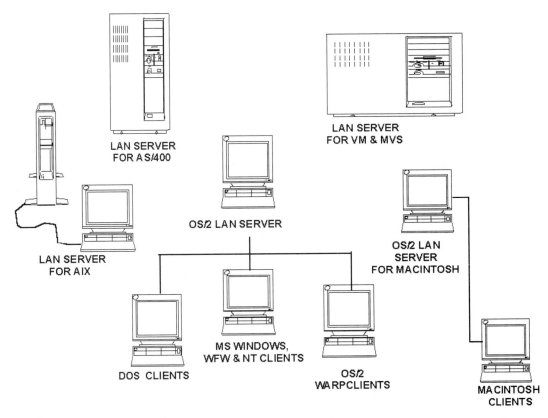

Figure 4.1 **LAN Server operating system and hardware platforms.**

Most of this book focuses on the PC platform, which scales well to many different organizations and has the largest install base.

For LAN Server clients, you currently have four options:

- OS/2 2.1 or higher
- DOS 3.3 and 5.0 (later releases supported by LAN Server 3.01 and 4.0)
- Preceding versions of DOS with Windows 3.11 and Windows for Workgroups 3.1 and 3.11
- System 6.0.5 or higher for AppleTalk-capable Macintosh workstations (requires IBM OS/2 LAN Server for Macintosh to be installed on the server)

The best advice for selecting operating system and hardware platforms is to keep things as simple and uniform as possible. While LAN Server is capable of supporting many combinations of hardware and software, the fewer platforms you choose, the easier your job will be in supplying future network services, training, and maintenance.

One of the most important considerations if you decide to use DOS workstations for requesters will be your requirements for low memory. Low memory is the 640KB of memory that comprises the total memory available to DOS for the operating system and device driver support. When DOS was first architected, 640KB seemed like an ample amount of memory, but today's software requires work-arounds for DOS's low memory constraints. Extended memory, which directly addresses the high memory area above the 1MB address, and expanded memory, which maps an area of low memory into a larger area of high memory, are the two most popular methods for gaining more space. Use of high memory requires an Intel 80286 or later processor. Applications loaded in high memory cannot interface directly with I/O devices. DOS 5.0 and later versions have eased the situation slightly by allowing much of the operating system itself to be loaded into the first 64KB of high memory, thus yielding additional space for applications. Unfortunately, the architecture of DOS precludes the possibility of ever completely alleviating DOS's low memory constraints.

If you read our biographical information, you are probably not surprised to hear that our operating system of choice for PCs is OS/2. OS/2 does not have the low memory constraints of DOS and is considerably more crash-proof. OS/2's installable HPFS is not subject to the disk fragmentation problems of DOS's FAT file system. With OS/2, we can have the best of all possible worlds (or, at least, all possible applications), because DOS, Windows, and OS/2 applications are all supported. Because OS/2 is a preemptive multi-tasking operating system, rather than simply a time-sliced application manager, we can run multiple applications that require real-time processing, such as communications and multimedia, without a flaw. The user interface has improved with every release. The OS/2 3.0 Warp we are currently using, for example, combined several of the most frequently used functions on a *launchpad* conveniently located on the desktop.

The nature of our work causes us to use our systems heavily for numerous tasks that get interrupted and reprioritized several times a day. I estimate that the ability to run background processes in OS/2 has saved more than 20 percent of my time on hectic days when I have needed it most. OS/2 does take longer to boot up than Windows (I turn my system on in the morning before I get my coffee), but once booted, OS/2 is both spritely and bulletproof. A long boot time is less of an annoyance if you never have to reboot during the day because you encountered an unrecoverable error. My OS/2 Server has been running several months having last been rebooted after a required power shutdown for building maintenance.

What Will be Needed on the Server?

The server will be the hardest working system on the network. It should, therefore, have the fastest CPU and more memory and hard disk than any requester or stand-alone PC. How fast does the server CPU need to be? The answer will vary, depending on the number of requesters and types of services and applications it will be supporting. A 20 MHz 80386 processor is often adequate for file and print sharing on a network of 20 users. As the number of concurrent users increases, the CPU should be upgraded accordingly. A faster CPU should also be considered when supporting such services as Remote IPL and such applications as multimedia. Remote IPL puts a large workload on the server when the remote workstations are first booting; the added CPU speed shortens the time users will have to wait for access. Multimedia is what is known as a *real-time* application. Information must be available within a small timing window for real-time applications to work. In a multimedia application, a server with inadequate CPU support would result in the picture and sound being jerky and distorted.

The speed of other workstations should also determine your server's CPU speed. Whereas a 20 MHz server would seem blindingly fast to users accustomed to PC-ATs, if your workstations are now 50 or 66 MHz 80486s, using the same server would appear painfully slow. In addition, fast requesters can generate a higher workload for the network. The workload generated by faster requesters can overwhelm a slow server by exhausting the number of buffers and resource elements set aside to handle work requests.

Once the server is installed, the best way to ensure that the CPU is adequate is to regularly monitor the server's CPU utilization. A rough estimate can be made by running the Pulse application, a productivity aid that comes with OS/2. More accurate information can be gathered by investing in one of the many performance tools available, such as IBM's System Performance Monitor/2, IBM LAN Netview Monitor, or CSN Inc's Watchit. The server's CPU utilization should average less than 70 percent and not exceed 80 percent for more than three or four minutes during peak usage. If the server CPU is inadequate, the server should either be upgraded to a faster CPU, or another server should be added to split the workload.

Tables 4.1 and 4.2 show the approximate amount of memory and hard disk space you will need on your server. Table 4.1 provides estimated resources needed for the Entry version of LAN Server, while Table 4.2 shows resources needed for the Advanced version. These tables are based on information provided by the workstation planning worksheets in Volume 1 of the

IBM OS/2 LAN Server 3.0 and 4.0 Network Administrator References. Notice that the two tables are similar with the following exceptions: the HPFS and HPFS386 file systems, cache, and slightly higher requirements to support additional functionality within the Advanced version. For estimating resources required for remote IPL, the tables assume 20 requesters are attached to the network. Due to the added complexity of calculating the hard disk requirements for remote IPL, details for these calculations are provided in Table 4.3.

If you are installing a network of more than 20 requesters, you must increase requirements for remote IPL and possibly the applications and data allowance to accommodate the larger number of users. If installing the Advanced version on a larger network, the HPFS386 cache will also change. The Advanced version of LAN Server creates a default cache size of 20 percent of the total memory. For example, the memory allocated to cache on a system with 10MB of memory installed will be 2MB. This default can be

Table 4.1 **LAN Server (Entry) Memory and Hard Disk Requirements (MB)**

Description	v3.0 RAM	v3.0 Disk	v4.0 RAM	v4.0 Disk
OS/2 Base (v2.1)—Required	2.8	31.7	2.8	31.7
Segment Swap Data Set—Required	N/A	10.0	N/A	10.0
HPFS—Recommended	0.2	N/A	0.2	N/A
HPFS Cache—Recommended	2.0	N/A	2.0	N/A
Active spooling (while printing)—Recommended	0.8	N/A	0.8	N/A
Subtotal for OS/2	5.8	41.7	5.8	41.7
LAN Server Domain Controller—Required	3.6	<10.1	2.2	<18.3
Temporary Space for Installation—Required	N/A	2.2	N/A	1.1
LAN Server Administration GUI—Recommended	N/A	N/A	4.5	*
Subtotal for LAN Server Base	3.6	<12.3	6.7	<19.4
Advanced/Tailored Install Components—Optional	N/A	<1.4	N/A	<1.4
DOS Remote IPL Service—Optional (for 10 users)	0.6	12.4	0.7	23.0
OS/2 Remote IPL Service—Optional (for 10 users)	0.8	81.3	0.8	71.4
Subtotal for LAN Server Optional Features	1.4	<95.1	1.4	<95.8
Allowance for Data and Applications	>3.2	>66.0	>2.1	>58.0
Total Base Requirement	12	120	15	120
Total Base Requirement Plus Optional Features	14	220	16	220

*Administration GUI disk requirement is included in Domain Controller requirement.

overridden by changing the values of the CACHESIZE parameter line within the HPFS386.INI file after LAN Server has been installed. This file is located in a subdirectory called IBM386FS. As stated in earlier chapters, the Advanced version is recommended for optimum file server performance on networks with greater than 80 concurrent users. The Entry server is recommended for networks of 80 or fewer concurrent users, but can support as many as 200 light users with an acceptable level of performance.

Table 4.2 **LAN Server (Advanced) Memory and Hard Disk Requirements (MB)**

Description	v3.0 RAM	v3.0 Disk	v4.0 RAM	v4.0 Disk
OS/2 Base (v2.1)—Required	2.8	31.7	2.8	31.7
Segment Swap Data Set—Required	N/A	10.0	N/A	10.0
HPFS386 Cache—Recommended	2.4	N/A	3.6	N/A
Active spooling (while printing)—Recommended	0.8	N/A	0.8	N/A
Subtotal for OS/2	6.0	41.7	7.2	41.7
LAN Server Domain Controller—Required	3.6	11.7	3.5	18.3
Temporary Space for Installation—Required	N/A	2.2	N/A	1.1
LAN Server Administration GUI—Recommended	N/A	N/A	4.5	*
Subtotal for LAN Server Base	3.6	13.9	8.0	19.4
Advanced/Tailored Install Components—Optional	N/A	1.4	N/A	1.4
DOS Remote IPL Service—Optional (for 10 users)	0.6	12.4	0.7	23.0
OS/2 Remote IPL Service—Optional (for 10 users)	0.8	81.3	0.8	71.4
Subtotal for LAN Server Optional Features	1.4	95.1	1.4	95.8
Allowance for Data and Applications	>2.4	>66	>2.8	>58
Total Base Requirement	12	120	18	120
Total Base Requirement Plus Optional Features	14	220	20	220

*Administration GUI disk requirement is included in Domain Controller requirement.

The rows of Tables 4.1 and 4.2 are divided into four sections: the OS/2 operating system, LAN Server, an allowance for data and applications, and totals. The first section contains the resources needed for the OS/2 operating system. The data is based on measurements of OS/2 version 2.1, which also closely matches the requirements for OS/2 2.0. These requirements include the base, HPFS, segment swap data set, cache, and active print spooling. HPFS provides performance advantages for accessing files within large directories. It reduces disk fragmentation, a problem common to the FAT file system. Disk fragmentation occurs when files written to a disk must be split into

Table 4.3 **LAN Server Remote IPL Hard Disk Requirements (MB)**

DOS Remote IPL	v3.0 Disk	v4.0 Disk
DOS Remote IPL Service	6.2	2.8
DOS Version (select one):		
DOS 3.3	0.5	0.5
DOS 5.0	2.2	2.2
DOS 6.3	N/A	10.3
Additional per DOS Remote IPL Workstation	0.4	0.7
OS/2 Remote IPL	v3.0 Disk	v4.0 Disk
OS/2 Remote IPL Service	10.9	2.2
OS/2 Version (select one):		
OS/2 2.0	40.4	40.4
OS/2 2.1	52.6	52.6
Additional per OS/2 Remote IPL Workstation	3.0	0.2

lots of pieces to accommodate the free space available. The fragmentation worsens over time and causes file access performance to get progressively slower. HPFS uses a different algorithm for data storage, which better accommodates the future growth of files. When installing OS/2, select HPFS to be installed on the partition. You may also choose to create a separate partition for the OS/2 base operating system; this facilitates upgrading the operating system without having to reinstall applications and data files. The maximum cache size supported for HPFS is 2MB.

The HPFS386 of the Advanced version of LAN Server replaces the HPFS of OS/2 and offers all the advantages of HPFS. The requirements for HPFS386 are included with the domain controller requirements in Table 4.2. As noted earlier, the HPFS386 cache defaults to 20 percent of the total memory installed in the Advanced server, and can be adjusted by editing the CACHE-SIZE parameter line of HPFS386.INI. Another feature of the Advanced server is that it can use memory above 16MB for cache; this is controlled by the USEALLMEM parameter in HPFS386.INI. USEALLMEM requires that the NIC be able to address memory above 16MB to enable the adapter to access the cache for sending and receiving data. Information on Supported NICs can be found in Appendix C. Prior to LAN Server 4.0, the HPFS386 CACHESIZE and USEALLMEM were specified in CONFIG.SYS.

 You may notice two other parameters relating to cache in CONFIG.SYS: CACHE and DISKCACHE. CACHE is the cache set aside for HPFS; this should be set to the maximum value of 2MB when installing the Entry version of LAN Server, and should not be in CONFIG.SYS if the Advanced version of LAN Server is installed. DISKCACHE is cache set aside for the FAT file system; this is not needed if files accessed by LAN Server are stored on an HPFS partition. After hardware, cache is the parameter that has the greatest impact on improving network performance. Accessing information from cache is as much as 1,000 times faster than accessing from disk. The larger the cache, the greater the chance that the information you need will be there.

The segment swap data set is space allocated for data that is swapped out of memory. This data is contained in the SWAPPER.DAT file. CONFIG.SYS contains the location of SWAPPER.DAT, along with parameters that determine its size.

Active spooling should be installed on any server with attached printers. It allows other processes to continue while print jobs are spooled to the printer.

The LAN server section includes base requirements that are subtotaled for the domain controller, LAN Server installation, and the administrative GUI. The optional advanced/tailored install features and remote IPL are also included with LAN Server. The domain controller includes all the services and functions acquired using the Basic or Easy install. When LAN Server is installed, a temporary directory is used to unpack files and save values needed during configuration. Since this temporary disk space is returned to the system when installation is complete, the space has been added back to the available resource for applications and data. The LAN Server 4.0 administrative GUI is resident only when the GUI is in use. Though the memory is returned to the system for use with other applications when administration is complete, it was not included with the application allowance because of the likelihood that administration will be done concurrently with application usage. The hard disk requirement for the LAN Server 4.0 GUI is included with the domain controller requirements, as the LAN Server references do not break out the GUI as a separate component.

The advanced (or tailored) install path includes: First Failure Support Technology/2 (FFST/2), the generic alerter service, support for Uninterruptible Power Supply (UPS), disk fault tolerance, local security, Virtual DOS LAN API support, the loopback driver, and a migration import utility. Most of these features were described in the previous chapter on LAN Server. FFST/2 and the generic alerter service expand error handling capabilities with LAN Server. FFST/2 provides an externalized interface for error handling and reporting within a workstation, while the generic alerter service provides a common format for error reporting across the network. UPS is highly recommended for protecting data in the event of a power outage. Disk fault tolerance protects data in the event of a hard disk failure by replicating data across two disk drives. Local security protects resources on the Advanced Server from unauthorized local access.

Virtual DOS API support and the loopback driver are programming and test aids. The loopback driver, for example, simplifies testing by allowing a programmer to test both the send and receive side of a networking program on a single system. The migration utility is a holdout from the earliest days of LAN Server; it provides support for migrating LAN Server 1.0 servers to the current release level. As described in the previous chapter, other migration utilities are available from IBM and numerous electronic bulletin boards to migrate Netware and LAN Manager servers to the current release of LAN Server.

Remote IPL requires lots of disk space on the server, because the server must accommodate everything that would normally be present on the requester's local hard drive, including in the case of OS/2 the SWAPPER.DAT file. The hard disk requirements for remote IPL consist of a fixed requirement and a variable requirement that grows with the number of requesters supported. The number of requesters assumed for Tables 4.1 and 4.2 were ten OS/2 and ten DOS requesters for a total of 20 remote IPL requesters. The fixed requirement includes portions of the LAN Server product and the operating system being served to the requester. There is a very close relationship between the remote IPL service and the operating system it is loading. Care should be taken that remote IPL is used with supported versions of the operating system, and that OS/2 remote IPL images match the release of the server. Also, DOS hard disk requirements have greatly increased within recent versions. The LAN Server 3.0 requirements were measured with DOS 5.0, and the LAN Server 4.0 requirements use DOS 6.3. The increase in the DOS remote IPL requirements reflect the growth in DOS. LAN Server 4.0 reduced its hard disk requirements for larger numbers of OS/2 requesters by focusing on the variable requirement. Details for calculating remote IPL requirements for a varying number of requesters is given in Table 4.3.

The tables provide requirements for domain controllers. Remember that one domain controller is required for each domain. A second server configured as a backup domain controller requires the same amount of memory and disk space as the domain controller. Additional servers require approximately 1MB less hard disk space and memory than is required by domain controllers. The tables assume the language installed is English or another European-based language that uses a single-byte character set (SBCS). Asian-based languages, such as Japanese and Korean, use double-byte character sets and require approximately 3.5MB of additional memory and 13MB of hard disk.

The allowance for data and applications provides the approximate memory and disk space left over from the total recommended value. This allowance needs to include all shared applications, administrative tools, shared directories, user home directories, and anything else you need to install on the server. The numbers provided in this row of the table should be adjusted according to the applications and services you wish to include on the server. To do this, list all the services you want to provide on the server, along with their requirements for memory and disk space. Then add up these values to get a more accurate estimate of your total server requirements. Be sure to add contingency for future growth of applications, data files, and users.

If your data and application requirements are equal or less than the allowance provided in the table, the totals reflect the amount of memory and hard disk space you will need on the server. Otherwise, add your data and application requirements to the numbers provided for the services you will be using to get a new estimate of your total. The first total includes only the base and recommended services. The second total includes every LAN Server installable feature, including remote IPL support for ten OS/2 and ten DOS requesters.

What Will be Needed on the Workstations?

Table 4.4 provides the low memory and hard disk requirements for LAN Server version 3.0's DOS LAN Requester and Version 4.0's DOS LAN Services. The requirements were measured after installing the default configurations for each combination of features and products shown. Low memory

Table 4.4 **DOS Requester Low Memory and Hard Disk Requirements**

Description	v3.0 Low Memory (KB)	v3.0 Disk (MB)	v4.0 Low Memory (KB)	v4.0 Disk (MB)
DLS with DOS and DOS NetBEUI:				
DOS 5.0 with Low Memory	N/A	N/A	259.4	6.2
DOS 5.0 with High Memory	N/A	N/A	215.2	6.2
DOS 5.0 with UMB	N/A	N/A	137.8	6.2
DOS 6.3 with Low Memory	N/A	N/A	259.0	6.5
DOS 6.3 with High Memory	N/A	N/A	216.1	6.5
DOS 6.3 with UMB	N/A	N/A	133.5	6.5
DLS with DOS and LAN Support Program:				
DOS 5.0 with Low Memory	194.0	5.5	248.4	6.3
DOS 5.0 with High Memory	154.0	5.5	204.2	6.3
DOS 5.0 with UMB	76.0	5.5	126.8	6.3
DOS 6.3 with Low Memory	N/A	N/A	248.0	6.6
DOS 6.3 with High Memory	N/A	N/A	205.0	6.6
DOS 6.3 with UMB	N/A	N/A	122.5	6.6

rows indicate the low memory requirements on systems that have no high memory available. High memory indicates the low memory requirements available when standard extended memory is used. Upper Memory Blocks (UMBs) indicate the ability of the operating system and requester to utilize part of the 384KB of memory available above the 1MB address. DOS LAN Services will automatically use the Upper Memory Block and extended memory if it is available; DOS LAN Requester's high memory usage must be set up using the HIMEM memory configuration utility. Additional low memory can be freed up at the expense of optimum performance by tuning the LAN Requester to conserve memory. With LAN Server 4.0, the DOS LAN Services configuration can be tuned to use as little as 30KB of low memory;

instructions are provided in Volume 2 of the *LAN Server Network Administrator's Reference.* NetBEUI is faster than LAN Support Program but also uses more low memory.

Table 4.5 provides the memory and hard disk requirements for the OS/2 Requester. The 4.5MB shown for the version 4.0 Requester's base memory requirement is needed only if the Administrative GUI is loaded. As with the server, the memory allocated for the GUI is freed up for usage by other applications when the GUI is not in use.

As discussed earlier, diskless workstations can be supported using LAN Server's remote IPL. Memory requirements for these requesters would be the same as for other requester workstations.

Table 4.5 **OS/2 Requester Memory and Hard Disk Requirements (MB)**

Description	v3.0 RAM	v3.0 Disk	v4.0 RAM	v4.0 Disk
OS/2 Base (v2.0 or v2.1)—Required	2.8	31.7	2.8	31.7
Segment Swap Data Set—Required	N/A	2.5	N/A	2.5
HPFS—Recommended	0.2	N/A	0.2	N/A
HPFS Cache—Recommended	0.5	N/A	0.5	N/A
Active spooling (while printing)—Recommended	0.8	N/A	0.8	N/A
Subtotal for OS/2	4.3	34.2	4.3	34.2
Requester and Transports (LAPS/MPTS)—Required	1.9	4.2	2.1	7.1
Temporary Space for Installation—Required	N/A	2.2	N/A	1.1
LAN Requester Basic/Easy Install Options	0.2	3.6	*4.5	8.7
Subtotal for LAN Requester Base	2.1	10.0	6.6	16.9
LAN Requester Advanced/Tailored Install Options	0.9	1.2	1.4	2.3
Allowance for Data and Applications	>2.7	>74	>4.2	>66
Total Base Requirement	10	120	12	120
Total Base Requirement Plus Optional Features	10	120	12	120

*Only needed when Administrative GUI is loaded.

Network Interface Cards (NICs)

The servers and requesters attach to the network via a cable attached to a NIC located within each workstation. Normally requesters will have a single NIC, while servers may be configured with up to 4 NICs. Each NIC is capable of routing information to 254 addresses, so four NICs on a server can support a total of 1,016 concurrent connections. NICs, also commonly called *Adapters,* must conform to your workstation's internal bus architecture. PS/2s and compatibles use a 16- or 32-bit Microchannel Architecture (MCA). PS/1s and other PC-compatibles use either Industry Standard Architecture (ISA) or Extended Industry Standard Architecture (EISA). NICs interface to a piece of software called a Media Access Control (MAC) driver. LAN Server supplies the MAC drivers for some NICs, while others come packaged with the NIC itself; the MAC must be properly installed and configured for LAN Server to be able to communicate over the network. Appendix C provides the current list of NICs supported by LAN Server versions 3.0 and 4.0. As indicated by the tables, version 4.0 vastly expanded its coverage of NICs. LAN Server currently supports over 70 percent of the NICs currently on the market.

Ethernet or Token Ring?

Token Ring adapters support 4-megabit-per-second and 16-megabit-per-second capacities. A highly reliable network, its performance degrades smoothly with added load up to approximately 95 percent of its theoretical data capacity. For this reason, Token Ring is ideal for networks with heavy traffic. Token Ring can handle frame sizes of up to 16KB, though most general-purpose networks are tuned to a maximum frame size of 2 to 4KB. Larger frame sizes speed up file transfers and also preserve CPU capacity on the server and client workstations.

Ethernet is less efficient than Token Ring in coping with heavy network usage. Ethernet performance tends to degrade sharply when usage exceeds approximately 20 percent of its theoretical data capacity of 10 megabits per second. Ethernet does not lend itself well for filtering traffic between local and wide area networks, so remote LAN access products, such as LAN Distance, cannot support as many connections to an Ethernet network as they can with Token Ring. Ethernet offers superior performance, however, when supporting very large networks, where usage is constrained to a few users at a time. Maximum Frame sizes cannot exceed 1.5KB, so file transfers may be slower. One reason for considering Ethernet is that there are currently more choices of adapter manufacturers and hardware than there are for Token Ring. If you need to support a wide range of non-IBM equipment, you will probably want to examine the Ethernet option carefully.

Is 16 Megabits Per Second Faster than 4 or 10?

The portion of the time within a network transaction that can be attributed to the speed of the network is measured in fractions of milliseconds—far below our ability to perceive. Transaction response—the time it takes to hit an Enter key and observe the result of a server transaction on a client workstation—is mostly composed of time the application on the server requires to process the transaction. The performance advantage of 16-megabit Token Ring cards is important, however, in providing necessary capacity for very large or heavily used networks.

Busmaster adapters have their own processors. With the advanced version of LAN Server, busmaster adapters can transfer data directly from disk cache, thus eliminating much of the overhead for moving data. The top performing IBM LAN Streamer adapter, for example, is an enhancement to the busmaster adapters, which allows data to be transferred at a much higher rate by generating memory addresses only once per block rather than once per every 4 bytes of data. These high-end NICs can also address memory above the 16MB system address space, allowing servers configured with up to 64MB of memory to use this additional memory for caching.

Cables and Cabling Standards

In the early days of networks, the choice of Ethernet or Token Ring also implied a choice in cable type and network topology. Ethernet originally utilized thick coaxial cable and a bus structure (a central cable with offshoot cables connecting individual workstations). Token Ring utilized shielded twisted-pair cable and was originally conceived as a ring topology in which each workstation acted as a repeater to maintain signal strength throughout the network. These original designs were expensive and unreliable. Most of today's Ethernet and Token Ring networks utilize a combination of cable specifically targeted for the distance and amount of traffic generated.

Most networks use a star topology in which a hub forms the center of the star, with cable radiating out to each of the workstations (see Figure 4.2). Many star clusters may be joined together at the hub to form larger networks. This technique is also used to connect network hubs between floors in a multistory building, and hubs across multiple buildings.

The cabling used to connect multiple hubs is called a *backbone* (Figure 4.3). The backbone generally requires a more expensive type of cable than that used to connect the workstations to the hub. Cable such as fiber optic or thick coaxial allows the backbone to span a greater distance and support a higher data rate than is typically needed to join a workstation to a hub. When joined with a maximum of five repeaters, coaxial cable can support a distance of 2.5 kilometers, or 1.5 miles. Fiber optic cabling is becoming increasingly

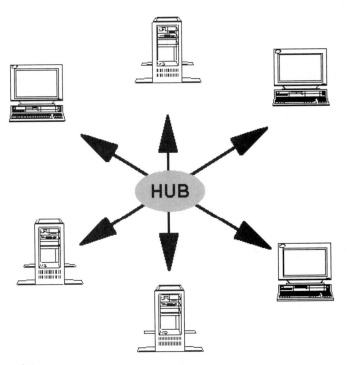

Figure 4.2 **Star topology.**

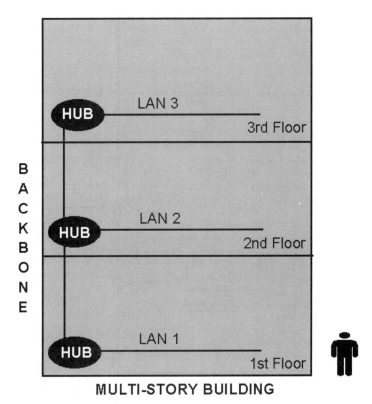

Figure 4.3 ***A backbone connecting multiple floors in a building.***

popular for backbones that must support longer distances or higher data rates. Fiber optic can support a distance of up to 100 kilometers, or 62 miles! The price, which was originally prohibitive, has been declining steadily against the price of coaxial cable in recent years. Let us take a closer look at some of the more popular cabling alternatives.

Coaxial Cabling (10Base2)

10Base2, shown in Figure 4.4, is sometimes called ThinNet or CheaperNet, and works only with Ethernet adapters. This is the least expensive option, and is easy to set up as long as you can string cable directly between PCs. 10Base2 is also the least flexible, expandable, and maintainable. Choose 10Base2 if you are setting up a simple LAN with only a few workstations in one room, or at most two adjoining rooms.

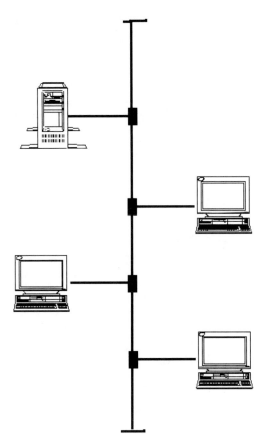

Figure 4.4 **10Base2 coaxial cabling.**

10Base2's biggest limitation is that the PCs are wired one after the other, in sequence—so a break or problem in any part of the connection brings down the whole network. 10Base2 also limits you to a maximum of 30 PCs per LAN (although it's possible to connect LANs with a device called a *repeater*).

10Base2 cabling is thin (5 mm—about 1/4 inch—in diameter) coaxial cable. Each PC has a T-shaped connector called a BNC connector. The bottom of the T in the BNC connector plugs into the PC's Ethernet adapter. One end of a 10Base2 cable plugs into each side of the T in the BNC connector, and the cable leads to the next PC in the string. The two PCs at either end of the string have a *terminator* in place of a cable connection. A terminator, as the name implies, terminates the string of PCs. The total length of all the cable must be less than 200 meters (about 600 feet), with no more than 30 PCs connected. If you cut your own cable, make each length a multiple of half a meter (about 18 inches).

UTP (Unshielded Twisted Pair) Cabling

For small networks and joining workstations to a hub, unshielded twisted-pair cabling is the next cheapest (after 10Base2) and the most easily installed choice. Unshielded twisted pair is similar to the telephone wire used in your home and office; it is a set of at least two pairs of copper wires encased in a single plastic sheath. While ordinary telephone wire is UTP Type 1 wire, you should use Type 3 or, better yet, Type 5 UTP for LANs. The type of UTP refers to various grades. Better grades have wires that are more tightly twisted than lower grades. The tighter twists help shield the wires from out-side electrical interference and allow reliable transmission at higher data rates. The higher grades of unshielded twisted pair can support both Ethernet and Token Ring reliably within offices and small businesses.

With UTP, each PC is connected by a length of cable to a special device called a *hub*—as contrasted with 10Base2, where each PC is connected to the next PC. This makes UTP more flexible, maintainable, and expandable than 10Base2, because you can easily add hubs to add more PCs—because the cable between PC and hub can be up to 300 feet long, and because you can put hubs in wiring closets in a larger building. Also, a problem in the cable connecting one PC doesn't affect the rest of the network, and the hubs can have intelligence to detect and report problems to a central administrator.

Cabling with UTP will cost more than 10Base2 initially, because you have to purchase at least one hub (although the cabling is a little less expensive). However, if you plan to grow and want to use Ethernet, this is the best choice.

The factors that may force you to consider a more expensive type of wiring are greater distances and higher data rates than may be needed for a small business. The maximum distance for a single segment of wire (work-station to hub) is 100 meters, or roughly 400 feet. Longer distances require another type of cabling, such as coaxial or fiber optic. While standard-grade unshielded twisted pair is adequate for 4 Mbit/second Token Ring and 10 Mbit/second Ethernet, 16 Mbit/second Token Ring requires the highest grade for reliable data transmission. At very high data rates of 100 Mbits/second, unshielded twisted-pair cabling is susceptible to producing high frequency electromagnetic emissions that may interfere with workstations and other equipment. Higher data rates will be increasingly common within the next decade.

STP (Shielded Twisted Pair) Cabling

Shielded twisted pair currently costs about 20 percent more than standard-grade unshielded twisted pair, and in some cases, less than the highest grades of unshielded twisted pair. Shielded twisted pair supports 16 mbit/second Token Ring as well as the higher 100 Mbit/second data rates. If you think you might want to take advantage of these higher rates, you may want to consider installing shielded twisted pair. Unfortunately, shielded twisted pair has the same distance limitations as unshielded twisted pair (100 meters), so it is not as useful as fiber optic for connecting between hubs.

Cabling Standards

Standards exist today that specify the structure of cabling within a building. The idea behind the standards is to specify a universal cabling system capable of satisfying a wide range of data transmission requirements (including support of either Token Ring or Ethernet). Cabling systems consist of vertical risers connecting multiple floors of a building, and horizontal cabling linking the risers with the computers on each floor. The vertical risers correspond to the backbone of the network while the horizontal cabling supports individual LANs that may be based on hubs.

A third consideration for structured cabling systems is access to services external to the building. Depending on distance, this may be handled through fiber optic cabling, or via the public telephone network with switched or leased telephone lines. Two commonly used standards are AT&T's Premised Distribution System, more commonly called Systimax, and the IBM Cabling System. Systimax specifies the use of unshielded twisted-pair and fiber-optic cabling. It requires the cable to be laid out in a star-shaped arrangement on each floor, linked back to wiring centers. The IBM Cabling System specifies a combination of unshielded twisted pair, shielded twisted pair, and fiber optic. While it may not be necessary for small networks, adherence to a cabling standard allows you to expand your network in an orderly way without requiring continual replacement of wiring and equipment.

Hubs

Another important component of both Ethernet and Token Ring networks, hubs provide a central point for connection and error detection, which allow physical networks to be conveniently managed from wiring closets. They can also provide a convenient point to monitor the network for traffic levels. Some hubs even come with built-in security features to prevent any unauthorized workstations or monitoring tools from connecting to the network. On Ethernet, hubs serve as repeaters to maintain signal strength; their central location helps reduce network congestion and collisions. The Ethernet standard, which gave rise to the use of hubs to support transmission of data at 10 Mbits/second over unshielded twisted-pair cable, is known as 10Base-T.

Token Ring looks to hubs to provide a mechanism for maintaining a logical closed ring by removing a section from the loop when it malfunctions. Recall that Token Rings rely on a token being passed from workstation to workstation to grant permission to transmit data. The actual data transmission follows in this same logical circuit. Before hubs, if a portion of the network was detached or malfunctioning, it was very difficult to locate the area causing the problem, because the entire network would become disabled. The first evolution toward Token Ring hubs, called Multistation Access Units (MAUs) connected workstations together in groups of eight. The MAUs could then be cabled to each other to form a large logical ring. If a workstation was disconnected or a NIC malfunctioned, the MAU closed off the affected section, in effect, *healing* the ring. The shortcoming of the MAU is that a bad connection between MAUs would still result in disabling the entire network. This realization led to the introduction of Concentrator Access Units (CAUs), which eliminate the interconnection of MAUs.

Today, there are many choices of hubs to fit the needs of Ethernet, Token Ring, and even combinations of the two networks. Choices of special interest to small businesses include low-cost and PC-based hubs that target networks of fewer than 20 users. The low-cost hubs feature a connector box, while PC-based hubs use a special card installed in the Server workstation. The main caution in using these lower-cost options is that many are not expandable; if the network outgrows the hub, you may be forced to reinvest in more flexible standard equipment.

Bridges, Routers, and Gateways

Repeaters join two network segments and extend the distance a signal can travel over a physical network by regenerating, or repeating, the signal. Ethernet hubs also perform this function on Ethernet networks, as do workstations on Token Ring networks. Bridges are another means of connecting two physical network segments together. In addition to repeating the data signal, bridges can make use of destination addresses within the packets to filter data. This allows bridges to reduce network traffic by only retransmitting data addressed to workstations on the other side of the bridge. Use of a bridge to subdivide a network is an effective way of reducing traffic on a network that has become too large. Two algorithms, *spanning tree* and *source routing*, are used by bridges to help determine which frames to forward and which to discard. Traditionally, Ethernet employs the spanning tree algorithm, while Token Ring employs source routing—although crossovers in support (particularly on Token Ring) are beginning to emerge. Some bridges also provide the ability to join a Token Ring and Ethernet segment together by providing the necessary translation in address packets.

Where bridges make very simple binary decisions to forward or not to forward data based on the destination address, routers can make more complex routing decisions based on address, protocol, packet type, and other criteria. Some routers can even select the fastest route based on current traffic conditions on the network. Where bridges can handle only bidirectional support, routers can support more complex network topologies that contain multiple links between a given pair of segments. Multiple links can aid in reducing traffic congestion by spreading traffic across the links; they can also provide another means of access in the event that one of the links fail.

Gateways provide still one more level in functionality: Gateways not only route data, but are also capable of translating between two different protocol sets. One common use of a gateway is to allow network clients configured with only NetBIOS to communicate over a wide area network that uses a protocol such as TCP/IP. An alternative to using the gateway would be to install the TCP/IP protocol along with NetBIOS on each client, but this approach may not be feasible if memory on the client is constrained. A major advantage of a gateway is that its use does not require any changes to the network clients.

Printers

Printers can be attached to a network in a variety of ways, but are most commonly attached via the LAN Server or via a LAN Server client running peer services. LAN Server utilizes the OS/2 printer drivers listed in the PRDESC.LST file found in the OS2/INSTALL subdirectory to support multiple print attachments. A list of printers derived from the OS/2 Warp Version 3.0 PRDESC.LST is shown in Appendix D. Attaching multiple printers to a single print queue, called *pooling*, allows LAN Server to efficiently route jobs to the first available printer. When defining ports for multiple printers, the fastest printer should be assigned the highest port. For example, if two printers are installed and printer A is faster than printer B, assign printer B to LPT1 and assign printer A to LPT2. If both printers are available when a job arrives, the printer assigned to the highest port will be used to print the job. Assigning the fastest printer to the highest port provides the most efficient processing.

To Contract or Not to Contract

The previous section is only a brief introduction to network hardware. The intention is to familiarize you with the terminology and components so that you can ask the right questions and more easily explore the current hardware offerings. Cable installation can be as simple as plugging eight or fewer workstations into a single MAU concealed between desks and a wall, or it can be as complex as employing cabling standards in a construction plan to connect multiple buildings outfitted with a full array of intelligent hubs, bridges, routers, and gateways. Except in the simplest arrangements, this phase of network installation is the one that will most likely require expert assistance. With that in mind, this section addresses some considerations for contracting your network installation.

The expertise needed to select and install new network hardware is available from many sources; each has its own strengths and weaknesses. These sources include: hardware/software dealers, cabling companies, software companies, network consultants, and network management companies.

Large hardware dealers may include in-house expertise and installation services. If so, this could be a simple and economical way to both acquire and install the necessary hardware. A possible disadvantage is that the dealer is motivated to sell you the products it supplies: The dealer's advice may not be totally impartial and your choice in products may be somewhat limited.

Companies that specialize in cabling can offer the most economical prices for its cabling, as well as a high level of experience in its installation. Unfortunately, cabling companies rarely offer installation services for other network components. This means you will need to deal with multiple vendors to supply the rest of your hardware needs.

Most application software companies can provide advice on hardware support for their applications. When using these services, be aware that some of the customer support and sales people supplying these services will probably not have direct experience with network hardware components; the information they supply may not be complete or totally accurate. It is a good idea to request documentation that lists hardware and software that are compatible with applications you intend to use. The documentation is more likely to be accurate and may include important information regarding use restrictions that might not be otherwise conveyed.

IBM performs extensive compatibility testing with LAN Server and sponsors programs called *Tested and Approved* and *Ready for . . .* Products that carry the *Tested and Approved* or *Ready for* marks shown in Figure 4.5 have been tested in an environment designed to ensure the ability to interoperate and coexist with LAN Server and other IBM LAN Systems products. Lists of compatible products and, in some instances, their test results are provided through several channels, including CompuServe, the (800)IBM-4FAX support number, and IBM's Sources and Solution's catalog.

Network consultants specialize in network installations and network integration. Network management specialists focus on network integration and tools for managing the network. Competent consultants should have experience in installing networks in environments similar to your own and provide impartial advice on the best alternatives for your situation. The downside of using a consultant or network management specialist is that this expertise is not guaranteed or cheap. It is up to you as a potential customer to establish that the consultant has the level of experience needed for your network installation and that you are getting the best value for your money.

Before signing any contracts, obtain references from at least three of the consultant's recent customers. Request the references to be from customers

Figure 4.5 **Compatability marks.**

with similar network installations to the one proposed for you. Verify these references by contacting the customers and asking about their overall satisfaction with the network and services rendered by the consultant.

During the initial interview with the consultant, gather information on relevant experience, stability of the consultant's business practice, and how well you and the consultant communicate. Ask such questions as: How many years has the consultant been in business? How many installations has he or she completed? Which ones were similar to your own? How many jobs is the consultant currently handling? You want the consultant to be in demand but not overcommitted. Too few jobs, even if the references are positive, may indicate financial instability, which could result in your job never being completed. Too many jobs may mean that you will not get the level of attention and service you desire.

Does the consultant have any product affiliations? Product affiliations may result in discounted prices and added expertise, or they could signal partiality toward products that may not give you the best value. Does the consultant have engineering certification in one or more network operating systems? Certification credentials, such as LAN Server's Engineering Certification and Novell's Certified Network Engineer, should not be accepted in lieu of hands-on experience, but do indicate a level of competency within a fairly broad range of current network topics.

Does the consultant listen to you and make valid recommendations that fit your needs or try to impose a *one size fits all* solution? This again is a good indicator of the consultant's competency and impartiality. In addition, it is very important that you and the consultant can communicate effectively throughout the project. Toward that end, be sure to define clearly what you want the consultant to achieve and what the scope of the consultant's job will be.

Discuss what this work will cost. If you agree to an hourly rate, insist on an estimate and upper bounds for the total cost. Discuss any contingencies that may affect the scope, cost, and timing of the job. Agree on checkpoints and include dates and standards for each checkpoint's completion. Agree on a reporting structure that includes how often the consultant will provide you with status reports and who should be contacted for questions when you are not available. Specify the documentation to be provided by the consultant at the completion of the job. This should include layouts of the hardware and cabling, hardware configurations for all equipment installed, list of suppliers, copies of all warantees, and copies of all hardware and software documentation needed for installation and maintenance. All agreements should be documented in the contract, including some guarantee of satisfaction with the consultant's services and how unsatisfactory performance, such as missed deadlines or other contract discrepancies, will be addressed.

If You Install Your Own Network

This section provides a few general tips from those of us who have participated in numerous network installations over the last decade. Many of these could be listed under the general heading of *common sense.* However, for many of us, common sense was not gained without a price. When installing or upgrading a network, there is tremendous temptation to jump in with the belief that all will go smoothly—that there is no need to back up data or test components one at a time. When something does not go as anticipated, the optimistic approach can result in lost data and even more lost time spent trying to step back through the process to pinpoint the source of the problem. The temptation to cut corners never goes away. Only when one is *bitten* sufficiently hard and often does prudence overtake optimism.

First and foremost, do your homework before you purchase or install any hardware or software. Start with a list of applications and capabilities you want to support and ensure that each component that you select interoperates with the others. It is not unusual to be planning your ideal network configuration and find that a key component is incompatible with other selected components. It is much less painful to start over on a network design that exists only on paper than to patch or rip out a physical installation.

It is generally good practice to stick with mainstream designs and products, as these are most likely to be understood and supported by other vendors. One example is adherence to a cabling standard that provides a tested environment with maximum flexibility to accommodate growth and change. Another example is limiting your choice of networks to the two dominant ones: Ethernet and Token Ring. Choosing a less common network type, such as PC Net, will severely limit your choice of network interface cards and peripheral hardware.

Whenever possible, set up new hardware and software in a small test environment before introducing it to your production network or to new users. This creates minimum disruption to your business as you set up the network, and allows you to deal with any problems you might encounter without added pressure. Your test environment need not be extensive but it must be realistic in including the same network components and applications that will be operating in your regular production environment. For example, after the cable and hubs are in place, install LAN Server and a single Requester with the applications you plan to use before installing additional workstations.

When applying changes, such as new releases of a NOS, to an established network, the most foolproof approach is to install the new release on a separate test system, test it, then move it onto the network to replace the older workstation component. If you do not have an extra workstation that can be used in this way, the next safest approach is to back up, reconfigure, and test the workstation during a time when it will not be in use, such as a weekend. If unsuccessful, the old configuration can be restored before the next workday. Information gathered during a successful installation and test period can be applied toward more efficiently propagating changes to additional workstations on the network.

Whenever possible, test new components one piece at a time. This helps you more easily isolate problems. For example, before ripping out walls to install cabling, test each section of cable by connecting it to the hub and a single workstation. Information provided by the device driver will inform you of whether the NIC could successfully initialize. A simple *ping* test does not require the services of a NOS, and will tell you if you are able to successfully send data over the network. Use the diagnostics provided with the product to test NICs and other hardware. Keep notes on the problems you encounter and any actions you take to address them. These notes come in very handy when setting up additional hardware, performing network maintenance, and talking with customer support personnel.

Table 4.6 **A Sample Cost Estimate for 15 Users**

Unshielded Twisted-Pair Cabling	$2,000
Hub	$750
NIC (16 @ $120/card)	$1,920
Server Workstation (1 @ $2,800)	$2,800
Client Workstations (15 @ $1,200)	$18,000
OS/2 (16 @ $89)	$1,424
Laser Printer	$1,000
LAN Server + 15 Client Licenses	$1,110
Application Licenses (E-mail, Database, etc.)	$4,000
Total	$33,004

Putting It All Together

With a few calls, you should be able to put together a reasonably good cost estimate for installing a network within your business. Table 4.6 provides a sample cost estimate for a small business installing an Ethernet network with 15 clients. Please note that these numbers are approximations. They are based on the current going rate for hardware and services in Austin, Texas.

This chapter introduced the various hardware components that make up a network and, hopefully, provided you with some *food for thought* in planning how your network will be installed and implemented. Tips for selecting and managing a contractor were included, as well as advice for the *do-it-yourselfer.* The next chapter fine-tunes the information you have received thus far by providing you with planning worksheets and advice for configuring your network today so as to save time and money later.

CHAPTER 5

Planning to Do Now to Save Time and Money Later

Plans are worthless, but planning is invaluable.

—*Peter Drucker*

The first four chapters introduced the concepts employed in modern networks and, hopefully, gave you some ideas on how you would like to use the network to benefit your business. This last chapter on planning pulls together several ideas and tips under the general topic of things all experienced network administrators wished they would have considered *before* installing their first networks. This chapter is important, because networks tend to g-r-o-w. Today, you are looking at a comparatively simple job of installing server resources, creating user accounts, and then enabling access by requesters. Tomorrow, you may have a more complex problem in adding or upgrading resources without disrupting the services already in use. It is tempting to rush into just getting the network up and running, and it is easy to get into a mode of reacting to situations rather than anticipating them, but you can save yourself a great deal of effort if you have a plan from which to work.

 ## Principle 1: Keep It Simple

Networks are less difficult to set up and maintain than ever before, but they are still far from simple. The development effort put into simplifying network installation and maintenance is largely offset by the increased function and flexibility that networks now offer. Networks are inherently more flexible and more complex than stand-alone PCs; the number of variations within a network is infinite. While hardware and software vendors try to test as many configurations as they can, it is impossible to anticipate every combination. Networking hardware and software can seem like a collection of parts that you have to make work together, rather than a smoothly integrated system. The first principle of setting up a reliable, easy-to-maintain network is to eliminate all unneeded variances: Keep it simple (Figure 5.1).

Do not forego any function that will benefit your business, but consider your investment in maintenance whenever you purchase equipment or install customizable features. By keeping it simple, your chances of coming up with a robust, low-maintenance network will be much greater. You will avoid dead-end products, unsupported combinations, and untested leading-edge technologies that may still have bugs. When you *do* encounter prob-

Figure 5.1 **Keep it simple!**

lems, a smaller number of variables will make the problems easier to resolve. Examples of variations you want to minimize include the following:

- Protocols such as:
  —NetBIOS
  —TCP/IP
  —IPX (Netware standard)
  —AppleTalk
  —SNA
- Operating systems and releases:
  —OS/2
  —DOS
  —Windows
  —Macintosh OS
  —UNIX
  —OS/400 (AS/400 OS)
- Types and vendors of hardware:
  —Workstations
  —Printers
  —Network interface cards
  —Cabling
  —Network types (i.e., supporting Ethernet *and* Token Ring)
  —Serial devices
  —Bridges and routers
  —Hubs
- Types and vendors of software and software releases:
  —Network operating systems
  —Network applications
  —Other communication software (i.e., host emulation, file transfer, E-mail, and remote LAN access)
  —Other applications, such as editors, spreadsheets, and databases

Simpler networks not only mean easier maintenance, but they also generally exhibit better performance and require less memory and disk storage to support. The point here is not to discourage you from pulling together the level of functionality you need, but to remind you to factor in the maintenance and support costs when considering whether to mix and match many different types of hardware and software, versus possibly spending a bit more to use or upgrade to a more integrated platform.

For example, you may have different types of Ethernet adapter cards in your network, some of which are from vendors who are no longer in business, and you may have different types of cabling that has been strung between machines as the need arose. Rather than investing an increasing amount of time and money in a patch-up approach, it may be wiser to make the initial investment in a single set of cabling and network adapters that will pay you back with better reliability and performance later. You are the best judge of the value of a low-maintenance network to you and your users!

Standardizing workstation configurations and popular applications makes it easier for you to provide better support for upgrading software and automatically accessing shared resources than is possible if users take a *roll-their-own* approach. Eliminating the variance in workstations also allows users the flexibility to log on and work from whichever workstation is available, rather than be assigned to a particular workstation. This can be particularly handy in a retail or manufacturing business in which employees are moving between workstations.

Principle 2: Anticipate Future Needs

You do not have to have a weighty, all-encompassing *master plan,* but it is wise to spend some time thinking about and writing down what your future needs will be (Figure 5.2). It is easy to fall into the trap of creating a limited, inflexible network that has to be scrapped when your business grows or changes. Initial, tangible costs always seem much more real than less tangible future costs. If you include the costs of maintenance, growth, and possible hardware replacement in your plans for the future, you will most likely thank yourself later. In particular, the physical LAN (the cabling, connectors, and LAN adapters) is one of the hardest-to-change decisions you will make, and has definite implications for your ability to grow. Once cabling and LAN adapters are installed, they are expensive to replace. If you anticipate any growth at all, it is important to install a physical LAN that will accommodate that growth.

Another important area to consider is the type of network you want to install, and how you want to distribute your resources. An earlier chapter described the pros and cons of a peer versus a server-based network. Peer networks do not require a dedicated server but they are difficult to manage and

Figure 5.2 **Anticipate future needs.**

cannot accommodate many users. LAN Server provides a very flexible base for growth, since a single server can accommodate hundreds of users and multiple servers can be organized into a single domain or multidomain network. While adding additional servers to a LAN Server network is easy, you may want to think about how you want to organize the servers and the resources each supports. Some ideas for this will be provided later in the chapter.

A third area to cover is a plan for creating and maintaining backups and other tools necessary for disaster recovery. This task is another one that is easy to neglect, because we are busy people and this type of maintenance and planning does not bubble up to the top of our to-do lists until a serious problem sends it there. The mechanism you choose for backing up data may have a strong influence on how you organize your resources. For example, if you choose to use tape for nightly backups, you may want to save time and tape by separating the data from the application directories. Since data changes more often than applications, this would allow you to back up your data nightly, and back up applications only when you first install them. On the other hand, if you were using the replication service to back up changes to a directory as they occur, separating data from applications becomes less useful.

 After you have installed and feel comfortable with LAN Server, compare your disaster recovery plans with the procedures and suggestions in Chapter 14. Have you covered all the important areas in keeping your network up and running? By familiarizing yourself with problem determination procedures and tools, and providing for regular backups, you will be ready for any problem that might occur.

Defining the Network

 Now is a good time to take out the notes you made while reading Chapter 1 about how you would like to use the network. If you do not have any notes, take a few minutes to think about what you want out of the network, then try to write down answers to the questions that follow. The answers will provide a blueprint for installing and configuring LAN Server, network resources, and user accounts. You may also want to look at the planning worksheets provided in Appendix A of volume 1 of the *LAN Server Network Administrator Reference*. The planning worksheets closely approximate the information you will be asked to supply when sharing resources, creating accounts, and configuring services on LAN Server:

- What resources do you want to share?
  —What files or directories?
  —What applications?
  —What printers?
  —What CD-ROMs, modems, or other devices?
- How do you want to support network applications?
  —Do you want to let users choose their own *private* applications from a set of shared applications you provide? Or do you want to set up *public* applications for your users, which will automatically appear on their desktop when they log on to the network?

—Do you want to purchase application licenses or purchase shrink-wrapped copies?

■ How do you want to control access to the resources you provide?

—Do all users require the same level of access to a resource? Or do different users require different levels of access?

—What levels of access are required for each resource?

—Do you want to allow guest access to some resources? (Guests do not require a separate user account; this is useful if many people need only occasional access to a nonconfidential resource.)

—Can you leave the server unsecured? Or do you need to secure the server in a locked room, or use the local server security feature provided by LAN Server Advanced?

—Do you have other special security needs that require data encryption or protection against someone monitoring the physical network?

■ How do you want to organize your user accounts?

—Do you want to define each user individually? (This is the simplest approach for a small organization.)

—Do you want to group users by department or function? (This is useful for medium-size businesses that do not have a lot of organizational changes.)

—Do you want to group users by privilege level? (For very large organizations, this maximizes the number of users that can be defined, and minimizes the amount of maintenance due to reorganization.)

If you are able to answer the preceding questions, you are well on your way toward putting together a network that will serve your needs! The next few sections provide some tips for organizing your network. Tips for larger networks that require multiple servers will be covered first, so if you are installing a single server network, feel free to skip to the later sections on organizing directories and applications.

 ## Tips for Organizing Multiple Servers on a Network

LAN Server domains provide flexibility in organizing multiple servers within a network. As described in earlier chapters, a domain is a collection of servers that share a common administrative database. Users can log on to a domain and access any server within the domain. A single domain can support up to 1,016 concurrent users. This is a theoretical limit based on the maximum connections that can be handled by four NICs in a high-end LAN Server PC. This limit has also been successfully tested numerous times in our laboratories, and so would also be considered a *practical* limit for the use of LAN Server Advanced.

When you read comparisons between products, such as the one provided in Appendix A, you will note that many products will provide a theoretical limit that is far beyond what the product could demonstrate in a laboratory (or in your business network). Some products will even state that a capacity parameter is *unlimited*. Whenever you see *unlimited*, you must realize that this actually means *unknown* and *untested*. Every parameter has a theoretical limit that is governed by the design of the software. Every parameter also has a practical limit that is the maximum level at which the product can be successfully tested or run on the current hardware technology. Be very cautious about advertisements and comparisons that blur the distinction between the two.

Multiple domains can be configured on a single network (Figure 5.3). Though each domain must have its own separately maintained administrative database, users who log on to one domain can access any other domain that supports their user account. Multiple domains are used to provide a scalable option for very large networks, to isolate portions of a network for management or security purposes, and to limit traffic across bridges or wide area networks.

Many organizations, including ours, support a large number of domains simply because individual departments or users created their own domains as a convenient way to share resources. From a user's perspective, accessing resources from multiple domains is fairly transparent. LAN Server provides a number of tools, such as Network Signon Coordinator and NEWPW, to aid users in managing passwords and sessions in multiple domains. These tools are discussed in Chapter 12. However, if a network is to be centrally managed, the administrator will generally want to minimize the number of domains to avoid having to maintain separate domain control databases.

Every domain must have a server designated as a domain controller. A domain controller is designated by setting the server role to *primary* when you install LAN Server. If you are creating a large network with multiple servers, you have tremendous flexibility and a number of decisions to make

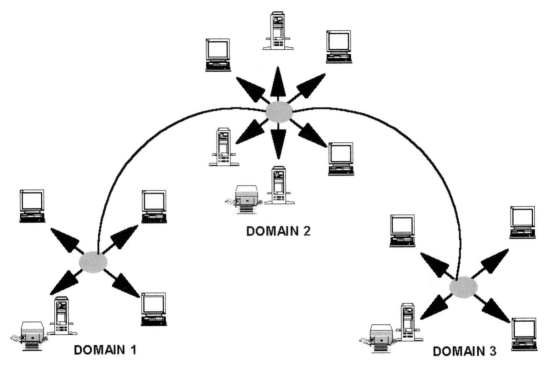

Figure 5.3 **Multiple domains on a single network.**

in organizing resources on the servers (Figure 5.4). Three common strategies are to:

- Organize servers by function
- Organize servers by location
- Organize servers by department

Organizing servers by specialized functions, such as printing, sharing files, and sharing applications, makes efficient use of server resources and allows you to take best advantage of the performance optimizations created for file sharing in the Advanced version of LAN Server. Memory and cache usage is optimized, because there is a higher concentration of users using a smaller set of resources. CPU utilization is optimized because of reduced operating system overhead. Hard disk space requirements are reduced, because there are fewer instances of duplicate programs and data being installed on multiple servers, as happens with the second and third option.

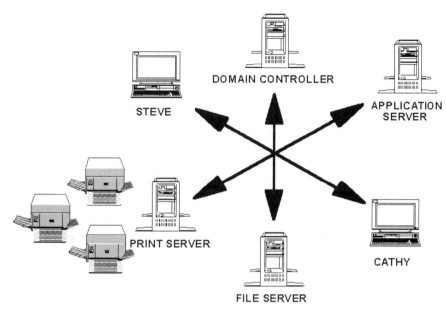

Figure 5.4 **Servers organized by function.**

Efficient use of printers and modems is made possible through the ability to manage multiple devices from a single queue. Data files can be backed up efficiently, because they are concentrated in a few locations.

Organizing servers by function can start with as few as two servers. It is often useful to separate print services from file and application sharing. If the workload for file sharing is heavy, installing the file and code sharing functions on the Advanced version of LAN Server will provide optimum use of the server hardware. Leave printers, modems, domain control services, and interactive applications on the Entry version of LAN Server, as these services do not get added benefit from the performance optimizations provided by the more costly Advanced Version (Figure 5.5).

Sometimes, it is not practical to split server resources by function. Different departments have different needs for resources, security, and response. It may be more convenient to organize the servers by departments (Figure 5.6). For example, an advertising agency might want a separate server for its graphics department, and a second server for its business accounts and payroll. While there may be overlap between the applications provided by the two servers (for example, an editor), the differences in use and security requirements justify this arrangement.

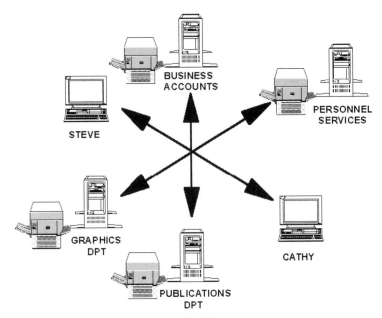

Figure 5.5 **Servers organized by department.**

Another situation that calls for a different approach to organizing servers is when the network is spread over a large area. It is much more convenient for users to pick up a print job from a printer located near them than to hike out to a bank of printers at a far end of the building. Printers can be made more accessible by dispersing them across multiple servers or by using peer services to provide access to auxiliary printers connected to requesters. See Chapter 8 for details on how to set this up.

In widely dispersed networks, it is important to provide a reliable high-speed connection between users and the resources they use most often. Plan to minimize the traffic over wide area networks, gateways, and bridges by providing the heaviest utilized services close to the user on the local network segment.

Ready access to the domain controller for user authentication, logon assignments, and network administration is also very important. You can improve access and protect yourself from the possibility of a failure on the domain controller by installing a second server as a backup. The backup

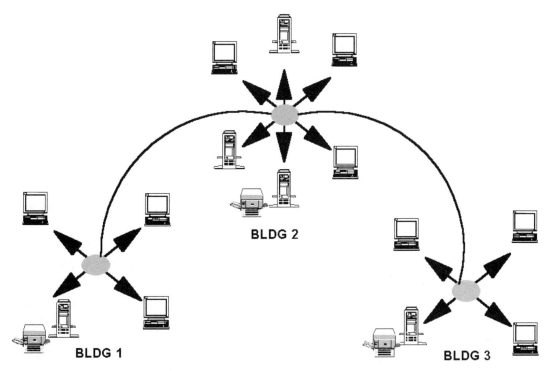

Figure 5.6 **Servers organized by location.**

domain controller maintains a copy of the domain control database to use in processing logon requests whenever the primary domain controller is unable to respond. This could happen because the domain controller is busy with other requests, or because the domain controller is not functioning.

The only thing the backup domain controller does not normally do is take requests from users and administrators to make changes to the domain control database. Requests for changing logon assignments, passwords, and shared resource definitions are accepted only by the primary domain controller to avoid any possible conflicts that could occur if changes were allowed to be made to multiple copies of the database. The backup domain controller can be readily switched over to the role of primary, however, by issuing the NET ACCOUNTS command from a local or remote workstation with the parameter */ROLE:PRIMARY.*

Tips for Organizing Directories and Files on the Server

Through the assignment of access permissions, you can create directories for both public and private use. A directory assigned to one or more users for their private usage is called a *home directory*. Home directories are used for storing important data that the user wants backed up on a regular basis, or in the case of remote IPL, they could contain all of a user's private data.

Disk space can become an issue whenever users are granted write or create permissions within server directories. The enforcement of hard-disk-space (DASD) limits for these directories is an important consideration *before* you have to send out your first urgent housekeeping message! The Entry and Advanced versions of LAN Server handle this problem in different ways. The Entry version, as well as Advanced versions released before LAN Server 4.0, allow you to set a limit on home directories—but the limit is not enforced. A utility, CHKSTOR, is used to check the status of disk storage used. If a user has exceeded the space you allocated, an alert is sent to the user, administrators, and any other designated recipients, informing them of the problem. It is left to you and the user to negotiate how to handle the situation.

LAN Server 4.0 Advanced introduced the ability to enforce these limits. Requests that would result in the limits being exceeded are blocked with an error message returned to the requester. An alert is also sent to the user warning whenever thresholds are exceeded that he or she may be getting close to the limit. One approach taken by administrators to enforce limits on the Entry version is to create separate disk partitions for users to use as their private work areas. This technique is not advocated unless it is certain that the alerts will not be effective in getting your users to control their space usage. Creating separate partitions is an extremely rigid approach; it is difficult to impossible to reconfigure a partition that is no longer adequate in size without causing a major disruption to the server.

Organizing directories by type of access is a good step toward minimizing long-term network maintenance. Applications, shared data, and private directories should always be kept separate from system resources, such as the operating system, LAN Server, and communication service directories. System resources on the server should be accessible only to administrators. Access to other resources can be most easily handled if you can separate them into categories based on the type of access, such as those listed here:

- Nonconfidential read-only resources (i.e., bulletin boards, price lists)
- Applications
- Data requiring read and write access (i.e., inventories)
- Highly sensitive or confidential read/write data (i.e., payroll, personnel records)
- Home directories

When you create a shared resource, you will install the resource in a subdirectory and associate an access control profile with it. The access control profile contains all the users and groups assigned to the resource, along with their associated access permissions. Organizing resources by type of access allows you to install them in a way that minimizes the separate access control profiles you have to set up and maintain. You can, for instance, create a subdirectory below the root for each category listed in the preceding to share as a single resource. You can then create subdirectories under each category for individual applications, home directories, and databases (Figure 5.7). Access permissions created for a subdirectory can be propagated to all subdirectories below it. There are a number of tricks of the trade for fine-tuning how these access permissions are propagated, which will be described in Chapter 8.

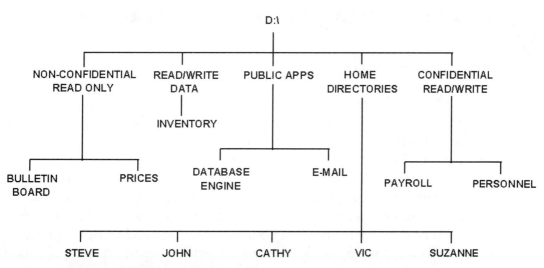

Figure 5.7 **Organize subdirectories by type of access.**

Guest access was mentioned earlier in this chapter; let's take a closer look at what it can do for reducing LAN Server administration. Guest is a special user account provided by LAN server for users who do not have their own user account to occasionally log on and access nonconfidential resources. If you provide applications or information to lots of users who only access the network occasionally, you can avoid the effort of creating and maintaining the extra accounts by providing access to these resources through use of the Guest UserID. On the other hand, you must carefully monitor the use of any directories accessible via the Guest account, since your guest could be invited or uninvited. The LAN Server audit utility can be used to monitor access to any resource.

Some last tips for this section are to be sure the names you assign to resources are adequately descriptive. Your users will thank you, and you will thank yourself when you later must maintain or upgrade your resources. You do not want to have to open every resource icon to determine its identity. Last, leave room for growth. Do not pile resources and users onto a server until it is at capacity and expect the server to maintain this level. Intermittent fixes applied under crisis conditions tend to not last long. It is much better to leave room for growth and then monitor your resource usage so that you can always maintain a buffer. The important resources to monitor are server memory usage, hard disk, and CPU utilization.

Tips for Selecting Software Applications

Whenever possible, choose mainstream applications that are fully network enabled. Talk to technical personnel and other users to see if the application runs well within your specific environment. Look for compatibility marks on the package, such as OS/2, Warp, and LAN Server Tested and Approved (Figure 5.8). Look for written instructions for how to install and configure the application. Check for any constraints the application may have when running in your environment. Be cautious when buying hardware or software that does not specify support for the exact environment that you are configuring. For example, some software applications are not network enabled; they assume they are running on your local machine and must be copied to your workstation to be used, rather than directly shared from an application server.

Figure 5.8 **Compatability marks.**

If OS/2 is installed on your workstations, you have the flexibility of choosing between OS/2, Windows, or DOS applications. Many applications offer versions for all three environments. Which should you choose? Native OS/2 applications usually provide the most consistency within an OS/2 environment, but because applications vary widely, there are other factors you should consider:

1. Are all application functions supported on the OS/2 platform? A good OS/2 application will take advantage of multitasking and the OS/2 GUI, while providing a consistent set of functions with those offered on other platforms. Reduced functionality and delayed availability of

the product on OS/2 indicates that the product is likely to be a port of the DOS or Windows version. It is sometimes better to run a fully supported Windows application under WINOS/2 than to run a less than full function OS/2 application natively.

2. Which applications will be the easiest to maintain and use? This is, to some extent, a matter of personal preference. DOS, Windows, and OS/2 each has its own set of fans. Until recently, the authors favored the OS/2 command line because we found it to be the fastest approach for experienced users. However, with the latest improvements offered by OS/2 Warp, LAN Server 4.0, and other GUI applications, we have gradually been transformed into full-fledged OS/2 GUI users. The ability to connect to resources by selecting a network icon and manipulating resources and accounts through drag-and-drop techniques are a boon to new and experienced users alike.

3. Will you be able to provide consistent applications for all users? As described at the beginning of this chapter, it is much easier to maintain a small number of applications within a consistent environment than it is to maintain lots of individual configurations. If you have older or less equipped PCs that cannot support Windows or OS/2 environments, you may want to either upgrade the PCs or consider providing DOS applications as a common base.

The OS/2 Windows environment provided by WINOS/2 provides an excellent base for running DOS- and Windows-based applications. OS/2 manages multiple DOS and Windows sessions within its preemptive multi-tasking environment, so you get smoother mouse and keyboard response when running multiple tasks than you do when running applications natively in Windows. OS/2 also isolates memory usage for each application, which provides protection against system crashes. The disadvantages in using DOS and Windows programs within OS/2 are a slightly less consistent environment for users, and a slightly more complex setup for the application.

Client/Server versus Shared File Applications

When you are considering a workgroup or distributed application, such as e-mail or a distributed database application, you should consider how it handles the split between its client and its server function—because you may not realize some of its built-in limitations until you have already acquired and installed the application.

Many early, or simple, applications rely on file sharing to access the server. These applications may have been designed when Netware file sharing was the only distributed capability available to PC users. For example, a distributed application's client may read and write directly to a shared file that resides on a server. Or, an e-mail application's client may retrieve and store a user's mail by reading and writing shared files. This technique is simple and straightforward to implement; however, it has significant drawbacks. First, the client does most of the work, and the server does simple file sharing. This does not take advantage of the processing power of the server the way it could. Second, the volume of traffic over the network can be very high. For example, a database query that must search every record will transfer the entire database to the client for searching. Third, security is a problem, because determined users can access parts of shared files from which they would otherwise be restricted. For example, users might be able to read each other's mail without authorization.

A better design for distributed applications is a client/server design. The client simply formulates a request and passes it to the server that executes it. For example, the request might be "search database X for records matching A." The server can search the database locally and return only the few matching records. Or the request could be "return all my e-mail that I have not read yet." The server can return just that person's e-mail without exposing anyone else's.

It is recommended that you choose network applications that use the client/server model. They solve the problems previously mentioned: The server is exploited more than the client, network traffic is minimized, and security can be enforced in terms that apply to the application.

E-Mail

E-mail is a popular network add-on. The simplest e-mail programs provide a *post office*, where incoming messages are filed under a user's ID. They also typically provide an editor for composing notes and responses, and a send feature for sending mail to others. A file system is sometimes provided so that you can file mail away for later viewing. In addition to these functions, you may want to look for:

- User notification when mail is received
- Directory support for locating people and addresses

- A good quality editor with support for printing, copying, and pasting documents
- An efficient filing system, such as a database, which allows you to categorize and search the information that you wish to keep by file name, date, subject, sender, and key words

Databases

Databases are the central information repository of many businesses. It is extremely important to select a database that is designed for a distributed network environment! The characteristics of a distributed database are:

- The database can be composed of several smaller databases that can be assembled using a common identifier, called a *key*, such as a Social Security number or customer account.
- The database allows for extended path names (i.e., does not assume all components to be on a single workstation).
- The database provides an efficient mechanism for remotely querying information.

System Query Language (SQL) is an example of a syntax commonly used for querying databases. The query language greatly reduces network overhead by allowing the database application to sort and parse the data at the location where the data is stored. Only the query and answer are transmitted over the network.

Other Considerations for Network Applications

Primary considerations for setting up and maintaining network applications are:

- Who will use the application?
- How will the application be accessed?
- Where will the application run?
- How will the application and resulting data be managed?

Are your users comfortable with the network, or do you need a turnkey solution for providing a consistent and easy-to-use interface? Experienced users often like to customize their desktop environments. They tend to use more network resources and be more experimental in their approach to trying out new applications and browsing the network. Experienced users may prefer to set up their own applications from a pool of applications you share on the application server. They may also prefer upgrading their own requesters and applications by accessing code provided by you on a code server.

On the other extreme, you may have very novice users. In this environment, you will want to provide a perfectly consistent interface across all requesters. Remote IPL is sometimes used in this environment, because it is easy to create consistency with a minimum investment in requester resources. Logon assignments can be used to automatically assign printers, applications, and other resources. Network security may be simplified by providing a minimal level of access privileges and inputting the user ID and password using the STARTUP.CMD file. You may want to further customize your applications with menus and other aids to simplify their access and use.

Tips for Maintaining the Network

The following actions, taken during planning and installation, will help minimize the amount of time and resources you spend later maintaining the network:

- Separate the data you will need to back up regularly from applications and other low maintenance files.
- Use group accounts to organize user entries.
- Record the maintenance you will need to do on a regular basis, and automate it using command and/or REXX files.
- Test all new applications before sharing them for general use over the network.
- Consider the use of LAN Server's Configuration/Installation/Distribution tools for installing OS/2 and OS/2 LAN Requester and subsequent upgrades on your client PCs.
- Create system recovery diskettes after you install, and keep them up to date.
- Start a system log to use in maintaining your network.

The System Log

The System Log is a diary of information you keep on your network. While not everyone maintains a System Log, those who do find the information a valuable asset in keeping their networks maintained in peak condition. The kind of information to keep in a System Log includes:

- A diagram of your network topology
- A User/Workstation matrix with locations, account names, and phone numbers
- Workstation addresses and hardware configurations
- Key configuration files, including:
  —CONFIG.SYS
  —IBMLAN.INI
  —PROTOCOL.INI
  —DOSLAN.INI (DOS)
  —AUTOEXEC.BAT (DOS)
  —STARTUP.CMD (OS/2)
- User and access information:
  —Domain definition
  —NET ACCESS output
  —NET GROUP output
  —NET USER output
  —CHKSTOR output
- Shared application notes
- Network drive assignments
- Server performance statistics, including:
  —NET ERROR output
  —NET STAT output
  —Cache size and cache hit ratios from CACHE386 output
  —Memory working set
  —Disk space in use and free
  —Server CPU utilization
- Backup/recovery procedures
- Problem/backup/recovery log
- Planned actions
- Changes to configuration, software, or accounts

Much of the information is generated as the output of LAN Server utilities and productivity aids. These tools are discussed in Chapter 12. How often you generate these reports depends on the size of your network and how fast it changes. If you are a new administrator, generate reports every few weeks until you establish a pattern for *normal* levels and variance within your network. At that point, you can adjust your monitoring frequency accordingly. If your network is approaching a capacity threshold, such as 1,000 concurrent users on an Advanced LAN Server, or if you are experiencing any problems on the network, you will want to monitor more closely until the problem is stabilized.

Other information, such as the problem/backup/recovery log, planned actions, and network changes, consist of notes you make when maintaining the network. These are very valuable in troubleshooting, as described later in Chapter 14. Your problem/backup/recovery log should record a full description of any problems encountered. All error messages or other *hints* at the cause should be noted. If you make changes in an attempt to fix or get around the problem, record what was done and what result (even if none) the action had on the problem. Finally, if you do find a fix or work-around, record it so that you will be able to quickly draw on this resource if you encounter the problem again. Your change log should include all hardware changes, major account changes (such as adding a large number of new users), new software added, and software upgrades, including any corrective service diskettes (CSDs) applied.

If you are installing a large network of more than 200 users, you may want to acquire some tools for monitoring performance and managing the network. There are many tools offered by IBM and third-party vendors, which simplify maintenance of large networks. Some provide additional support for monitoring network performance. Some focus on monitoring the network and pinpointing problems. Others provide support for integrating a diverse set of products on the network. Others provide a security mechanism for detecting unregistered devices that attempt to connect to the network.

This chapter concludes the suggestions and tips for planning your network. Are you ready to dig into installing it? Bravo! That is the topic of Chapter 6.

CHAPTER 6

Installing and Configuring LAN Server

I will build my castle one brick at a time for I know that small attempts, repeated, will complete my undertaking.

—*Og Mandino,* The Greatest Salesman in the World

 This chapter will show you how to install, configure, and bring up your first server; Chapter 7 will later show you how to create and use your first user account, shared directory, and shared printer on the LAN.

All this will be done on one PC, because LAN Server, unlike Novell NetWare, lets every server PC also act as a fully functional OS/2 requester and workstation PC. So, you can use the server PC to try out any LAN Server function or feature, or run any DOS, Windows, or OS/2 application, at the same time that you are sharing the server PC's files and printers with other requesters. When you want to install additional requester PCs, see Chapter 9 for install procedures and guidelines.

Think of this as a trial installation. Try a simple, quick install first, get it working, then add to it later. You will gain experience and understanding that you will need later when trying more complex things. If nothing serious goes wrong, a simple trial installation and bringup of OS/2 and LAN Server should take no more than an hour or two, especially if you use CD-ROM.

If you make a mistake or change your mind about something, it's easy to back out or change any installation or configuration that you did. You can even easily delete all of LAN Server and start over from scratch. You can also add components or features, reconfigure the server, or move most of the server product from one partition to another.

Selecting Hardware for Your Server PC

For your first trial installation of OS/2 and LAN Server, your server PC should ideally be a test machine, with no *live* data or production applications that you need to save. If you do have data or applications you want to save, it's wise to do a complete backup using your normal procedures. OS/2 and LAN Server should not damage any existing data or applications, but things can always go wrong and you should always have a backup available.

Your server PC should have at least a 386 processor. See Chapter 4 for a general discussion of server PC requirements, and Tables 4.1 and 4.2 for specific memory (RAM) and hard disk requirements. You will need either a CD-ROM drive or a 3.5-inch high-density diskette drive to perform your installation, depending on the media included in your LAN Server package. If you want to share a printer, you'll need a printer attached to one of your parallel ports.

Next, you need a network adapter (NIC) for your server PC, so you can attach it to your LAN. See Chapter 4 for guidelines on network adapters, and

Appendix C for a list of supported network adapters. It's important that LAN Server supports your network adapter. Beware of network adapters that claim they are compatible with a well-known brand—sometimes they are and sometimes they are not. When in doubt, ask the manufacturer if they support use of their network adapter with OS/2 and LAN Server.

It is possible to install LAN Server without a network adapter by using the Loopback Driver—a special driver that simulates a LAN inside your server PC. You can later install a real network adapter. Installing the Loopback Driver will be discussed later in this chapter.

Selecting, Planning, and Installing OS/2 on Your Server PC

It is recommended that you use OS/2 Warp (version 3) for your initial installation. It is the latest version of OS/2 and is the most readily available. You can use an earlier release of OS/2—version 2.11 or later is recommended.

As of this writing, there are four different OS/2 Warp packages available: OS/2 Warp, OS/2 Warp with WINOS2, OS/2 Warp Connect, and OS/2 Warp Connect with WINOS2. The OS/2 Warp Connect packages are available only on CD-ROM, but the others are available on CD-ROM or 3.5-inch diskette. If you have a CD-ROM drive that's supported by OS/2 Warp, use CD-ROM to install OS/2 and LAN Server; it's faster and easier than swapping diskettes.

The two OS/2 Warp Connect packages include the OS/2 Requester component from LAN Server 4.0 and OS/2 Peer, plus the NetWare Requester 2.11, OS/2 TCP/IP 3.0 with Internet access, and LAN Distance Remote 1.1. You can use OS/2 Warp Connect on a server PC, but don't install OS/2 Peer or the OS/2 Requester, because LAN Server provides that function.

OS/2 Warp with WINOS2 comes in a blue-sided box and includes WINOS2, a version of Microsoft Windows 3.1 tailored for OS/2 Warp. OS/2 Warp with WINOS2 will run DOS, Windows, and OS/2 applications all by itself—no separate DOS or Windows installation is needed.

OS/2 Warp without WINOS2 comes in a red-sided box and does not include WINOS2. OS/2 Warp without WINOS2 will run DOS and OS/2 applications all by itself, without the DOS operating system.

If you have a separate copy of Microsoft Windows or Windows for Workgroups (versions 3.1 or 3.11), OS/2 Warp without WINOS2 can use it to run Windows applications. Before installing OS/2 Warp without WINOS2, make sure you have installed Microsoft Windows on your hard disk, and you have the original or backup Windows diskettes or Windows CD-ROM (they will be needed during OS/2 install). You can also install Microsoft Windows after installing OS/2 Warp without WINOS2.

If you just need to run OS/2 and DOS applications on your PC, and no Windows applications, choose OS/2 Warp without WINOS2—it's the lowest-cost option. Many server PCs will fall into this category unless you are also using them as user workstations.

If you do need to run Windows applications along with OS/2 and DOS applications, you have a choice to make between OS/2 Warp with or without WINOS2. Choose OS/2 Warp without WINOS2 if you have an already installed Windows setup that you want to preserve. OS/2 Warp with WINOS2 is best if you don't have Windows installed, or if you are reformatting the Windows partition while installing (perhaps to use HPFS instead of FAT).

Planning Your Hard Disk Setup

Speaking of partitions, formatting, HPFS, and FAT—let's spend a few minutes learning about these topics, because they are frequently misunderstood and are a source of confusion for OS/2 newcomers.

Your PC has one or more hard disks physically installed inside the chassis. Each hard disk can have one or multiple partitions. Each partition has a fixed size measured in megabytes, where 1 megabyte is actually 1,048,576 bytes (2 to the 20th power for the mathematically inclined). Any space on the hard disk not occupied by partitions is called *free space*, and you can add new partitions as long as there is free space left. You can't change the size of a partition—you have to delete and recreate it. When you delete a partition, all its data is lost—you must back up and later restore any data or programs that you want to keep.

Each partition has a drive letter, C through Z, which is used to access it under DOS or OS/2. CD-ROM drives are also assigned a drive letter, normally one higher than the last partition's drive letter. Usually, PC manufacturers create partitions and install an operating system at the factory before you buy your PC. You will often want to change the partitioning scheme when installing a server or requester PC with OS/2.

There are two types of partitions: *primary partitions* and *logical drives.* A primary partition is normally used to hold a bootable operating system, such as DOS or OS/2, while logical drives hold applications and data.

It is recommended that you create one primary partition on your first hard disk, and use logical drives for all your other partitions (if any). Multiple primary partitions are difficult to set up and maintain. If you think you want to create multiple primary partitions, read Chapters 17 and 18 of your *User's Guide to OS/2 Warp* carefully before proceeding.

Should you simply create one large partition on each hard disk, or should you divide your hard disks into multiple partitions? There is no one answer to this question. One large partition can be the most efficient way to use hard disk space, because there is just one pool of free space for new files. On the other hand, many people prefer to keep their operating system and their applications and data on separate partitions so that it's easier to redo one or the other if necessary. Also, if you are using the FAT file system (see the following) and you have large hard disks, you will want to partition them, because FAT does not handle large partitions well.

 If you do create multiple partitions, plan carefully, because it's difficult to change partitions once they are set up. If you have to change the size of a partition, you must delete and recreate it, losing all its data. And if you delete or insert a partition, all partitions following it change their drive letters—usually requiring applications to be reconfigured or reinstalled.

Before you can use a new partition, you must format it, which installs a blank file system ready to store new files. You can also reformat a partition that's already in use, which erases all the data stored on that partition.

When you format a partition, you choose the file system for that partition. The DOS operating system supports only the file system called FAT (File Allocation Table). OS/2 supports FAT, and also supports HPFS (High Performance File System). Diskettes are always FAT format—you can't have an HPFS diskette.

Should you format your partitions with FAT or HPFS? The advantages of HPFS are many, and it is recommended that you strongly consider using it on your server PC (see Table 6.1).

 Table 6.1 **Choosing HPFS or FAT**

Advantages of HPFS

Better performance than FAT in most cases.

Compatible with LAN Server Advanced's HPFS386 file system.

Uses space on large partitions more efficiently than FAT.

Supports partitions larger than FAT's limit of 2 gigabytes (2,048 megabytes).

Supports file names up to 254 characters long for OS/2 applications. FAT limits OS/2 applications to 12-character file names (up to 8 characters, optionally followed by a period and up to 3 more characters).

Sorts directories by file name automatically.

Supports user IDs longer than 8 characters, when LAN Server is installed on HPFS partitions FAT partitions limit the user IDs to 8 characters.

Advantages of FAT

Uses about 500K less RAM in your OS/2 PC.

You must use FAT for any partitions to be accessed by DOS. However, DOS and Windows applications running under OS/2 can use HPFS partitions.

You must install Microsoft Windows on a FAT partition before installing OS/2 Warp without WINOS2.

Setting Up Both DOS and OS/2 on Your PC

You may have DOS (with or without Windows) already installed on your PC, and you may wish to install OS/2 but keep the ability to boot either DOS or OS/2. Your reason may be that you have DOS or Windows applications that you can't run under OS/2, or that you are just trying out OS/2 and want to be able to switch back to DOS whenever you want to.

An easy way to accomplish this is to simply install OS/2 on the C partition where DOS is installed, without reformatting. Once OS/2 is up and running and you wish to boot DOS next, open an OS/2 command window and type **BOOT /DOS /N**.

The next time you shut down OS/2 and reboot, DOS will start. To switch back to OS/2, type this at a DOS command prompt: **C:\OS2\BOOT /OS2 /N**. The next time you reboot your PC, OS/2 will start.

If you want to install OS/2 in a different partition from DOS, you can do this by installing the OS/2 Boot Manager. The Boot Manager comes up first when you reboot your PC and lets you choose which partition you want to boot. Boot Manager also supports installing and booting OS/2 in a logical drive rather than a primary partition. If you want to set up Boot Manager on your PC, read Chapters 17 and 18 of your *User's Guide to OS/2 Warp* carefully and follow one of the excellent, detailed examples.

Installing OS/2 Warp on Your Server PC

Once you have decided how to set up your hard disks and backed up any data or applications you want to save, you can go on to install OS/2 Warp on your server PC. Insert the OS/2 Installation diskette in your A drive, and boot your PC. Insert Diskette 1 when asked. If you are installing from CD-ROM, insert the CD-ROM in the CD-ROM drive. You will soon see a *Welcome to OS/2* screen with two choices: Easy Install or Advanced Install. Advanced Install is accompanied by a warning that it's for "experienced, technical" users—but if you have followed the discussion in this section, you have plenty of technical experience to get through Advanced Installation. Select Advanced Installation and press Enter.

The next window is Installation Drive Selection. The OS/2 install program has selected a drive (partition) on which it will install OS/2. You can accept this selection or you can invoke the FDISK program with the "Specify a different drive or partition" option. FDISK lets you select a different partition for OS/2 installation by marking it *Installable*. With FDISK, you can also reconfigure your partitions in any way you desire, and to install Boot Manager if you wish. If you run FDISK and change your partitions, you will need to reinsert the OS/2 Installation diskette and reboot—the on-screen instructions will guide you. When you have run FDISK to your heart's content, choose to accept the selected drive.

If the install partition is already formatted, the next window asks if you want to reformat it. Choose Yes if you want to change the file system on the partition, or if you want to erase all the files. Choose No if you want to preserve the files—for example, if you are installing OS/2 in a DOS partition for the dual boot method.

If the install partition is not formatted or you choose to reformat it, the next window asks what file system you want to install—HPFS or FAT. Make your choice (see Table 6.1) and press Enter. After a short wait, the installation continues.

Now, OS/2 files are copied to the OS/2 partition from diskettes 1 through 6 and the install diskette. You are prompted to insert diskettes if you are not using CD-ROM. Then, OS/2 install asks you to remove the diskette from the drive and press Enter, and reboots itself automatically from the OS/2 partition.

The next window is labeled System Configuration, and lets you select your locale (country and keyboard layout) and PC hardware setup (see Figure 6.1). You are actually picking the device drivers you will install to adapt your hardware devices to OS/2. It's very important to choose the right device drivers for your hardware setup. LAN Server, in particular, needs the correct printer device drivers loaded so that it can share access to the printer with requesters on the LAN. To find out more about any device on this window, click on its icon, then click Help. Also, you can consult your *User's Guide to OS/2 Warp.*

A good strategy to follow is: If in doubt, leave it out. After you install and reboot OS/2, you can get right back to the System Configuration window with OS/2 Selective Install, and add any drivers you are missing. When you have the System Configuration to your liking, click on OK. If you didn't install a printer, you will see a window asking you to select one—do so if you wish.

The OS/2 Setup and Installation window comes up next, and lets you select OS/2 features and tailor OS/2 (see Figure 6.2). If you have enough space on your partition, installing all the features is OK—but consider deselecting the Multimedia feature, which is installed by default. Unless someone is using

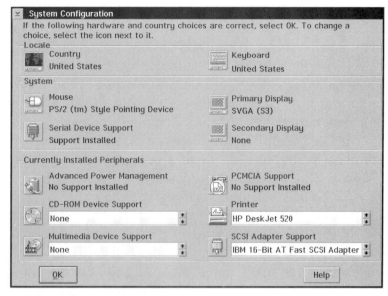

Figure 6.1 **OS/2 Warp System Configuration.**

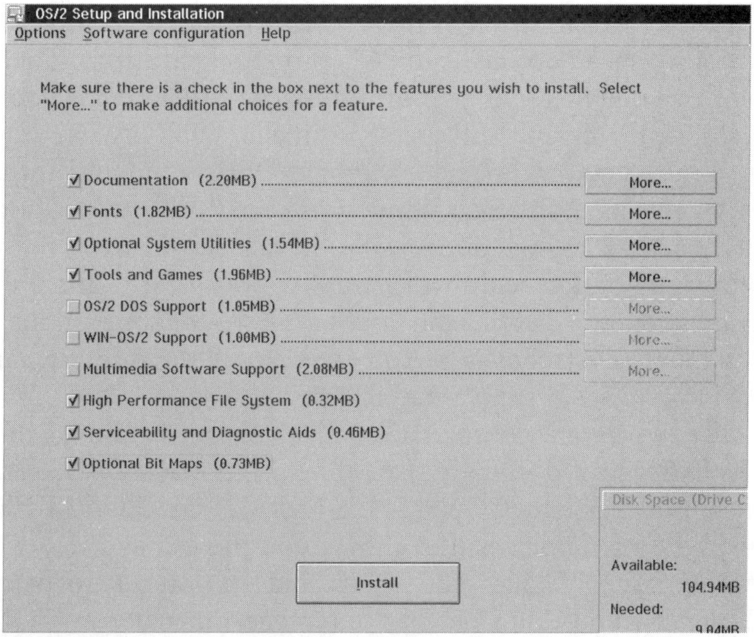

Figure 6.2 **OS/2 Warp Setup and Installation.**

your server PC as a workstation, the Multimedia feature uses RAM and processor for no benefit. Also, consider deselecting DOS and Windows support unless you want to run DOS or Windows applications on your server PC.

As with the System Configuration window, a good strategy is to install only what you think you need. OS/2 Selective Install allows you to revisit the Setup and Installation window later. Also, OS/2 Warp provides Selective Uninstall so that you can remove features you have previously installed.

The OS/2 Setup and Installation window's Options menu lets you format additional partitions, or exit to a command prompt temporarily. And the Software Configuration menu can tailor OS/2 and DOS parameters in the CONFIG.SYS file. Consider tailoring the OS/2 SWAPPATH and DISKCACHE parameters.

SWAPPATH allows you to specify where OS/2 keeps its *swap file*—a file used by OS/2 to swap out applications and data temporarily. If you run large applications, run many applications at once, or have limited RAM installed on your PC, your swap file can get as large as 20 or 30 megabytes or more. And if you run out of space for your swap file, applications can stop working—or OS/2 can even stop. If the OS/2 partition doesn't have enough room for your swap file, move it to a different partition with the SWAPPATH parameter.

DISKCACHE specifies how much RAM in your server PC is set aside as a *cache* to speed up access to FAT-formatted partitions. The default is 10 percent of your RAM. If you are primarily using HPFS, you don't need this. Override the default and specify a smaller DISKCACHE setting.

When you are finished with the OS/2 Setup and Installation window, click on Install. The next window is called Advanced Options, and lets you select actions to take during OS/2 install (see Figure 6.3). The "Add existing programs" option will invoke the OS/2 Add Programs utility at the end of installation, which will scan your partitions for applications it recognizes and add them to your desktop. You can also run the Add Programs utility later—it's in the OS/2 System Setup folder.

The "Migrate configuration files" option will take the existing CONFIG.SYS and AUTOEXEC.BAT files from your OS/2 partition and merge them with the new CONFIG.SYS and AUTOEXEC.BAT files. Finally, "View and edit migration results" shows you the old and new CONFIG.SYS and AUTOEXEC.BAT files side by side and lets you cut and paste between them. Generally, you don't need to intervene manually in CONFIG.SYS at this time—CONFIG.SYS settings will be discussed later in this chapter.

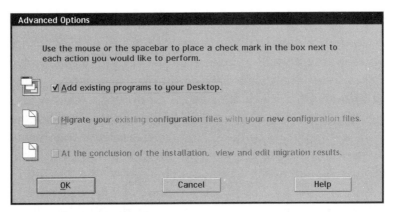

Figure 6.3 **OS/2 Warp Advanced Options.**

Deselect the Advanced Options you don't want, and click OK on the Advanced options window to finish the install process.

Now the rest of the OS/2 files are copied to your OS/2 partition as needed. If you are installing from diskettes, you will be prompted to insert diskettes as needed. If you are installing a *without WINOS2* version of OS/2 and you chose to install Windows support, you will also be prompted to insert your original or backup Windows diskettes or CD-ROM so that OS/2 can copy certain files it needs.

Congratulations! You have completed installing OS/2 Warp. You will see a window telling you that OS/2 installation is complete, and you should reboot your PC. Remove any diskette from the drive and use Ctrl-Alt-Del to reboot.

First Startup of OS/2 on Your Server PC

OS/2 should display a logo screen, followed by a pause of a few seconds as OS/2 builds its Workplace Shell desktop. You should also see the OS/2 Tutorial. Take a few minutes to go through the tutorial, regardless of whether you have used OS/2 before. Then make sure that all your partitions are accessible by opening the Drives folder inside the OS/2 System folder and opening each drive in turn.

It's a good idea to shut down and reboot your OS/2 system once you have checked it out. You should see a faster reboot to the newly built desktop, and you should not see the OS/2 Tutorial this time. If you have any problems, see your *User's Guide to OS/2 Warp*, Chapters 14 and 15.

Stopping OS/2 Gracefully

It's very important that you always shut down OS/2 properly before rebooting it. Shutdown will write all data to the hard disk and save the desktop correctly. If you don't shut down, you may lose data or corrupt your desktop. Shut down OS/2 by clicking on "Shut down" in the OS/2 Launch Pad, or by selecting "Shut down" from the OS/2 desktop's pop-up menu.

If OS/2 appears to hang, don't reach for the on-off button immediately. Try pressing the Ctrl-Esc key combination a few times, and waiting about 30 seconds. You may see a window that says "This program is not responding to system requests. Select Enter to end it. Data will not be saved." If you click on Enter, with any luck the stuck application will be terminated and you can continue operation. If this doesn't work, the next best option for stopping OS/2 is the Ctrl-Alt-Del key combination. This will at least close out the hard disks correctly, even if the OS/2 desktop isn't saved. Resort to the on-off switch only if Ctrl-Alt-Del doesn't work.

Tailoring Your OS/2 System

Open the System Setup folder by clicking mouse button 2 on an empty spot of your OS/2 desktop, then selecting System Setup from the pop-up menu. You will see the Selective Install and Selective Uninstall utilities. Selective Install lets you redo your OS/2 install, changing device settings, adding features, and tailoring OS/2. Selective Uninstall lets you remove features. Also, see the section later in this chapter on the CONFIG.SYS file, and consider tailoring some of its key parameters—particularly the CONNECTIONS parameter of the SET AUTOSTART=line, and the /IRQ parameter of the BASEDEV=PRINT0x.SYS line.

Understanding OS/2 Printers
and How They Work with LAN Server

OS/2 supports a large number of printers (see Appendix D) by providing printer drivers that adapt the printer's individual characteristics to OS/2. OS/2 installs only the printer drivers you request, so if you add a new printer to your system, you may need to install a new printer driver. It's very important to match the printer driver to the printer, otherwise you may get garbled output, no output at all, or error messages when you try to print.

You attach a printer or plotter to your PC by plugging its cable into a parallel or serial port. The parallel ports are named LPT1:, LPT2:, and so on; the serial ports are named COM1:, COM2:, and so forth. Serial and parallel ports have different connectors, so you won't get them confused. Most printers use parallel ports because they are faster.

When you print under OS/2, you are not usually printing directly to a printer attached to a serial or parallel port. Instead, OS/2 captures the data being printed in a special file on your hard disk, called a *print job*. Print jobs are kept in a *print queue,* which is a list of print jobs waiting to be printed on a printer. OS/2 removes print jobs from the print queue one at a time, and prints them on the printer. Because OS/2 is a multitasking operating system, it can print jobs on the printer at the same time as other applications are working. Your application does not have to wait!

OS/2 lets you manage the print queue—you can delete jobs, change the ordering of jobs in the queue, request multiple copies of a job to be printed, and hold or release the print queue (when the queue is held, no jobs are printed).

When you install a printer under OS/2, a printer icon is created on your desktop. It's important to realize that this printer object in OS/2 is really a print queue. If you double-click it to open it up, you will see a folder full of print jobs. A print queue is connected to a parallel or serial port, and has a printer driver to handle the unique characteristics of the attached printer. You can change the printer driver or port attachment of a print queue whenever you wish. You can even ask that the print data be output to a file rather than sent to a printer port. This is useful when you want to capture the printed output and send it to someone as a data file.

It's not unusual to have more than one print queue connected to the same output port, and printing on the same printer. OS/2 will share use of the printer between the print queues automatically.

LAN Server can share OS/2 print queues on the server for use by requesters on the LAN. Requesters can print jobs to shared print queues, and the server will print the jobs on its printer. Requesters can also manage shared print queues on the server—deleting jobs, holding and releasing the queues, and so on—if they are logged on with the proper administrative authority.

OS/2 requesters have both local and network print queues, represented by Printer and Network Printer objects on the OS/2 desktop. Network print queues point to a shared print queue on a server. When an OS/2 requester prints to a network print queue, the data is actually sent across the LAN to the server, and not stored on the requester's local hard disk. Printing to a network print queue is usually faster than printing to a local print queue, from the requester's point of view. The printer driver for a network print queue must match the printer driver for the shared print queue on the server, or output may be garbled or lost.

An OS/2 requester can also manage a server's shared print queue, working through the network print queue. In Chapter 9, you will learn more about installing OS/2 requesters and setting up network print queues.

Installing OS/2 Printers

You can use Selective Install to install new printers, but it's easier and faster to use the Printer template. Open the Templates folder on the OS/2 desktop, find the Printer template, and drag it to an empty spot on the OS/2 desktop (using mouse button 2). You will see the Create a Printer window (Figure 6.4).

Remember, we are really creating a new print queue, even though OS/2 calls it a *printer.* Type the name for the print queue. The name you type is used to refer to the print queue on the OS/2 desktop. The actual name of the print queue is the first 8 characters of this name, with blanks squeezed out.

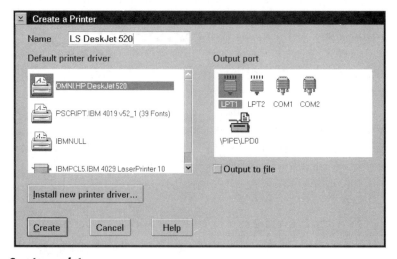

Figure 6.4 **Create a printer.**

Select the correct printer driver from the displayed list. If you don't have the correct printer driver installed, click on "Install new printer driver." This will bring up a list of supported printers. Choose a printer and click Install. You will be prompted to insert the correct OS/2 printer driver diskette. You can also install printer drivers from any source by typing a new path in the Directory field—for example, you can install printer drivers from CD-ROM or from a network drive.

You can also delete unwanted printer drivers from the displayed list. Click on the unwanted driver with mouse button 2 and select Delete from the pop-up menu.

Finally, select the port to which the printer is attached. You can check "Output to File," and the print data will be written to a file instead of being sent to an output port. If a port is shaded, that means it's already in use by another print queue. You can still select it, and it will be shared with the other print queue. You can also change port settings by double-clicking on the port icon. Now click Create, and the printer object is created on your desktop.

Try printing a small file (for example, CONFIG.SYS) to make sure the printer you installed is working correctly. Open the OS/2 System folder, then the Drives folder. Now click on the C drive with mouse button 2, click on the arrow to the right of Open, and select Icon View from the cascaded menu. (If you installed OS/2 on a different drive, use that drive instead.) Find the CONFIG.SYS icon in the C drive icon view and click on it with mouse button 2. Select the Print item from the pop-up menu. A window pops up asking you if the file is plain text or printer-specific data. Click on plain text, and the CONFIG.SYS file should print on the printer. If you have problems print-ing this file, see the online book *Printing in OS/2* that's located in the Information folder on your desktop—reference the section called "Solving Printing Problems."

Selecting, Planning, and Installing LAN Server on Your Server PC

It is recommended that you use LAN Server version 4.0, because it's the latest release and has significant enhancements over version 3.0, including a brand-new administrative GUI and a much-improved install procedure. If you have LAN Server 3.0 already, consider an upgrade to 4.0. If you do use

LAN Server 3.0, the details of the install procedures in this chapter will differ, sometimes significantly. The differences will be briefly covered, but for details, see the *LAN Server 3.0 Installation and Configuration Guide.* Another good resource for LAN Server 3.0 is the Redbook, *LAN Server 3.0 Experiences.* See Appendix B for more information on these publications.

LAN Server comes in two versions: LAN Server Entry and LAN Server Advanced. LAN Server Advanced has all the features and functions of LAN Server Entry, plus the HPFS386 file system—but it costs more than LAN Server Entry. HPFS386 provides better performance and supports more users than the HPFS file system that comes with OS/2. See chapter 4 for guidelines on which version of LAN Server to choose. With either version of LAN Server, you have a choice of media—CD-ROM or 3.5-inch diskette. LAN Server also supports remote installation from a server—see Chapter 13 for details.

If you have another IBM or non-IBM LAN product licensed on your server PC, inquire about an upgrade version of LAN Server—you may save some money. Upgrades are available from LAN Server Entry to LAN Server Advanced, and from older releases of LAN Server to LAN Server 4.0. Upgrades are also available from other networking products, such as Novell NetWare, Microsoft LAN Manager, and IBM PC LAN Program. Promotions and special upgrade programs are continually revised—call IBM or your reseller for details.

What's in the LAN Server Package?

The LAN Server 4.0 product is available in a package with 27 3.5-inch high-density diskettes (5.25-inch diskettes are not available), or a package with one CD-ROM. If you have a CD-ROM drive that's supported by OS/2, purchase the CD-ROM package. You can create 3.5-inch diskettes from the CD-ROM as needed, or install directly from the CD-ROM.

LAN Server has components that are separately installable (see Table 6.2). LAN Server includes extensive documentation, and additional documentation is available from IBM. Table 6.3 summarizes the available documentation and its availability.

Overview of the Server Install Procedure

Three LAN Server components are required to install a server PC: MPTS, OS/2 Requester, and OS/2 Server. The OS/2 Server install program will auto-

Table 6.2 **LAN Server 4.0 Software Components**

Name	Description	Diskettes
MPTS	OS/2 Multiprotocol Transport Services—OS/2 NetBIOS and TCP/IP transports. Diskette 3 has utilities and toolkits for MPTS.	3
OS/2 Requester	Installs MPTS if needed. Diskettes 4/5 have the administrative GUI.	5
OS/2 Server	Installs OS/2 Requester and MPTS if needed.	3
Productivity Aids	Diskettes 1 and 2: many useful utilities. Diskettes 3 and 4: LAN Server Specialist. Diskette 4: Mobile File Synchronization.	4
NSC	Network Sign-on Coordinator for DOS and OS/2.	1
DLS	DOS LAN Services—DOS and Windows requester and NetBIOS transports.	3
LSP	DOS LAN Support Program—802.2 (DLC) and NetBIOS transports for DOS. Install program is called DXMAID.	1
DOS TCP/IP	DOS TCP/IP transports with NetBIOS emulation.	3
OS/2 Softcopy Books	OS/2 Viewable softcopy books in hypertext format. Can also be printed.	4
Windows Softcopy Books	Windows viewable and printable soft-copy books.	CD only

matically install MPTS and the OS/2 Requester if they are not already installed.

There are two paths through the server install procedure—Easy and Tailored; use Easy install the first time you install a server. You can run the install program again, using the Tailored path, to make any required changes.

 If you need to add or remove LAN Server components or features, move LAN Server to another partition, or remove LAN Server completely—use the server install program's Tailored path. Don't attempt to delete, copy, or move individual LAN Server files or directories yourself—it's too easy to mess things up.

The server install program guides you through a sequence of windows, asking you to enter information and click on buttons. You can go backward in the sequence of panels any time by using the Cancel button.

Table 6.3 **LAN Server 4.0 Information**

Document Name	OS/2 Soft Copy	Windows Soft Copy	Hard Copy Included	Hard Copy Included in SBOF-8553	Hard Copy Order Number
Easy Start	X	X	X	X	S10H-9743
Up and Running!	X	X	X	X	S10H-9679
DOS LAN Services and Windows User's Guide	X	X	X	X	S10H-9684
Guide to LAN Server Books		X	X	X	S10H-9688
Planning, Installation, and Configuration	X	X		X	S10H-9680
Performance Tuning	X	X		X	S10H-9681
Network Administrator's Tasks	X	X		X	S10H-9682
OS/2 LAN Requester User's Guide	X	X		X	S10H-9683
Problem Determination Guide	X	X		X	S10H-9685
Error Messages (ASCII file ERROR.TXT)	X				
Glossary	X				
Commands and Utilities	X	X		X	S10H-9686
Programming Guide and Reference	X	X		X	S10H-9687
DOS Client Access for TCP/IP: Setup			X	X	S10H-9384
MPTS/2 Configuration Guide	X	X		X	S10H-9693
MPTS/2 Programmer's Reference				X	S10H-9694
MPTS/2 Error Messages and Problem Determination Guide				X	S10H-9695
LAN CID Utility Guide	X	X		X	S10H-9742

Table 6.3 **(continued)**

Document Name	OS/2 Soft Copy	Windows Soft Copy	Hard Copy Included	Hard Copy Included in SBOF-8553	Hard Copy Order Number
Migrating from Microsoft LAN Manager					GG24-4387
Migrating from NetWare					GG24-4388
Understanding Performance Tuning Theory					GG24-4430

Key:

OS/2 Soft Copy	Soft-copy (online) version of document provided with LAN Server in OS/2 viewable (hypertext) and printable format.
Windows Soft Copy	Soft-copy (online) version of document provided with LAN Server CD-ROM package in Windows or WINOS2 viewable and printable format.
Hard Copy Included	Hard-copy (paper) version of document provided with LAN Server.
Hard Copy Included in SBOF-8553	Hard-copy (paper) version of document included in Bill of Forms package SBOF-8553, which can be ordered from IBM (see Appendix C for information).
Hard Copy Order Number	Used to order individual copies of documents from IBM. See Appendix B for ordering information.

If you are installing LAN Server 3.0, there are some differences from LAN Server 4.0. The server install procedure will *not* automatically install the transport component. You must install it individually, before installing the OS/2 Server, and reboot. The OS/2 transport component in LAN Server 3.0 is called LAPS (LAN Adapter and Protocol Support) and does not support TCP/IP. Also, the LAN Server 3.0 calls the two paths through install Basic and Advanced, rather than Easy and Tailored.

Installing LAN Server on Your Server PC

If you are installing from CD-ROM, insert the CD-ROM, open an OS/2 command window, and type **d: INSTALL**, where **d:** is your CD-ROM drive. You will see a Welcome window; click OK. Then you will see a menu of choices (Figure 6.5). Select "Install OS/2 LAN Server 4.0" on this window and click OK. Click OK on the Welcome window for OS/2 LAN Server installation.

If you are installing from diskettes, insert Server Diskette 1, open an OS/2 command window, and type **a: INSTALL**, where **a:** is your diskette drive. Click OK on the Welcome window for OS/2 LAN Server installation.

```
┌─────────────────────────────────────────────────────┐
│ CD-ROM Installation                                   │
├───────────────────────────────────────────────────── │
│                                                       │
│   Select an option from below.                        │
│                                                       │
│    ● Install OS/2 LAN Server 4.0                      │
│                                                       │
│    ○ Install OS/2 LAN Requester 4.0                   │
│                                                       │
│    ○ Make 3.5-inch product diskettes                  │
│                                                       │
│    ○ Install Online Books                             │
│                                                       │
│    ○ View Online Books                                │
│                                                       │
│                                                       │
│    ┌──────┐   ┌──────┐   ┌──────┐                     │
│    │  OK  │   │ Exit │   │ Help │                     │
│    └──────┘   └──────┘   └──────┘                     │
└─────────────────────────────────────────────────────┘
```

Figure 6.5 **LAN Server CD-ROM Installation Choices.**

Next, you see a window asking if you wish to use the Easy or Tailored path (Figure 6.6). You can click on Help for this window and see a detailed description of the things that Tailored install will do that Easy won't. For now, choose the Easy path by clicking the Easy button.

If your server PC has more than one hard disk partition (drive), the next window asks you to choose a drive for the installation (Figure 6.7). The default is to install on the OS/2 boot drive. You can install LAN Server on any

```
┌───────────────────────────────────────────────────────────┐
│ Easy or Tailored Installation/Configuration                 │
├───────────────────────────────────────────────────────────┤
│   Easy installation allows you to get up and running with   │
│   default features.                                         │
│                                                             │
│   Tailored installation allows you to selectively install   │
│   and configure LAN Server features.                        │
│                                                             │
│   Select Help for a complete description of the Easy and    │
│   Tailored choices.                                         │
│                                                             │
│   ┌──────┐  ┌──────────┐  ┌──────┐  ┌──────┐                │
│   │ Easy │  │ Tailored │  │ Exit │  │ Help │                │
│   └──────┘  └──────────┘  └──────┘  └──────┘                │
└───────────────────────────────────────────────────────────┘
```

Figure 6.6 **LAN Server Easy or Tailored installation.**

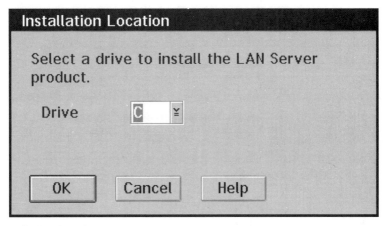

Figure 6.7 ***Installation location.***

drive with enough space. However, some features of LAN Server are always installed on the OS/2 boot drive (see Table 6.4 for details). Choose a drive and click OK.

Next, you are asked to enter a unique name for this server PC (Figure 6.8). Type **LSSERVER** and click OK or press Enter. (LSSERVER is the name used in the next few chapters for our examples. You may, of course, choose a different name. Just remember to substitute your name for LSSERVER when going through the examples in this book.) Both server and requester PCs have names. Remember this rule when installing additional servers or requesters later:

A Server Name or Requester Name cannot match any other Server Name, Requester Name, or Domain Name of any PC in the LAN.

The next window asks you to enter the name of the domain (Figure 6.9). Type **LSDOMAIN** and press Enter. (Again, you can substitute your own name if you wish.) The server PC will be the domain controller for the new domain, called LSDOMAIN. If you later install additional servers for this domain, you would also enter LSDOMAIN when you install them. When assigning domain names, remember this rule:

A Domain Name cannot match any other Server Name or Requester Name of any PC in the LAN.

If you have Microsoft Windows for Workgroups PCs on your LAN, it's a good idea to use their Workgroup Name for your Domain Name. That way,

Table 6.4 **LAN Server Directories**

Directory	LAN Server Use
\IBMLAN	All OS/2 Server and OS/2 Requester files except UPM
\IBMLAN\INSTALL	Install program and installation logs
\IBMLAN\ACCOUNTS	User/group definitions (NET.ACC) and user logon scripts
\IBMLAN\BACKUP	Backup copies of configuration files created by install programs
\IBMLAN\BOOKS	Soft copy books
\IBMLAN\LOGS	Error and audit logs
\IBMLAN\NETPROG	Programs
\IBMLAN\NETLIB	Programs (dynamic link library (DLL))
\IBMLAN\NETSRC	Development toolkit files for writing LAN Server applications
\IBMLAN\PRODAIDS	Productivity aids (see Chapter 12)
\IBMLAN\REPL	Replicator service control files
\IBMLAN\SERVICES	Programs that are LAN Server services
\IBMLAN\XPG4	Programs to adapt LAN Server for different languages
\IBMLAN\USERS	Origin for home directories for users
\IBMLAN\DCDB	The Domain Control Database
\IBMLAN\DOSLAN	Images for Remote IPL of DOS requesters
\IBM386FS	HPFS386 program files (LS Advanced only)
\MUGLIB	User Profile Management programs
\MUGLIB\DLL	User Profile Management programs (DLL)
\IBMCOM	LAN Adapter and Protocol support from MPTS component
\IBMCOM\DLL	LAPS programs (DLL)
\IBMCOM\MACS	LAPS MAC drivers (network adapters drivers)
\IBMCOM\PROTOCOL	LAPS Protocol drivers
\MPTN	TCP/IP and Socket support from MPTS component
\MPTN\BIN	Programs for TCP/IP and Sockets
\MPTN\DLL	Programs for TCP/IP and Sockets (DLL)
\MPTN\PROTOCOL	Protocol drivers for TCP/IP and TCPBEUI
\MPTN\ETC	Control files for TCP/IP

The \IIBM386FS, \MUGLIB, and \IBMCOM directories are always installed on the OS/2 boot drive. \IBMLAN and \MPTN may be installed on a drive of your choice. \IBMLAN can be moved to another drive after installation.

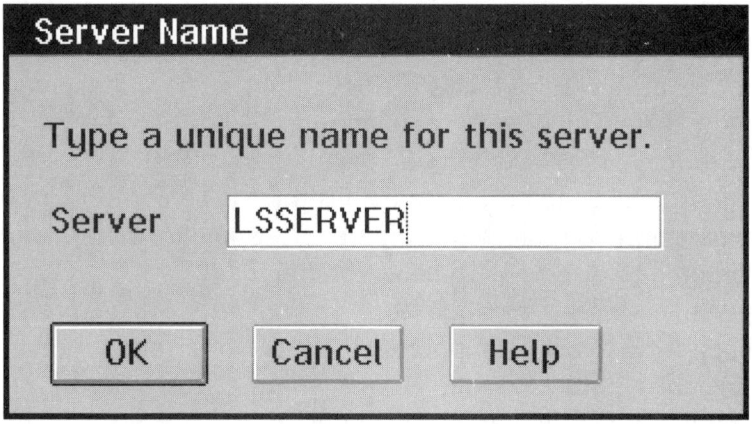

Server Name

Type a unique name for this server.

Server   LSSERVER

OK   Cancel   Help

Figure 6.8 **Choose a server name.**

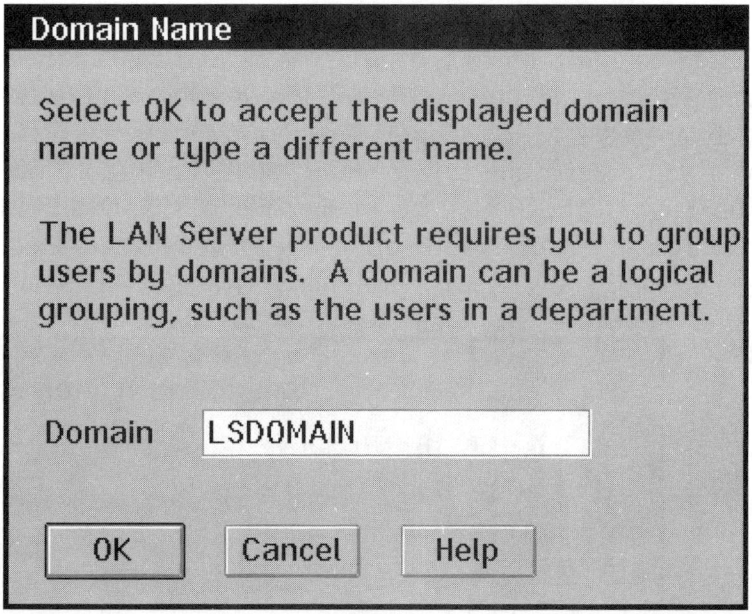

Domain Name

Select OK to accept the displayed domain
name or type a different name.

The LAN Server product requires you to group
users by domains. A domain can be a logical
grouping, such as the users in a department.

Domain   LSDOMAIN

OK   Cancel   Help

Figure 6.9 **Choose a domain name.**

LAN Server shared files and printers will be visible when your Windows for Workgroups users browse network resources.

The next window asks if this is the first or only server for this domain (Figure 6.10). Click Yes. If you later install additional servers for this domain, you would click No when you install them.

Now, the install program copies the MPTS component (see Table 6.2) to the partition you selected in Figure 6.7. If you are using diskettes, you will be prompted to insert MPTS diskettes 1 and 2.

While MPTS is installing, look up your network adapter type and model in Appendix C. See if it's supported by LAN Server, and whether the MAC driver is included with LAN Server, and whether LAN Server can autodetect the adapter. If your adapter is not supported by LAN Server, you may not be successful in installing and running LAN Server. Beware of adapters advertised as compatible with a well-known adapter—they are not always compatible.

MPTS attempts to automatically detect the type of network adapter that you have installed on your server PC (Figure 6.11). If it is successful, you will see a window telling you the adapter type that was detected. If the displayed adapter is correct, click OK. Otherwise, click "Change adapter."

If MPTS was unsuccessful in detecting your adapter type, you will see the Select Network Adapter window, so you can choose an adapter (Figure 6.12). If your adapter type does not appear on the list but is supported, click on "Other Adapter" to install the driver software that was supplied by the adapter manufacturer on a diskette. Be sure to consult the instructions that come with your adapter for the proper procedures in this case.

In rare cases, MPTS adapter detection can cause your PC to hang or lock up. If you suspect this is happening, start the installation procedure over again, but type the INSTALL command like this: **x: INSTALL /NS**, where **x:** is your CD-ROM or diskette drive letter. The adapter detection step will be bypassed and you will select your network adapter manually.

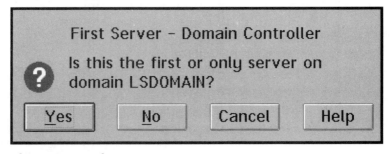

Figure 6.10 **Choose server role.**

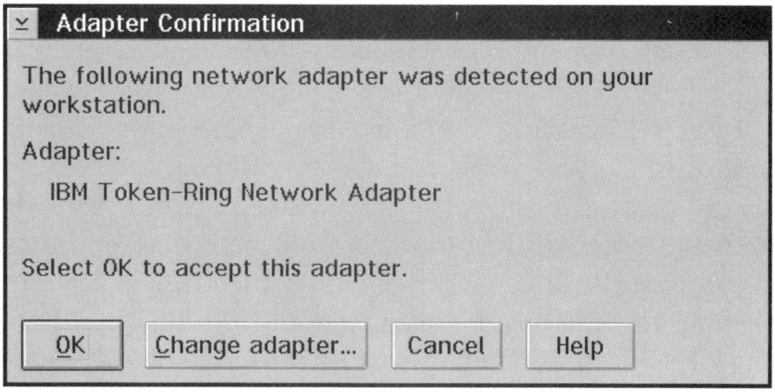

Adapter Confirmation

The following network adapter was detected on your workstation.

Adapter:

IBM Token-Ring Network Adapter

Select OK to accept this adapter.

[OK] [Change adapter...] [Cancel] [Help]

Figure 6.11 **Adapter confirmation.**

Now, the install program copies the OS/2 Requester and OS/2 Server components to the drive you chose in Figure 6.7. If you are installing from diskettes, you are prompted to insert Requester diskettes 1 through 5, and Server diskettes 1 and 2.

Then you will see a window informing you about the default user ID and password. Click OK. If you are installing LAN Server Entry, you will next see a window asking you to shut down and reboot the system. Click Exit, close

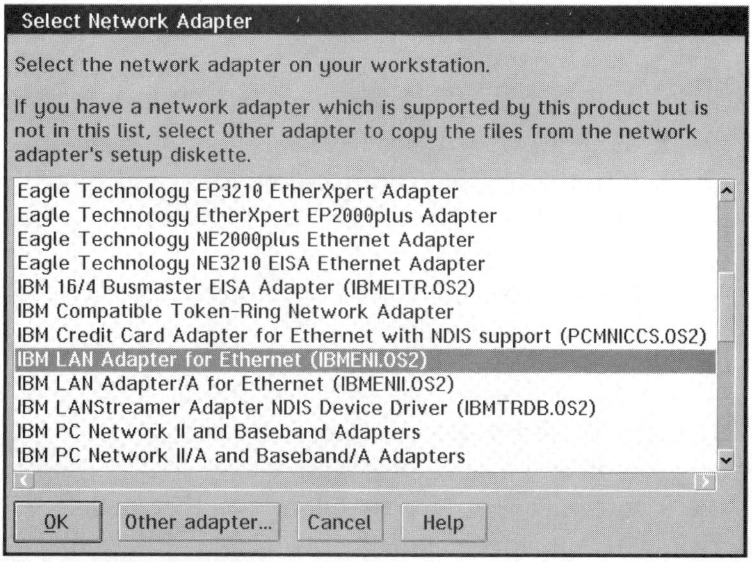

Select Network Adapter

Select the network adapter on your workstation.

If you have a network adapter which is supported by this product but is not in this list, select Other adapter to copy the files from the network adapter's setup diskette.

Eagle Technology EP3210 EtherXpert Adapter
Eagle Technology EtherXpert EP2000plus Adapter
Eagle Technology NE2000plus Ethernet Adapter
Eagle Technology NE3210 EISA Ethernet Adapter
IBM 16/4 Busmaster EISA Adapter (IBMEITR.OS2)
IBM Compatible Token-Ring Network Adapter
IBM Credit Card Adapter for Ethernet with NDIS support (PCMNICCS.OS2)
IBM LAN Adapter for Ethernet (IBMENI.OS2)
IBM LAN Adapter/A for Ethernet (IBMENII.OS2)
IBM LANStreamer Adapter NDIS Device Driver (IBMTRDB.OS2)
IBM PC Network II and Baseband Adapters
IBM PC Network II/A and Baseband/A Adapters

[OK] [Other adapter...] [Cancel] [Help]

Figure 6.12 **Select network adapter.**

any other applications or windows that are open, and shut down OS/2 as you normally would. Then reboot OS/2 Warp with the Ctrl-Alt-Del key combination (affectionately known as the *three-finger salute*).

If you are installing LAN Server Advanced with HPFS386, you will see a window asking you to create a startup diskette. You should create a startup diskette, because it's important to be able to boot from diskette if your hard disk fails, or the OS/2 system on your hard disk becomes unbootable for some reason. With LAN Server Entry, the OS/2 Warp install diskette and diskette 1 together can be used to boot from diskette. However, if you are using HPFS386, these will not work as is—you have to create a modified version of OS/2 Warp diskette 1 that contains the HPFS386 file system. If you want to create your startup diskette later, you can bypass this step now and use the MAKEDISK utility later. To create your HPFS386 startup diskette now, follow these steps:

1. Get a blank, formatted diskette to be used for the modified Diskette 1.
2. Minimize the server install program and start another OS/2 command window.
3. Type the command **DISKCOPY a: a:**, where **a:** is your diskette drive.
4. Insert the OS/2 Warp diskette 1 and press Enter in response to the "Insert the source diskette" message.
5. When you see the "Insert the target diskette" message, insert the blank, formatted diskette in the diskette drive and press Enter.
6. After the DISKCOPY command finishes copying the diskette, type **N** in response to the "Copy another diskette?" message. Then type **ERASE a:BUNDLE**, where **a:** is your diskette drive.
7. Exit from the OS/2 command window and switch back to the server install program. Now click Yes on the window asking if you want to create a startup diskette.
8. When the startup diskette is completed, remove it and label it "LAN Server startup diskette 1."

When the need arises, use your new startup diskette by booting the OS/2 Warp install diskette, and inserting your new LAN Server startup diskette 1 when prompted to insert OS/2 Warp diskette 1.

Last, you will see a window telling you that installation is complete, and you should shut down and reboot. Click Exit on this window, then shut down and reboot your server PC.

Booting Your Server PC for the First Time

Watch the screen carefully as your newly installed LAN Server boots for the first time. You will see lots of new messages on the screen after the initial OS/2 logo and before the OS/2 desktop appears. In a normal boot, you will see the following messages:

```
Locked file device driver loaded. Processing files
. . .
```

- This message should appear only the first time you reboot the server. It indicates that the installation process is completing and putting all the LAN Server files in the proper directories.

```
IBM OS/2 LANMSGDD. . . .
IBM OS/2 LAN Protocol Manager . . .
IBM OS/2 NETBEUI . . .
Adapter 0 has . . .
NETBIOS 4.0 loaded and operational
```

- These messages are normal and indicate that the NetBIOS protocol stack is loading.
- A message from the MAC driver that you have selected. Each MAC driver can and does create a unique message. Watch carefully to see if any errors are displayed.
- The screen will switch to the OS/2 desktop. You should see a command window processing the STARTUP.CMD file, which should have the NET START SERVER command in it. Watch the window to make sure the OS/2 Requester and Server components start up properly, without any errors.

If there are problems loading the MAC driver, typical error messages will be:

- PRO0025: An error occurred when the program tried to bind . . .
  This error indicates that the MAC driver failed to initialize properly. There should be another error message displayed by the driver previously. If you didn't see it, try rebooting and watching again.
- NET3087: The requester detected a problem with the cable connection. You will see this error message after the OS/2 desktop appears in the window where NET START SERVER is executing. This message can

mean that the cable to your LAN is not connected, or that there is a configuration error of some other type.

If you see other error messages, you can get online Help for them. For example, to see the Help for the NET3087 message, open an OS/2 command window and type **HELP NET3087**.

The LAN Server error messages are also documented in the file called ERROR.TXT that was installed in your \IBMLAN directory.

Fixing Problems with Initial Server Boot

If you see a MAC driver-related error, check the following items:

- Is your network adapter supported by LAN Server? See Appendix C for a list of supported network adapters. If your network adapter is not supported, you may want to continue trying to make it work—or you may decide to purchase a supported adapter. In the long run it's usually less expensive to use supported adapters.
- Is your network adapter correctly installed in your PC? Review your network adapter's installation manual to make sure you have correctly installed and configured your network adapter. Many network adapters come with a configuration utility that must be run before the network adapter is activated. Also, you must be sure that the IRQ, I/O port, and shared memory addresses you choose do not conflict with others already defined on your PC.

  If you are using a Token Ring adapter, make sure the adapter is set to the correct speed—4 or 16 megabits per second—for your Token Ring LAN. Some newer adapters will automatically sense this, but many require that you set the speed with switches on the card or with a configuration utility. If the speed is set incorrectly, the adapter will fail to connect to the LAN.
- Did you install the correct MAC driver for your network adapter? Sometimes the model names for network adapters are confusing. Check Appendix C again and see if there's a different choice you should or could be making.
- Are the network adapter parameters correctly specified to LAN Server? LAN Server Easy Install provides defaults for network adapter parameters and does not give you an opportunity to change them. If your net-

work adapter requires parameters to be specified to LAN Server, and the defaults are not correct, your network adapter may not work.

Many network adapters, such as the Eagle Technology NE2000, require you to specify the IRQ, I/O address, and shared RAM address for the adapter. These are set with jumpers or switches on the card, and you must then provide those settings for MPTS as parameters. If these are set incorrectly, the network adapter will not work. Other network adapters are smarter and allow the driver to automatically sense these settings, so you don't have to specify them. Typically, these network adapters are set up with a configuration program rather than jumper settings or switches on the network adapter itself.

Always review your adapter's manual for instructions on setting up with LAN Server and OS/2. You may also want to call the adapter manufacturer's technical support line for help. They may have a later version of the MAC driver, or they may be able to help you with OS/2 configuration questions.

If you need to change the MAC driver for your network adapter, or change its parameters, you need to run the MPTS configuration program— see the following section titled "Configuring and Tailoring MPTS."

First LAN Server Command

To make sure your server PC is working correctly and can communicate on the LAN, open an OS/2 command window and type **LOGON**. When the LAN Server Logon window appears, type **USERID** in the User ID field, and **PASSWORD** in the Password field. The domain name should be LSDO-MAIN, so you don't need to change it. Then press Enter or click on OK. If you see a "Logon Successful" message, your server PC is up and operational! Now type **LOGOFF** to log off your server PC.

At this point, you can continue with Chapter 7 to learn about basic LAN Server use while performing some simple administrative actions. The rest of this chapter covers additional material on server installation.

Recovering the IBM LAN Services Folder

If you have to rebuild your OS/2 desktop, you may lose your IBM LAN Services folder. To get it back, simply run through a Tailored Install of LAN

Server (see the following), but don't change anything. Reboot your server PC when asked. Your IBM LAN Services folder will be recreated on the desktop.

Recovering from Locked Files

If you had a problem during one of the install procedures, you may not be able to proceed because locked files still exist. If you are getting this message, delete the file IBMLANLK.LST from the \OS2\INSTALL directory. This file is used by LAN Server install to specify the locked files to be replaced by the Locked Files Device Driver.

Tailoring LAN Server

Use LAN Server Tailored Install to selectively add, remove, or tailor LAN Server components and features. LAN Server Tailored Install will also configure MPTS and allow you to add, delete, and change LAN adapters and their protocol stacks.

If you just want to configure MPTS and not the OS/2 Server or Requester components, you can invoke MPTS configuration directly by double-clicking the MPTS icon on the OS/2 desktop. However, if you add or remove an adapter, the OS/2 Server and Requester will not be aware of that change unless you run LAN Server Tailored Install.

If you installed from CD-ROM, insert the LAN Server CD-ROM, open an OS/2 command window, and type **d:INSTALL**, where **d:** is the CD-ROM drive. Click OK on the Welcome window, then choose "Install LAN Server 4.0" from the CD-ROM Installation window (Figure 6.5) and click OK.

If you installed from diskette, open the IBM LAN Services folder on your desktop and double-click the LAN Server Installation/Configuration icon.

Click OK on the Welcome window for server installation, and then click on Tailored on the Easy or Tailored Installation/Configuration window (Figure 6.6).

The next window you see is titled Installation Tasks (Figure 6.13). The first two tasks are relevant to tailoring this workstation; the rest of the tasks have to do with remote installation, which is covered in Chapter 13. If you

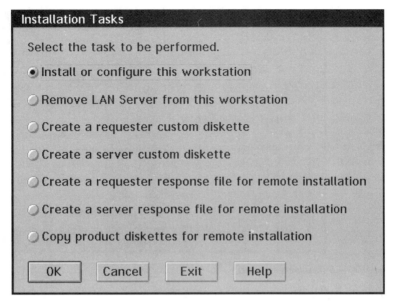

Figure 6.13 **Installation tasks for Tailored Install.**

want to remove LAN Server completely, select "Remove LAN Server from this workstation" and click on OK. Follow the prompts, and LAN Server will be removed. You will have a choice of removing MPTS as well or leaving it intact. If you want to tailor LAN Server, select "Install or configure this workstation," and click OK.

If you have more than one partition defined on your server PC, the next window asks you to choose a drive (Figure 6.7). LAN Server will move most of its code to a different drive if you change the drive letter (see Table 6.4).

The next window asks you to select the server type: Domain controller, Additional server, or Backup domain controller (Figure 6.14). See Chapter 2 for a discussion of server roles. You can change a server from one type to another on this window.

The next window asks if you wish to reinstall MPTS. Normally, you would click No, since it's already installed.

Now, the LAPS (LAN Adapter and Protocol Support) part of MPTS scans your server PC to detect the network adapters (LAN adapters) that are installed. As in Easy install, you can accept what's been detected or choose your adapter (Figures 6.11 and 6.12). When you have the proper adapter identified, click OK.

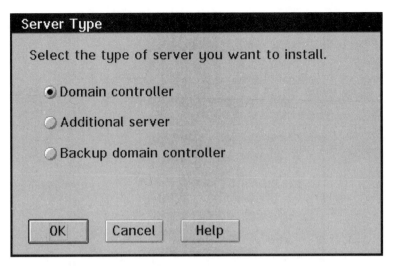

Figure 6.14 **Select server type.**

Next, you see the complex yet powerful LAPS Configuration window (Figure 6.15). LAPS stands for LAN Adapter and Protocol Support. This window allows you to specify your network adapters and protocols, and tailor their parameters any way you wish. You can configure multiple network adapters, and configure multiple protocols for each adapter.

The resulting configuration is visible in the lower part of the window, in the area labeled Current Configuration. The building blocks are in the upper part of the window, with Network Adapters on the left and Protocols on the right. No changes are actually made until you click OK; if you click Cancel, any changes you made are discarded—so feel free to experiment.

To tailor the parameters for an installed protocol or network adapter, highlight it in the Current Configuration list and click on Edit, or simply double-click it.

A window pops up with the parameters for that driver or protocol, and you can view or change any parameter. For example, in Figure 6.16 you can set the Interrupt Level (IRQ) for the IBM Ethernet adapter to match the IRQ setting on the card's jumpers or switches. If you are not familiar with a parameter, click on its value and then click Range to see the possible values. In Figure 6.16, this has been done for the Interrupt Level parameter.

To add a new adapter, double-click on the adapter in the Network Adapters list. To add a protocol to an adapter, highlight the adapter in the

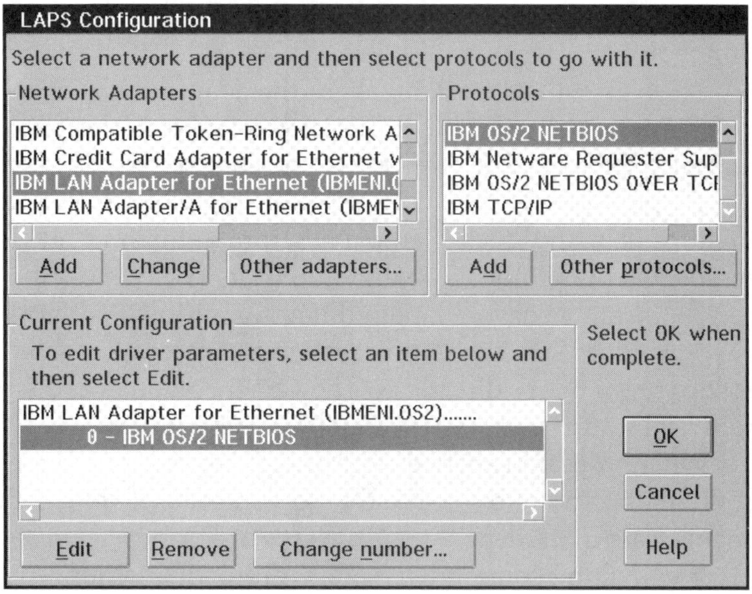

Figure 6.15 **LAPS Configuration.**

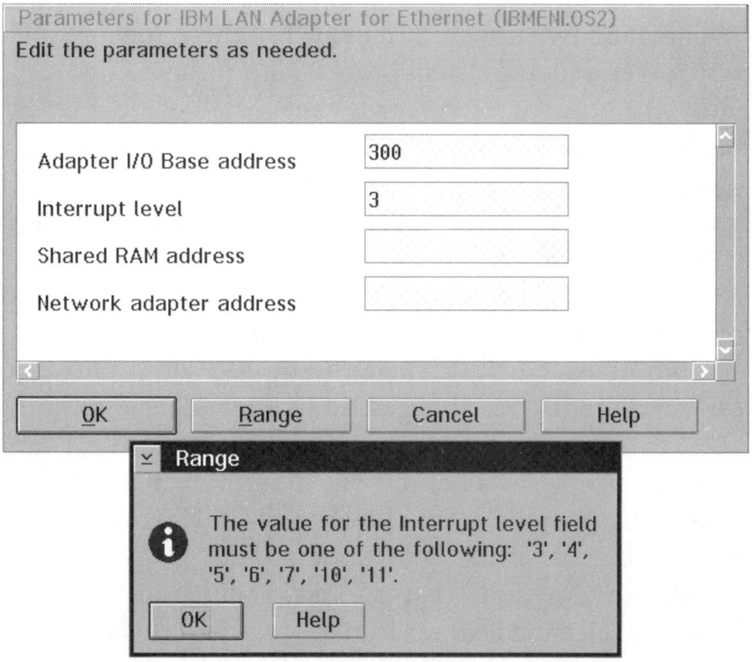

Figure 6.16 **Edit parameters.**

Current Configuration list, then double-click the new protocol in the Protocols list.

To change an adapter, highlight the adapter to be changed in the Current Configurations list, highlight the new adapter in the Network Adapters list, and click Change. The adapter will be changed to the new one you selected.

To remove a protocol or adapter, highlight it in the Current Configurations list and click Remove. Before removing an adapter, you must remove all the protocols configured for it.

To install a new adapter driver or protocol driver—for example, an adapter driver supplied on diskette with an adapter you have purchased—follow the vendor's directions. The Other Adapters and Other Protocols buttons will start the process of installing these drivers.

When you are satisfied with the changes you have made on the LAPS configuration window, click OK to continue. If you click Cancel, all your changes are discarded.

If you didn't configure the 802.2 protocol on your LAN adapter, the window shown in Figure 6.17 is warning you that you can't use the LAN Server Remote IPL feature. You don't have to worry about this unless you are planning to use Remote IPL now. Click Yes and you will return to the task of configuring and tailoring LAN Server.

The window shown in Figure 6.18 acts as the *control center* for the rest of LAN Server Tailored install process. From this window, you can install and remove LAN Server features via the "Install or remove a component" selection. You can also configure and tailor LAN Server features via the "Configure a component" selection. When you are done installing, removing, and configuring features, select "Apply the changes" to complete the Tailored install process and make the changes you have specified. If new features must be installed, you will be prompted to insert diskettes as needed. You should shut down and reboot your server PC after a Tailored install.

Nothing is actually changed until you select "Apply the changes," and you can discard your changes by clicking Cancel on this window—so feel free to experiment.

If you select "Install or remove a component," and click OK, you will see the Install and Remove window shown in Figure 6.19. This window shows you the current install status of all the LAN Server features, and the install/remove actions that are planned to be taken. You specify install actions by selecting features from the list, and clicking Install or Remove. The actions you specify will display in the Actions column of the list. You can

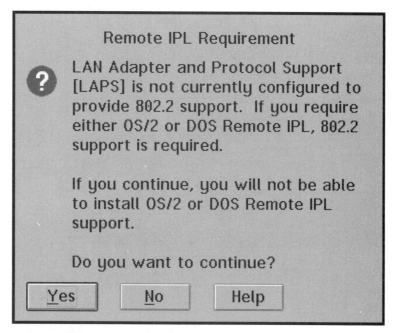

Figure 6.17 **802.2 warning.**

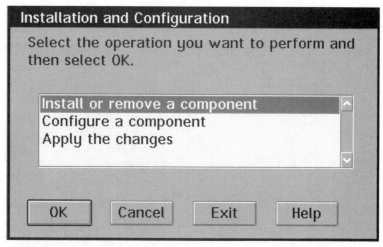

Figure 6.18 **Installation and Configuration tasks.**

also remove an action specification by highlighting it in the Action column and clicking "Cancel action." You can highlight more than one feature at a time if you wish, and the Install, Remove, or Cancel action buttons will apply to all the highlighted features.

For example, in Figure 6.19, Install was clicked for the Uninterruptible Power Supply and Timesource features, and Remove for the 386 HPFS feature. Since Timesource Support was already installed, the Action column shows "Replace" rather than "Install."

When you are done specifying install actions for the LAN Server features, click OK to return to the window shown in Figure 6.18. If you click Cancel, your specified actions are discarded.

If you select "Configure a component" from the window shown in Figure 6.18 and click OK, you will see the Configure window shown in Figure 6.20.

From the Configure window, select a feature and click Configure. Windows will appear asking for configuration and tailoring information. When you have filled in all the information, click OK to return to the Configure window. You can then select another feature and click Configure. When you are done configuring features, click OK on the Configure window to return to the Installation and Configuration window (Figure 6.18).

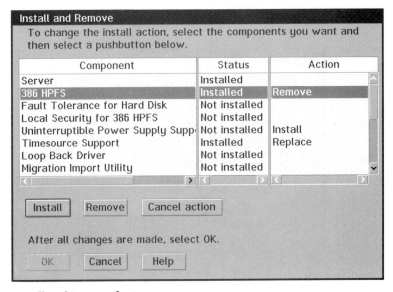

Figure 6.19 **Install and Remove features.**

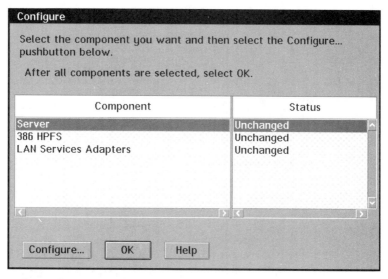

Figure 6.20 **Configure features.**

When you configure the Server feature, you can choose:

- The Server Name and Domain Name for this server. The Server Name is the name of this server PC, and the Domain Name is the name of the domain to which this server PC belongs. If you are tailoring a previously installed LAN Server, you can change the Server Name or Domain Name that was previously specified. Follow these rules for assigning Server Names and Domain Names, or your requesters and servers will not start correctly:

    A Server Name or Requester Name cannot match any other Server Name, Requester Name, or Domain Name of any PC in the LAN. A Domain Name cannot match any other Server Name or Requester Name of any PC in the LAN.
- Whether to start the server automatically when the server PC boots. This creates a STARTUP.CMD file with a NET START SERVER command in it.
- Whether you have any network adapters that use 24-bit direct memory addressing (DMA). A network adapter with 24-bit DMA cannot use RAM in your server PC above 16 megabytes. When you specify this option, LAN Server will compensate for the network adapter's limitations. Very few network adapters have this problem—some that do

are the IBM Token Ring Busmaster adapter and the IBM LANStreamer MC-16 adapter.

- Which services to start automatically when the server starts. See Table 6.5 for a list of services and a brief description of each.
- Whether you want to reinitialize the Domain Control Database (DCDB). If you want to keep your alias and user definitions, do *not* reinitialize the DCDB.

When you configure the LAN Services Adapters feature, you choose:

- Which adapters to use with LAN Server. You can have more than one adapter configured with MPTS. Here, you choose which adapter(s) LAN Server will utilize.
- The NetBIOS resources for each LAN adapter (see Figure 6.21). Refer to the section "LAN Server Tuning" later in this chapter for an explanation of these resources, and guidelines for how to tune them if needed.
- If you need to change the NetBIOS resources in LAPS Configuration, click on Cancel to return to the LAPS Configuration window and edit the parameters for the NetBIOS protocol.

When you are done configuring LAN Server features, click OK on the Configure window (Figure 6.20) and you will return to the Install and Configure window (Figure 6.18). You can then select "Apply the changes," which will complete the Tailored Install process.

Configuring and Tailoring MPTS

Double-click on the MPTS icon on your desktop to run the MPTS configuration and installation program. If you are adding or removing an adapter, you must run the LAN Server install program and take the Tailored install path. This will in turn invoke the MPTS configuration program, but will also configure the OS/2 Requester and Server properly for the added or removed adapters.

You have three choices on the initial window: Install, Configure, and Remove. Pick Configure, and you will see a window asking what you want to configure. The default choice is "LAN Adapters and Protocols," which is

Table 6.5 **LAN Server Services**

Requester Services (also run on server)

Service	Description
Requester	Accesses shared resources on a server.
Messenger	Receives and logs network messages.
Peer	Shares resources in a limited way with requesters. Cannot be run on server.
Replicator	Replicates files between a requester and a server, or two servers.

Server Services

Service	Description
Server	Provides shared resources for requesters.
LSServer	Handles the Domain Control Database (DCDB). Normally started with the Server service.
Netlogon	Supports domain logon and replication of user and group definitions between servers in a domain. Normally started with the Server service.
Alerter	Sends messages to users when events occur, such as printer errors or server disks running out of space. Normally started with the Server service.
DCDBRepl	Handles replication of Domain Control Database (DCDB) information to backup Domain Controllers.
Netrun	Allows users to run command-line applications on the server.
RemoteBoot	Handles requesters booting DOS or OS/2 from the server rather than from their local hard disk.
UPS	Handles signals from an attached Uninterruptible Power Supply (UPS) device, sending warning messages or shutting down the server when power problems occur
GenAlert	Sends alerts to an enterprise NetView console.
Timesource	Designates a server as a reliable time source.

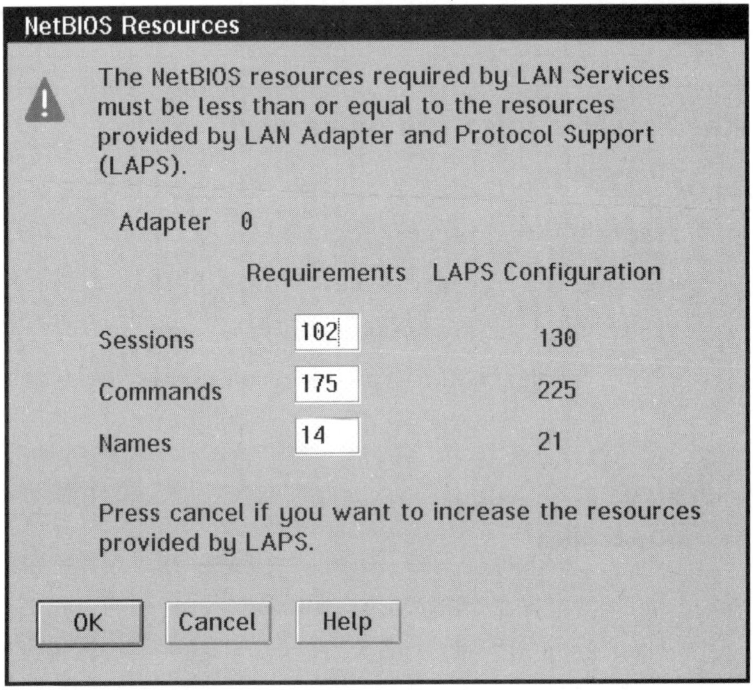

NetBIOS Resources

⚠ The NetBIOS resources required by LAN Services
must be less than or equal to the resources
provided by LAN Adapter and Protocol Support
(LAPS).

Adapter   0

	Requirements	LAPS Configuration
Sessions	102	130
Commands	175	225
Names	14	21

Press cancel if you want to increase the resources
provided by LAPS.

OK   Cancel   Help

*Figure 6.21 **NetBIOS resources.***

what you want. Click on Configure, which will take you to the LAPS Configuration window (see Figure 6.15). Follow the directions for Figure 6.15 to tailor your network adapters and protocols. When you click OK on the LAPS Configuration window, you will be asked to shut down and reboot your PC.

This procedure will put an MPTS icon on your desktop, and remove the MPTS icon from your IBM LAN Services folder. This is normal. If you see a *broken* MPTS icon left inside your IBM LAN Services folder, just delete it.

Installing LAN Server with the Loopback Driver

If you don't have a network adapter supported by LAN Server, or if you aren't connected to a LAN and want to try out LAN Server, you can install the Loopback Driver in your server PC. This will simulate a LAN inside your PC, letting the OS/2 Requester on your server PC talk to the OS/2 Server on the same PC without any network adapter or LAN connection.

To install the Loopback Driver, follow the Tailored Install procedure shown earlier. When you get to the LAPS Configuration window, remove all adapters and protocols from the Current Configuration window of the LAPS Configuration window. Then click OK. The next window asks a question: Do you want to use the Loopback driver instead of LAPS? Click Yes. Then proceed with the Tailored Install procedure as described, making sure that the Loopback Driver feature is installed from the window in Figure 6.19. When your server reboots, you will see only one driver loaded: the NetBIOS Loopback Driver.

Installing and Viewing LAN Server Soft Copy Books

To view or install the soft-copy books from CD-ROM, open an OS/2 command window and type **d:INSTALL**, where **d:** is your CD-ROM drive. You will see the CD-ROM Installation window (Figure 6.5). To view a soft-copy book from the CD-ROM, select "View Online Books" and click on OK; then choose the book you want to view. When you close the book, you are returned to the CD-ROM Installation window.

To install the soft-copy books from CD-ROM, select "Install Online Books" and click OK. Click OK on the Welcome window, then select "Install all books" and click OK. You can also select specific books you wish to install on this window. The online books are copied to your hard disk, and a LAN Server Books folder is placed inside the IBM LAN Services folder on the desktop. Click Exit on the Installation Complete window, and click Exit on the CD-ROM Install window.

To install the soft-copy books from diskette, insert the Online Books diskette 1, open an OS/2 command window, and type **a:INSTALL**, where **a:** is your diskette drive. Click OK on the Welcome window, then select "Install all books" and click OK. You can also select specific books you wish to install. The online books are copied to your hard disk, and a LAN Server Books folder is placed inside the IBM LAN Services folder on your desktop. Click Exit on the Installation Complete window, and click Exit on the CD-ROM Install window.

To view the soft-copy books from your hard disk, open the IBM LAN Services folder on your desktop, open the LAN Server Books folder, and double-click on the book you wish to view.

Setting Up the License Tracking Utility Icon

The License Tracking Utility (LTU) helps you track and manage licenses for LAN Server and Requester software in your network. It is installed on all domain controllers by default, but no icon is created for it. You can easily create an icon for LTU in your LAN Services folder.

Open the Templates folder and the IBM LAN Services folder. Drag a Program template from the Templates folder and drop it inside the IBM LAN Services folder. In the Settings notebook, set the Path to LTU.EXE, set the Title on the General page to "License Tracking Utility," and close the Settings notebook. You will see a License Tracking Utility icon appear in the IBM LAN Services folder.

You can run the License Tracking Utility by double-clicking on its icon. Look at its online Help to learn what it does and how it works.

Creating 3.5-Inch Diskettes from the LAN Server CD-ROM

To create 3.5-inch diskettes from your LAN Server CD-ROM, first obtain the correct number of blank, formatted 3.5-inch diskettes (see Table 6.2). Insert the CD-ROM into the drive and type **d:INSTALL**, where **d:** is your CD-ROM drive. You will see the CD-ROM Installation window (Figure 6.5). Select "Make 3.5-inch product diskettes," and click OK.

The next window asks you what diskettes you want to create. Your choices are: OS/2 LAN Requester (8 diskettes), OS/2 LAN Server (19 diskettes), DOS LAN Services (4 diskettes), and MPTS (3 diskettes). Select OS/2 LAN Server and click OK. You can now create diskettes for MPTS, OS/2 Requester, OS/2 Server, Productivity Aids, DLS, and LSP (see Table 6.2). You are prompted for each diskette, and you can skip creating any diskettes you don't need.

Installing the MPTS Utilities and Toolkits

If you have the LAN Server CD-ROM, follow the procedure given earlier to create a 3.5-inch diskette for MPTS diskette 3. To install the MPTS utilities and toolkits, insert MPTS diskette 3, open an OS/2 command window, and type:

```
MD c:\MPTN\APPLETS
PKUNZIP2 a:\APPLETS\MPTSAPLT.ZIP c:\MPTN\APPLETS
MD c:\MPTN\CASSETUP
PKUNZIP2 a:\APPLETS\CASSETUP.ZIP c:\MPTN\CASSETUP
PKUNZIP2 -D a:\TOOLKIT\*.ZIP c:\
```

where **a:** is your diskette drive and **c:** is the drive where MPTS is installed.

The MPTS utilities and toolkits are documented in the file called README.UTL that is installed to the \MPTN\APPLETS directory by this procedure.

Installing LAN Server Productivity Aids

The Productivity Aids are most easily installed from diskettes. If you have the LAN Server CD-ROM, make four 3.5-inch diskettes for the Productivity Aids, using the procedure given earlier. Now, open an OS/2 command window, insert Productivity Aids diskette 1, and type **a:INSTALL**, where **a:** is your diskette drive. You will see the Productivity Aids Installation window shown in Figure 6.22.

Set the Source Drive to your diskette drive. Set the Target Drive to the drive where LAN Server is installed. You must install each productivity aid individually by selecting it and clicking on Install. You are prompted to insert diskettes as needed. If you install all the aids in the list, they will take about 4 megabytes of hard disk space. The aids are installed to the \IBMLAN\PRO-DAIDS directory, along with a file called README that describes the aids. A LAN Services Productivity Aids folder is created inside your IBM LAN Services folder, with icons for the aids you installed.

Six productivity aids are not installed by this procedure—LAN Server Specialist, Remote File Synchronization, DISCUSER, EXTALIAS, REMUSER, and LSRXUTIL. These aids are discussed in Chapter 12.

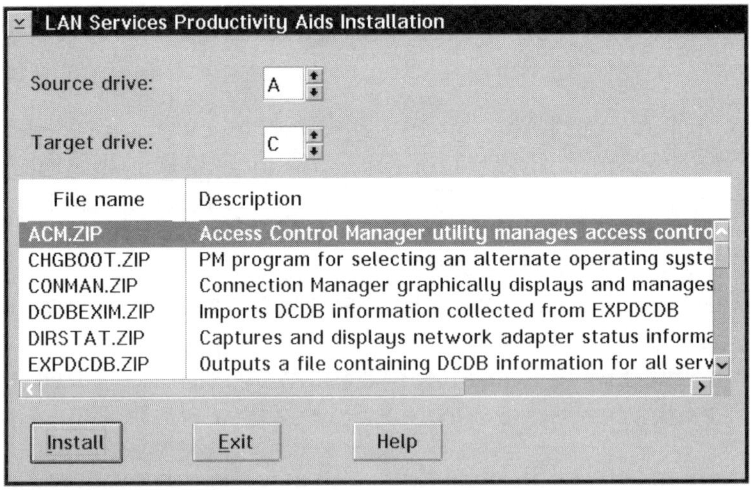

Figure 6.22 **Productivity Aids install.**

Installing the DISCUSER, EXTALIAS, REMUSER, and LSRXUTIL Productivity Aids

Open an OS/2 command window, insert the Productivity Aids diskette 2, and type:

```
PKUNZIP2 -D a:DISCUSER.ZIP c:\
PKUNZIP2 -D a:EXTALIAS.ZIP c:\
PKUNZIP2 -D a:REMUSER.ZIP c:\
PKUNZIP2 -D a:LSRXUTIL.ZIP c:\
COPY c:\IBMLAN\PRODAIDS\LSRXUT.40 c:\IBMLAN\NETLIB\LSRXUT.DLL
```

where **a:** is your diskette drive, and **c:** is the drive where LAN Server was installed.

Installing the LAN Server Specialist Productivity Aid

The LAN Server Specialist (LSS) aid helps you track and diagnose LAN Server problems in your server and in your requesters. See Chapter 12 for more information on LSS. LSS requires that the OS/2 Serviceability and Diagnostic

Aids be installed. If you haven't installed these, do so using OS/2 Selective Install in the System Startup folder. LSS also requires that you install FFST/2 support with LAN Server. If you haven't done so already, use LAN Server Tailored Install to select and install the FFST/2 feature.

To install LAN Server Specialist, insert Productivity Aids diskette 3, open an OS/2 command window, and type **a:LSSINST /T:c:**, where **a:** is your diskette drive, and **c:** is the drive where LAN Server was installed. Follow directions when asked to switch diskettes.

After installation of LAN Server Specialist, you should see a LAN Server Specialist folder on your desktop. Open it and review the online documentation for instructions on installation of LAN Server Specialist Agents on your requester PCs, and for information on use of LAN Server Specialist.

Installing the Remote File Synchronization Productivity Aid

The Remote File Synchronization aid helps users work with shared files when the user is sometimes disconnected from the server—for example, a user with a laptop PC and a docking station. To install the Remote File Synchronization aid, you must first create an installation diskette. Get a blank, formatted diskette, put the Productivity Aids diskette 4 in the diskette drive, open an OS/2 command window, and type **COPY a:REMOTEFS.ZIP c:\IBMLAN\ INSTALL**, where **a:** is your diskette drive, and **c:** is the drive where LAN Server is installed. Now, remove the Productivity Aids diskette 4, insert the blank diskette, and type:

```
FORMAT a: /V:MARS1 /ONCE
PKUNZIP2 c:\IBMLAN\INSTALL\REMOTEFS.ZIP a:
DEL c:\IBMLAN\INSTALL\REMOTEFS.ZIP
```

where **a:** is your diskette drive, and **c:** is the drive where LAN Server is installed. Label the blank diskette "Remote File Synchronization Productivity Aid—Install Disk."

To install the Remote File Synchronization, insert the install disk you created, open an OS/2 command window, and type **a:INSTALL**, where **a:** is your diskette drive. Follow the install instructions. When installation is complete, shut down and reboot your PC. You should see a folder on your desktop labeled Mobile File Sync. Review the online documentation in that folder for information on how to set up and use Remote File Synchronization.

Tailoring the System by Editing Configuration Files

Many system parameters are specified within files that can be edited with a standard text editor (so-called ASCII text files). These files are shown in Table 6.6.

Making a copy of the original configuration file before editing it is highly recommended. To edit a control file with the OS/2 System Editor, open an OS/2 command window and type, for example, **E c:\IBMLAN\IBMLAN.INI**, where **c:** is the drive where LAN Server was installed. This will open the System Editor and edit the IBMLAN.INI file. Make sure the editor is *not* in word-wrap mode.

If you prefer to use a character-mode editor, use TEDIT instead of E. Do *not* use the EPM editor to edit CONFIG.SYS, because it does not support lines longer than 255 characters.

To learn how to use these editors, see the online Help for them. Make whatever modifications you wish, then save the file. You will usually have to shut down OS/2 and reboot for the modifications to take effect. Changes to most sections of IBMLAN.INI can be put into effect by stopping and starting the service whose section you changed.

Table 6.6 **LAN Server Configuration Files**

Name	Drive	Directory	LAN Server Use
IBMLAN.INI	LAN Server install	\IBMLAN	Startup parameters for LAN Server services
PROTOCOL.INI	OS/2 boot	\IBMCOM	LAN Adapter and Protocol support parameters
HPFS386.INI	OS/2 boot	\IBM386FS	HPFS386 file system parameters (LAN Server Advanced only)
CONFIG.SYS	OS/2 boot	\(root)	OS/2 system startup parameters and drivers
STARTUP.CMD	OS/2 boot	\(root)	OS/2 startup commands

The IBMLAN.INI File

The IBMLAN.INI file is organized by LAN Server service (see Table 6.5 for names and descriptions of LAN Server services). Each service can have a section in IBMLAN.INI. A section starts with the service name inside square brackets, followed by keyword lines. Each keyword line has a keyword, an equal sign, and a value or values. Lines that start with a semicolon are comments and are ignored by LAN Server. Keywords and section names can be uppercase or lowercase.

For example, the IBMLAN.INI section for the Requester service starts as follows:

```
[requester]
; Parameters for the Requester service.
  COMPUTERNAME = LSSERVER
  DOMAIN = LSDOMAIN
```

As each service starts, it reads its parameters from its section in IBM-LAN.INI. If you change IBMLAN.INI, you must stop and start the service whose section you changed for the change to take effect. Some parameters can be overridden in the NET START command. See NET START in the *LAN Server Command Reference* online book for details.

The services section in IBMLAN.INI is a special section that specifies which services exist and where the service programs are located. For example:

```
[services]
  messenger = services\msrvinit.exe
  peer = services\netpsini.exe
  replicator = services\replicat.exe
  requester = services\wksta.exe
```

is a typical services section for a requester, which defines four services and specifies where their service programs are (relative to the IBMLAN directory).

The networks section in IBMLAN.INI is another special section, which specifies the logical networks that LAN Server will use. It is read at OS/2 boot time, before any service starts up. If you change this section, you must shut down and reboot your server PC before the changes take effect. Here's an example of the networks section:

```
[networks]
net1 = NETBEUI$,0,LM10,34,70,14
```

This example specifies that LAN Server has one logical network defined, called net1, which will use the LM10 interface to network adapter number 0 with the NetBEUI protocol (the default for LAN Server). LAN Server will use up to 34 sessions, 70 commands, and 14 names on this adapter. If additional logical networks were in use, additional lines would appear here.

Table 6.7 lists some key IBMLAN.INI parameters. Also look at the IBMLAN.INI file itself for LAN Server 4.0; it contains comments that document the WRKHEURISTICS and SRVHEURISTICS settings quite well—only a few

Table 6.7 **Key IBMLAN.INI Parameters**

Requester Service Parameters

Parameter Name	Description
ComputerName	Name of this PC (whether it's a requester or server). Must be unique among all ComputerNames in the LAN, and must not match any Domain name in the LAN.
Domain	Name of the primary domain for this PC (whether requester or server).
OthDomains	Comma-separated list of up to four domain names. These *other domains* will be monitored by the requester, and you can browse and connect to their resources. Also, the LAN Server Administrative GUI will recognize these other domains and let you administer them.
UseAllMem	Yes if all network adapters do not use 24-bit DMA. No otherwise.
WrkHeuristics	40 flags for fine-tuning of the requester. Some notable flags are documented following. See the IBMLAN.INI file for documentation on the others.
WrkHeuristics 36	If 1, synchronize requester PC's clock with Domain Controller's clock at domain logon. If 0, do not synchronize.
WrkHeuristics 37	Default validation for logons. 0: no validation. 1: local validation. 2: domain logon.
WrkServices	List of services, separated by commas, that should be started when the Requester service starts. For example: WrkServices = Messenger.
WrkNets	List of logical networks, separated by commas, that the Requester service will use. For example: WrkNets = net1, net2.

Table 6.7 **(continued)**

Server and Peer Service Parameters

Parameter Name	Description
AlertNames	List of user IDs to receive administrative alert messages.
GuestAcct	User ID to be used for guest validation. See Chapter 8.
AutoDisconnect	Number of minutes to allow idle sessions to remain without disconnecting. A value of −1 disables idle session disconnection.
MaxConnections	Maximum number of connections to shared resources supported by Server. (Not applicable to HFPS386 shared file resources.)
MaxShares	Maximum number of shared resources supported by Server.
MaxUsers	Maximum number of sessions supported by Server.
SrvHidden	If Yes, the server is not visible to users browsing the network.
Security	Peer only. If User, specifies user level security for the Peer Services. If Share, specifies share level security for the Peer Services. See Chapter 14.
UserName	Peer only. For Security=user, specifies the user ID of the user who is considered the *owner* of the peer services PC.
SrvHeuristics	20 flags for fine tuning the server. See the IBMLAN.INI file for documentation.
SrvServices	List of services to be started when the Server service starts. For example: SrvServices = NetLogon, LSServer.
SrvNets	List of logical networks that the Server service supports. For example: SrvNets = net1, net2.

of these settings have been highlighted in Table 6.7. For a complete explanation of all IBMLAN.INI parameters, see the LAN Server 4.0 online book *Performance Tuning*.

The CONFIG.SYS File

The CONFIG.SYS file is in the root directory of the OS/2 boot drive. OS/2 reads CONFIG.SYS at boot time to set startup parameters and to load device drivers. See Table 6.8 for key CONFIG.SYS parameters and settings you can try. For more information on any of these, open the OS/2 Command Reference from the Information folder and search on the keywords.

The HPFS386.INI File

The HPFS386.INI file is in the IBM386FS directory of the OS/2 boot drive. HPFS386 reads this file at boot time to set startup parameters. See Table 6.9 for key HPFS386.INI parameters. For more information on HFPS386.INI parameters, see the LAN Server 4.0 online book *Performance Tuning*, or simply

Table 6.8 *Key CONFIG.SYS Parameters*

SET AUTOSTART=	Remove the CONNECTIONS parameter from this statement, or OS/2 will probably ask you to log in to the network every time you boot your PC.
IFS=c:\OS2\HPFS.IFS	This is the OS/2 HPFS file system. You can tune the size of its cache with the /CACHE:n parameter, *n* is the cache size in units of kilobytes (1024 bytes). The maximum is /CACHE:2048, which is a 2-megabyte cache.
SET RESTARTOBJECTS=	Use the STARTUPFOLDERSONLY parameter to suppress OS/2's habit of restarting applications that were active when you shut down your system.
DISKCACHE=	The first parameter is the size of the cache used for FAT-formatted partitions. If your server PC uses mostly HPFS partitions, you can change this from D, which is 10 percent of the available RAM, to a number that specifies the size of the cache in kilobytes (1,024 bytes). A good choice for an HPFS-only system is 64.
SWAPPATH=	The first parameter is the location of your OS/2 swap file (SWAPPER.DAT). You can change this to point to a directory on a different partition if you don't have enough space on your OS/2 boot drive. If you do this, don't forget to delete the original SWAPPER.DAT file when you reboot.
BASEDEV=PRINT0x.SYS	*x* is either 1 or 2. Try adding the /IRQ parameter to this statement. On most PCs, printing will take less overhead. On some PCs, printing will stop working. If this happens, simply remove the /IRQ parameter.

Table 6.9 **Key HPFS386.INI Parameters**

Cachesize=	The size of the RAM cache for HPFS386 files, in kilobytes. For example, Cachesize=16384 is a 16-megabyte cache. If not specified, the default is to use 20 percent of the RAM up to 20 megabytes, then 60 percent of the remaining RAM (if any).
UseAllMem=	If Yes, the file cache can use all memory in the server PC. If No, the file cache will be kept in the first 16 megabytes of memory. Use No if your disk controller cannot address memory above 16 megabytes.

edit the HPFS386.INI file and look at it—there are many comments describing its use in the file.

The PROTOCOL.INI File

The PROTOCOL.INI file is in the \IBMCOM directory of the OS/2 boot drive. It tells the LAN Adapter and Protocol Support how to load the network adapter drivers and protocols, how to bind them together, and what the startup parameters are for them. Use the MPTS Configuration program to work on PROTOCOL.INI if you are adding, deleting, or changing drivers or protocols. If you simply want to change a parameter, then editing the file directly is reasonable.

The PROTOCOL.INI file is structured into sections, similar to the IBM-LAN.INI file. Each section represents a network adapter driver or a protocol driver that you have configured.

Tuning LAN Server

Tuning is the task of modifying LAN Server parameters so that you get the capacity and performance you need from your server, within the limits of your hardware. Tuning can be a complex task. The *LAN Server 4.0 Network Administrator's Reference, Volume 2* on *Performance Tuning*, covers this subject in detail, and it is recommended for further study.

Here, you are given a brief overview of LAN Server tuning, and told how to use the LAN Server 4.0 Performance Tuning Assistant.

LAN Server 4.0 Performance Tuning Assistant

The LAN Server 4.0 Performance Tuning Assistant is installed for you on every server PC. It's represented by an icon in the LAN Services folder. Double-click on it to start the tuning assistant.

The Tuning Assistant presents itself as a notebook with five major sections—Server, Assumptions, System Files, Test Data, and Warnings (Figure 6.23). The major sections are denoted by tabs on the right-hand side of the notebook. Each major section has individual pages, denoted by tabs on the bottom side of the notebook. As you click on a major section tab, you will see the individual page tabs change.

You describe your server configuration in the pages of the Server and Assumptions sections. When you click Calculate, the Tuning Assistant creates new versions of the system files IBMLAN.INI, CONFIG.SYS, PROTOCOL.INI, and HPFS386.INI. You can review old and new versions of the system files in the System Files section—the changes are highlighted for you. You can go back to the Server and Assumptions sections and make more changes and click Calculate again.

When you are satisfied with your configuration, you can activate the new system files with the Apply button on the System Files page (the previous

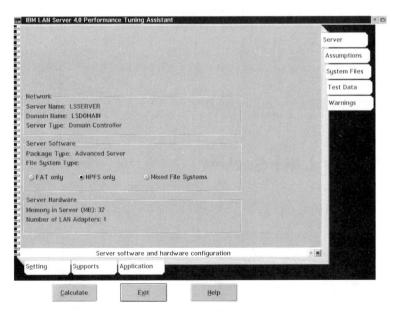

Figure 6.23 **LAN Server 4.0 Performance Tuning Assistant.**

versions of the files are saved in a backup directory). The Test Data section gives you details on the parameters that the Tuning Assistant is working with, and the Warnings section shows you messages about your configuration for your information and action.

Use the Tuning Assistant to *rough out* your tuning parameters. Then, review the information in the following "LAN Server Tuning" section and use those guidelines to further tailor your LAN Server parameters.

LAN Server Tuning Overview

There are two kinds of tuning you perform: *capacity* tuning and *performance* tuning. Capacity tuning is setting parameters to allow the server to handle the expected load of users without running out of some resource. Performance tuning is setting parameters to allow the server to handle its workload efficiently. There are two, sometimes conflicting, performance tuning goals: to maximize the overall throughput of the server, and to minimize the server response time (the time taken by the server to respond to a request). Concentrate on capacity tuning first, then turn to performance tuning.

LAN Server can share many resources: files, print queues, named pipes, and serial devices. LAN Server Entry has one server, called the Ring 3 server, that handles all of these shared resources. LAN Server Advanced has the Ring 3 server, and also has the HPFS386 server for optimized access to shared files on an HPFS partition. When you are running LAN Server Advanced, you are actually running two different servers at the same time: the HPFS386 server for shared HPFS files, and the Ring 3 server for shared FAT files, print queues, named pipes, and serial services. You need to be aware of this when tuning LAN Server Advanced. Tune the Ring 3 server parameters first, then the HPFS386 parameters.

LAN Server 4.0 has made the task of tuning much easier than LAN Server 3.0. LAN Server 4.0 installation will set reasonable defaults for tuning parameters. These defaults should be sufficient to handle 20 to 30 simultaneous users for the Entry version, or 100 simultaneous users for the Advanced version. Also, LAN Server 4.0 provides the Tuning Assistant, which will automatically generate tuning parameter settings for you when you describe your server setup. If you are using LAN Server 3.0, be prepared to tune your server. There is a LAN Server 3.0 tuning aid available in the form of a spreadsheet. It's called CNFGLS30 and it's available for downloading from IBM (see Appendix B for details).

Capacity Tuning Summary

A good strategy for capacity tuning is to leave the defaults set by installation, and run your server for a while. If a resource is needed but not available, an error message will be logged. Check the error log periodically with the Error Log display utility in the LAN Services folder or the NET ERROR command. You can do this from a remote administrator's workstation if you wish. If you see a pattern of resource exhaustion, tune the server by increasing that resource.

There are two basic types of resource used by the server: *server* resources and *NetBIOS* resources. The NetBIOS resources required by LAN Server are sessions, commands (also known as NCBs), and names. A NetBIOS session represents a link between one requester PC and the server, so you must have enough sessions to support the expected number of simultaneous requesters for your server. A NetBIOS command represents an operation—as a rule of thumb, provide between 1.5 and 2 commands per session. A NetBIOS name represents a contact point for requesters to the server—you would increase this only if LAN Server services or NetBIOS applications failed to start properly.

Each network adapter has its own pool of NetBIOS resources. Each NetBIOS resource has two specifications: an overall value set in the PROTO-COL.INI file, and a LAN Server value set in the **netx=** line of the IBMLAN.INI file. The LAN Server value for a NetBIOS resource is subtracted from the overall value, and whatever is left over is available for other NetBIOS applications running on the server (such as IBM Database/2). For example, the PROTOCOL.INI file could specify:

```
SESSIONS = 130
NCBS = 225
NAMES = 21
```

and the IBMLAN.INI file could specify:

```
net1 = NETBEUI$,0,LM10,102,175,14
```

where the last three parameters represent sessions, commands, and names, respectively. In this example, there are 28 sessions, 50 commands, and 7 names left over for other NetBIOS applications.

Each adapter is limited to 254 sessions. Also, the number of commands and names is limited by a complex formula. If you start getting a message such as:

```
LTO0097 System resources exceeded. . . .
```

when you reboot your server PC, you need to lower some of the NetBIOS resources. See the file \IBMCOM\README.MPT for details on how to calculate NetBIOS resources.

Server resources are described in Table 6.10.

Table 6.10 **Server Resources for Capacity Tuning**

These parameters are located in the IBMLAN.INI file, in the [server] section.

Resource	IBMLAN.INI Parameter	Description
Session	maxusers	One required for each requester PC that is using the server simultaneously. Only one Session is needed per requester, no matter how many different shared resources are accessed. A NetBIOS session resource is also needed for each simultaneous requester (see preceding).
Share	maxshares	One required for each name, shared resource at the server. A print queue, a directory alias, or a shared serial device counts as a shared resource.
Request buffer	numreqbuf	One required for each active request from a requester. As a rule of thumb, allocate two request buffers per active requester.

The following parameters do not apply to HPFS386 shared file resources. HPFS386 manages these resources internally and does not require capacity tuning. If you are using HPFS386, tune these parameters only for non-HPFS386 shared file resources.

Resource	IBMLAN.INI Parameter	Description
Connection	maxconnections	One required for each connection of a requester to a shared resource.
Open file	maxopens	One required for each opened shared file at the server.
File lock	maxlocks	One required for each locked shared file at the server.
File search	maxsearches	One required for each active directory scan at the server.
Big buffer	numbigbuf	One required for each active large-block file transfer request from a requester. As a rule of thumb, allocate two big buffers per active requester moving large blocks of data. However, each big buffer takes 64K of RAM, so don't overdo it.

Performance Tuning Summary

Usually, file sharing performance is very important to users. To get good file sharing performance, these are the important factors:

- Fast hard drives at the server
- Sufficient file cache at the server
- Use of LAN Server Advanced and HPFS386

If you are using HPFS386, you can get an idea of the efficiency of your file cache by opening an OS/2 command window at the server and typing **CACHE386 /STATS:D**. You will see a dynamically updated display of the running total of bytes read and written, and a read and write cache hit ratio. For example, if the read cache hit ratio is 88 percent, this means that out of 100 read requests to the server, 88 are satisfied from the server's RAM cache without having to read from the hard disk. If your cache hit ratio is less than 80 or 90 percent, you may want to consider increasing your HPFS386 cache, which may require adding more RAM to your server PC.

The easiest way to tune your cache size is to go through a LAN Server tailored install, and select to configure the HPFS386 feature from the window in figure 6.20. Then, change the cache size in the configuration windows that you see. You can also edit the \IBM386FS\HPFS386.INI file directly, and modify the parameter there—it's called *cachesize=* in the *[filesystem]* section.

If your server PC has more than 16 megabytes of RAM, be sure to specify the *useallmem=yes* parameter in HPFS386.INI—unless you happen to have a disk controller that uses 24-bit DMA and cannot address memory above 16 megabytes. You can also specify this parameter through the Tailored install path as you configure HPFS386. If you set this parameter to *useallmem=no*, you won't be able to use memory above 16 megabytes for file cache.

CHAPTER 7

A Guided Tour of LAN Server Administration

> **Throw your heart over the bar and your body will follow.**
>
> —*Norman Vincent Peale,* The Power of Positive Thinking

This chapter will walk you through simple administration steps for your newly installed server. Chapter 8 will cover some of the more advanced tasks and concepts in LAN Server administration. You should invest an hour or two of your time to walk through these steps; you will learn the basics of LAN Server administration in an efficient and simple way, and you will accomplish some useful work as well.

You will create a new administrative account for yourself, create a user account for one of your users, define a shared directory on your server, provide access control for the directory, and create a shared printer. You will also log on as a user and use the shared directory and printer.

You will see how to accomplish each task with the LAN Server 4.0 Administrative Graphical User Interface (GUI). If you are using LAN Server 3.0, there is no GUI, but there is a full-screen interface that can handle all the tasks in this chapter. See the *LAN Server 3.0 Network Administrator's Reference*, volume 3, for details.

The examples given assume you are using OS/2 Warp on your server and requester. If you are using an earlier release of OS/2, you can accomplish the same tasks, but the exact interface will look a little different.

You will also see the LAN Server commands you can use in a command window or a command file to accomplish the same tasks. Knowing both is helpful—you can use the GUI for less familiar or more complex tasks, and use commands for familiar, quick tasks. You also put commands in an OS/2 command file to automate repetitive tasks.

Before We Start

If you are not experienced in working with OS/2, take the OS/2 Tutorial now. Even if you have some experience, consider taking it—you will probably learn something you didn't know, and it's quick and fun! The OS/2 Tutorial should be displayed the first time you start your new OS/2 system, or you can find it in the Information folder. (If it wasn't installed with OS/2, you can install it now using Selective Install from the System Setup folder.)

It is assumed in these examples that you have installed a server called LSSERVER in a domain called LSDOMAIN, and you are sitting at the keyboard and screen of that server. (If you chose other names, simply substitute your own names in the examples.)

You should see a folder on your desktop called IBM LAN Services (Figure 7.1). Open the LAN Services folder, and you'll see several program objects. For now, only the LAN Server Administration, Logon, and Logoff programs will be used.

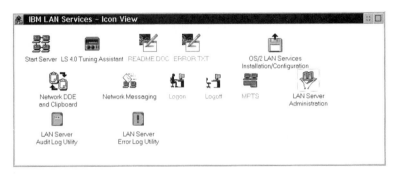

Figure 7.1 **IBM LAN Services folder–Icon View.**

Log On to the Domain

Your first task is to log on to your new LAN Server domain. Start (open) the Logon program in the IBM LAN Services folder. You will see the LAN Server Logon dialog box (Figure 7.2).

Type **USERID** for your user ID, then tab to or click in the password entry field. Type **PASSWORD** for your password. Don't type any spaces before or after USERID or PASSWORD. You shouldn't have to change the displayed domain name. Now press Enter or click on OK.

After a few seconds, you should see a message: Logon successful. You may first see an information message: Your user ID can not receive messages. If you do, ignore this message (just click on OK or press the Enter key). Chapter 10 will explain how LAN Server network messaging works and what this message means.

The equivalent command would be:

```
LOGON USERID /P:PASSWORD
```

```
┌─────────────────────────────────────────────┐
│ LAN Server Logon                              │
├─────────────────────────────────────────────┤
│                                               │
│  Note: The password will not display.         │
│                                               │
│  Verification:     Domain                      │
│                                               │
│  User ID          │ USERID              │      │
│                                               │
│  Password         │                     │      │
│                                               │
│  Domain name      │ LSDOMAIN            │      │
│                                               │
│   ┌───────┐  ┌─────────┐  ┌───────┐          │
│   │  OK   │  │ Cancel  │  │ Help  │          │
│   └───────┘  └─────────┘  └───────┘          │
└─────────────────────────────────────────────┘
```

Figure 7.2 **LAN Server Logon.**

Create Your Own Administrative Account

Your next task is to create your own administrative account, and delete the default USERID administrative account. If you don't do this, anyone familiar with LAN Server could log on as USERID with password PASSWORD, and gain administrative access to your domain. In other words, they could create and delete user accounts, change passwords, and access any resource in the domain.

Open the LAN Server Administration GUI from the IBM LAN Services folder (Figure 7.3). It will take a few seconds for the GUI to start up. If your server has less than 16 megabytes of memory, you may find the GUI too slow. You can use commands instead, or you can run the GUI from a remote requester with more memory.

The first window the GUI presents is titled "LAN Server Administration —Icon View" and contains three objects. One is a domain container, whose icon is a medieval castle and whose name is LSDOMAIN. You will do most of your work inside this domain container. The other two objects are your local server workstation, and a container for shadowed servers that you use frequently. For now, just use the LSDOMAIN container (Figure 7.4). Open it up by double-clicking mouse button 1.

The domain container, in turn, holds five containers. All of your domain's administrative data is in these five containers. In this chapter, you will work with the User Accounts and the Resource Definitions containers.

Now, open the user accounts container to see the domain's user account objects, which are represented by icons that look like picture ID cards or driver's licenses (Figure 7.5).

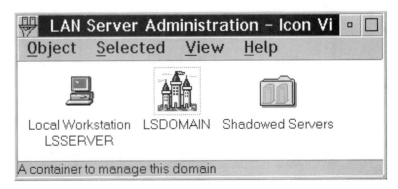

Figure 7.3 ***LAN Server Administration–Icon View.***

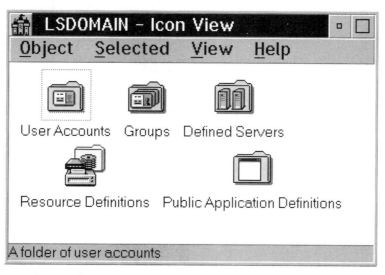

Figure 7.4 **Domain container.**

You should see these objects in the User Accounts container:

- UserID Template—the template used to create new user accounts.
- USERID—the default administrative account, which will be deleted soon.
- GUEST—the default guest account. How guest accounts work will be explained later.
- LSSERVER—used by LAN Server to help manage the server. Do not delete or change this account.

Figure 7.5 **User Accounts—Icon View.**

If you don't see all of these, you may need to scroll the container window or select Arrange from the container's pop-up menu.

To create your new administrative account, drag the UserID Template to an empty spot in the User Accounts window. (Remember to use mouse button 2 to drag objects, as the OS/2 Tutorial teaches.) You will see a settings notebook with many pages and choices. On the Identity page, which is displayed first, type LSADMIN in the "User account name" field. You can also type a Description if you wish (Figure 7.6).

Now turn to the Password page in the notebook by clicking on the Password tab. Check the "Change password" checkbox. Then, click inside the "New password" entry field and type a new password, at least four characters long, of your own choosing. (Chapter 8 will show how to change the minimum required password length from the default of 4.) Use the Tab key to jump to the "Confirmation" entry field, and type the password again to

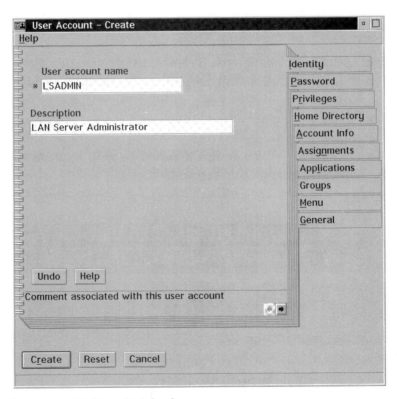

Figure 7.6 **User Account Settings Notebook.**

confirm that you've typed it correctly. Be sure to remember this password! If you forget it, you will not be able to administer your LAN Server anymore.

Now turn to the Privileges page and select Administrator. Last, click the Create button (or simply close the notebook) to create the new account. You should see a new user account object called LSADMIN in the User Accounts container.

Finally, delete the USERID account object by selecting Delete from its pop-up menu. (Click mouse button 2 on the object to get the pop-up menu, as described in the OS/2 Tutorial.) Note that you cannot drag a LAN Server GUI object to the OS/2 Shredder to delete it.

The equivalent commands for these tasks are (substitute your chosen password, at least 4 characters long, in the first command):

```
NET USER LSADMIN password /ADD /PRIV:ADMIN
NET USER USERID /DELETE
```

It's a very good idea to create a backup administrative account identical to the LSADMIN account, but with a different user ID and password. Write down the backup account's user ID and password and lock them in a safe place. If you ever forget the password for your administrative account, or it is lost or deleted for some reason, you can use your backup administrative account to fix it.

Log On with Your New Administrative Account

Your next task is to log off from USERID, and log on with your new administrative account, LSADMIN. To log off, open (double-click) the Logoff program from the LAN Services folder. You will see a dialog box listing all the logons you have active (there should only be one). Click on "Log off All" to log off. This will cause the Administration GUI to stop, and you'll have to click OK on a dialog box helpfully informing you of this fact.

Now, open (double-click) the Logon program, and log on with LSADMIN as your user ID, and your chosen password.

If you want to do this from the command line, enter these commands:

```
LOGOFF
LOGON LSADMIN /P:password
```

Create a New User Account

Your new LAN wouldn't be much use without some users. So, let's create one! Start up the LAN Server Administration GUI again, and open the domain container, then the User Accounts container. Drag the User ID Template to an empty spot on the window, just as you did before, to create a new user account.

You will see the user account object settings notebook. On the Identity page, type LSUSER and (optionally) a description. On the Password page, check Change Password, then type LSUSER's password (twice), remembering that it must be at least four characters long. Click on Create (or close the notebook) to create the new account.

This new user account does not have administrator privileges. This user will not be able to create new accounts, delete accounts, or perform other administrative actions.

The equivalent command is:

```
NET USER LSUSER password /ADD
```

Create a Directory Alias

Now let's share a directory on the server by creating a directory alias. This is a name for a shared directory on a server. Users on the LAN can access shared directories by the alias name—they don't have to know the server name, drive letter, or path of the shared directory.

Open the Resource Definitions container that's inside the domain container (Figure 7.7). You will see three templates: a Directory Template, a Printer Template, and a Serial Device template.

Create a directory alias object from the Directory Template (drag the template to an empty spot in the Resource Definitions container window, or select Create Another from its pop-up menu). You will see the settings notebook for the new alias object. Type a name for the alias, and a description if you wish. Now, click on the Server Name pull-down list and choose your server from the list. Finally, type the full pathname of the directory you want to share in the Path field. For example, your directory alias definition might look like this, for an alias called LSDATA on a server called LSSERVER, for the directory C:\DATA\SALES (Figure 7.8).

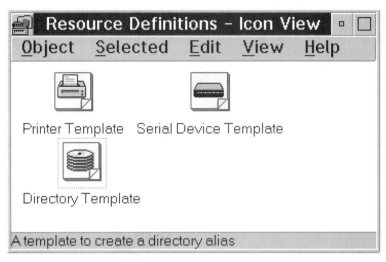

Figure 7.7 **Shared Resource Definitions.**

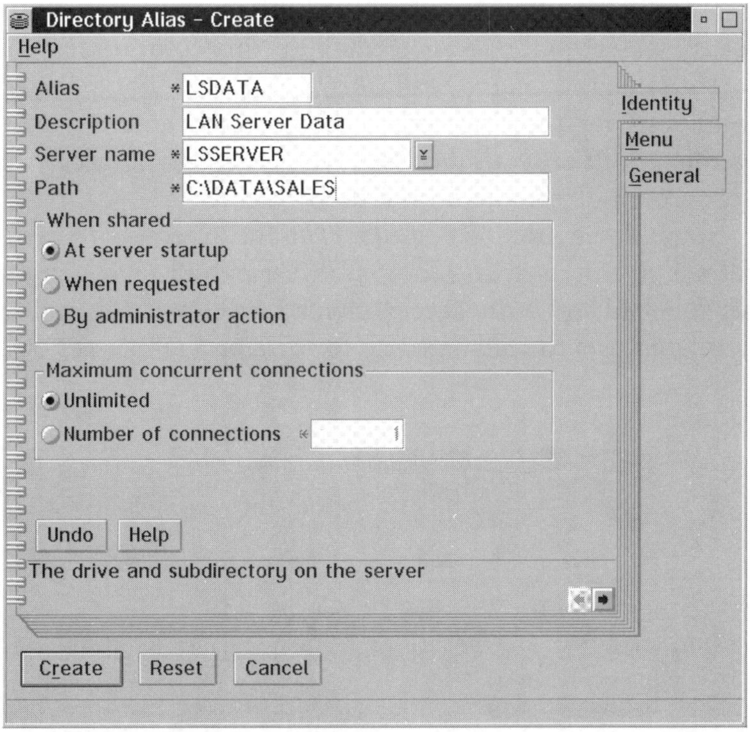

Figure 7.8 **Directory Alias settings notebook.**

Now, click the Create button (or close the settings notebook) to create the new directory alias object.

There is one more step: granting access to the directory. Access is granted through an access control profile. If your new shared directory has no access control profile, you'll see a message giving you a chance to create one. For now, click on Cancel, because access will be granted when the alias to the user account is assigned in the next step.

To create this directory alias from the command line, use the following command:

```
NET ALIAS LSDATA \\LSSERVER C:\DATA\SALES
```

Assign the Directory Alias to the User Account

The easiest way to set up your new user, LSUSER, with your new directory alias, LSDATA, is to assign the directory alias to the user account. This will connect the directory to the user when the user logs on, and also gives you an easy way to grant access to the directory for the user.

To assign the directory alias to the user account, open both the Resource Definitions and the User Accounts containers and move them until you can see them both on your desktop. Now, drag the directory alias object to the user account object and drop it there (Figure 7.9).

You will see a dialog box titled "Grant Access to a Resource." LAN Server will not give users access to your directory unless you grant it. To give your user full read and write access, check the R, W, C, D, and A permissions. To allow your user to read data and execute programs but not create, modify, or

Figure 7.9 **Assigning a Directory Alias to a user.**

delete any files or directories, check only the R permission. Then click on Set (Figure 7.10).

Next, you will see a message asking if you wish to propagate access control to all the subdirectories. Click on OK to make sure that all subdirectories have the same access control as your shared directory. If you don't propagate access control, users may not be able to read or write in subdirectories of your shared directory.

Finally, you will see a dialog box titled "Administer Logon Assignments" (Figure 7.11). If you want the shared directory to appear at a specific drive letter when the user logs on, pick the drive letter in the "Local Drive Name" field, then click OK.

The equivalent commands are:

```
NET USER LSUSER /ASSIGN D:LSDATA
NET ACCESS LSDATA /ADD LSUSER:RWCDA
NET ACCESS LSDATA /APPLY
```

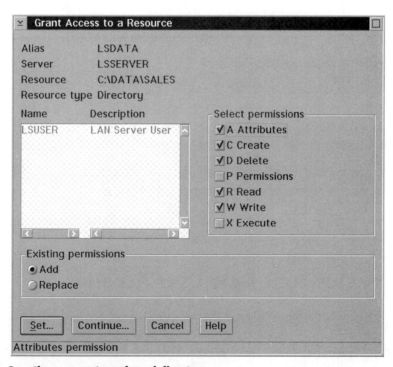

Figure 7.10 **Granting access to a shared directory.**

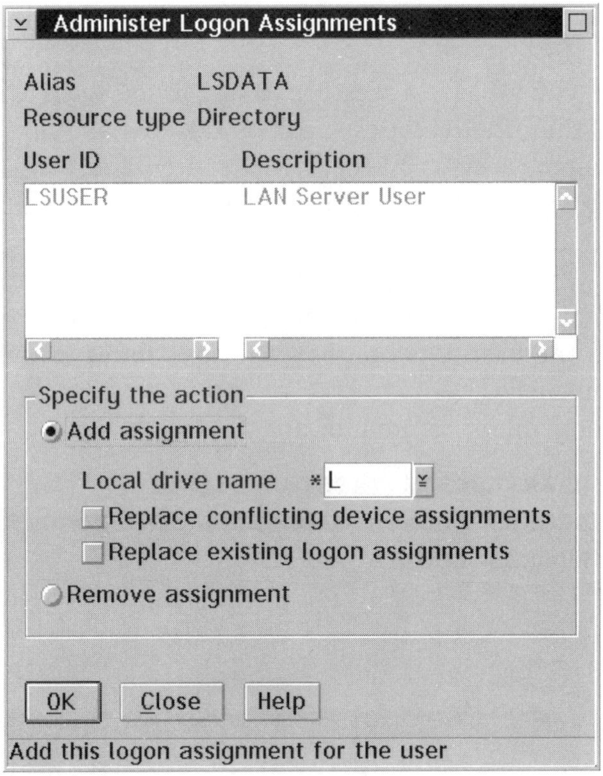

Figure 7.11 **Logon assignments.**

or, to assign read-only access:

```
NET USER LSUSER /ASSIGN D:LSDATA
NET ACCESS LSDATA /ADD LSUSER:R
NET ACCESS LSDATA /APPLY
```

Try Out Your New User Account

You have created a new administrative account, a new user account, and a directory alias. You have assigned the directory alias to the user account at logon, and granted access to the directory. Congratulations! These are the key tasks that a LAN Server administrator needs to know. Now it's time to try out your work.

Using the LAN Services folder, log off your administrative account and log on to your new user account. You should see a "Logon successful" message, and your shared directory should be connected and ready to view. Open the Drives folder (it's normally inside the OS/2 System folder). You should see a network drive icon for your shared directory, with a little server PC picture sitting on top of the disk drive icon. If you open the network drive, you should see the files and directories inside that shared directory on the server.

Using commands to do the same thing, you would enter:

```
LOGOFF
LOGON LSUSER /P:password
     (logon successful message)
DIR D:
     (shows files/directories on server)
```

Create a Printer Alias

Now, let's let our user share a printer that's attached to the server. First, you must install the printer on the server PC as a normal OS/2-usable printer. To do this, go to the server machine and open the Templates folder. Drag the Printer template (not the Network Printer template!) to the desktop, and fill in the resulting dialog box. You will have to pick a name for the printer, a print driver (you can install a new driver here if needed), and the output port that the printer is attached to (usually LPT1).

When you are done, you should be able to open the Drives folder, find a short data file with text in it (such as CONFIG.SYS), and drag it to the printer object. A dialog box will pop up asking you if the file is plain text or printer-specific data. Choose "plain text," and the file should print successfully. This verifies that your printer is operational and correctly defined to OS/2 on the server.

Now, log off and log on with your administrative account, and start the administrative GUI as before. Open the Resource Definitions container that's inside the domain container. Create a new printer alias by dragging the Printer Template to an empty spot in the window. You will see the settings notebook for the printer alias object. Type a name for the alias, and a description if you wish. Then pick a server from the drop-down list of server names—this is the computer name of your server; and pick a print queue name from the drop-down list—this is the name of the printer that you just installed. Click on Create or close the settings notebook to create the printer alias.

You will see a message asking you to click OK if you want to create an access control profile. Click on Cancel instead. The default for LAN Server printers is to allow access for all logged-on users, and you don't need to create an access control profile to allow access.

There is no command available to install an OS/2 printer—you must use the Printer template in the Workplace Shell. The following command will create a printer alias called LSPRT for the printer called OS2PRINT on the LSSERV server:

```
NET ALIAS LSPRT \\LSSERV OS2PRINT /PRINT
```

Use the Printer Alias

Let's use the newly defined printer alias to print to the server from a requester. Log off and log on as your user account, either at the server PC or at a requester PC. Now, open the Templates folder and locate the Network Printer template (not the Printer template!). Drag this onto your desktop, and a dialog box opens so that you can define the printer. Click on the arrow on the right-hand side of the Server drop-down list, and you will see a list of domains and servers in your network. Select your domain name from the list—it will have an asterisk in front of it. Now, click on the Resource drop-down list and select the printer alias. Finally, click on OK and your network printer object is created.

OS/2 will, at this point, prompt you to install a printer driver if it can't find the proper printer driver on your requester. It is very important that you install a printer driver on your requester that matches the one on the server. If you don't, your output will be garbled or missing, or strange errors will occur.

Now, try to print a file to the server using drag-and-drop. Find a small text file somewhere in the Drives folder (the CONFIG.SYS file on your boot drive is a good choice). Now, drag that file to the network printer object you just created, and drop it. A dialog box pops up asking you if the file's data is plain text or printer-specific. Select "plain text." Now, the file should print on the printer attached to the server. Network printing is that easy!

Another way to print a file is to use the OS/2 COPY command. The following command would print the CONFIG.SYS file to the printer called OS2PRINT on the LSSERV server:

```
COPY CONFIG.SYS \\LSSERV\OS2PRINT
```

However, if the printer cannot handle straight ASCII files, this COPY command won't work. Most PostScript printers, for example, cannot handle straight ASCII files, but require PostScript files. In this case, the file you copy to the printer must be in PostScript format.

Thus ends the quick tour of LAN Server administration. While it's been easy and maybe even fun, a lot has been accomplished. We've closed a security loophole by defining our own administrative account, defined a user and some shared file and print resources, assigned the resources to the user—and shown that it all works.

In the next chapter, you will learn more about LAN Server administration and accomplish more administrator tasks. Chapter 9 will guide you through the process of installing a requester, and Chapter 10 will show you how to surf the LAN Server network as an expert user on a requester PC.

More about LAN Server Administration

Thy gift, thy tables are within my brain
Full character'd with lasting memory
Which shall above that idle rank remain
Beyond all date, even to eternity.

—*William Shakespeare, "Sonnet 72"*

In this chapter, you will learn all the skills you need to administer a LAN Server domain, including setup, routine changes and maintenance, and day-to-day monitoring of the domain. This chapter is meant to be a reference; when you need to know more about a topic, you can read about it here. You should read the first section, "Working with the Administrative GUI"—it will help you do all your work more effectively.

Here's a quick roadmap to Chapter 8.

Working with the Administrative GUI	How to exploit the object-oriented features of the Administrative GUI to the fullest extent
More about/Working with LAN Server Security	What LAN Server provides for security, and how to set it up and work with it
More about Resource Definitions	Some hints, tips, and cautions on setting up resource definitions

More about Shared Print Queues | Some advanced information on setting up and using shared print queues—and guidance on setting up remote printers for your server

Setting up Home Directories | Home directories can be a time-saver and a boon for your users—how to make them work for you

Setting up Network Applications | Network applications are one of the most attractive features of LAN Server—how to set them up and use them

Managing Multiple Domains | For advanced users—if you have more than one domain, here's how to set it up and manage it

Monitoring your Network from day to day | How to automatically and manually monitor your domain and its servers

Working with the Administrative GUI

The LAN Server Administrative GUI is an object-oriented graphical user interface with advanced features. This section will give you some general guidelines for getting the most out of the GUI.

Remote Administration Using the GUI

You can run the GUI on the server PC, but running the GUI on a requester PC is for many the most convenient way to administer their servers. Also, the GUI takes significant RAM and processor resources to run, which may slow down server performance if you run it on the server PC. Simply log on to the domain as a user with administrator privilege, and you can do everything through the GUI that you could do if you were running it from the server PC.

Working with GUI Containers

The GUI is organized around *containers*, *objects*, and *templates*. Containers contain objects or other containers. Templates are special objects that can create new objects.

Containers, objects, and templates are represented by icons. Container icons usually look like manila folders (see Figure 7.4). When you open a container, a window appears showing the container's contents. Template icons look like yellow sticky pads (see the user ID template in Figure 7.5).

Containers, objects, and templates all have settings, which are parameters and options. Settings are displayed in settings notebooks.

The first window you see when starting the GUI (see Figure 7.3) is the LAN Services Administration container. It holds the Local Workstation container, the Shadowed Servers container, and up to six Domain containers. Each Domain container (see Figure 7.5), in turn, holds five containers: User Accounts, Groups, Resource Definitions, Defined Servers, and Public Application Definitions.

Working with containers is easy. To open a container, double-click on its icon with mouse button 1. You will see a window open up, showing the container's contents—icons representing other containers or objects. You can have many containers open on your desktop at once. To close an open container, double-click on the small icon in the window's upper left-hand corner with mouse button 1. You can also resize, move, minimize, maximize, restore, tile, and cascade open container windows just like any other window on the OS/2 desktop. If you are not familiar with these operations, you should review the OS/2 Tutorial—a fun, fast, and simple online introduction to the OS/2 desktop.

To issue commands on a container, get its pop-up menu by clicking on its icon with mouse button 2—or, if it's already open, click on an empty spot in its window with mouse button 2.

Figure 8.1 shows the pop-up menu for the main container, LAN Services Administration. To issue a command, click on the command with mouse button 1. Some commands, such as Open, have additional commands that you can see by clicking on the small arrow to the right of the command. In Figure 8.1, this has been done for the Open command. Different containers may have different commands on their pop-up menus.

To view or modify the settings for a container, click on Settings. To sort the objects in a container into alphabetical order, click on Sort. To arrange the icons in a container in an orderly fashion, click on Arrange. To reevaluate and redisplay the objects in a container, click on Refresh Now.

At this point, you should take a tour through the containers, using the preceding description as a guide. Starting with the first LAN Services Administration container, open each container, see what's inside it, and look

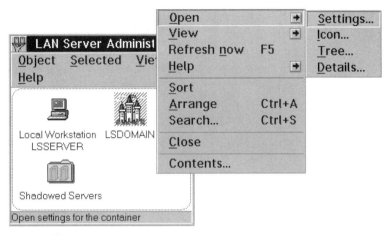

Figure 8.1 **Container pop-up menu.**

at the commands on its pop-up menu. Also, bring up each container's settings notebook, and page through it to get an idea of what settings are available for that container. If there's something you don't understand, you can always press the F1 key to get Help on what you are seeing.

Working with GUI Objects

The administrative GUI has many types of objects. The most common types are: User Account, Group, Resource Definition, Public Application Definition, and Service.

To open the settings notebook for an object, double-click on its icon with mouse button 1. To see an object's pop-up menu, click on its icon with mouse button 2. To issue a command from the pop-up menu, click on it with mouse button 1. To move an object to another spot in the container window, drag its icon with mouse button 2 to an empty spot in the container window. (*Drag* means to click and hold the mouse button, then move the mouse, and release the mouse button in the new location.) To create a copy of an object, hold down the Ctrl key while dragging its icon. You can also create a copy of an object by selecting "Create another" from its pop-up menu. To delete an object, select Delete from its pop-up menu.

Many objects in the GUI support drag-and-drop—in other words, you can drag an object, drop it onto another object, and cause an action to take place. For example, you can add a user account to a group by opening the

User Accounts and Groups containers so that their windows are both visible on the screen, and dragging a user account to a group with mouse button 2. A window appears confirming the action taken.

 You can save time and effort by working with several objects at once. It takes a little practice, but it's worth the effort to learn if you spend much time with the administrative GUI.

First, select the objects you want to work with. To select a single object, click on it with mouse button 1. To select several objects, you can:

- Click and hold mouse button 1 on the first object. While holding the button, touch each of the other objects with the mouse pointer. Release the button.
- Click and hold mouse button 1 on an empty spot in the window. Drag out a rectangle around the objects you want to select. Release mouse button 1.

You can combine these selection techniques by holding down the Ctrl key while selecting. For example, you can hold down Ctrl while selecting three single objects by clicking on them, and selecting a group of four objects by dragging a rectangle around them. All seven objects are selected when you are done. If you don't hold down the Ctrl key, each selection cancels the previous selections.

Once you have finished selecting your objects, you can operate on them all at once. If you click on any of the selected icons with mouse button 2, you will see a pop-up menu that applies to all the selected objects. You can, for example, select Delete from the pop-up menu, and all the objects will be deleted. If you drag any of the selected icons with mouse button 2, all the objects are dragged. You can, for example, add several user accounts to a group by selecting the user accounts and dragging them all to the group.

At this point, you should look at the different object types in the GUI, and display the pop-up menu and settings notebook for each object type to get an idea of what it can do. You should also practice selecting objects and using drag-and-drop techniques.

Working with GUI Templates

A template is a special kind of object that can be used to create new objects. To create a new object, find its template in the container window, and drag the template to an empty spot in the window using mouse button 2. The new object's settings notebook will open automatically so that you can specify the object's name and other settings.

Templates have default settings that are passed on to objects created from them. You can make your own custom templates with the defaults you want. To do this, create an object and change its settings as you wish. Then turn to the General page of the object's settings notebook, and select the Template check box. When you save the settings, the object's icon changes to indicate it is a template. Then, to create a new object from your custom template, just drag it to an empty spot on the container's window, as you would for a normal template.

Custom templates are handy if you often create objects with similar settings. For example, you can create a user account custom template, called SALESTEMPLATE, that has all the settings you normally give to a user in the sales department—group memberships, logon assignments, expiration date, and so on. When you need to create a new user account for the sales department, just drag the SALESTEMPLATE to an empty spot, fill in the new user's ID and password, and you are done.

A custom template is still an object in its own right. In the preceding example, you have created a user account called SALESTEMPLATE, which someone could use to log on. It's a good idea to give this user account a password that you keep secret so that no one can use it. When you create a new user account from a custom template, the password is *not* copied from the custom template—you must specify a new password.

Working with GUI Settings Notebooks

Settings notebooks are where most of the settings for LAN Server containers and objects reside. You will be working with them frequently. A settings notebook organizes many settings into sections and pages. Each section has a major tab on the right side of the notebook. Click on the tab to see the section.

Most sections have only one page, but some have more than one. If a section has more than one page, you can see the other pages by clicking the small right-pointing arrow at the bottom of the page. You will also see "Page 1 of n" at the bottom of the page to alert you that there are multiple pages.

To make changes on a settings notebook page, use the mouse to select fields, and use the keyboard as needed. The following types of fields are seen on notebook pages:

Pushbutton	Rectangle with text inside it. Click to take immediate action.
Entry field	White rectangle. Click then type the needed information.
Check box	Small square with text to the right. Click to choose between two alternatives. Check mark appears in square to indicate choice.
Radio button	Group of small circles with text to the right. Click one to choose among a set of alternatives. Dot appears inside circle to indicate choice.
List box	A list of items. Select one or more items from the list. Scroll the list by clicking on the arrows if necessary.
Drop-down list	Like an entry field, but with a downward-pointing arrow next to it. Click on the arrow to see a list of choices for the entry field, and click on a choice—or type in the entry field.

You will see an Undo button at the bottom of most notebook pages. Click Undo to discard unsaved changes on that page. Many notebook pages also have a Default button—click it to set the settings on that page back to their original default values. All notebook pages have a Help button to get Help on that page.

When you are done changing notebook pages, you need to save your changes or discard them. Unlike the OS/2 Desktop, changes that you make in a LAN Server settings notebook do not take effect immediately. You decide when and if changes are saved, using the buttons at the bottom of every settings notebook.

When you are modifying the settings of an existing object or container, there are four buttons at the bottom of the notebook:

Set	Save your changes to all notebook pages, and close the notebook.
Apply	Save your changes, but leave the notebook open.
Reset	Discard your unsaved changes to all notebook pages, restore the last saved settings.
Cancel	Discard your unsaved changes, restore the last saved settings, and close the notebook.

When you are creating a new object, there are three buttons at the bottom of the notebook:

Create   Save your changes, create the object, and close the notebook.
Reset   Discard your changes, and leave the notebook open.
Cancel   Close the notebook without creating the object.

More about LAN Server Security

LAN Server security is powerful and flexible. You need to understand the basics of how it is managed and enforced, so you can take the greatest advantage of that power and flexibility.

LAN Server security is managed through two separate but related sets of data: the *user accounts database*, and the *access control profiles*. The user accounts database contains all the user accounts for the domain. Each user account has a user ID and password, and other information about the user. The user accounts database is maintained on the domain controller, and is automatically copied to each server in the domain. Any changes to the user accounts database must be made at the domain controller, and changes are automatically sent to each server in the domain.

Each server in a domain has its own access control profiles that specify the access rights or permissions that users have to resources on that server. By default, all users have access to shared print queues and shared serial device queues, but no users have access to shared directories—you must specify shared directory access control profiles. Users with full administrative privilege, however, can access any shared resource regardless of access control profiles.

LAN Server security is enforced in two ways: *user validation* and *access control*. User validation is enforced when a user logs on to the domain, and when a user contacts a server. The user's ID and password are checked against the user accounts database, and other restrictions specified in the user account are also checked. Access control is enforced after user validation, when a user tries to access a resource at a server. The server checks the user's ID and group memberships against the access control profile for the resource, and grants or denies access based on the permissions it finds there. If the user has Administrative privilege, access control is not checked. However, you can assign special privileges to users, which allows them to perform some administrative functions but does not give them unchecked access to shared resources. For example, you can designate a user as a print operator, which allows the user to delete and reorder print jobs in the domain's shared print queues.

You can specify that a user account expires after a certain date, or you can disable a user account temporarily without deleting it. This is useful if, for example, you have users who are on temporary assignments, or taking leaves of absence. You can also specify that a user account is valid only during certain hours of the day and week, or only when used from certain requesters.

Password management is an important part of security, because LAN Server security depends on passwords being secret and difficult to guess. Users are normally allowed to change their passwords—but you can remove that ability from any or all users, and set the passwords yourself. If you allow users to change their passwords, you can specify a minimum password length, require periodic password changes, and disallow reuse of previously used passwords.

The passwords in the user accounts database are stored in a scrambled format—no one, not even an administrator, can discover a password by looking at the user accounts database or by intercepting transmissions across the LAN. If a user forgets his or her password, you can reset it to a new value. You can also mark a password expired, which forces users to change it the next time they logon.

You can create up to 250 groups per domain, and add user accounts to groups—a user account can belong to as many groups as needed. You can think of groups as a filing system for user accounts—for example, you could create a SALES group for the sales staff, and a WORDPERFECT group for the WordPerfect users. Once your groups are defined, you can specify access control and resource assignments by group, and you can send messages to a group rather than to each individual user account. Group definitions are maintained in the user accounts database.

You can set up auditing to log successful or unsuccessful attempts by users to logon or access resources. You can also set up alerts to send you a message if repeated security violations occur.

Working with LAN Server Security

This section will walk you through how to set up and use LAN Server security features, give you several ideas to help make your job easier, and warn you about several pitfalls you may encounter while administering LAN Server security.

Working with Domain Security Policies

To set domain security policies, open the settings notebook for the domain container. (Review the earlier section, "Working with the Administrative GUI," if you don't know how to do this.) Go to the Policy page and you will see Figure 8.2. This example specified that user passwords expire if they haven't been changed in 30 days (the default is never to expire). When a password expires, users cannot log on or access resources until they change the password.

When users change their passwords, it was specified that the new password must be at least six characters long (the default is four)—and the new password cannot match any of their last six passwords (the default is eight). It was also specified that users cannot change their passwords more than once every five days (the default is to allow them to change their passwords

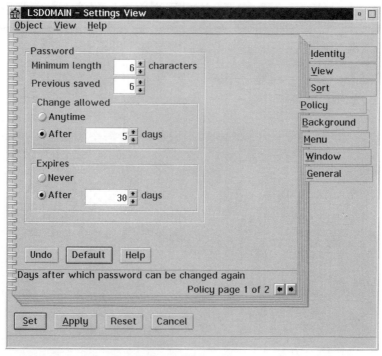

Figure 8.2 **Domain security policy settings (page 1).**

any time). This last restriction prevents users from simply changing their passwords six times in a row, then going back to their original password, thus defeating the purpose of requiring periodic password changes.

Now turn to page 2 of the policy settings (see Figure 8.3). Here, a logon grace period of 20 minutes has been allowed (the default is an indefinite period). If a user's account expires or becomes inactive, or the specified logon hours are past, then the user is allowed 20 minutes before access to resources is cut off. A warning message is sent to the user when the grace period starts.

You can also use the NET ACCOUNTS command to set these domain security policies, like this (type the command all on one line even though it is shown on two lines here):

```
NET ACCOUNTS /MAXPWAGE:30 /MINPWLEN:6
/UNIQUEPW:6 /MINPWAGE:5 /FORCELOG:20
```

 Be sure you enter the NET ACCOUNTS command at the domain controller PC's keyboard, or use the NET ADMIN command to send it remotely

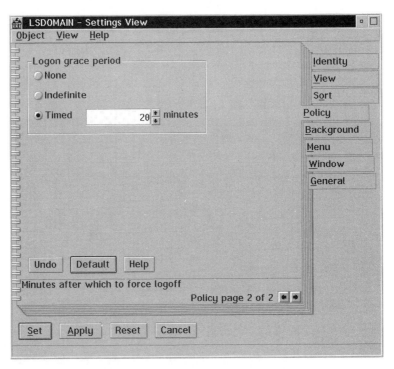

Figure 8.3 **Domain security policy settings (page 2).**

to the domain controller. See Chapter 11 for more information on LAN Server commands and how to use them from a remote requester.

Working with User Accounts

To work with user accounts, open the user accounts container for the domain. You will see some user accounts with the names of the servers in your domain—do not modify or delete those accounts, as LAN Server uses them to manage servers. The user accounts you see in the container window are objects. You can create, delete, copy, and move user account objects, as described in the earlier section "Working with GUI Objects."

Each user account has a user ID, up to 20 characters long, that is unique in the domain. User IDs can be entered in upper- or lowercase. If you want to use user IDs longer than eight characters, you must use HPFS on the server partition where LAN Server is installed.

Let's create a new user account and review all the security-related settings for it. As described earlier in "Working with GUI Objects," drag the User ID template to an empty spot on the window, and you'll see the user account settings notebook for your new user account. Turn to the Password page (Figure 8.4).

To set a password, select the "Change password" check box, then type the new password twice (the password will not display on the screen). Passwords can be up to 14 characters long, and can be typed in upper- or lowercase. If you select "Change password" but don't type a password, the user account will have no password. If the password is shorter than allowed by the domain security policies, you will see an error message when you try to save the new account by clicking on Set or Apply.

To force the user to change the new password at the first log on, select the "Expire password" check box. This is a good way to force users to choose and remember their own passwords.

This example set the password for the LSUSER account, and specified that it is expired and will have to be changed by the user. The equivalent command, when issued at the domain controller, is:

```
NET USER LSUSER newpas /ADD /PASSWORDEXP:YES
```

where *newpas* is the new password for the user. Use */ADD* to create a new user account, or omit */ADD* if you are modifying an existing user account. You can also type the command like this:

```
NET USER LSUSER * /ADD /PASSWORDEXP:YES
```

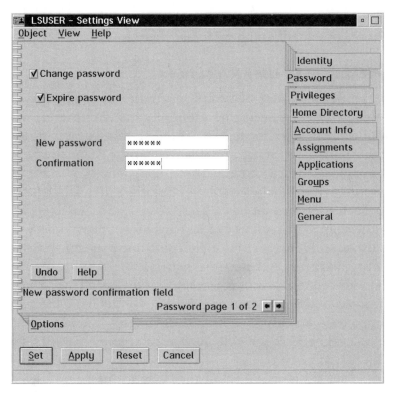

Figure 8.4 **User account–Password settings (page 1).**

and LAN Server will let you type the new password without displaying it on the screen.

Now click on the Options tab at the bottom of the notebook, and you will see the second page of the Password settings (Figure 8.5). "Age in days" is the number of days since this user's password was changed or reset. "Bad password count" is the number of times this user has attempted to use an incorrect password during logon or resource access. The bad password count is reset to zero when the correct password is used.

The "Account must have password" option is selected by default. It specifies that the user cannot remove the password, and that the user must follow the domain policies for password changes—expiration, reuse, and interval between changes. If this option is not selected, the user may remove the password and need not follow the domain security policies for password changes.

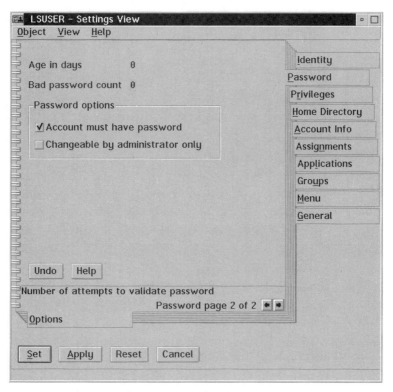

Figure 8.5 **User account–Password settings (page 2).**

The "Changeable by administrator only" option, when selected, does not allow the user to change the password (the administrator can always reset the password to a new value). By default, this option is not selected, which allows the user to change the password.

The following command, when issued at the domain controller, would set the options from this notebook page (the command is to be typed all on one line):

```
NET USER LSUSER /PASSWORDREQ:YES
/PASSWORDCHG:YES
```

Now turn to the Account Info page in the notebook (Figure 8.6). The Last Logon and Last Logoff fields indicate the last time a successful logon and logoff for this domain were accomplished. The Disabled option, when selected, disables the user account—the user cannot log on or use resources.

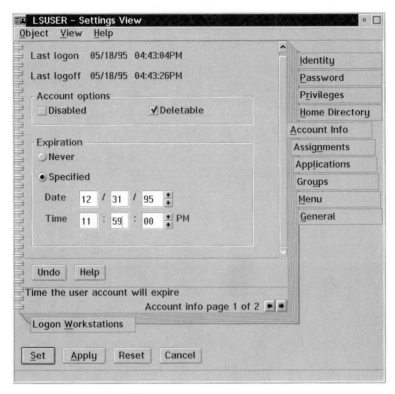

Figure 8.6 **User account—Account Info.**

The Deletable option, when selected, allows the administrator to delete this user account. The defaults are Disabled not selected, and Deletable selected.

You can use the Disabled option to disable a user account temporarily without deleting it. For example, if one of your users takes a leave of absence, you can disable his or her user account until he or she returns. You can use the Deletable option to protect yourself against accidentally deleting important user accounts (such as your administrative account).

The Expiration parameter allows you to specify a date and time when this account will expire. An expired account cannot be used to log on or access resources. The user will be given a grace period before access is cut off (see Figure 8.3). Figure 8.6 specified that LSUSER will expire one minute before midnight on New Year's Eve 1995. To change the date and time, click inside the number you want to change, then click on the Up and Down arrows.

The NET USER command provides a subset of the function on this notebook page. A command to enable the user account and set an expiration date is:

NET USER LSUSER /ACTIVE:YES /EXPIRES:12/31/95

Now, turn to the Logon Workstations page (Figure 8.7). If "Any" is selected (the default), the user can log on from any requester. We have selected "Allowable names," typed LSSERVER, and clicked Add. Now this user can log on only from the requester whose name is LSSERVER (in this example, the server PC).

You can also set logon hours for user accounts, but not with the administrative GUI—only with the NET USER command. You can select any of the 168 hours in a 7-day week, and specify that an account can log on or use resources during only those hours. The command to specify the logon workstations, and log on from 8 A.M. to 5 P.M. Monday through Friday, and 9 A.M. to noon on Saturday, is (type this all on one line):

NET USER LSUSER /WORKSTATIONS:LSSERVER
/TIMES:M-F,8:00-17:00;S,9:00-12:00

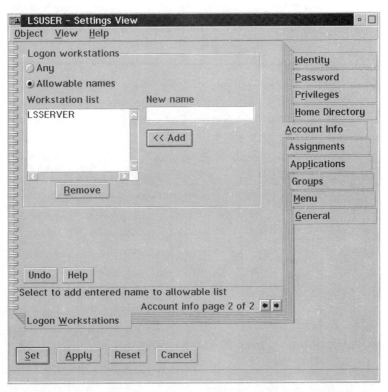

Figure 8.7 **User account Logon Workstations.**

Click the Privileges tab, and you will see the Privileges page (Figure 8.8). The default is User privilege, which gives the user account no special administrative privileges. If you select Administrator privilege, this user can perform all administrative activities for the domain, and can access any shared resource in the domain regardless of access control.

The Special Privileges are useful when you want to allow a user to perform some administrative tasks, but not get free access to all shared resources. You can give any or all of these special privileges to a user. They include:

- *Accounts operator*—The user can administer user accounts and groups, except for user accounts with Administrator or Special privileges. The administrative GUI can be used by an accounts operator.
- *Print operator*—The user can administer shared server print queues.
- *Server operator*—The user can administer server shared resources.
- *Comm operator*—The user can administer shared serial device queues.

Figure 8.8 **User account Privileges.**

This example assigned the Accounts and Print special privileges to LSUSER. The equivalent command is (typed on one line):

```
NET USER LSUSER /PRIV:USER
/OPERATOR:ACCOUNTS,PRINT
```

 If you find that you are creating user accounts with similar settings, a good way to save time is to create a custom user account template with the settings you most frequently use. See the preceding section, "Working with GUI Templates," for how-to information. When you want to create a new user, use your custom template rather than the User ID template. The password for the custom template is not copied; you must specify a new password for the new user account. If you keep the custom template's password secret, no one can log on to it.

Working with Groups

You can create up to 250 groups per domain, and put user accounts into groups. A user account can belong to as many groups as you wish. LAN Server automatically creates and maintains six special groups for you: USERS, GUESTS, ADMINS, LOCAL, SERVERS, and RPLGROUP. The USERS group contains all user accounts with User privilege; the GUESTS group contains all user accounts with Guest privilege; and the ADMINS group contains all user accounts with Administrator privilege. The LOCAL group is used only with LAN Server Advanced, and only when Local Security is installed. LOCAL is used to manage access for local applications running on the server, when no user is logged on there.

 The SERVERS group is created and maintained by LAN Server to keep track of the servers included in the domain. The RPLGROUP group is created and maintained by LAN Server to keep track of the Remote IPL requesters in the domain. Do not modify or delete the SERVERS or RPLGROUP groups or the user accounts in them, or LAN Server could lose track of its servers or Remote IPL requesters.

To work with groups, open the Groups container located in the domain container for your domain. You will see group objects representing the defined groups in the domain. You can create new groups and delete groups, as outlined in the earlier section "Working with GUI Objects." You can add user accounts to the group, and delete user accounts from the group, by working with the Users page of the group's settings notebook. You can also work with the Groups page of a user account's settings notebook to add the user account to groups, or delete the user account from groups.

You can also use drag-and-drop to add users to groups (but not delete users from groups). To do this, open the Groups container and the User Accounts container, and place them side by side on your desktop. Now select User Accounts and drag them to a group—the user accounts are added to the group. Or, select Groups and drag them to a User Account—the user account is added to all the groups.

Working with Access Control

Normally, you don't have to manage access for shared print queues or shared serial device queues. LAN Server, by default, allows all valid users (those in the USERS group) to access those resources (as well as shared named pipes). When you create a shared print queue or serial device queue resource definition, the administrative GUI will ask you if you want to create an access control profile. It is recommended that you not create one unless you want to limit access to certain users or groups.

You do need to manage access control for shared directory resources. LAN Server, by default, allows no access to shared directory resources. (Users with Administrative privilege, however, are not subject to access control, and can access any shared resource.)

When you create a shared directory resource, the GUI prompts you to create or modify the directory's access control profile. You can also modify access control for an existing shared directory resource by selecting "Manage access" from its pop-up menu. In either case, you will see a settings notebook for the access control profile shown in Figure 8.9.

This example granted read-only access for the group LSGROUP, and read-write access for the user BROWNCS. You should use the R permission to grant read-only access to a shared directory, and the ACDRW permissions to grant read-write access to a shared directory. Other combinations of these permissions are possible but not generally useful in practice (see Table 8.1 for details).

This was done by turning to the Permission page, clicking Add, choosing LSGROUP from the list of users and groups, choosing the R permission, clicking OK, then clicking Add again and adding BROWNCS with the proper permissions. You can also remove users and groups from the access control

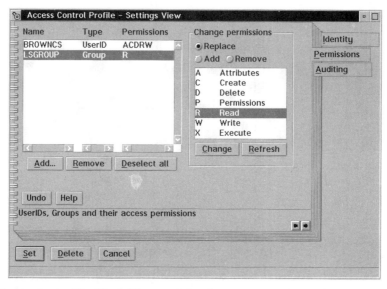

Figure 8.9 **Access Control Profile settings notebook.**

profile by selecting them and clicking Remove, or you can completely delete
the access control profile by clicking Delete.

To change permissions for users and groups that are already on the list,
first highlight the users and groups whose permissions you want to change.
Then choose whether you want the new permissions to replace, add to, or

Table 8.1 **LAN Server Access Permissions for Shared Directories and Files**

Letter	Name	Permission
R	Read	Existing files may be read, including copying files or executing programs.
X	Execute	Existing files that are OS/2.EXE programs may be executed.
W	Write	Existing files may be updated.
C	Create	New files and subdirectories may be created.
D	Delete	Existing files and subdirectories may be deleted.
A	Attributes	Existing file and subdirectory attributes may be changed.
P	Permissions	Access Control Profile may be viewed and modified.

remove from the existing permissions by selecting Replace, Add, or Remove. Finally, highlight the new permissions, and click Change. For example, we could change the permissions for LSGROUP to full read-write access by clicking on LSGROUP; clicking Add; clicking on the A, C, D, and W permissions; and clicking Change.

You can also use drag-and-drop to manage access control. Open the user accounts or groups container, and the resource definitions container, so they are both visible on the screen. Select some user accounts or groups and drag them to a resource definition.

You will see the Grant Access to a Resource window (Figure 8.10). Simply select the desired permissions, and select whether the new permissions should replace or add to existing permissions for the listed users or groups. (Other users or groups in the access control profile won't be affected.) This example dragged the groups LSGROUP and ANOTHER to the resource LSALIAS2, and selected to replace the existing permissions for LSGROUP and ANOTHER with the R permission. When you click Set, the access con-

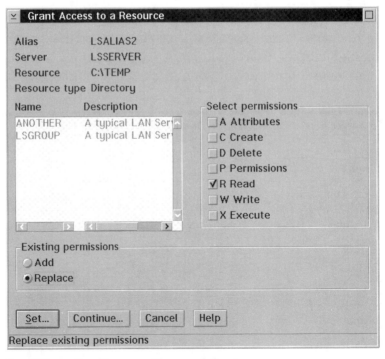

Figure 8.10 **Grant Access to a Resource (drag-and-drop).**

trol profile is updated. You will then be asked whether you wish to propagate the access control profile (click Yes, normally). Then you will get a chance to add or remove the resource as a logon assignment for the selected users or groups.

You can set up groups based on your users' needs for access to resources. For example, set up a group for users who need access to a particular set of applications and data directories, and create access profiles for those resources to your group. Then, adding a user account to that group automatically gives the user access to all the group's resources. If you want to grant access to all valid users, use the special group USERS, which automatically includes all user accounts with User privilege.

After you create or modify an access control profile, you will be asked if you wish to propagate the access control profile to subdirectories. If you do, then the access control profile that you created or changed will be applied to all subdirectories of your shared directory.

You should propagate access control profiles. If you do not, you may find that subdirectories of your shared directory are not accessible to users, when you intended them to be. If you set up overlapping shared directories, then propagating access control profiles can cause problems. In other words, if you define a shared directory resource A that is a subdirectory of another shared directory resource B, then A's access control profiles will be wiped out if you propagate B's access control profiles. If you do set up overlapping shared directories, be very careful about propagating access control profiles.

If you are managing access control for a shared directory resource with LAN Server Entry, or within a FAT-formatted partition with LAN Server Advanced, you should be aware of a potential problem with access control propagation. If you create a new subdirectory while working at the server PC, the access control profile is not propagated to the new subdirectory. This may happen when you install a new application at the server. If this occurs, your users may complain that they are getting *access denied* errors when they shouldn't be. You can propagate the access control profiles again through the "Propagate access . . ." command on the pop-up menu of the shared directory resource. This problem does not occur if the shared directory resource resides on an HPFS386 partition with LAN Server Advanced, or if you create the new subdirectories while working at a requester PC.

If you want to share a CD-ROM drive, you can take advantage of the default access control profile that is associated with the drive letter. The default access control profile for a drive is used whenever there is no access control profile on the directory. This makes sense for a CD-ROM drive, because whenever the CD-ROM is changed, the directories change.

First, create a shared directory resource for the root directory of the CD-ROM drive, but do *not* create an access control profile for it. Instead, open the Drives folder on the OS/2 desktop, and select the "Manage access . . ." command from the CD-ROM drive's pop-up menu. (The Drives folder is normally inside the OS/2 System folder). You will see a settings notebook similar to Figure 8.9, but the Identity page will show D: as the Resource Name, rather than D:\, which is the name of the shared directory. Now, set whatever permissions you wish on this page, and do *not* propagate the access control profile. You should find that your users can access any directories on any CD-ROM in the drive.

If you are spending a lot of time managing access control, you should look at the Access Control Manager productivity aid that's shipped with LAN Server 4.0. You may find it easier and faster to use than the administrative GUI once you have gained experience. See Chapter 12 for information on productivity aids, and Chapter 6 for information on installing productivity aids.

When LAN Server is checking access control for a user, the user's ID may appear on the permissions list, along with several groups that have that user as a member. In this case, LAN Server's rules are:

- If the user ID appears on the permissions list, then the permissions granted are those for that user ID. The user's group memberships are not checked.
- If the user ID does not appear on the permissions list, then the user's group memberships are checked. The permissions granted are those for all groups on the list that have the user as a member.

If a user has any permissions on a shared directory, the user can read the directory (read the names of files and subdirectories and their attributes). Table 8.1 describes the other access granted by permissions. If you grant the P permission to a user or group, they can modify the access control profile— grant or revoke any permission to any other user for the shared directory resource. You would give the P permission to a user whom you trust to manage access control for that shared directory resource and its subdirectories. A user without special or administrative privileges must use the NET ACCESS command to manage access control profiles. They can also use the Access Control Manager productivity aid (see Chapter 12).

Understanding Logon, Logoff, and User Validation

User validation occurs when the user logs on to a domain, and is handled by the domain controller or a backup domain controller. User validation occurs again when a requester sets up a session with a server, and is handled by that server. A session is set up the first time a requester tries to access a server in any way, and is used for all access to that server until the user logs off or the session is disconnected in some other way, such as a network error or administrator action.

You may wonder why user validation is done twice. There are two situations in which user validation at session setup is required for security. First, the server may not belong to the domain the user logged on to; second, the user may have logged on locally before trying to set up a session with a server.

If a user logs on to domain A and then tries to set up a session with a server in domain B, then the user is validated against domain B's user accounts database. This means that the user must have a valid user account with the same password in both domains A and B, or domain B must have guest access capability. See *Managing Multiple Domains* in this chapter for more information on this.

A user can log on locally at the requester, rather than doing a domain logon. The requester can accept any user ID and password for local logon, since it's not checked against the domain's user accounts database. In this case, the user is validated by the server when session setup is attempted.

From this discussion, it should be clear that logon is a convenience for the user, rather than a way to enforce security. From a security point of view, logon is just a way to store a user ID and password in the requester. Later, when the requester tries to set up a session with a server, the requester sends the user ID and password to the server for validation. This occurs for each new server contacted by the requester.

When a user logs off, all the user's sessions are disconnected, and the user's ID and password are erased from the requester. You (the administrator) cannot force a user to logoff. You can, however, make the user's account invalid (for example, by setting the Disabled flag). If you do this, then user validation will fail when the user tries to set up a new session to the server. However, existing sessions are not affected, unless you delete those sessions also. LAN Server 4.0 includes a productivity aid called DISCUSER that will disable a user account and delete all the sessions for that user. See Chapter 12 for details on productivity aids, and chapter 6 for information on installing productivity aids.

Here's a list of the steps required for user validation to succeed:

1. The user's ID must be defined as a user account. If it is not, and this is an attempt to set up a session to a server, the guest account is used instead. See the section "Managing multiple domains" later in this chapter for more information.
2. The user account must be active.
3. The user account must not have expired.
4. The user account's list of logon workstations, if any, must include the name of the user's requester.
5. The user account's logon hours, if any, must include the current time.
6. The user account's password must not have expired. (If the password expired, the LOGON command will prompt the user to change the password.)
7. If the user account has a password, the supplied password must match it. If not, the supplied password is ignored.

More about Shared Print Queues

 The "Understanding OS/2 Printers and How They Work with LAN Server" section (Chapter 6) explained some of the basics of OS/2 printing, and covered how to install printer drivers and create a print queue. Chapter 10 will cover how to use shared print queues from a requester. This chapter will cover how to manage and administer shared print queues. You may also wish to review the online book, *Printing in OS/2*, that comes with OS/2 Warp. Look in the Information folder for it.

As described in Chapter 6, you create a print queue under OS/2 by creating a printer object on the OS/2 desktop. It's really a print queue, even though OS/2 calls it a printer. A print queue has an object name, which is the title of its icon, and a physical name, which is an eight-character or less abbreviation of the object name. The physical name is used by LAN Server when defining a shared print queue resource. A print queue also has a default printer driver associated with it, and an output port.

If you have more than one printer of the same type, using the same printer driver, you can pool these printers under a single print queue. OS/2 will keep all the printers in the pool busy as long as there are jobs in the print queue. To do this, simply select multiple output ports from the Output page of the print queue's settings notebook.

You can have more than one print queue for the same printer. To do this, select the same output port for more than one print queue. The print queues will share the printer. Multiple print queues are useful for printers that support more than one type of data—for example, a printer that supports both PostScript and PCL5 data streams can be configured with two print queues, one with the PostScript printer driver and one with a PCL5 printer driver. Another use of multiple print queues is to define different job properties, different settings pages, or different operating times for the different queues.

You may find that you need more than three parallel ports for your server PC. OS/2 installs only LPT1:, LPT2:, and LPT3: by default. To create additional parallel ports under OS/2, enter the following command procedure into a file called ADDLPT.CMD, using the System Editor:

```
/* ADDLPT.CMD: Add LPT4 through LPT9 to OS/2 */
call RxFuncAdd 'SysIni', 'RexxUtil', 'SysIni'
do i = 4 to 9
 call SysIni 'SYSTEM', 'PM_SPOOLER_PORT', 'LPT'||I,
 ';'||'00'x
end
```

Save the file and exit the System Editor. Now run the command procedure by typing **ADDLPT** in an OS/2 command window, after changing to the directory where the command file is stored. You will find that you can access parallel ports LPT4: through LPT9:.

You can manage a print queue at the server by issuing commands from its pop-up menu. You can manage the jobs in a print queue by opening the print queue and working with the jobs you see in its window. You can manage a print queue and its print jobs from a remote OS/2 requester by defining an OS/2 network printer, and working with its pop-up menu and its print jobs.

To define an OS/2 network printer, open the OS/2 Templates folder, drag a Network Printer template onto the desktop, and type the server name and print queue name into the window that pops up. Or, you can open the Network folder and use the LAN Server Resource Browser to find the network printer object, and drag it onto your desktop. See Chapter 10 for specific procedures on creating an OS/2 network printer.

Whether you are working with the print queue at the server PC, or remotely from a requester, you can manage a print queue with commands from its pop-up menu. You can hold or release the queue with the Change Status command (when it is held, no jobs will print). You can delete all jobs from the queue. If you are working remotely, you can even create and delete print queues on the server by using the Remote Admin command on the pop-up menu.

You can also view the print jobs by opening the print queue object. Try opening it in both an icon view and a details view, and decide which you like better. You can set the default view in the object's settings notebook. In either case, you will see all the current print jobs. By issuing commands from its pop-up menu, you can delete a print job, specify a print job to print next, or hold or release a print job. A print job that is held will not print even when the print queue is released. You can also open the settings for a print job from its pop-up menu. From a print job's settings notebook, you can change the number of copies to be printed for that job, or change its priority in the queue.

If you are working with a network print queue on a remote requester, and have opened an icon or details view, changes to the queue are not displayed immediately—the view is refreshed periodically. You can adjust the refresh period through the settings notebook for the network print queue. You can also request an immediate refresh through the pop-up menu for the network print queue.

If a printer is having a problem, the icon for the print job currently printing will change appearance. If you are viewing the print queue in detail mode, the displayed status of the job will change.

Setting Up Remote Printers

LAN Server can support printers that are not attached directly to the server PC's parallel or serial ports. There are three ways that this can be set up:

1. Some printers can be attached directly to a LAN, and emulate LAN Server or other network print servers. These appear to the user like another print server.
2. Several companies market a device that attaches to the LAN and provides a parallel port or two for attaching printers. Examples are the Lexmark 4033 and the Hewlet-Packard JetDirect. These devices come with software that is installed on an OS/2 print server. This software redirects print output across the LAN to the device. To OS/2, these

printers appear the same as locally attached printers. If LAN Server is installed, you can share print queues that print to these remotely attached printers.

3. If you have a requester PC with a locally attached printer, you can install Peer Services with the OS/2 Requester, or DOS Peer Services, and make that printer available to other users for printing. The disadvantage of this approach is that only one user at a time can be using the printer, and the print queue is not centrally managed and administered at a server. You can also install OS/2 Warp Connect with OS/2 Peer, which allows unlimited use of shared print queues.

It's possible to create a print queue on a server PC that sends its output to a printer attached to a DOS or OS/2 requester PC. To do this for an OS/2 requester PC, follow these steps:

1. Make sure that OS/2 and the OS/2 requester are installed and operational on your requester PC, and that the printer works when printing jobs locally at the requester PC.

2. Install and start Peer Services at the requester PC using Tailored Install. See Chapter 9 for install procedures.
3. Delete the printer object for the printer at the requester PC.
4. Enter this command at the requester PC:

   NET SHARE REMOTE=LPT1: /COMM

   where *LPT1:* is the port that the printer is attached to.
5. Log on at the server PC with the user account you normally use. Enter the command:

   NET USE LPT3: \\LSPEER\REMOTE /COMM

   where *LPT3:* is an unused parallel port at your server PC, and *LSPEER* is the name of the requester PC. If you don't have any unused parallel ports at the server PC, see the preceding procedure for adding parallel ports.
6. Create a print queue (printer object) at the server PC using normal OS/2 procedures. Assign the appropriate printer driver. Use LPT3: as the output port.
7. Create a shared printer resource at the server PC to share the print queue defined in the previous step.

To do this for a DOS requester PC, use these steps:

1. Install DOS and the LAN Server DOS requester (DLS) with Peer Services at the requester PC. Make sure the attached printer is operational and that you can print to it locally.
2. Share the printer at the requester PC as you normally would with DLS Peer. This example assumes that the printer is called *REMOTE* and the DLS Peer requester PC is called *LSPEER.*
3. Log on at the server PC with the user account you normally use. Enter the command:

   NET USE LPT3: \\LSPEER\REMOTE

   where *LPT3:* is an unused parallel port at your server PC, and *LSPEER* is the name of the requester PC. If you don't have any unused parallel ports at the server PC, see the preceding procedure for adding parallel ports.
4. Create a print queue (printer object) at the server PC using normal OS/2 procedures. Assign the appropriate printer driver. Use LPT3: as the output port.
5. Create a shared printer resource at the server PC to share the print queue defined in the previous step.

One disadvantage of this procedure is that you must leave a user logged on at the server PC.

More about Resource Definitions

 Chapter 7 showed how to create a shared print queue resource and a shared directory resource, and how to add a logon assignment to a user account with drag-and-drop. That's most of what you need to know about shared resource definitions, but here's a few more tidbits of information to help you do your job more effectively.

You can stop and start the sharing of a resource through the resource definition's pop-up menu. If sharing is stopped, current users lose their connections, and new users cannot connect to the resource. You can work with the list of currently shared resources at a server through the "Current shares" command on the pop-up menu for that server.

Before you delete a shared resource, you should stop sharing for that resource. If you don't, the resource is still shared even though you deleted it. Even if you create a new resource with the same name, the old resource is still shared under that name until you stop and restart sharing for the new resource.

The settings notebook for a shared resource (see Figure 7.8) lets you control when a resource is shared. You should always specify to share resources at server startup. The other choices allow you to share resources only when a user requests access, or only when the administrator specifies that the resource should be shared. Selecting these choices can cause the resource to be unavailable to some users.

If you want to limit the number of concurrent users for a shared resource, select "Number of connections" from the settings notebook, and type a number. This is useful if you have installed an application that is licensed for only a certain number of users at a time.

Be sure that the *maxshares=* parameter in the IBMLAN.INI file is set to a value large enough to support all your shared resource definitions and all your users with home directories, combined.

You can manage logon assignments by group. Simply drag a group to a resource, or a resource to a group, and you can assign the resource to all the user accounts in the group at the same time. You can also remove logon assignments, using drag-and-drop, for user accounts or groups. The Logon Assignments window (see Figure 7.11) has a "Remove assignment" radio button. If you select it, the logon assignment is removed from the listed user accounts.

You can also manage logon assignments for a user account from the Assignments page of the user account's settings notebook if you don't wish to use drag-and-drop.

Setting Up Home Directories

Assigning a home directory is an easy, one-step way to provide a user, or a group of users, with a directory on a server that they can read and write. If assigned to one user, think of it as a way to provide an additional hard disk for that user, which actually resides at the server. If assigned to a group of users, think of it as a working area for the group to create, update, and review files.

For example, the authors created this book using LAN Server to store their word processor files on a common server. One of us would write a chapter and ask the other to review it. The other would use the word processor's annotation feature to attach comments, then save the file. The first person would then review the notes and update the document.

To assign a home directory to a user, first decide where you want to put the home directory. LAN Server provides a directory called \IBMLAN\USERS for use by home directories, but you can put home directories on any directory on any server. Our example gives each user a subdirectory of D:\HOME-DIRS, with a name that's the same as the user's ID. (You would want to use HPFS on your LAN Server partition in this case, to support home directories for user IDs that are over eight characters long.)

Then, bring up the user account's settings notebook and turn to the Home Directory page (Figure 8.11). You see that the home directory has been assigned to the user's H drive, and that it's located on the server LSSERVER on the directory D:\HOMEDIRS\LSUSER. When you save the notebook, the directory is

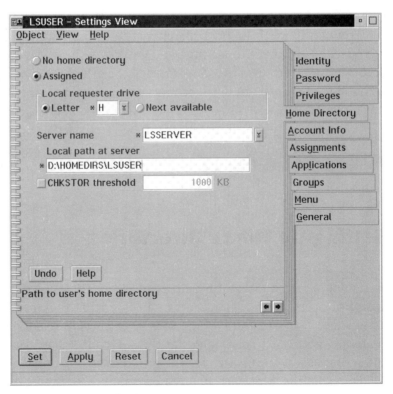

Figure 8.11 **User account Home Directory page.**

created if it doesn't exist; an access control profile is created for the directory automatically, giving the user full permission to access the directory.

To assign the same home directory to multiple users, simply specify the same home directory server and path for those users. Each user will be added to the access control profile for the directory. If the home directory already has subdirectories, you should propagate the access control for the home directory each time you assign the home directory to a user. To propagate access control, navigate to the directory through the OS/2 Drives folder, bring up the pop-up menu for the directory, and select "Propagate access."

In this example, the next time LSUSER logs on to the domain, he or she will have an H drive that points to the D:\HOMEDIRS\LSUSER directory on the server, and can work on files or subdirectories there.

Since the user is assigned the P permission, the user can also grant access to their home directory to other users without having to bother the administrator. For example, LSUSER can use this command:

NET ACCESS H: /GRANT LSGROUP:R

which will grant read access to everyone in the group LSGROUP for LSUSER's home directory.

Home directories are managed internally by LAN Server by creating a directory share whose name is the user ID. If you have already defined a shared directory resource with that name, the home directory assignment will not work. Delete and re-create the shared directory resource with a different name.

If you have set the *cleanup=yes* parameter in the [lsserver] section of the IBMLAN.INI file, your users may complain that their home directories are being disconnected, and they must log off and log on again to recover. If this happens, change the parameter to **cleanup=no**, and stop and restart the

server. See Chapter 6 for more information on editing the IBMLAN.INI file.

When you remove a home directory assignment from a user, or delete a user with a home directory assignment, the home directory itself is not deleted. You must delete the directory manually.

Setting Up Network Applications

Network applications are a convenient, easy way to provide your users with applications that are resident on your server. The beauty of network applications is that you do not have to install anything on the requester itself (unless the application requires it for some reason). You simply create the network application on the server and assign it to a user. The next time that user logs on, he or she will see the application displayed on the desktop, and can run it.

Before you create a network application, you must create a shared directory resource for the directory containing the application's program files. You should create an access control profile for this directory, giving read access to the users or groups who will be using the network application. It's most convenient to create a group, representing users of this application, and granting access to the group rather than to each individual user.

If the application requires any other shared directories or print queues during execution, create shared resource definitions for them, and give them appropriate access control profiles.

To create the network application, open the Public Application Definitions container inside the domain container. Create your application from the OS/2 or DOS application template, depending on what type of application it is. (If it's a Windows application, create a DOS application.) If it's an OS/2 application, you'll see a settings notebook like the one shown in Figure 8.12.

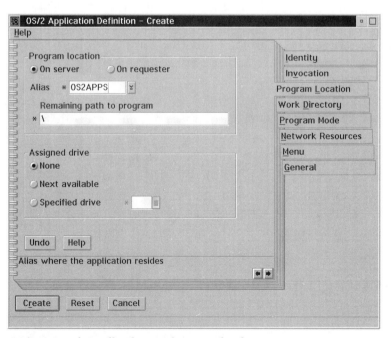

Figure 8.12 **OS/2 Network Application settings notebook.**

An alias called OS2APPS has already been created, which points to the directory where our application resides. And, the first two pages of this notebook have been filled in: The Identity page gave the application a name, SOLITARE; and the Invocation page provided the command used to start the application, KLONDIKE. (This is the OS/2 Klondike Solitare application provided with OS/2 Warp.) The Program Location page shown in Figure 8.12 specifies the shared directory resource (alias) where the program files are located, OS2APPS. If the program were located in a subdirectory, that subdirectory would be specified in the "Remaining path to program" field. A drive letter can also be assigned to the program location—then the user would have that drive letter assigned to the program directory when the user runs the network application. Since this is a well-written network-aware OS/2 application, it doesn't need to have a drive letter assigned.

The "Work directory" and "Network resources" pages allow you to assign other shared directories or shared print queues when the network application is run. This application doesn't need any other directories, but this flexible setup allows you to run even complex applications that use many different directories as network applications. The "Program mode" page allows you to run nongraphical or full-screen applications.

Once you have finished filling in the notebook, click Create to create the network application definition. To assign the network application to a user, open the user accounts folder, select the user or users you wish to assign, and drag them to the network application. If you have already defined a group of users for the application, you can simply open the groups container and drag the group to the network application. All the users in the group will have the application assigned to them. You can also assign network applications to a user account by opening its settings notebook and using the Applications page.

Once you have assigned the SOLITARE application to an OS/2 user, try logging on as that user from an OS/2 requester. You will see a Network Applications folder appear on the desktop. Open the folder and you will see the SOLITARE application, complete with its normal icon. If you double-click the icon, the OS/2 Solitare program should start.

To define a DOS or Windows network application, use the DOS Application template. The settings notebook is similar to the one in Figure 8.12. One difference is that you must assign drive letters for the program location shared directory and any other network resources—because DOS and Windows applications know how to work only with drive letters.

DOS or Windows network applications can, of course, be run on a LAN Server DOS or Windows requester. They can also be run on a LAN Server OS/2 requester, because OS/2 supports execution of DOS and Windows applications. DOS and Windows applications often require special settings to run properly under OS/2. To assign these settings for network applications, use the OS/2 Drives folder to navigate to the program's execution file (normally with a file type of .EXE). Bring up the Settings notebook for the execution file and modify the DOS Settings for that file. The next time an OS/2 user with that application assigned logs on, the Network Applications folder will include the new settings.

Managing Multiple Domains

You can use the administrative GUI to remotely administer up to six domains at a time if each domain has your logged-on user ID and password defined as a user account with Administrative privilege. One domain is the domain you logged on to. A second domain is the default domain you specified when you installed the OS/2 LAN Requester (this is specified by the *domain=* parameter in your requester's IBMLAN.INI). The other four domains are specified in the *othdomain=* parameter in your requester's IBMLAN.INI. You can also specify the other four domains temporarily with a command, like this:

```
NET CONFIG REQ /OTHDOMAINS:dom1,dom2,dom3,dom4
```

where *dom1* and so on are the names of the other domains you want to administer.

If you have multiple domains, your users may want to log on to one domain and access resources on a server in another domain. The easiest way to support this is to create resource definitions on the logon domain for the resources on the other domain. With this technique, your users will view those resources as if they were attached to their logon domain. They should not be aware that the resources really belong to another domain. These are known as *cross-domain resources.*

Creating a cross-domain resource is very similar to creating a local resource. Simply type the name of the server on which the resource is located in the Server name field of the resource's settings notebook. Managing access control is a little trickier, because when the user tries to access the cross-domain resource, the user will have to be validated using the other domain's user accounts database.

There are two basic approaches to managing access control for cross-domain resources: using guest access, or defining the user in both domains. Defining the user in both domains is straightforward; simply add the user account to the other domain's user accounts database, specifying the same information (including password), and also add the user to whatever groups are necessary. Then, you can grant permissions for the user in the other domain just as you would in their logon domain.

Users who are defined in multiple domains should change their passwords in all domains at once. LAN Server 4.0 provides two productivity aids that will help users do this:

- Network Signon Coordinator, a comprehensive logon and password change manager for LAN Server and other IBM network products for DOS and OS/2 requesters.
- NEWPW, a simple OS/2 utility that handles password changes across multiple LAN Server domains for OS/2 requesters. See Figure 12.2 in Chapter 12 for more information.

Another way to manage access control across multiple domains is with guest users. When a user tries to use a cross-domain resource and the user is not defined in the other domain's user accounts database, the user is validated as a guest user. By default, guest users have Guest privilege and are added to the special group called GUESTS. So, you manage access control for guest users by granting access to the GUESTS group.

Guest user validation is actually done using the user account called GUEST. By default, the GUEST user account has no password, and has the Guest privilege. You can change how guest users are validated by changing the settings of the GUEST user account. You can stop all guest user validation by disabling the GUEST user account. You can require guests to use a password by adding a password to the GUEST user account. You can even give the GUEST account Administrator privilege if you want to allow all guest users full access to your domain!

If you want to give your guest users access to all shared print queues, use the following command at the domain controller:

```
NET ACCESS \PRINT /GRANT GUESTS:C
```

If you create an access control profile for a specific print queue, that access control profile will override this default.

Monitoring Your Network Day to Day

In this section, you'll learn how to check up on your LAN's health, how to set up your LAN to tell you when there are problems, and how to smoothly shut down your LAN.

Viewing the Error Log

OS/2 Requesters and OS/2 Servers keep a detailed error log, describing any errors that occur in any of the services that are running. Whenever you suspect a problem with an OS/2 server or OS/2 requester, it's a good idea to look at its error log.

The error log is kept in the file \IBMLAN\LOGS\NET.ERR. You can set a maximum size for the error log file—once the maximum is reached, the oldest entries in the log are overwritten. The maximum size is 100 kilobytes by default, and can be changed with the *maxerrorlog=nnn* parameter in IBM-LAN.INI (see Chapter 6 for information on changing IBMLAN.INI).

The best way to view the error log is with the LAN Server Error Log utility. This is a graphical OS/2 application that displays the error log. You can view the local log, or view a remote server's log if you have administrative privilege on that server. You can sort the log by earliest or latest first or by the service that logged the error, you can print the log or output it to an ASCII file, you can clear the log, and you can view the detailed cause and suggested action information for any log message.

You can also use the NET ERROR command (see Chapter 11) to output the error log to the screen or clear the error log.

Setting Up Alerts

Alerts are messages that are sent to designated users when events occur on servers. To send alerts, your servers must have the Alerter service running. You can specify that the Alerter service is automatically started with the server during Tailored Install, or by adding alerter to the *srvservices=* list in IBMLAN.INI.

To receive alerts, your OS/2 or DOS requester must have the Messenger service running. If you want to see the alerts as pop-up messages, you must have the OS/2 Network Messaging utility running and configured to pop up incoming messages, or the DOS NetPopUp service running. You can configure your OS/2 requester to automatically start the Messenger service during install, or you can add messenger to the *wrkservices=* list in IBMLAN.INI. You can also automatically start the Network Messaging utility by putting a shadow of its icon in the OS/2 Startup folder.

Administrative alerts are sent to the users listed in the *alertnames=* parameter of IBMLAN.INI. You can also put group names in the list, and alerts will be sent to all users in the group. A good group to put in the list is ADMINS, which automatically sends alerts to all logged-on users with Administrative privilege.

Alerts are also sent to other users, as appropriate—for example, when a print job completes or there is an error on a printer, an alert is sent to the user who submitted the print job.

Many alerts are reported only when certain thresholds are exceeded during a specified time interval. If the thresholds are not exceeded, the events are logged but no alerts are generated. You can configure the threshold settings in IBMLAN.INI—see Table 8.2 for details. After you change these settings, you must stop and restart the server before they take effect.

The UPS service generates alerts if there is an impending power failure or other power condition that should be reported to administrators. The Fault Tolerance facility (available only with LAN Server Advanced) generates extensive alerts to monitor hard disk problems and recovery actions taken by Fault Tolerance. If you initiate Disk Space Limits (available only with LAN Server 4.0 Advanced), it will send alerts to administrators and users whenever individual directory limits are exceeded or are nearing a threshold.

Logged-On Users

If you read and understood the section "Understanding Logon, Logoff, and User Validation" in this chapter, you can appreciate that Who is logged on to the domain? is not an easy question to answer. To see LAN Server's attempt, bring up the pop-up menu of the domain container, click on the arrow next to Open, then select Logged-on Users from the cascaded menu. You will see a list of users. This represents requesters who have performed a domain logon, and who are continuing to respond to a periodic poll that the domain

Table 8.2 **Alert settings in IBMLAN.INI**

IBMLAN.INI parameter	Default Value	Explanation
ErrorAlert=	5	Threshold for number of errors logged to the error log.
LogonAlert=	5	Threshold for number of logon attempts that failed due to security violations.
AccessAlert=	5	Threshold for number of resource access attempts that failed due to security violations.
DiskAlert=	5,000	Threshold for free disk space available on server volumes (measured in kilobytes)
NetIOAlert=	5	Threshold for number of network I/O errors.
AlertSched=	5	Alert interval in minutes; if any of the thresholds listed above is exceeded during an interval, an alert is generated.
AlertNames=	(none)	Names of users and groups who will receive alert messages.

controller sends out. If a requester is down or not responding for some reason, it is eventually dropped from the list. It seems that DOS requesters don't respond very well, and the list tends to be incomplete.

The NET WHO command can be issued from any logged-on requester, and provides a somewhat more complete list. It includes both requesters that have logged on to the domain and are responding to the periodic poll, and also requesters that have a session set up with any server in the domain.

Monitoring Servers

From the administrative GUI, you can open a domain container, then open the Defined Servers container and you will see the servers in the domain. Bring up the pop-up menu on any server, click on the arrow next to Open, and you will see menu choices for Active Sessions, Open Files, Statistics, and Current Shares.

Click on Active Sessions and you will see a list of all the requesters that are currently accessing the server, along with the logged-on user name, number of connections (number of shared resources being accessed), number of open files, and how long the session has been there. You can forcibly disconnect sessions by highlighting them and clicking Delete.

If a requester has a session with a server, and the server disconnects the session, the requester will try to reconnect the session the next time that a resource on the server is accessed. This will force a revalidation of the logged-on user at the server. So, if you want to completely remove a user from your domain, you must disable the user's account and disconnect all the user's sessions. LAN Server 4.0 has a productivity aid, DISCUSER, that does this for you.

The Statistics command on the server's pop-up menu gives you a set of interesting statistics about the server. Of particular interest are "Password Violations" and "Access permission errors." These indicate how many times the server rejected a session setup request, and how many times the server denied access to a resource. If these numbers become large, you may want to enable auditing and start checking the audit log to see who is responsible. Also of interest are the "Request buffer failures" and "Big buffer failures." If these events happen often, you may want to consider tuning your server (see Chapter 6).

If there are servers you monitor frequently, open the Shadowed Servers container and drag them into it. *Shadows* of the server objects will be created in the Shadowed Servers container, making it faster and easier for you to access them.

Setting Up Auditing

LAN Server auditing records many security-related events and writes them to the audit log. Auditing is a good way to keep records that you can review in case you suspect security problems. Knowing what violations occurred when and where can help in tracking down the cause of a security problem.

Auditing is individually enabled, disabled, and recorded for each server. The audit log is kept in the file \IBMLAN\LOGS\NET.AUD. Its maximum size is controlled by the *maxauditlog=* parameter of IBMLAN.INI, and the default is 100 for 100 kilobytes. If the audit log becomes larger than the maximum, old records are erased by new ones.

The best way to view the audit log is with the LAN Server Audit Log utility. This is a graphical OS/2 application that displays the audit log. You can view the local log or a remote server's log if you have administrative privilege on that server. You can sort the log by earliest or latest first, by the user ID, or by the type of event; you can print the log or output it to an ASCII file; you can clear the log; and you can view the detailed information for any audit event. You can also use the NET AUDIT command to display or clear the audit log.

You can specify which events are audited for each server in great detail, with the *auditing=* parameter of IBMLAN.INI. The valid values for this parameter are listed in Table 8.3. You can specify multiple values separated by semicolons.

If *Resource* auditing is enabled on a server, then the access control profile for a resource determines what auditing is enabled for that resource. If you bring up the settings notebook for a resource definition, and turn to the Auditing page, you can choose to audit nothing, failed access attempts, successful access attempts, or all access attempts. Even more fine-grained auditing is possible by

Table 8.3 **Audit Events**

Auditing= Parameter Value	Audited Events
No	None—no audit log is generated
Yes	All events
BadNetLogon	Invalid domain logons
GoodNetLogon	Valid domain logons
NetLogon	All domain logons
BadSessLogon	Invalid session setups to a server
GoodSessLogon	Valid session setups
SessLogon	All session setups
Logon	All domain logons and session setups
BadUse	Invalid connections to shared resources
GoodUse	Valid connections to shared resources
Use	All connections to shared resources
LogonLimit	Users exceeding their valid logon hours
UserList	Modifications made to the user accounts database
Permissions	Modifications made to access control profiles
Resource	As defined in the access control profile for a resource

using the NET ACCESS command—you can choose to audit opens, writes, deletes, and/or attempts to change the access control profile.

Bringing Down a Server or Domain

Use the following steps to bring down a server:

1. Use the Active Sessions display for the server to determine who has a session to the server. Disconnect any sessions that have no open files—these users are not actively using the server.
2. Notify the remaining users that the server is about to go down. If you have enabled Network Messaging, you may want to send them a message. Use the /USERS option of the NET SEND command to send a message to all users who have sessions at this server, who have messaging enabled. You will receive an error message for each user who doesn't have messaging enabled.
3. Stop the Server service on the server. You cannot do this remotely; you must log on locally at the server PC. Then open a command window and type **NET STOP SERVER**.
4. Your server PC is now running as a requester.

To bring down a domain, follow these steps:

1. Stop new users from logging on by stopping the NETLOGON service on the domain controller and each backup domain controller. You can do this remotely. Open the Defined Servers container for the domain, open each server in turn, and open its Services container. Find the NETLOGON service, bring up its pop-up menu, and select Stop. If you want to use LAN Server commands, open a command window and type:

    ```
    NET ADMIN \\server /C NET STOP NETLOGON
    ```

    where *server* is the Server name of the server. Do this for the domain controller and for each backup domain controller.
2. Stop each server in the domain by using the preceding procedure for stopping a server.

 You can create command files that will accomplish many of these day to day monitoring tasks more easily—see Chapter 11 for more information.

CHAPTER 9

Installing and Configuring the Requesters

In all negotiations of difficulty, a man may not look to sow and reap at once; but must prepare business and so ripen it by degrees.

—*Sir Francis Bacon,* Essays or Counsels Civil and Moral

This chapter will cover installation and configuration of the requesters for your LAN, and how to work with Windows for Workgroups requesters and peers on your LAN.

The LAN Server package includes two different requesters: the DOS requester, also called DOS LAN Services, or DLS, and the OS/2 requester. Each requester PC that you install requires a separate license for the requester software (whether DOS or OS/2), called a *requester license* or a *distributed feature license.* You can acquire these licenses from IBM or from your original place of purchase for LAN Server. You need only one requester license for each requester PC, no matter how many different servers or domains you access.

IBM provides a utility called the License Tracking Utility, or LTU, to help you keep track of the requesters on your LAN. You can search for requesters, and tag which are licensed. See Chapter 6 for more information on installing and starting LTU.

The OS/2 requester is also included with the OS/2 Warp Connect product. If you are using Warp Connect for your requester PC, you don't need the requester from the LAN Server package, or a separate requester license. The Warp Connect install procedure gives you the option of installing the OS/2 Requester.

This chapter covers installing the LAN Server 4.0 versions of the DOS and OS/2 requesters. The installation and configuration of the LAN Server 3.0 OS/2 requester is similar to LAN Server 4.0, except that you must install the OS/2 transport component (called LAPS) before you install the OS/2 requester. The installation and configuration of the LAN Server 3.0 DOS requester is quite different from the 4.0 version, as the DOS requester was rewritten for the 4.0 release. For information on installing and configuring the LAN Server 3.0 requesters, see the book *LAN Server 3.0 Network Administrator Reference, Volume 1: Planning and Installation.*

Installing the DOS Requester

You must install the requester under DOS. If Windows is running, stop it to return to a DOS command prompt.

If you are using diskettes, insert DOS LAN Services diskette 1 and type **a:INSTALL**, where *a:* is your diskette drive.

If you are using CD-ROM, insert the LAN Server CD-ROM and type **d:\DLS\INSTALL**, where *d:* is your CD-ROM drive.

Press Enter on the Welcome to DLS screen. The next screen lets you specify where DLS is to be installed—the default is C:\NET. You can specify a different installation directory if you wish. Press Enter to continue.

The next screen asks you to select the network adapter that's installed in your PC. DLS tries to identify the type of adapter, and highlights it on the screen. If it's wrong or if it didn't select an adapter, move the highlighting to the correct adapter. See Appendix C for more details on supported adapters. Press Enter when you've selected the correct adapter, and DLS will configure your network drivers.

In some cases, the attempt to identify the network adapter can cause the install procedure to hang or terminate. If this happens to you, reboot your PC and rerun the INSTALL command with the /I option to suppress adapter identification.

The next screen asks you to enter your machine ID. This is the requester name for this PC. The requester name must not duplicate any other requester name, server name, or domain name in the LAN. Enter the requester name and press Enter.

The next screen asks for your user name, which is your user ID. This will be used as the default when you log on. This does not limit the user IDs that can be used but simply provides a default for convenience. Type a user ID and press Enter to continue.

The next screen asks for the domain name. This will be used as the default domain when you log on. You can use a different domain when you log on if you wish. Type a domain name and press Enter to continue.

The next screen lets you choose what features to install, and what NetBIOS drivers to use (Figure 9.1). The features you can optionally install are:

- *The DOS GUI*—This allows DOS users, without Windows, to log on, browse, connect, and manage peer shared resources through a graphical user interface that's very similar to the DLS Windows GUI. The GUI is started with the NETGUI command. If you don't install the GUI, then the NET command is available to perform these functions from the DOS command prompt.
- *Peer Services*—This feature allows DOS users to share directories and printers with other DOS and OS/2 requesters on the network.
- *Windows Support*—This allows Windows users to log on, browse, connect, and manage peer shared resources with a Windows GUI. Also, the Windows File Manager and Print Manager will support network operations, such as browsing and connecting to resources, and Windows applications that are network-enabled will support the LAN Server network.

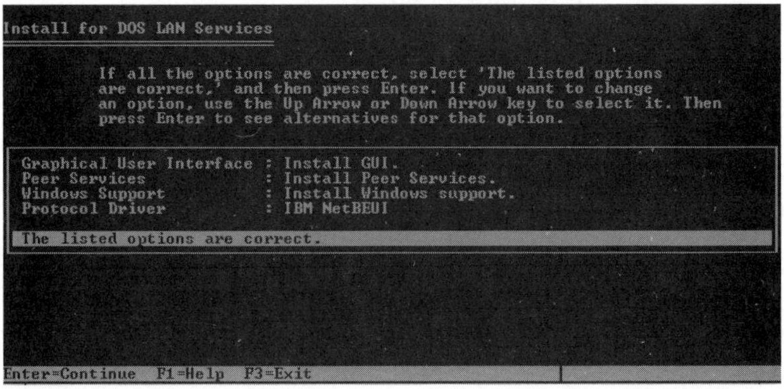

Figure 9.1 **DLS install features.**

If you have sufficient hard disk space, feel free to install all the features. They don't use any resources unless you invoke them. To choose not to install a feature, highlight its line and press Enter.

 The choice of NetBIOS protocol driver is important. The default is IBM NetBEUI. You can optionally choose IBM 802.2 NetBIOS drivers, also known as the LAN Support Program, or LSP, drivers. The advantages of each are shown in Table 9.1.

To change NetBIOS drivers, highlight the Protocol Driver line and press Enter. Then highlight "Change driver for protocol" and press Enter. Choose "Install 802.2 Support" for the IBM 802.2 NetBIOS driver, or "Do not install 802.2 support" for the IBM NetBEUI driver.

When you are done deciding which features and NetBIOS driver to install, highlight "The listed options are correct." and press Enter.

The next screen allows you to tailor your DLS configuration (Figure 9.2). On this screen, you can change your choices for requester name (machine ID), default user name, and default logon domain.

Another key choice is the type of *redirector*. The redirector is the driver that handles connecting to remote resources and transferring data. You can choose the basic, full, or virtual redirector as a default. You can also specifically start either the basic or full redirector. The advantages of each are shown in Table 9.2.

The Full Redirector is usually recommended for DOS users who occasionally use Windows, and the Virtual Redirector is recommended for full time Windows users with 32-bit processors. If you need to conserve the most memory, you can use the Basic Redirector but you will lose the ability to log

Table 9.1 **NetBEUI vs. LAN Support Program drivers**

Advantages of NetBEUI:

- Fastest performance.
- Supports more non-IBM adapters.

Advantages of LAN Support Program:

- Supports applications using the 802.2 protocol, such as certain mainframe terminal emulators.
- Uses less memory than NetBEUI, particularly with Token Ring adapters.

Table 9.2 **Choosing a Redirector for DLS**

Advantages of the Basic Redirector:

■ Good performance.

■ Supports access to file and print resources.

■ Uses 49K less memory than the Full Redirector.

■ Usable with or without Windows.

■ Supports all processor types.

Advantages of the Full Redirector:

■ Better performance than the Basic Redirector.

■ Supports domain logon, network browsing, and aliases; as well as file and print access.

■ Usable with or without Windows.

■ Supports 80286 and above processor types.

Advantages of the Virtual Redirector:

■ Performance equal to Full Redirector.

■ Supports all functions.

■ Takes no conventional memory.

■ Usable only when Windows is running.

■ Supports 32-bit processors only: Intel 80386 and above.

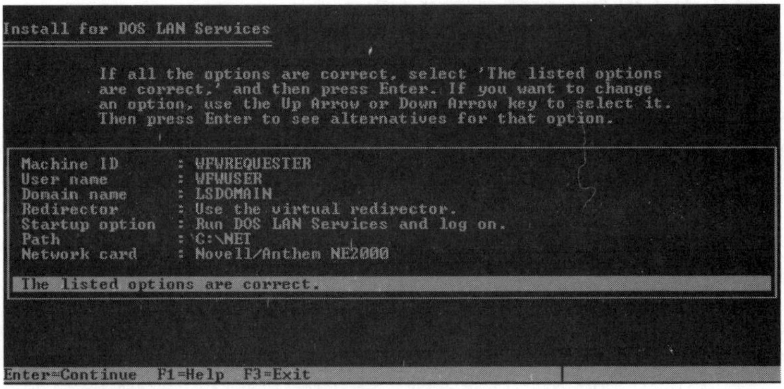

```
Install for DOS LAN Services

         If all the options are correct, select 'The listed options
         are correct,' and then press Enter. If you want to change
         an option, use the Up Arrow or Down Arrow key to select it.
         Then press Enter to see alternatives for that option.

    Machine ID       : WFWREQUESTER
    User name        : WFWUSER
    Domain name      : LSDOMAIN
    Redirector       : Use the virtual redirector.
    Startup option   : Run DOS LAN Services and log on.
    Path             : C:\NET
    Network card     : Novell/Anthem NE2000

    The listed options are correct.


Enter=Continue   F1=Help   F3=Exit
```

Figure 9.2 **DOS LAN Services Configuration Tailoring**

on to a domain and use LAN Server resource definitions—you will have to access resources by server name.

You can also choose a startup option on this screen, which will add appropriate commands to AUTOEXEC.BAT. Also, on this screen, you can change your network adapter or its settings.

 Many network adapters, such as the Eagle NE2000, have manual settings on the adapter for the IRQ, the shared RAM address, and so on. You must specify these settings when you install DLS, or the adapter driver won't work right when you reboot your PC. To view or change the settings, highlight the network adapter and press Enter; then highlight "Edit settings for network card driver" and press Enter (Figure 9.3).

If you have an Eagle NE2000, you will see the settings in Figure 9.3 (each network driver is different). Modify these settings to match the manual settings on the adapter. Once you get all these settings right, the installation will start. Insert diskettes as requested. When complete, reboot your PC.

Initial Requester Startup and Troubleshooting

Check the screen carefully for error messages from your network drivers. If you see any error messages, or the PC appears to hang, you may have a problem with your network driver configuration. You can restart the DLS Install and edit the network adapter driver settings, as described previously. Or, you can manually edit the PROTOCOL.INI file, found in the DLS directory, to change the adapter settings if you are familiar with them.

Figure 9.3 **DLS network adapter settings.**

If you start Windows, another setup program will run after asking you for confirmation. This setup program will modify Windows settings. You should stop and restart Windows after this setup is complete.

A common error message from Windows is "The FULL redirector was not loaded," followed by the message "Cannot find DLSNET.DLL." If you see these messages, do not look for a file called DLSNET.DLL—none exists! The actual cause of these messages is that the network drivers were not properly started before Windows was started. Try exiting from Windows and checking your AUTOEXEC.BAT file. If you find that there is no NET START command in the AUTOEXEC.BAT file, or the NET START command appears *after* the WIN command, edit the AUTOEXEC.BAT file and insert a NET START command *before* the WIN command. Reboot your PC and try starting Windows again.

If you are still having problems with Windows, check the SYSTEM.INI file (found in the Windows directory). The SYSTEM.INI file should have the following parameters:

In the [boot] section:
```
network.drv=dlsnet.drv
```

In the [boot.description] section:
```
network.drv=IBM DOS LAN Services
```

In the [386Enh] section, for enhanced mode Windows:
```
network=vnetbios.386,vnetsup.386,vredir.386
```

In the [386Enh] section, for standard mode Windows:
```
network=*dosnet,*vnetbios
```

If you are installing with Windows for Workgroups, be sure to remove the Windows networking support before you install DLS. After installation, you may need to correct your CONFIG.SYS file. Here's an example of the DLS drivers that should be loaded in your CONFIG.SYS file if you selected the NetBEUI driver:

```
REM DEVICE=C:\WINDOWS\IFSHLP.SYS
device=C:\NET\protman.sys /i:C:\NET
device=C:\NET\ne2000.dos
device=C:\NET\dlshlp.sys
```

The *ne2000.dos* driver is specific to the NE2000 adapter, and will vary based on your adapter type. Notice that the Windows for Workgroups

IFSHLP.SYS driver has been removed (by putting *REM* in front of it), and the DLS driver DLSHLP.SYS is loaded. If your CONFIG.SYS is loading the IFSHLP.SYS driver instead of DLSHLP.SYS, manually edit the file and make it right.

You may also need to update the Windows for Workgroups networking drivers with the DLS versions if the DLS install program hasn't done this correctly. To do this, use these commands:

```
REPLACE C:\NET\*.DLL C:\WINDOWS /S
REPLACE C:\NET\*.386 C:\WINDOWS /S
```

Configuring and Tuning a DOS Requester

You can rerun the DLS install program any time to add features or tailor the installation options. However, many configuration and tailoring options are best done by manually editing the AUTOEXEC.BAT and NETWORK.INI files. This section will explain how DLS features and options work, and how to configure and tailor them.

Starting Services and Memory Use

You can start and stop services manually with the NET START and NET STOP commands. You can specify the name of a service to start or stop. If you use NET START with no service name, the default service that's started is controlled by the *autostart=* parameter in the NETWORK.INI file. When you start a service that requires other services, they will be started automatically. For example, NET START MESSENGER will start the Full redirector if it's not already started.

You should put a NET START command in the AUTOEXEC.BAT file to automate starting the network. DLS Install will do this for you if you choose. If you are using Windows, the NET START command must be issued before Windows is started (with the WIN command). A list of the available services, what they do, what other services they require, and how much memory they require are shown in Table 9.3.

All DLS services can be loaded into Upper Memory Blocks (UMBs) in DOS, thus reducing the impact of these services on DOS low memory. When a service starts, it will load itself into a UMB if there is a large enough UMB

Table 9.3 **DLS Services**

Service	Memory Use	Description
NetBind	Varies	Initializes network adapter drivers, releases unneeded memory. Memory use varies by network adapter, typically about 15K. Not used with LAN Support Program drivers.
NetBEUI	50K	Provides high-performance NetBIOS transport. Not used with LAN Support Program drivers.
Basic	49K	Basic redirector. Accesses resources without full domain services. Requires NETBEUI to be started, or LAN Support Program drivers to be installed.
Full	98K	Full redirector. Use instead of basic redirector for full domain services. Requires NETBEUI to be started, or LAN Support Program drivers to be installed.
Messenger	18K	Receives messages sent to this requester. Requires basic or full redirector to be started.
NetPopUp	22K	Displays received messages in a pop-up window. Requires messenger to be started.
Peer	63K	Shares file and print resources. Requires basic or full redirector to be started.

available. Setting up DOS to provide and use UMBs is a difficult task. Most versions of DOS today provide utilities to optimize memory use—use the one that comes with your version of DOS. For example, IBM PC DOS has the RAMBOOST utility that is set up with the RAMSETUP command. If you want to get the most out of your DOS memory, there are many good DOS books available that explain DOS memory management and how to use it.

If you need network access only when you are using Windows, you can start just the NetBEUI service (or install the LSP drivers), then start Windows. The virtual redirector will take over, which uses 32-bit Windows memory, not DOS memory. You cannot use the Messenger, NetPopUp, or Peer services with the virtual redirector.

If you are using the NetBEUI driver and you haven't issued any NET START command since booting DOS, you will notice that 79K of DOS memory is being used for no apparent reason. To release this memory, issue any NET START command. NET START NETBIND will release the memory without starting any services.

Tailoring Logon Options

DOS LAN Services provides a *password caching* feature that you can enable or disable (it's enabled by default). With password caching, DLS stores the user's domain passwords in an encrypted password list file on the requester. The user provides a workstation password at logon, which is used to decrypt the password list file and recover the domain password.

If your users access multiple domains or peers with different passwords, this can be a useful feature, because the user has to remember just the workstation password. This feature has some disadvantages: If the user moves to a different requester, the password list file may be nonexistent or out of date; and, password list files may be considered a security problem, because the administrator can't set policies for workstation passwords, such as minimum length and frequency of change.

If you want to disable the password caching feature, edit the NETWORK.INI file and change the *passwordcaching=* parameter from *Yes* to *No*. Once this feature is disabled, the user provides the domain password at each logon, and no password list file is maintained. The NETWORK.INI file is found in the DLS directory (C:\NET, unless you specified a different one at install). You may also want to delete the password list file. It's called *user.PWL*, where *user* is the first eight characters of the user ID, and the file is stored in the DLS directory (C:\NET by default).

When a user logs on, DLS by default performs a domain logon. The user's logon assignments and network applications are processed, and the user's ID and password are validated. You can change this default by changing the NETWORK.INI file's *lslogon=* parameter from *Yes* to *No*. Once this change is made, user logon will be local and no logon assignments or network applications will be provided. If the basic redirector is being used, all logons are local regardless of the *lslogon=* parameter setting.

You might consider changing the *lslogon=* option if the user normally works with peers rather than domains, as peers don't support domain logon. The user can always request a domain logon through the /DOMAIN: option of the NET LOGON command when needed.

When a user connects to a resource, DLS saves the connection information. If the user logs off and logs on again, DLS restores the connections, using the saved information. You can disable this feature by changing the *reconnect=* parameter in NETWORK.INI from *Yes* to *No.*

When a user logs on to a domain, DLS sets the requester PC's clock to match the domain controller's clock. This is called *time synchronization.* If the requester and the server are in different time zones, this can be a problem. You can disable this feature by changing the *timesync=* parameter in NET-WORK.INI from *Yes* to *No.*

Installing the OS/2 Requester

The first steps are to select hardware for your OS/2 requester PC, and to install OS/2 on the PC. The sections "Selecting Hardware for Your Server PC" and "Selecting, Planning, and Installing OS/2 on Your Server PC" in Chapter 6 also apply to an OS/2 requester PC, and you should review and use the information from these sections, with the following exceptions:

- You cannot install a LAN Requester with the Loopback Driver. You must have a network adapter in the requester PC.
- You can use OS/2 Warp Connect for your requester PC. OS/2 Warp Connect includes the OS/2 Requester and the OS/2 Peer. See the section, "Installing OS/2 Warp Connect as a Requester," in this chapter for more information on this option.

This section will cover installing the OS/2 requester from LAN Server 4.0 using a PC on which OS/2 has already been installed. There are two paths through the OS/2 requester install procedure—Easy and Tailored. You should use the Easy path at first—you can always go back and use the Tailored path later to add or remove features, or to tailor your configuration. If you need to reconfigure the OS/2 requester or remove it completely, use the Tailored path of the install program. Don't try to move or delete files yourself—it's much easier and more reliable to let the install program do it for you.

Before installing the OS/2 requester, you should review the information in "Selecting, Planning, and Installing LAN Server on Your Server PC" in Chapter 6. There are many similarities in the install procedures.

Installing the OS/2 Requester Using the Easy Path

If you are installing from CD-ROM, insert the CD-ROM, open an OS/2 command window, and type **d: INSTALL**, where *d:* is your CD-ROM drive. You will see a Welcome window; click OK. Then you will see a menu of choices, as shown in Figure 9.4. Select "Install OS/2 LAN Requester 4.0" on this window and click OK. Click OK on the Welcome window for OS/2 LAN Requester installation.

If you are installing from diskettes, insert Requester Diskette 1, open an OS/2 command window, and type **a: INSTALL**, where *a:* is your diskette drive. Click OK on the Welcome window for OS/2 LAN Requester installation.

The next window, Important Licensing Information, informs you that a license is required for requester software. See the beginning of this chapter for more information on requester licensing. Click OK on this window.

Next, you see a window asking if you wish to use the Easy or Tailored path (Figure 9.5). You can click on Help for this window and see a detailed description of the things that Tailored install will do that Easy won't. For now, choose the Easy path by clicking the Easy button.

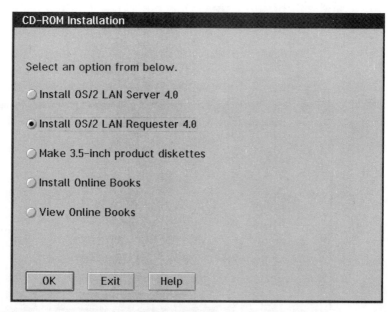

Figure 9.4 **LAN Server CD-ROM installation choices.**

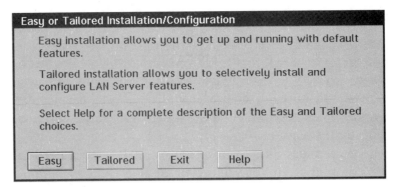

Figure 9.5 **Easy or Tailored installation.**

If your requester PC has more than one hard disk partition (drive), the next window asks you to choose a drive for the installation (Figure 9.6). The default is to install on the OS/2 boot drive. You can install the OS/2 requester on any drive with enough space. However, some features of the OS/2 requester are always installed on the OS/2 boot drive (see Table 6.5 for details). Choose a drive and click OK.

The next window asks for a requester name. This is the name for the requester PC. It must be different from all other requester names, all server names, and all domain names on your LAN. The requester name uniquely identifies the requester PC in the LAN.

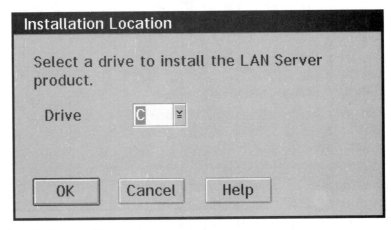

Figure 9.6 **Installation location.**

The next window asks for the domain name. Specify the domain that this requester will use most frequently. When a user logs on at this requester PC, this will be the default logon domain.

Now, the MPTS component is installed from MPTS diskettes 1 and 2, or from the CD-ROM. Once MPTS finishes installing, it will try to detect the type of network adapter that you have installed in your requester PC (Figure 9.7). If successful, you will see the Adapter Confirmation window. You can accept the detected adapter, or click "Change adapter" to get to the Select Network Adapter window (Figure 9.8). If MPTS is not successful in detecting the network adapter, you will see the Select Network Adapter window right away.

 Pick your adapter from the list, using Appendix C as a guide.

With some PC and network adapter hardware, the adapter detection logic in MPTS will cause hangs or other errors. If this happens to you, restart the install procedure using the /NS option on the INSTALL command.

Once your adapter is chosen or confirmed, the rest of the OS/2 requester is installed from diskette or CD-ROM, and you are informed that installation is complete. Shut down the OS/2 system and reboot your PC.

 Review the sections "Booting Your Server PC for the First Time" and "Fixing Problems with Initial Server Boot" in Chapter 6. All of the guidance and advice in those sections apply to your requester PC as well.

When your requester PC finishes booting, verify that it's operating properly by opening an OS/2 command window and issuing the LOGON command. Enter your user ID and password for your logon domain, and check that logon is successful.

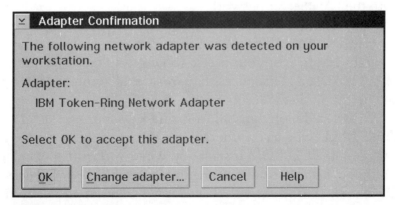

Figure 9.7 **Adapter confirmation.**

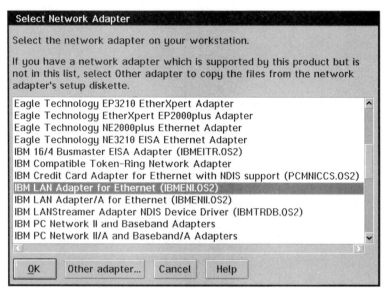

Figure 9.8 **Select network adapter.**

Installing the OS/2 Requester Using the Tailored Path

The Easy install, by default, installs the LAN Server Administrative GUI feature, and does not install the Virtual DOS LAN API feature. Most nonadministrative users do not need the Administrative GUI, although it does allow some amount of end-user tailoring. Most users who run DOS or Windows applications will benefit from the Virtual DOS LAN API feature, because it allows network-enabled DOS and Windows applications to see and work with the LAN Server network.

You can save some disk space and memory, and support network-enabled DOS and Windows applications, by using Tailored Install to select the right features for your users. You can also modify your network adapter settings, change the services that are started automatically by the requester, and perform other tailoring tasks.

To start a Tailored install from CD-ROM, insert the CD-ROM and type **d:INSTALL**, where *d:* is your CD-ROM drive. Select "Install LAN Requester 4.0" from the CD-ROM Installation window (Figure 9.4) and click OK.

If you installed from diskette, open the IBM LAN Services folder on your OS/2 desktop and start the OS/2 LAN Services Installation/Configuration program.

Click OK on the Welcome window, and click OK on the Licensing Information window. Then click Tailored on the Easy or Tailored window (Figure 9.5). You will see an Installation Tasks window, from which you can "Install or configure this workstation" or "Remove LAN Requester from this workstation." If you want to simply remove the requester, choose the Remove option and click OK. You will be given the opportunity to remove MPTS also, if you wish (Figure 9.9)

To tailor this installation, select "Install or configure this workstation" and click OK. If your requester PC has more than one drive, you will see the Installation Location window (Figure 9.6). If you change the drive where LAN Requester is currently installed, the LAN Requester will be moved to the new drive (but the MPTS and User Profile Manager components will not be moved).

You will then be asked if you want to reinstall MPTS. Normally, you don't, so click No. Then you will be asked to confirm the adapter choice or select a different adapter, just as in Easy install (Figures 9.7 and 9.8).

At this point, you will see the LAPS Configuration window, and you can work with the network adapter drivers and protocol drivers. Review Figures 6.15 and 6.16 in Chapter 6, and the accompanying text—it's the same for requesters and servers.

When you are done configuring adapters, you will see the Installation and Configuration window (Figure 9.10). As with the server install, you first select which features to install and remove, then configure your features, and finally apply the changes.

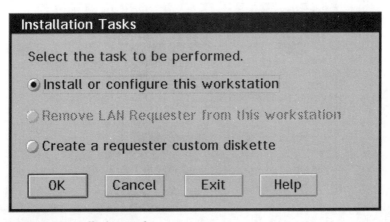

Figure 9.9 ***Requester Installation Tasks.***

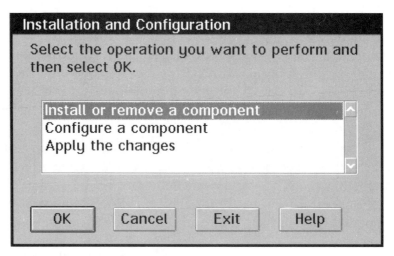

Figure 9.10 **Installation and Configuration tasks.**

Select "Install or remove a component" and you'll see the window in Figure 9.11. The Administrative GUI was removed, since most nonadministrative users won't need it. The Virtual DOS LAN API support was installed so that DOS and Windows applications can see the LAN Server network. Peer Services were installed, so we can share resources with other requesters.

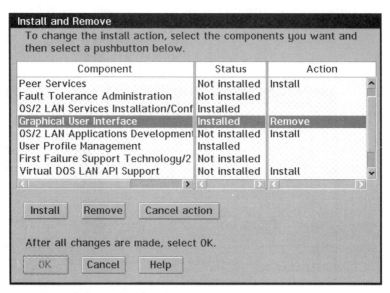

Figure 9.11 **Install and Remove features for Requester.**

And the OS/2 LAN Applications Development Toolkit was installed, so we can write C or C++ programs using the LAN Server APIs. Click OK and you return to the Installation and Configuration window (Figure 9.10).

Select "Configure a component" and you'll see the Configure window, which allows you to configure features (Figure 9.12). To configure a feature, highlight it and click Configure. Fill in the requested information until you return to the Configure window.

When you configure the Requester feature, you can choose:

- The Requester Name and Domain Name for this requester.
- Whether to start the requester automatically when the PC boots. This adds a command, NET START REQ, to the OS/2 STARTUP.CMD file.

- Which services to start automatically when the requester starts. See Table 6.4 for a list of services and a brief description of each.

When you configure the Peer Services feature, you can choose:

- Security mode as Share Level or User Level, and the owner's user ID if User Level was chosen. See the following section for more information on Peer Services.

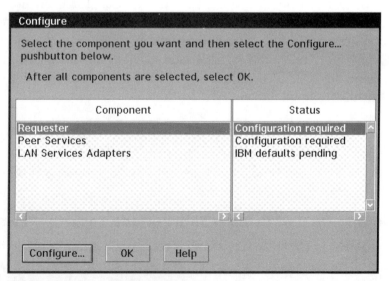

Figure 9.12 **Configure features for Requester.**

Installing and Configuring Peer Services in an OS/2 Requester

As previously described, use the Tailored Install path to install Peer Services on an OS/2 requester. Peer Services allows a requester PC to share one print queue, one serial device queue, and several directories with other requesters on the LAN. The term *peer PC* will be used for a requester PC running Peer Services and sharing resources.

When you install Peer Services, the default logon type is changed from domain logon to local logon. This is not always the desired default. If your peer PC is normally used as a requester to a LAN Server domain, you want to log on to the domain. To change the default back to domain logon, edit the peer PC's IBMLAN.INI file and change character number 37 of the *wrkheuristics=* parameter from 1 to 2.

When you configure Peer Services, you must choose *share-mode* security or *user-mode* security. User-mode security is more complex to set up, but is more flexible and secure. User-mode security is similar to security on a server PC, so it may be more familiar to you if you are used to administering a LAN Server domain. User-mode security also allows you to designate an owner— a user ID that is always allowed to access the peer PC from a remote requester. This would usually be the user who owns the peer PC and uses it as a requester to the LAN Server domain. Share-mode security is easier to set up, and is useful for peer PCs on which security is not a concern.

Only one user at a time, plus the owner (for user-mode security), can remotely access the shared resources on a peer PC. If a second user tries to access resources on a peer PC, he or she will receive the message "SYS0071: The network request was not accepted." If you receive this message, you can use the NET SESS command to find out who is using the peer at this time, like this:

```
NET SESS \\LSPEER /PEER
```

where *LSPEER* is the name of the peer PC. Once you find out who is using the peer, you can send a message to their PC and request that they release it.

Setting Up and Using a Share-Mode Security Peer

A good way to set up a peer PC is to create a command file to start the peer and share the desired resources. For share-mode security, here's a command file example (do not type the numbers, they have been added only for reference). You can place these commands in the STARTUP.CMD file, and they will be executed when the peer PC starts up:

1. **NET START PEER**
2. **NET SHARE IPC$**
3. **NET SHARE ADMIN$ PEERADMIN**
4. **NET SHARE SALES=C:\MYSALES**
5. **NET SHARE APPL=C:\MYAPPL /PERM:R**
6. **NET SHARE SECRET=C:\HUSH CLEFS**
7. **NET SHARE MYPRINT /PRINT**

Command 1 starts the peer service on the peer PC. To stop sharing resources, type **NET STOP PEER**. Command 2 allows users to browse the resources on the peer PC. Command 3 allows remote administration of the peer PC, and assigns the administration password PEERADMIN. To remotely administer the peer PC, issue the commands:

NET USE \\LSPEER\ADMIN$ PEERADMIN
NET ADMIN \\LSPEER /C <some command>

where *LSPEER* is the name of the peer PC. Command 4 shares the directory C:\MYSALES as a shared resource called SALES. Any user can read or write all files in this directory or its subdirectories. Command 5 shares the directory C:\MYAPPL as a read-only resource called APPL. Any user can read (but not write) all files in this directory or its subdirectories. Command 6 shares the directory C:\HUSH as the resource called SECRET, with the password CLEFS. A user who knows the password accesses the resource with the following:

NET USE x: \\LSPEER\SECRET CLEFS

Command 7 shares the print queue MYPRINT. Any OS/2 user can print to the queue through a network printer object. Create the object by dragging a Network Printer template from the Templates folder, and filling in LSPEER as the server and MYPRINT as the queue name. Any DLS user can print to the queue by connecting to the resource, as they would normally.

 For more information on these and other commands, see Chapter 11.

Setting Up and Using a User-Mode Security Peer

With user-mode security, the peer PC has a user accounts database and access control profiles that are very similar to those found on a server PC.

There are two differences: The peer does not have any domain-wide resource definitions, such as aliases; and the peer does not replicate its user accounts database with anyone—it's stand-alone. You must perform a certain amount of setup and tailoring of the peer's user accounts database for user-mode security. Here's an example of setting up the user accounts database (the numbers have been added for reference; don't type them):

1. `LOGOFF`
2. `LOGON USERID /P:PASSWORD /V:LOCAL`
3. `NET ACCOUNTS /MINPWLEN:0`
4. `NET USER PEERUSER DOMPW /ADD /PRIV:ADMIN`
5. `NET USER USERID /DELETE`
6. `LOGOFF`
7. `LOGON PEERUSER /P:DOMPW`
8. `NET USER USERA USERA /ADD`

This example assumes Peer Services was installed on a requester PC whose user normally logs on to a domain. Commands 1 and 2 log you on locally at the peer with the default administrative user ID. If you don't do this, you will not be able to issue the NET USER commands, because you don't have administrative privilege at the peer PC. Command 3 resets the minimum password length requirement to zero for the peer PC. Command 4 adds the user's normal domain logon user ID, *PEERUSER,* as a local administrative user ID, with the user's domain password, *DOMPW.* Command 5 deletes the default ID, because it's too well-known to be secure. Commands 6 and 7 log on to the domain again, but now the user is also an administrator of the local peer PC. Command 8 adds a user, called *USERA,* as a valid user for the peer, with password *USERA.* USERA is someone that you want to have access to peer resources.

The user USERA can now change his or her initial password at the peer PC to match his or her domain password, from his requester PC, with this command:

`NET PASSWORD \\LSPEER USERA USERA DOMAINPW`

where *LSPEER* is the name of the peer PC, and *DOMAINPW* is USERA's normal domain password. Now, when USERA logs on to his or her normal domain, he or she will also be a valid user at the LSPEER peer PC—and USERA did not have to reveal his or her domain password to the peer PC's owner.

To share a directory resource at the peer PC with user-mode security, you must first create an access control profile and apply it to the subdirectories, as you do at a server PC. For example:

```
NET ACCESS C:\MYSALES /ADD USERS:Y
NET ACCESS C:\MYAPPL /ADD USERS:R GUESTS:R
NET ACCESS C:\HUSH /ADD USERA:Y
```

These commands give all valid users at the peer PC read-write access to the C:\MYSALES directory; all valid users and guest users (users not defined in the peer's user accounts database) read access to the C:\MYAPPL directory; and USERA read-write access to the C:\HUSH directory. If there are subdirectories, you should propagate the access control profiles, like this:

```
NET ACCESS C:\HUSH /APPLY
```

Here's a command file to start the user-mode peer service and share the resources. These commands could be added to STARTUP.CMD if you wish to share these resources all the time:

```
NET START PEER
NET SHARE SALES=C:\MYSALES
NET SHARE APPL=C:\MYAPPL
NET SHARE SECRET=C:\HUSH
NET SHARE MYPRINT /PRINT
```

The resources will be accessible only to the users or groups to whom you have granted access through access control profiles.

The owner of the user-mode security peer PC can administer it from a remote requester PC like this (for example):

1. **LOGOFF**
2. **LOGON PEERUSER /P:DOMPW**
3. **NET ADMIN \\LSPEER /C NET USER USERX USERX /ADD**
4. **COPY \\LSPEER\C$\HUSH\SECRET.DAT C:\XYZ**
   LOGOFF

Commands 1 and 2 log on to the domain with the peer owner's user ID. Command 3 issues a remote command to the *LSPEER* peer PC to add a new user to the peer's user accounts database. Command 4 shows how the user-mode peer owner can access any directory on the peer PC remotely, even if no NET SHARE has been issued to share that directory. In this case, the file *C:\HUSH\SECRET.DAT* is copied from the peer PC to the requester's *C:\XYZ* directory. If the peer owner has been designated as the *owner user ID* when configuring the peer, the owner can always access the peer remotely even if someone else is currently connected.

Other OS/2 Requester Installation and Tailoring

 See the following sections of Chapter 6 for other installation and configuration procedures that are applicable to an OS/2 requester:

- "Configuring and Tailoring MPTS"
- "Installing and Viewing LAN Server Soft-Copy Books"
- "Installing the MPTS Utilities and Toolkits"
- "Installing LAN Server Productivity Aids"
- "LAN Server Internals—Services, Files, and Directories"

Installing OS/2 Warp Connect as a Requester

OS/2 Warp Connect is an exciting new version of OS/2 Warp that includes a host of LAN networking features:

- *OS/2 LAN Requester*—The MPTS, OS/2 Requester, and Productivity Aids components from LAN Server 4.0.
- *OS/2 Peer*—A special version of the LAN Requester optimized for use in a peer-to-peer networking environment. Compatible with LAN Server.
- *NetWare Requester*—Connection to Novell NetWare servers.
- *LAN Distance Remote*—Turns a telephone link-up between two Warp Connect PCs into a virtual LAN. Also supports dialing into the LAN Distance Connection Server (sold separately) for full LAN access.
- *TCP/IP 3.0*—Latest version of IBM's OS/2 TCP/IP software, with the ability to connect to UNIX systems and use the Internet.

Perhaps the best feature of Warp Connect is its simple, integrated install and configure program. You can install OS/2 and any combination of the Warp

Connect networking features with ease. You can also set up a Warp Connect PC as a code server, and install other Warp Connect PCs across the LAN.

Warp Connect comes in two versions—with and without WINOS2. It is available only on CD-ROM, so you'll need a PC with a CD-ROM drive that's supported by OS/2 for your initial Warp Connect installation. Other PCs without CD-ROM drives can be installed across the LAN using Warp Connect's remote installation feature.

This section will focus on installing the OS/2 Warp and LAN Requester components of Warp Connect.

Installing Warp Connect from CD-ROM

With Warp Connect, you can install the OS/2 operating system and any combination of the networking features at the same time. To start the install, insert the Warp Connect CD-ROM and the installation diskette, and reboot the PC. Insert Warp Connect diskette 1 when asked. You'll see a Welcome screen explaining the components of Warp Select, then you'll install the OS/2 Warp operating system, as described in Chapter 6, "Installing OS/2 Warp on Your Server PC." Be sure to select Advanced Installation, as described in Chapter 6, because Warp Connect will not install LAN Requester if you select the Easy path.

When the PC reboots with the installed OS/2 Warp operating system, the Warp Connect networking feature installation program takes over automatically. The first window you see asks if you want to install any networking support. If you select No, you have installed the equivalent of the OS/2 Warp product. You can restart the installation later with the Warp Connect Selective Install for Networking (see Figure 9.17). If you select Yes, to install networking products, you will see Figure 9.13. From this window, you choose the products you want to install. You can install OS/2 Peer as a requester for LAN Server, but this does not include the Administrative GUI. If your users are primarily accessing server-based resources, you should install the LAN Requester. You can also select to install the Novell NetWare Client for access to Novell NetWare servers on the LAN; TCP/IP for OS/2, which connects to other TCP/IP systems and also provides access to the Internet; or LAN Distance Remote, which supports dial-up access between Warp Connect systems or to a LAN Distance Connection Server. This section will cover only LAN Requester installation. When you select the LAN Requester and click OK, you will see Figure 9.14.

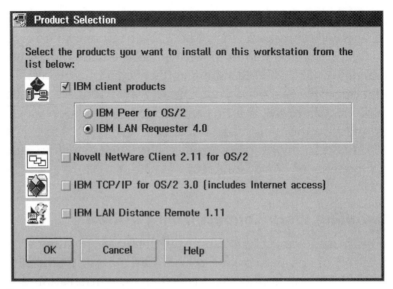

Figure 9.13 **Warp Connect Product Selection.**

The setup notebook in Figure 9.14 has sections for each product you selected, plus a page for the network adapter setup. Your network adapter should be highlighted in the list if it was detected by Warp Connect. If the wrong adapter is highlighted, pick the right one. If the driver for your adapter is not included with Warp Connect, click "Other adapter" to install it from the diskette provided by the adapter manufacturer.

Many adapters (such as the Eagle NE2000 selected in Figure 9.14) have switches and jumpers on the adapter to select the IRQ, the shared RAM address, and other key settings. You must configure the settings in Warp Connect to match the switch and jumper settings, or your network products won't function. Click "Settings" to see Figure 9.15.

Notice the IRQ setting defaults to 3. Many PCs require that you change the network adapter IRQ from 3 to another value, such as 10 or 11, to avoid conflicts with the second serial port. You must also change the setting here to match the hardware switch settings. Click "Change" to see the list of acceptable values, and to select a new value. Additional settings can be viewed and changed by clicking "More."

Some adapters can be configured by software. Typically, these adapters do not require you to specify IRQ and other settings here, because the adapter driver can read these settings from the adapter itself.

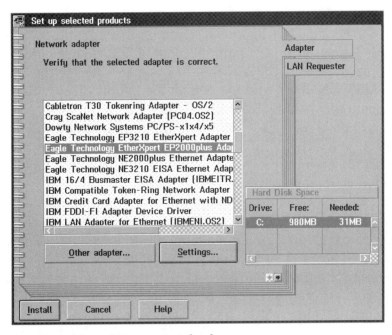

Figure 9.14 **Warp Connect product setup notebook.**

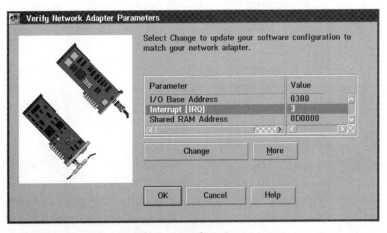

Figure 9.15 **Warp Connect Network Adapter settings.**

Once you have completed changing adapter settings, click OK and return to the notebook of figure 9.6. Click on the "LAN Requester" tab to see the LAN Requester configuration settings, as shown in Figure 9.16.

In Figure 9.16, the requester has been installed on the C: drive and named WARPCONNECT, and the default logon domain specified as LSDOMAIN. The protocol setting is NetBIOS. Installing NetBIOS over TCP/IP as the LAN Server protocol is possible, but is not covered in this book. You would use this if you wanted LAN Server and LAN Requester to communicate across a TCP/IP network, perhaps one installed in your company to communicate between remote offices.

When you are done configuring the settings notebook, click "Install" to complete the install process. Warp Connect will install the rest of OS/2, the MPTS component, perform a reboot, install the LAN Requester component, then tell you that installation is completed. When you click OK, your PC will reboot with the LAN Requester installed and started. Be patient during this process—it may seem that nothing is happening for a minute or two, but eventually things will start moving again.

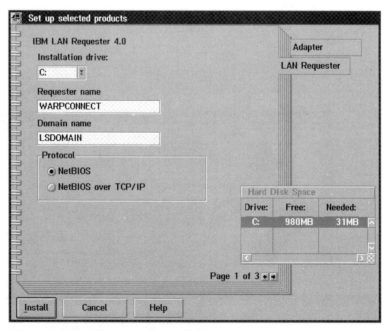

Figure 9.16 **Warp Connect LAN Requester settings.**

If you have any problems with the initial startup of the new LAN Requester, see the section "Booting Your Server PC for the First Time" in Chapter 6.

Tailoring Warp Connect

If you open the OS/2 System folder, then the OS/2 Warp Connect Install/Remove folder, you'll see the collection of installation and configuration programs shown in Figure 9.17.

Here's a list of the programs and their purposes:

LAN Requester Install/Remove	Invokes the standard LAN Requester install program, as described in the previous section "Installing the OS/2 Requester." Do not use to install new features, since it requires diskettes. Use the PRODINST command from the CD-ROM instead.
MPTS Install/Remove	Invokes the MPTS configuration program, as described in "Configuring and Tailoring MPTS" in Chapter 6.
NSC Remove	Removes the Network Sign-on Coordinator program that's installed by default.
OS/2 Warp Selective Install	Use to selectively install OS/2 Warp features. Same as the Selective Install program in the System Setup folder.

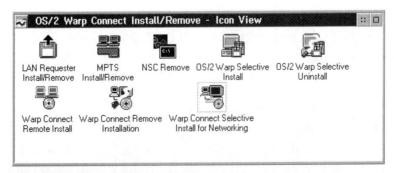

Figure 9.17 **Warp Connect Install/Remove folder.**

OS/2 Warp Selective Uninstall	Use to selectively remove OS/2 Warp features. Same as the Selective Uninstall program in the System Setup folder.
Warp Connect Remote Install	Use to install Warp Connect PCs over the LAN. See "Installing Warp Connect from a Code Server" in this chapter.
Warp Connect Remove Installation	Removes the Warp Connect installation program from your hard disk. It takes about 3 megabytes of space. To restore it later, insert the CD-ROM and run the INSTALL command.
Warp Connect Selective Install for Networking	Runs the Warp Connect install program for local or remote installation of Warp Connect networking features.

The Warp Connect installation program is designed to install with the most used options. To perform advanced or tailored installations, use the install procedures from the individual products by opening an OS/2 command window and typing **d:PRODINST**, where *d:* is your CD-ROM drive. PRODINST will give you a menu of products and let you install them individually with their unique install programs. PRODINST will also let you create 3.5-inch diskettes for the individual products.

Installing Warp Connect from a Code Server

Once you have installed Warp Connect on a PC with a CD-ROM drive, you can use it as a *code server* to install Warp Connect on additional LAN-connected PCs without requiring a CD-ROM drive on the additional PCs. Of course, each PC that you install with Warp Connect requires a separate license.

You can save money on additional copies of Warp Connect by purchasing *additional license* packages, which don't include the CD-ROM or books, and installing them over the LAN with remote installation.

The Warp Connect Remote Install program creates two remote installation diskettes. Then, you leave the Warp Connect Remote Install program running with the CD-ROM in the drive, take the remote installation diskettes to the LAN-connected PC, and boot the PC from the diskettes. Then, you install Warp Connect on the LAN-connected PC, as usual. It will load the software across the LAN, from the CD-ROM on the code server PC.

To do this, start Warp Connect Remote Install from the folder in Figure 9.17, and have two blank, formatted 3.5-inch high-density diskettes ready. As the Remote Install program walks you through creating the remote install diskettes, you will select a network adapter for the remote PC and specify the settings, as you did in Figures 9.15 and 9.16. When you have the diskettes, the Warp Connect Remote Installation Service will start automatically and wait for you to take the diskettes to the remote workstation and reboot.

Insert the first diskette and reboot the remote PC. Insert the second diskette, as requested. You will proceed through a normal-appearing Warp Connect install, as previously described. The only difference is that the software is loaded across the LAN, from the CD-ROM on the code server PC that you set up.

At the code server PC, you can see the status of the remote install. When the install is complete, close the Remote Install program at the code server PC.

The remote install diskettes are specific to the code server where they were created. They will not work with another code server. Also, the remote install diskettes are specific to a network adapter type and the settings for that network adapter. You will need to create separate sets of remote install diskettes if you have more than one code server, or multiple network adapter types.

The code server is set up to support only one remote install at a time. To allow multiple installs, you can edit the file GRPWARE.INI, which is found in the code server's c:\GRPWARE\CLIENTS directory. Locate the MaxClients parameter and change its value from 1 to the maximum number of simultaneous installs you require. Note: The status display for the Remote Install program won't be correct when you have more than one client installing at the same time.

Tailoring Warp Connect from a Code Server

You can run the Warp Connect install program again from the code server to install another networking product. Reboot the remote with the same remote install diskettes after starting the Remote Install program on the code server. You can reinstall OS/2 or just the networking products.

If you want to run the individual product install programs from the CD-ROM remotely, set up the code server with the Peer Services feature of the

LAN Requester, or with the OS/2 Peer product. Share the CD-ROM drive at the code server and connect to the CD-ROM drive from the remote PC, using the LAN Requester or OS/2 Peer that's installed there. Then use the command **x:\PRODINST**, where *x:* is the redirected drive letter for the remote CD-ROM drive. You can install, remove, or tailor any of the networking products this way without a CD-ROM drive in your remote PC.

Working with Windows for Workgroups PCs

If you have a PC with Microsoft Windows for Workgroups installed, you can use it as a requester and peer for LAN Server networks without installing DLS. You will be able to log on to the LAN Server domain, and browse and connect to resources, when acting as a requester. You will be able to share directory and printer resources with OS/2 and DOS requesters when acting as a peer.

Windows for Workgroups as a Requester

The following features are not supported by Windows for Workgroups as a requester to a LAN Server domain:

- *Logon assignments*—Any resources assigned to the user are ignored at domain logon.
- *Home directories*—Not supported at domain logon.
- *Network applications*—Applications assigned to the user are ignored at domain logon.
- *Aliases (domain resource definitions)*—Not supported; you connect to resources by server, not by domain.
- The Windows for Workgroups Network DDE and Clipboard is not compatible with the LAN Server version.

You can provide these features by installing DLS with Windows for Workgroups. See the section "Installing the DOS Requester" in this chapter for guidance.

Windows for Workgroups requesters can browse resources on a LAN Server domain if at least one Windows for Workgroups PC has a workgroup name equal to the LAN Server domain name, and is set up for sharing resources.

Windows for Workgroups as a Peer

Windows for Workgroups shares resources much like the DLS Peer Services, or the OS/2 Peer Services with share-mode security. If a resource has a password, you must provide the password in a NET USE command to access the resource from an OS/2 or DOS requester.

OS/2 requesters encounter restrictions when accessing Windows for Workgroups shared directories. Windows for Workgroups does not support long file names or OS/2 extended file attributes, and you cannot use the OS/2 Drives folder or Network folder to browse Windows for Workgroups shared directories. You must use OS/2 and LAN Server commands.

Summary

This chapter showed how to install and configure both DOS and OS/2 requesters. The next chapter will show how to use those requesters—from a user's point of view.

CHAPTER 10

A User's Tour of the Network

That which we persist in doing becomes easier—not that the nature of the task has changed, but our ability to do has increased.

—*Ralph Waldo Emerson*

This chapter will look at the LAN from a user's perspective. It will begin with some general information about LAN Server logons, then take you on a guided tour of the network using the DOS and the OS/2 requesters. These sections will focus mainly on using the new graphical user interfaces to log on, change the password, browse the network, connect to resources, use remote printers, and send messages. Coverage of the command line interface is provided in Chapter 11. The tour will be augmented at regular intervals by a discussion of information related to the functions just explored, and the chapter will conclude with information on useful tools you may want to try after you are comfortable with the basic LAN Server functions: the clipboard and Dynamic Data Exchange (DDE).

Understanding Logon and Logoff

You log on by providing a user ID and password to the requester. The requester supports only one logon at a time—if you want to log on with a different user ID, you have to log off first. However, you can log on at several different requester PCs using the same user ID at the same time. (Note: LAN

Server 3.0 does not allow you to log on from more than one requester using the same user ID. This restriction was removed in LAN Server 4.0.)

LAN Server requesters provide two types of logon: *domain* and *local.* You can change the logon type when you log on, and you can change the default logon type. For DOS, the default is determined by the *lslogon=* parameter in the NETWORK.INI file; for OS/2, the default is determined by character 37 of the *wrkheuristics=* parameter in the IBMLAN.INI file. If you have started the DOS basic redirector, logon is always local.

When you log on to a domain, you receive logon assignments and network applications as specified by your user account definition in the domain, and your clock is synchronized to the domain controller's clock. When you log on locally, no domain is involved, you don't receive any logon assignments or network applications, and your clock doesn't change.

Your logon assignments are shared resources that are automatically connected when you log on. For example, you may have a shared print queue resource automatically assigned as LPT2:, and a shared directory assigned as the Q drive.

Your network applications are shared applications that you can run at your requester. You don't have to install or configure these applications. If you use OS/2, you will see a new Network Applications folder appear on your desktop after you log on. When you log off, the folder is deleted from your desktop. When you run a network application, the resources that it needs are automatically connected. When the application terminates, the connections are removed.

When you log off, all connections to shared resources are removed, and network application assignments are also removed. If you are using OS/2 and running any applications that use network resources, those applications are terminated.

During domain or local logon, the requester attempts to add the user ID as a messaging name. If this works, users can send messages to the user ID. If more than one requester is logged on with the same user ID, only the first to log on can receive messages sent to the user ID.

A Tour of the DOS Requester

The DOS requester was almost completely rewritten in the LAN Server 4.0 release. This information pertains to the 4.0 level of the DOS requester, also known as DOS LAN Services, or DLS. For information on the 3.0 level of the DOS requester, see the *IBM OS/2 LAN Server Version 3.0 DOS LAN Requester User's Guide.*

Logon

To log on under DOS with DLS, type **NET LOGON** at the DOS command prompt. You can specify the user ID and password with NET LOGON, or let DLS prompt you to enter them.

To log on under Windows, follow the configuration instructions described in the following discussion of "Logging On via Windows" to make sure that the logon screen appears when Windows is invoked. Enter your user ID, password, and domain—if different from those displayed—at the logon window.

Discussion—Logging On via DOS

The password you enter with NET LOGON is your *workstation password*, not your domain password. Your workstation password unlocks a password list file, which contains the passwords for the domains you access. No one can read the file without the password. When you log on to a domain for the first time, DLS asks you for the domain password, then stores it in the password list file. Your password list file is called *userid.PWL* (where *userid* is the first eight characters of your user ID). If you log on with a different user ID, another password list file is created for the new user ID. If you change a domain password, it is changed at the domain and in the password list file.

You can change your workstation password any time without changing any domain passwords. If you can delete a password list file, a new one will be created when you next log on. Password list files can also be copied and used on another PC.

If you are only accessing a single domain, you may not want to use password list files at all. Editing the NETWORK.INI file in the DLS directory and changing the *passwordcaching=* parameter from *Yes* to *No* will disable this feature. Once you do this, you log on with your domain password, and no workstation password is required. You can use the /DOMAIN:dom option to log on to a different domain than the one you normally use.

Discussion—Logging On via Windows

There are two ways to use Windows with DLS: You can log on first in DOS, then start Windows; or you can log on in Windows. If you log on in DOS, you can start Windows, use network resources, stop Windows, and continue to use network resources under DOS. The downside is that you will use more DOS low memory by logging on in DOS, to accommodate the basic or full redirector. See Table 4.4 for DOS low memory requirements.

To log on in Windows, install the DLS Windows support, choosing the "virtual redirector" and "start DLS and logon" configuration options. Your AUTOEXEC.BAT file should have a NET START command, which will start the NetBIOS protocol drivers. This NET START command must appear before the WIN command that starts Windows. If the NetBIOS protocol drivers are not started when you start Windows, you will see an error message saying "The FULL redirector was not loaded," followed by the message "Cannot find DLSNET.DLL." If you see these messages, change the AUTOEXEC.BAT file to include a NET START command before the WIN command that starts Windows, and reboot your PC.

You should see a logon window as soon as you start Windows. You can choose local or domain logon, and you can choose the logon domain. As in DOS Logon, the password you enter is your workstation password, not your domain password. This can be manipulated and altered using the same processes described in the previous section.

Browsing and Connecting to Resources

The network can be browsed using commands described in Chapter 11 or the DLS GUI. Start the DLS GUI by entering NETGUI at the DOS command prompt. Or, if using Windows, double-click mouse button 1 on "DOS LAN Services" in the IBM DOS LAN Services group. The GUI within DOS and Windows is nearly identical (Figure 10.1). Take time to familiarize yourself with the options available for each function. Simply choose a command from the menu bar, click on it, and take a look at what information is requested. To get more information on specific parameters, select the online Help. The available functions are:

- Change domain and workstation password, and user comment.
- Log on and log off, and list logged-on users in the domain.

- Configure and run network applications.
- Connect to network drives and printers, and manage logon assignments.
- Share network drives and printers if Peer Services is running.
- Send, receive, view, and log messages.

Take a look at the shared directories available for your use. To do this, select Drives from the menu bar and then select Connections. To the right of the Network path parameter of the Drive Connections screen, you will see a Find button. Select it and you will see a screen that displays a list of available aliases and another list of available peers and servers. To see what resources are on a particular peer or server, select the name of the workstation in the Peer or Server List. Now, let's connect to one of these resources by selecting one from either the Network Name list or the Alias list. The resource is now displayed in the Selected Network Path field. Select OK and you will find the same resource displayed in the Network Path field of the Drive Connections window.

You assign the resource to a drive letter by selecting the down arrow next to the Drive field and selecting a letter from the list of available drives. Leave the password field blank for now. If one is required, you will be notified by an error message when you attempt to connect. You can then come back and supply one. Last, decide whether you want to automatically reconnect to this resource each time you log on. If you do not want to reconnect at logon, select No. Select Connect to connect to the resource you just configured.

Now let's see if we can connect to a network printer. Close the Drive Connections window by selecting Close on the right-hand side and open the Printer Connections window. Do this by selecting Printers from the menu and Connections from the pull-down menu. As you see, the Printer Connections screen is very similar to the Drive Connections screen, except that

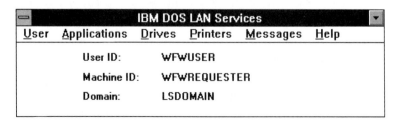

Figure 10.1 **DOS and Windows GUI.**

one of the fields reads Devices rather than Drives. You can look at available shared printers by selecting Find, and browse the print resources either by alias or by a specific peer or server. Select the printer you would like to use, and select OK to return to the Printer Connection window. Select the Down arrow next to Device and select an LPT connection from the ones displayed. Select whether you want to automatically connect to the printer when you log on. Select Connect, then select Close to return to the main DOS LAN Services screen.

Let's see if everything works! Return to a DOS command prompt by selecting the DOS arrow icon, or closing the DOS LAN Services screen. Browse the files and directories on the network drive you just configured by entering **DIR n:**, where *n* is the letter you just configured for your network drive. Print your AUTOEXEC.BAT file on the network printer you just configured by entering **COPY C:\AUTOEXEC.BAT LPTn:**, where *n* is the number you just configured for your network device.

Discussion—Options for Browsing and Connecting

A shortcut for bringing up the Drive Connections Window is to select the Drive Connections icon below the menu bar. It looks like a stack of LP records (for those of us who can remember life before CDs) connected to a floor-standing PC. The LP record stack is actually a fair approximation of the physical disk it is meant to represent.

A shortcut for bringing up the Printers Connections Window is to select the Printers Connections icon below the menu bar. It is located below and to the left of Help, and looks like a printer connected to a floor-standing PC.

If you have Windows installed on your workstation, you can use the Windows file manager and print manager to browse and connect to shared file and print resources on the network.

Sending and Receiving Messages

If your messaging service is enabled, you can send messages to other users using the NET SEND command or the DLS GUI. Messages can be sent to a specific PC using its requester or server name, to a specific user using the user ID, to everyone on a specific domain, or to everyone on the entire network. Be aware that the latter two options, if abused, can be very disruptive to your fellow coworkers. Also, be careful that the workstation or user ID used is correct for the intended receiver. A coworker was once very embarrassed by sending a humorous message to a visiting executive who happened to be using the workstation, and did not take the humor particularly well.

With that said, let's try sending a message to a coworker! If you are not presently at the DLS GUI main screen, start the DLS GUI by entering NET-GUI at the DOS command prompt. Or, if using Windows, double-click mouse button 1 on "DOS LAN Services" in the IBM DOS LAN Services group. Check to see if your coworker is logged on by selecting User from the menu bar and then selecting List logged-on Users from the pull-down menu.

Return to the main DLS screen and select Messages from the menu bar, followed by Send Messages from the pull-down. In the Destination field, select User ID and type the User ID of your coworker. Type your message in the Message field and select Send.

Ask your coworker to send back a message to you. The message from your coworker may pop up on your screen. If it does not, view your message log by selecting Messages from the menu bar of the main DLS screen and then selecting View Message Log. To delete the messages after you have read them select Clear Log. Select Cancel to return to the main DLS screen.

Discussion—More about Sending and Receiving Messages

A shortcut for viewing logged-on users from the DLS GUI main screen is to select the icon below the menu bar, which looks like two people with a question mark. A shortcut for sending messages is to select the icon below the menu bar, which has an envelope with two PCs in the background. The Find button located in the Send Messages screen is another way to display the logged-on users.

If you see the error message "Your user ID was not added as a message name" or "Your user ID cannot receive messages," it means either your messaging service is not enabled or someone has logged on to another PC with your user ID. Only the first user to log on with a specific user ID will receive messages addressed to it.

Messages are logged to the file MESSAGE.LOG in the DLS directory and can also be displayed on your screen. To see messages displayed, start the NETPOPUP service on DOS, and start the WinPopUp application under Windows. With DLS, the Messenger service requires that you start the Full or Basic redirector, not the Virtual redirector.

End of DOS Requester Tour–Logging Off

Log off by selecting User from the menu bar of the DLS GUI main screen, and Log Off from the pull-down menu. A window will be displayed confirming when you have successfully logged off the network.

Congratulations! You have just completed your first successful tour of the network using the DOS Requester! For an extended stay, take a look at the information provided in the *DOS LAN Services and Window's User's Guide*. Soon you'll be whizzing around like a native!

A Tour of the OS/2 Requester

The graphical user interface provided by OS/2 and Warp adds additional flexibility and power in browsing, connecting, and managing LAN Server resources. One of the major differences you will notice between the OS/2 and DOS Requesters is that OS/2 icons can be used directly to connect to resources. The icons can also be dragged and dropped onto other icons to manipulate the resources they represent. For example, an icon representing a file can be dragged and dropped onto another icon representing a network printer to print the file. If you are a new user of OS/2 or Warp, spend a few minutes taking the OS/2 online tutorial before proceeding with the tour of the OS/2 requester.

Logon

Type **LOGON** at an OS/2 command line to log on with the OS/2 requester. Unless you have peer services installed on your workstation, you should see a Domain Logon screen. If so, type your User ID and password in the fields provided. Type the name of your domain if it is different from the one displayed.

If peer services is installed on your workstation, you may get a Local Logon screen. If this happens, select Cancel to cancel the local logon, and log on to the domain by typing **LOGON /V:DOMAIN /D:[domain]**, where [domain] is your domain name. A Domain Logon screen should appear, displaying the name of the domain you entered with the /D option. Type your User ID and password in the fields provided and press the Enter key.

Discussion—More about Logging On with OS/2

You can also use the OS/2 Workplace Shell to log on. If you open the the LAN Server Resource Browser inside the Network folder on the OS/2 desktop without having logged on, OS/2 will prompt you to log on through the Network folder. Only domain logon is supported. You can log on to the default domain, or type a different domain.

If you shut down OS/2 while you are logged on and are connected to resources, OS/2 will display this logon window when you restart OS/2. When you log on, your network connections will be reestablished. To stop OS/2 from restarting your network connections, edit the CONFIG.SYS file and remove the CONNECTIONS parameter from the SET AUTOSTART= line.

 With OS/2, if you use more than one user ID, always log off before you log on again. Multiple logons are ignored by the OS/2 requester! For example, if you log on as PAT, then log on as CHARLIE without first logging off, you are still considered to be logged on as PAT when you access shared LAN Server resources. To see if you have multiple logons, use the command LOGOFF /L.

You will see a window displaying all current logons. If there is more than one, log off all of them, then log on as normal. Likewise, if you are sharing workstations with other users, be sure to log off before leaving the workstation, as the next user could end up accessing all of your resources even after logging on with a separate user ID!

The OS/2 requester does not use a password list file, as the DOS requester does. You can change your password for the logon domain through the User Accounts Management program, which can be found inside the UPM Services folder on your desktop. Simply start User Accounts Management, click on Action—Change Password, and fill in the window.

 If you want to maintain the same user ID and password on more than one domain, the NEWPW productivity aid can be of assistance. See Chapter 6 for details on installing productivity aids and Chapter 12 for general information on NEWPW. Start the NEWPW program from the Productivity Aids folder that can be found inside the IBM LAN Services folder. You will see a window showing a list of domains, and fields to enter your new and old passwords. You can change the domain list, check your password age on the domains in the list, or change your password on the domains in the list. NEWPW will try to change the password on each selected domain, and report back success or failure on each.

If you want to maintain a user ID and password across LAN Server domains and other IBM products, such as mainframe systems or IBM DB2/2 servers, look into the Network Signon Coordinator productivity aid.

Browsing and Connecting to Resources

Use the OS/2 Network Folder to browse the network and find available servers and domains. Open the Network folder and you'll see the LAN Server Resource Browser. (If you have the NetWare requester from Warp Connect installed, you'll also see a folder for NetWare servers.) Open the LAN Server Resource Browser and you will see something like what is shown in Figure 10.2. You can see that the Resource Browser folder has a number of server objects within it, represented by icons that look like PCs in floor-standing cases. Some of these objects represent domains, some represent servers within domains, and some represent peers. The titles of the domain objects start with "Aliases for domain. . . ."

Open a server or domain object and you'll see resource objects. Two types of resource objects are contained inside the server or domain folder: *network directories* and *network printers*. These are represented by icons that look like normal folders and printers with little server PCs next to them. Open a few of the network directories by pointing at them and double-clicking mouse button 1. What do you see?

Locate the icon for a network printer you would like to use, and drag it to your desktop. This is done by using the mouse to point to the print icon. Pick up the icon by holding down mouse button 2, drag the icon to a clear area of

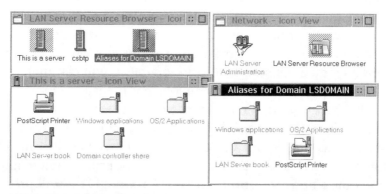

Figure 10.2 **LAN Server resource browser**

your OS/2 desktop, and drop it by releasing the mouse button. You have just placed the network printer on your desktop.

You may see a prompt from OS/2 to install the proper OS/2 and Windows printer drivers. The drivers to support the network printer must be installed on your workstation before you will be able to correctly print a file. Insert the requested diskettes if you want to install the print drivers now. Otherwise, select cancel to get out of the printer installation screen.

If you have the appropriate print drivers installed and were able to successfully drag the network printer, assign a port to the network printer. Click mouse button 2 on the network printer icon and select "Assign port" from the printer object's pop-up menu. You are now ready to print a file! Open your OS/2 drives folder, select your C drive and locate the icon for your CONFIG.SYS file. Drag and drop the CONFIG.SYS icon onto the network printer. You will see a window asking if your file is plain text or printer-specific. Select plain text. Double-click mouse button 1 on the network printer icon, and you should see your print job within the queue. Close the network printer window by double-clicking mouse button 1 on the little box at the top left corner of the window.

Discussion—Options for Browsing and Connecting

Network directories act much like normal directories on your desktop—you can open them to view the files and directories inside, and move or copy files and directories between network directories and ordinary directories. You can also select "Access Another" from a network directory's pop-up menu to create a new network directory object. And, you can select "Assign drive" from the pop-up menu to assign a local drive letter to the network directory object. You can create a shadow of a network directory on your desktop by simply dragging it there.

Network printers also act much like normal desktop printers. You can open them to view and manage the print jobs on the server's print queue. If you are an administrator or print operator, you can manage all print jobs. If you are a user, you can view all jobs but manage only your own.

It's best to drag the network printer to your desktop if you are going to use it often. The network printer object will move, rather than creating a shadow as a network directory does. However, if you refresh the server folder, or close and reopen it, the network printer will reappear there. When you drag a network printer to your desktop, OS/2 will prompt you to install the proper OS/2 and Windows printer drivers if they are not already installed. You can also use a network printer template from OS/2's Templates folder to create a network printer object if you wish.

A printer port can be assigned to the network printer with the "Assign port" command from the printer object's pop-up menu. Any OS/2 application that writes to an LPT port will be able to access the network print queue. DOS and Windows applications running under OS/2 can use the same LPT port.

You can install and use WINOS2 printers for remote print queues. To do this, assign an LPT port under OS/2, as described previously. Then, use the WINOS2 Control Panel to install a Windows printer, making sure that you use the right Windows printer driver. Finally, connect the Windows printer to LPTn.OS2, where *LPTn* is the LPT port that you assigned under OS/2. Select to not use the Windows print manager—network printing will work best that way. If you need more than the three available LPTn.OS2 ports, you can add more by editing the WINDOWS.INI file in the Windows directory.

Creating a shadow of a server object on your desktop is helpful when you want to access a server or domain quickly without going through the network folder. Simply open the network folder and drag the server icon onto an open space on your OS/2 desktop; a shadow will be created automatically.

You can delete a server object by selecting "Delete" from its pop-up menu. If you find that a server object is out of date or incorrect, a good way to fix it is to delete it, then select "Refresh now" from the Resource Browser folder's pop-up menu. The server object will be re-created.

If the LAN Server Resource Browser folder gets out of sync, as can occasionally happen, you can delete the entire folder. Shut down your requester PC and reboot, open the Network folder again, and you should see a newly created LAN Server Resource Browser folder. If you accidentally or purposely delete the Network Folder, it will also reappear on reboot.

Shared remote serial devices can be used only with OS/2 requesters, and can be used only by OS/2 applications—not DOS or Windows applications. You must use the OS/2 command line interface to browse and connect to shared serial devices. See Chapter 11 for more information.

Sending and Receiving Messages

If your messaging service is enabled, you can send messages to other users using the NET SEND command or the Network Messaging application within the LAN Services folder located on the OS/2 desktop. Messages can be sent to a specific PC using its requester or server name, to a specific user using the user ID, to everyone on a specific domain, or to everyone on the entire network. Be aware that the latter two options, if abused, can be very disruptive to your fellow coworkers. Also, be careful that the workstation or user ID used is correct for the intended receiver.

With that said, let's try sending a message to a coworker! Open the Network Messaging icon within the LAN Services folder. It looks like an envelope with two PCs in the background. In the Destination field, select User ID and type the User ID of your coworker. Type your message in the Message field and select Send.

Ask your coworker to send a message back to you. The message from your coworker may pop up on your screen. If it does not, view your message log by opening the OS/2 Drives folder. Navigate the C drive to find the MES-SAGE.LOG file in the \IBMLAN\LOGS subdirectory. Double-click mouse button 1 on the file object, and you will see your messages displayed within the OS/2 Editor. When you are through viewing your messages, return to the desktop by closing the OS/2 Editor and the Drive objects.

Discussion—More about Sending and Receiving Messages

Messages are normally logged to the file MESSAGE.LOG in the \IBMLAN\ LOGS directory for OS/2. Messages can also pop up on your screen. To see messages pop up, start the Network Messaging application, and configure it for message pop-ups.

It is important to enable messaging and message pop-ups on the administrator's workstation, because important alerts from the servers are sent to administrators as messages. (See Chapter 8 for information on configuring and enabling alerts). Messages are also used by the print server to inform users when the job is complete, or if an error has occurred on the print job.

If you log on to more than one workstation, only the first workstation will receive the message addressed to your user ID. If the messenger service is running when you log on, and you or someone else has already logged on with your user ID, you will see the error message "Your user ID was not added as a message name" or "Your user ID cannot receive messages."

End of OS/2 Requester Tour—Logging Off

Log off by selecting the Logoff Icon from the LAN Services folder and selecting Logoff All. A window will be displayed, confirming when you have successfully logged off the network.

Congratulations! You have just completed your first successful tour of the network using the OS/2 Requester! For an extended stay, take a look at the information provided in the *OS/2 LAN Requester User's Guide*. The next section provides information on a fun and convenient way to share data and applications with coworkers over the network.

Sharing Clipboard and DDE Information

LAN Server 4.0 added an exciting feature for collaboration between users— Network Clipboard and DDE (Dynamic Data Exchange). This feature enables you to copy information on your clipboard from one user to another on the LAN, and to share information between applications using DDE. For example, if you are using a presentation package on Windows, and your coworker is using a compatible package on OS/2, you can copy a drawing to your Windows clipboard, and your coworker can copy it to his or her clipboard across the LAN, then paste it into a document he or she is creating. If the applications are DDE-enabled, he or she can even set up a DDE link between the applications across the LAN so that when you change the drawing, the changes are incorporated into the document being created.

Network DDE and Clipboard is provided for both OS/2 and Windows requesters, and allows sharing between OS/2 and Windows applications across the LAN. Windows applications running under OS/2 can also use Network DDE and clipboard—make sure that the WINOS2 clipboard is set for public sharing. You can even cut and paste from DOS applications running in a DOS window under OS/2.

To use the Network Clipboard, both users must start up the Network Clipboard and DDE application. This makes their clipboards available to any user on the LAN for copying. One user simply clicks "Copy clipboard," types in the name of another user's requester PC, and clicks "Copy." The clipboard contents are copied across the LAN.

If you don't want to share your clipboard for other users, you can share *clippings,* which are copies of the clipboard that you save on your requester. Each clipping has a name. You can choose to share only your clippings by clicking "Control Access" and modifying the access selections. Users can copy any of your named clippings.

To establish a DDE link, copy information to the clipboard from a DDE-enabled application, then copy the clipboard to another requester across the LAN. Paste-link the information into another DDE-enabled application, just as you would do between two applications running on the same PC. If the information is changed at the source, these changes will appear where the linked copy has been pasted.

Summary

This Chapter introduced the basic functions of LAN Server by taking you on a guided tour of the network using the graphical user interface of the DOS and OS/2 requesters. Chapter 11 will look at how these and other tasks are accomplished using the DOS and OS/2 command line interfaces.

CHAPTER 11

LAN Server Commands

> *The cosmos itself is an integral whole, a web of interrelated things and events. Within this web of relationships and change, any entity can be defined only by its function, and has significance only as a part of the whole pattern.*

—*Ted J. Kaptchuk,* The Web That Has No Weaver

Although graphical user interfaces are easy to use, once you become familiar with a task, it's often easier to work with a command. And, you can put commands into command files to automate repetitive tasks. (There's an example showing use of a command file at the end of this chapter.)

LAN Server offers a large set of commands for using and administering the network. These commands are completely documented in the LAN Server book *Commands and Utilities*, which is available online. Also, each NET command has corresponding online Help available.

Trying to find the right command and parameters for a given task is often difficult, since there are so many and their names don't always describe what they do very well. To help you to find the right command to use, lots of short examples will be provided, rather than just describing the parameters and options of each command. A breakdown by task and role will also be provided. There are three main categories: general user commands, commands to manage servers and peers, and commands to manage domains. Within each category, there are several functional areas with several examples for each.

You should use this chapter by looking up the category and item you are interested in, checking out the applicable commands and the examples, then trying them out for yourself. If you can't make them work for you, or you need more information, you can use the online Help to get an exact description of the command's parameters and options.

First, you will be given some general information on commands and how to use them.

Getting Help on Commands

Here's a guide to getting on-screen help for the NET commands and other topics. If you are an OS/2 user, you can also view the online book *Command Reference*, which has a detailed description of DOS and OS/2 LAN Server commands.

Information Desired	OS/2 Command	DOS Command
General Help	NET HELP	NET HELP HELP
List of commands and topics for which Help is available	NET HELP	NET HELP
Help on a specific command or topic	NET HELP command	NET HELP command
Help on options for a specific command	NET HELP command /O	NET HELP command
Help on an error message NET*xxxx*	HELP NET*xxxx*	NET HELP *xxxx*
Help on other error message *abcxxxx*	HELP *abcxxxx*	N/A

If the information scrolls before you can read it, use the Pause key or add |MORE to the end of the command. For example:

NET HELP SHARE|MORE

will display the Help for the NET SHARE command, and pause at the end of each screen until you press a key.

Hints and Tips about Using Commands

If you need to use special characters or blanks within a parameter, you can enclose the parameter in double quotes ("). For example, if someone has defined a server or resource with embedded blanks in the name (as you can do easily with Windows for Workgroups), you can NET USE a resource on the server like this:

```
NET USE x: "\\WFW SERVER\A SHARED DISK"
```

Generally, you can abbreviate names of options and parameters.

Some commands ask for a confirmation before proceeding. You can usually specify a /Y option to bypass the confirmation. This is useful when you are putting commands in a command file.

Remote Administration Using Commands

Most LAN administrators don't use the server PC's keyboard, screen, and mouse to administer the server PC. Instead, they use their own requester PC. Almost every aspect of LAN Server administration can be accomplished from a requester. Simply log on to the domain you want to administer, with a user account with Administrative privilege. Then use the NET ADMIN command to direct commands to a server. The NET ADMIN command is available from OS/2 requesters and DOS DLS requesters.

If the command deals with domain-wide information—such as NET USER, NET GROUP, or NET ALIAS—direct the command to the server that is the domain controller. If the command deals with server-specific information—such as NET ACCESS or NET SHARE—direct the command to the server that has that information.

You can also use NET ADMIN to remotely administer OS/2 requesters that are running Peer Services, and PCs running OS/2 Warp Connect with OS/2 Peer. You must be logged on with a user ID and password that is defined with Administrative privilege in the peer's local user accounts database.

For example:

```
NET ADMIN \\LSSERVER /C NET USER
```

will issue the NET USER command at the domain controller called *LSSERVER*, and return the output to your workstation. And,

NET ADMIN \\LSABC /C NET SHARE

will issue the NET SHARE command at the server or peer *LSABC*, and route the output back to your requester.

Note that NET ADMIN does not work with commands that request additional information or confirmation. Most commands that request additional information also have a way to supply that information in options and parameters. For example, the NET STOP command has a /Y parameter that will bypass the normal request for confirmation. However, you must put the command in quotes, like this:

NET ADMIN \\LSABC /C "NET STOP SERVER /Y"

because if you don't, the /Y option will be processed by NET ADMIN rather than sent to the server as part of the NET STOP command.

You can run commands other than NET using NET ADMIN. For example, the following is perfectly legal:

NET ADMIN \\LSSERVER /C DATE 5-24-1995

will issue the OS/2 command *DATE 5-24-1995* at the server *LSSERVER*, thereby resetting its date. However, the command environment set up by NET ADMIN has no PATH variable set. This means that only commands in the \IBMLAN\NETPROG directory, or OS/2 internal commands, will be executed unless you provide an explicit path like this:

NET ADMIN \\LSSERVER /C \OS2\SYSLEVEL

to execute the OS/2 SYSLEVEL command at the server.

You can issue multiple commands to a remote server or peer without invoking NET ADMIN every time. For example:

NET ADMIN \\LSSERVER /C

will start a command session with the remote server *LSSERVER*. Any commands you type are executed at the server, and you will see the results. Use the EXIT command to stop the command session. An example of a remote command session is given in Table 11.1.

Table 11.1 **NET ADMIN with a Remote Command Session**

Your input is italicized. Note that the two NET USER commands are executed at the remote server LSSERVER.

```
[C:\]net admin \\lsserver /c
Type EXIT or press Ctrl+Z to exit.


[\\lsserver] net user


User accounts for \\LSSERVER
-----------------------------------------------------------------
BROWNCS  GUEST LSADMIN
LSSERVER
The command completed successfully.
[\\lsserver] net user lsadmin /priv:admin
The command completed successfully.
[\\lsserver] exit


[C:\]
```

Commands for General Users

Logon/Logoff (OS/2)

LOGON	Displays a window for you to log on.
LOGON uid	Attempts to logon as *uid* with no password, to your default domain. If unsuccessful, displays logon window.
LOGON uid /P:pw	Attempts to logon as *uid* with password *pw*, to your default domain. If unsuccessful, displays logon window.
LOGON uid /P:pw /V:N	Logs you on locally as *uid*, password *pw*. No validation is done.

LOGON uid /P:pw /D:dom   Attempts to logon as *uid* with password *pw* to domain *dom*. If unsuccessful, displays logon window.

LOGON uid /P:pw /R   Attempts to logon as *uid*, password *pw*, to your default domain. If unsuccessful, displays error message—does not display logon window.

LOGOFF   Logs you off.

Logon/Logoff (DOS)

NET LOGON   Prompts you for user ID and password, logs you on to your default domain.

NET LOGON uid pw   Logs on to your default domain as *uid* with password *pw*.

NET LOGON /DOM:dom   Prompts you for user ID and password; logs you on to domain *dom*.

NET LOGOFF   Logs you off.

Changing Your Password

NET PASSWORD   (OS/2) Prompts you for domain, user ID, old password, new password. Changes password.

NET PASSWORD /D:dom   (DOS) Prompts you for user ID, old password, new password. Changes password in domain *dom*.

NET PASSWORD uid opw npw   Changes the password for *uid* in your logon domain from *opw* to *npw*.

NET PASSWORD /D:dom uid opw npw   Changes the password for *uid* in domain *dom* from *opw* to *npw*.

NET PASSWORD \\srv uid opw npw   Changes the password for *uid* on server/peer *srv* from *opw* to *npw*.

Network Browsing

NET VIEW   Lists servers in your logon domain. (OS/2) also lists servers in your default domain and your other domains.

NET CONFIG REQ /OTH:dom1,dom2	(OS/2) temporarily adds up to four other domains to browse or administer. Set permanently with *othdomains=* in IBMLAN.INI.
NET VIEW \\srv	Lists shared resources on server/peer *srv*, which can be in any domain.
NET ALIAS	Lists shared resource definitions in your logon domain.
NET ALIAS /DOM:dom	Lists shared resource definitions in domain *dom*.
NET ALIAS ali	Displays details about the shared resource definition *ali* in your logon domain.
NET ALIAS ali /DOMAIN:dom	Displays details about the shared resource definition *ali* in domain *dom*.
NET APP	(OS/2) Lists public application definitions in your logon domain.
NET APP /DOMAIN:dom	(OS/2) Lists public application definitions in domain *dom*.
NET APP apl	(OS/2) Displays details about the public application definition *apl* in your logon domain.
NET APP apl /DOMAIN:dom	(OS/2) Displays details about the public application definition *apl* in domain *dom*.
NET WHO	Lists requesters logged on to or using resources in your logon domain.
NET WHO /D:dom	Lists requesters logged on to or using resources in domain *dom*.
NET WHO usr	Displays details about logged-on user *usr*.
NET WHO \\srv	Lists requesters using resources on server/peer *srv*, which can be in any domain.

Logs and Status

NET ERROR	(OS/2) Displays the error log, oldest error first.
NET ERROR /R	(OS/2) Displays the error log, newest error first.
NET ERROR /R /C:n	(OS/2) Displays the *n* most recent entries in the error log.

NET ERROR /D	(OS/2) Clears the error log.
NET CONFIG REQ	(OS/2) Displays lots of information about the requester, including its name, the logged-on user name, and the logon and other domains.
NET CONFIG	(DOS) Displays information about the requester, including its name, the logged-on user name, and the logon domain.
NET STATS REQ	(OS/2) Displays statistics on the requester.
NET STATS REQ /C	(OS/2) Clears requester statistics.

Shared Directories

DIR \\srv\res\path	(OS/2) Lists the subdirectory *path* of directory resource *res* at server/peer *srv*. You can use this style in most OS/2 commands and applications, rather than a redirected drive letter.
DIR \\srv\C$\IBMLAN	(OS/2) Lists the IBMLAN directory on the C drive of the server/peer *srv*. All the server's or peer's drives are shared like this. Access control prevents unauthorized reading or writing of files.
NET USE	Lists the redirected drives in effect, and also the connections that have no drive redirections associated with them.
NET USE d:	Displays details on the connection associated with redirected drive *d:*.
NET USE d: ali	Redirects the drive *d:* to the directory resource *ali* in the logon domain.
NET USE d: ali /DOMAIN: dom	(OS/2) Redirects the drive *d:* to the directory resource *ali* in the domain *dom*.
NET USE d: \\srv\res	Redirects the drive *d:* to the directory resource *res* at server/peer *srv*.
NET USE d: \\srv\res password	Redirects the drive *d:* to the directory resource *res* at the server/peer *srv*. Provides *password* to the server for validation.
NET USE d: /DEL	Removes the redirection of drive *d:*.

Shared Print Queues

COPY x.x \\srv\res	(OS/2) Copies the file *x.x* to the print queue resource *res* at serve/peer *srv*. The file must be in a format supported by the destination printer.
NET USE	Lists the redirected printer ports and the queues they are connected to.
NET USE lpt3:	Displays details about the print queue connected to by *lpt3:*.
NET USE lpt3: res	Redirects printer port *lpt3:* to the print queue resource *res* on the logon domain.
NET USE lpt3: res /DOMAIN:dom	(OS/2) Redirects printer port *lpt3:* to the print queue resource *res* on the domain *dom*.
NET USE lpt3: \\srv\res	Redirects printer port *lpt3:* to the print queue resource *res* on serve/peer *srv*.
NET USE lpt3: \\srv\res password	Redirects printer port *lpt3:* to the print queue resource *res* on server/peer *srv*. Provides *password* to the server for validation.
NET USE lpt3: /D	Removes the redirection of printer port *lpt3:*.
NET PRINT \\srv	Lists the print queues and waiting users at server/peer *srv*.
NET PRINT \\srv\res	Lists the print jobs for print queue *res* at server/peer *srv*.
NET PRINT lpt3:	Lists the print jobs for the print queue to which *lpt3:* is redirected.
NET PRINT \\srv 12 /DEL	Deletes print job number *12* from the server/peer *srv*. Each print job on a server has a unique job number. You can delete only your own print jobs.
NET PRINT \\srv 12 /HOL	Holds print job number *12* at the server/peer *srv*. The job won't print until it is released. You can hold only your own print jobs.
NET PRINT \\srv 12 /REL	Releases print job number *12* at the server/peer *srv*. You can release only your own print jobs.
NET PRINT lpt3: 12 /DEL	Deletes print job number *12* from the print queue to which *lpt3:* is redirected. You can delete only your own print jobs.

Shared Serial Devices (OS/2 Requesters Only)

COPY x.x \\srv\res	(OS/2) Copies the file *x.x* to the serial device resource *res* at server/peer *srv*. The file must be in a format supported by the serial device.
NET USE	Lists the redirected serial ports and the queues they are connected to.
NET USE com3:	Displays details about the serial device queue connected to by *com3:*.
NET USE com3: res	Redirects serial port *com3:* to the serial device queue resource *res* on the logon domain.
NET USE com3: res /DOMAIN:dom	Redirects serial port *com3:* to the serial device queue resource *res* on the domain *dom*.
NET USE com3: \\srv\res	Redirects serial port *com3:* to the serial device queue resource *res* on the server/peer *srv*.
NET USE com3: \\srv\res password	Redirects serial port *com3:* to the serial device queue resource *res* on the server/peer *srv*. Provides *password* to the server for validation.
NET USE com3: /D	Removes the redirection of *com3:*.
NET COMM \\srv	Lists the serial device queues and waiting users at server/peer *srv*.
NET COMM \\srv\res	Lists the waiting users for serial device queue *res* at server/peer *srv*.
NET COMM com3:	Lists the waiting users for the serial device queue to which *com3:* is redirected.
NET COMM \\srv\res /PURGE	Removes you from the list of waiting users for the serial device queue *res* at server/peer *srv*.
NET COMM com3: /PURGE	Removes you from the list of waiting users for the serial device queue to which *com3:* is redirected.

Time

NET TIME	Displays the time in your logon domain (at the domain controller).
NET TIME /SET	Sets the requester's clock to the time in your logon domain, after asking for confirmation.
NET TIME /YES	Sets the requester's clock to the time in your logon domain.

NET TIME /DOMAIN:dom	Displays the time in domain *dom*.
NET TIME \\srv	Displays the time on server/peer *srv*.
NET TIME \\srv /SET	Sets the requester's clock to the time on server *srv*, after asking for confirmation.

Messaging

NET START MESSENGER	Starts the Messenger service on your requester. Enables reception of messages sent to your logon user ID or your requester name.
NET START NETPOPUP	(DOS) Starts the NetPopUp service on your DOS requester. Messages you receive will pop up on your screen.
NETMSG	(OS/2) Starts the Network Messaging GUI, so you can see messages as they are received, and send messages.
NET SEND uid Hello.	Sends message *Hello.* to user *uid*.
NET SEND uid <hello.txt	Sends the contents of the file *hello.txt* to *uid* as a message.
NET SEND req Hello.	Sends message *Hello.* to requester *req*.
NET SEND /D Hello.	Sends message *Hello.* to all users in your default domain.
NET SEND /D:dom Hello.	Sends message *Hello.* to all users in domain *dom*.
NET SEND /BROAD Hello.	Sends message *Hello.* to all PCs on your LAN.

Commands to Manage Servers and OS/2 Peers

Logs and Status

NET START	Lists the services that have been started.
NET START PEER	(Peer only) Starts the peer service—allows requesters and peers to access resources.
NET START SERVER	(Server only) Starts the server service—allows requesters to access resources.
NET STOP SERVER	(Server only) Stops the server service.

NET STOP NETLOGON	(Server only) Stops the netlogon service—if executed on the domain controller and its backups, stops any new logons to the domain.
NET ERROR	Displays the error log, oldest error first.
NET ERROR /R	Displays the error log, newest error first.
NET ERROR /R /C:n	Displays the *n* most recent entries in the error log.
NET ERROR /D	Clears the error log.
NET AUDIT	Displays the audit log, oldest entry first.
NET AUDIT /R	Displays the audit log, newest entry first.
NET AUDIT /R /C:n	Displays the *n* most recent entries in the audit log.
NET AUDIT /D	Clears the audit log.
NET CONFIG SRV	Displays lots of information about the server.
NET STATUS	Displays combination of NET CONFIG SRV and NET SHARE.
NET STATS SRV	Displays statistics on the server.
NET STATS SRV /C	Clears server statistics.
CACHE386 /S:D	(LAN Server Advanced only) Displays HPFS386 cache statistics— dynamically updated.
CACHE386 /S:C	(LAN Server Advanced only) Clears HPFS386 cache statistics.
CACHE386 /O	(LAN Server Advanced only) Displays HPFS386 cache size and options set for all drives.

Shared Resources and Sessions (General)

These commands should be issued at the server for which they are intended. You can use NET ADMIN to issue them remotely. The exception is NET SESS with the /PEER option, which will execute remotely at the named server.

NET SHARE	Lists all shared resources.
NET SHARE res	Displays details of shared resource *res*.
NET SHARE res /D	Deletes (unshares) shared resource *res*.
NET SESS	Lists all active sessions by requester and user ID.

NET SESS /D	Deletes all active sessions.
NET SESS /D /Y	Deletes all active sessions without asking for confirmation.
NET SESS \\req	Displays details of the session with requester *req*.
NET SESS \\req /D	Deletes the session with requester *req*.
NET SESS \\srv /PEER	List all active sessions on server/peer *srv*.

Shared Files and Directories

NET SHARE res=x:\path	Shares the directory *x:path* as resource *res*. No resource definition is created and no access control profile is set up. This share goes away when the server is restarted.
NET FILE	Lists all server files currently open by requesters.
NET FILE fid	Displays details about the open file with file ID *fid*. The file ID can be seen in the NET FILE listing.
NET FILE fid /CLOSE	Forces closing of the open file with file ID *fid*.

Shared Print Queues

NET SHARE prtq /PRINT	Shares a print queue *prtq*. No resource definition is created. This share goes away when the server is restarted.
NET PRINT	Lists the print queues currently defined at your server.
NET PRINT res	Displays details about the print queue *res*.
NET PRINT res /PURGE	Removes all print jobs from the print queue *res*.
NET PRINT res /HOLD	Holds the print queue *res*—no jobs will be printed.
NET PRINT res /REL	Releases the print queue *res*—jobs can be printed again.
NET PRINT j /DEL	Deletes print job *j*. You can see *j* in the NET PRINT listing.
NET PRINT j /HOLD	Holds print job *j*. It will not print until released.

| NET PRINT j /REL | Releases print job *j*. |
| NET PRINT j /FIRST | Makes print job *j* first in the queue for printing next. |

Shared Serial Device Queues

NET SHARE res=com1:,com2: /COMM	Shares a pool of serial devices, *com1:* and *com2:*, as serial device queue resource *res*. No resource definition is created. This share goes away when the server is restarted.
NET COMM	Lists the serial device queues currently defined at your server.
NET COMM res	Displays details about the serial device queue *res*.
NET COMM res /PURGE	Removes all users waiting in the serial device queue *res*.
NET DEVICE com1:	Displays the status of serial device *com1:*.
NET DEVICE com1: /DEL	Removes the current user of serial device *com1:* and makes it available for assignment again.

Access Control

These commands should be issued at the server or peer where the resource exists, except as noted.

NET ACCESS	Lists all access control profiles to all resources on the server. Warning: Can take a long time if there are many access control profiles.
NET ACCESS ali	Displays the access control profile for shared directory resource definition *ali* in the logon domain. Can be issued from a requester.
NET ACCESS ali /TREE	Lists the access control profiles for the shared directory resource *ali*, and all its subdirectories.
NET ACCESS x:\path	Displays the access control profile for the directory *x:path*. *x:* can be a local drive on the server where NET ACCESS is issued, or it can be a redirected drive if NET ACCESS is issued from a requester.

NET ACCESS \PRINT\prtq	Displays the access control profile for the shared print queue *prtq*.
NET ACCESS \PRINT /TREE	Lists all access profiles for the shared print queues.
NET ACCESS \COMM\comq	Displays access control profile for the shared serial device queue *comq*.
NET ACCESS \PIPE\path	Displays access control profile for the named pipe resource *path*.

In the following NET ACCESS examples, *na* can take any of the forms in the preceding examples. It can be a shared directory resource definition, a directory path, a print queue, a serial device queue, or a pipe.

NET ACCESS na /ADD user:Y	Creates an access control profile for *na*, with one entry giving *user* the RWCDA permissions. (Y is shorthand for RWCDA.)
NET ACCESS na /DEL	Deletes the access control profile for *na*.
NET ACCESS na /GRANT USERS:r GUESTS:r	Adds two entries to the access control profile for *na*, giving the special groups USERS and GUESTS the *r* permission for *na*.
NET ACCESS na /REVOKE GUESTS	Removes the entry for the special group GUESTS from the access control profile for *na*.
NET ACCESS na /CHANGE user:r	In the access control profile for *na*, changes the entry for *user* to *r* permissions.
NET ACCESS na /APPLY	Applies the access control profile for *na* to all subdirectories of *na*.
NET ACCESS na /FAIL:ALL	Audits all failed attempts to access the resource *na*.
NET ACCESS na /FAIL:ALL /SUCC:ALL	Audits all attempts to access the resource *na*, whether successful or not.
NET ACCESS na /TRAIL:N	Audits nothing for resource *na*.

Commands to Administer Domains

The DSPDOMDF command will display all the user accounts, groups, aliases, and applications defined in a domain.

All of the domain administration commands should be executed at the domain controller.

Domain Policy Settings

NET ACCOUNTS	Displays the domain policy settings.
NET ACCOUNTS /ROLE:STANDALONE	Changes the role of the server to stand-alone, effectively removing it from the domain.
NET ACCOUNTS /ROLE:MEMBER	Changes the role of the server to an additional (member) server.
NET ACCOUNTS /MAXPWAGE:30 /MINPWAGE:6 /UNIQUEPW:5 /MINPWLEN:6	Sets domain password policies: Passwords expire every 30 days, can be changed only once every 6 days, cannot reuse any of the last 5 passwords, and must be at least 6 characters long.
NET ACCOUNTS /FORCELOGOFF:15	Sets the domain forced logoff policy when accounts expire or logon hours are past. Users will be given 15 minutes of grace.

User Accounts

NET USER	Lists all user accounts.
NET USER uid	Displays details about user account *uid*.
NET USER uid /DEL	Deletes user account *uid*.
NET USER uid pw	Resets user account *uid*'s password to *pw*.
NET USER uid *	Resets user account *uid*'s password—you type it after the command and it is not displayed.
NET USER uid pw /ADD	Creates a new user account *uid* with password *pw* and all defaults. You can specify any of the following options as well.
NET USER uid /PRIV:ADMIN /OPER:ACC,PRINT	Changes user account *uid* to have administrative privilege and accounts and print special privileges.
NET USER uid /PASSWORDCHG:YES /PASSWORDREQ:YES /PASSWORDEXP:YES	Changes user account *uid* to allow the user to change passwords, to require the user to have a password and follow domain password policies, and to set the password expired immediately.

NET USER uid /ACTIVE:YES /EXPIRES:12-31-95 /TIMES:M–F,8AM–5PM /WORKSTA:reqa;reqb	Changes user account *uid* to be active (enabled), to expire on 12/31/95, to be valid only from 8 A.M. to 5 P.M. Monday through Friday, and to be valid only when used from requesters *reqa* and *reqb*.
NET USER uid /ASSIGN x:ali,PUBLIC:apl	Assigns the resource *ali* to drive *x:*, and assigns public application *apl*, to the user account *uid*. Assignments take effect at the next logon.
NET USER uid /UNASSIGN x:ali, PUBLIC:ALL	Removes the assignments of the *ali* resource, and all public applications, from the user account *uid*.

Groups

NET GROUP	Lists all the groups.
NET GROUP grp	Lists the members of group *grp*.
NET GROUP grp /ADD	Creates a new group *grp*.
NET GROUP grp /DEL	Removes all the user accounts, and deletes the group *grp*.
NET GROUP grp uida uidb /ADD	Adds the user accounts *uida* and *uidb* to the group *grp*.
NET GROUP grp uida uidb /DEL	Removes the user accounts *uida* and *uidb* from the group *grp*.

Resource Definitions (Aliases) and Network Applications

NET ALIAS	Lists the aliases at your logon domain.
NET ALIAS /DOM:dom	Lists the aliases at domain *dom*.
NET ALIAS ali	Displays details about alias *ali* in your logon domain.
NET ALIAS ali /DOM:dom /DEL	Deletes alias *ali* from domain *dom*.
NET ALIAS ali \\srv x:\dir	Creates a shared directory resource definition *ali* in your logon domain, which points to the directory *x:\dir* on server/peer *srv*. Does not create an access control profile.

NET ALIAS ali \\srv prtq /PRINT	Creates a shared print queue resource definition *ali* in your logon domain, which points to the print queue *prtq* on server *srv*.
NET ALIAS ali \\srv com1: /COMM	Creates a shared device queue resource definition *ali* in your logon domain, which points to the serial device *com1:* on server *srv*.
NET APP	Lists the network applications in your logon domain.
NET APP /DOM:dom	Lists the network applications in domain *dom*. The /DOM option can be used with any NET APP command.
NET APP apl	Lists details about network application *apl*.
NET APP apl /DEL	Deletes network application *apl*.
NET APP apl /ADD /APPDIR:res /COMMAND:cmd /TYPE:OS2 /REM:"rem"	Creates an OS/2 network application *apl*, which resides in the directory pointed to by the shared directory resource definition *res*, which is invokedby the command *cmd*, and has the remark *rem*.

Time

| NET TIME /DATE:05-25-95 /TIME:07:42 | Sets the clock in the logon domain; all servers are synchronized. The time and date must be in exactly this format, with leading zeros, and you must use a 24-hour clock (no A.M. or P.M.). |
| NET TIME /DATE:05-25-95 /TIME:07:42 /DOMAIN:dom | Sets the clock in domain *dom*. |

Using Command Files

You can put LAN Server commands into command files to automate your tasks. Here are two simple examples. The first example uses OS/2's standard batch command language to automate shutting down a server. The proce-

Table 11.2 **Example Server Shutdown Command Procedure**

Save this procedure as *servdown.cmd*:

```
echo Bring down the server %1
pause
net admin \\%1 /c "net stop netlogon /y"
net admin \\%1 /c net send /users Server coming
down!
pause
net admin \\%1 /c "net stop server /y"
```

When the procedure is run, this is what the screen looks like:

```
[C:\]servdown lsserver
[C:\]echo Bring down the server lsserver
Bring down the server lsserver

[C:\]pause
Press any key when ready . . .

[C:\]net admin \\lsserver /c "net stop netlogon /y"
The NETLOGON service is stopping.
The NETLOGON service was successfully stopped.

[C:\]net admin \\lsserver /c net send /users Server
coming down!
The message was successfully sent to all users of
this server.

[C:\]pause
Press any key when ready . . .

[C:\]net admin \\lsserver /c "net stop server /y"
These requesters have sessions on this server:
CSBTP                               LSSERVER
The SERVER service is stopping. . . . . . . . .
The SERVER service was successfully stopped.
```

Table 11.3 **Example Procedure to Add a New User**

Save this procedure as *adduser.cmd*:

```
/* Command file to add a new user for the Sales
group */
/* Invoke as: ADDUSER userID password */

ARG userID randomPW

'net user' userID randomPW '/add /passwordexp:yes'
if rc < > 0 then signal error
'net group Sales' userID '/add'
if rc < > 0 then signal error
'net user' userID '/assign g:sdata,f:lotus'
if rc < > 0 then signal error
say 'New user' userID 'created OK.'
exit

error: say 'Error' rc 'creating user' userID
exit
```

When the procedure is run, this is what the screen looks like:

```
[C:\]adduser ann startpw

[C:\]net user ANN STARTPW /add /passwordexp:yes
The command completed successfully.

[C:\]net group Sales ANN /add
The command completed successfully.

[C:\]net user ANN /assign g:sdata,f:lotus
The command completed successfully.
New user ANN created OK.
```

dure issues three NET commands: NET STOP NETLOGON to prevent any-one else from logging on, NET SEND to send a warning message to all users, and NET STOP SERVER to finally stop the server service, disconnecting all remote users. The *%1* parameter in the procedure stands for the server name that's entered when the command procedure is invoked (Table 11.2).

The second example automates creating a new user, adding the user to a group, and adding two logon assignments for the user. The user is created with a password assigned by the administrator, but the password is marked *expired*, so the user will have to create his or her own password at the first logon. This procedure uses OS/2 REXX. It issues three commands: NET USER to create the user account, NET GROUP to add it to a group, and NET USER to add logon assignments. The return code is checked after each com-mand (Table 11.3).

CHAPTER 12

LAN Server Utilities and Productivity Aids

The criticism that a machine cannot have much diversity of behavior is just a way of saying that it cannot have much storage capacity

—*Alexander Turing, "Computing Machinery Intelligence"*

Two sets of LAN Server tools make life easier for those of you who will be administering the network. The first set of tools, called *utilities*, is automatically included when you install LAN Server. Help on the utility syntax is provided through the NET HELP command, in the *OS/2 Commands and Utilities* reference, and in Appendix B of the *Network Administrators' Reference*, Volume 3. Instructions for using the utilities are also found in the *Network Administrators' Reference*, Volume 3. Because the utilities are already well documented, only a brief overview of them will be included in this chapter.

The second set of tools, called *productivity aids* or *applets*, is provided on a separate set of diskettes (Figure 12.1). The productivity aids are small applications that have been collected from many sources. Most are not as well tested or as well documented as the utilities. Where documentation exists, it is generally in the form of README files accompanying the programs. Think of the productivity aids as diamonds in the rough; this chapter will help get you started in using them by providing information that may not be available elsewhere. Some productivity aids are *freeware* provided by vendors of more sophisticated products, some are programs that began life as personal tools employed by IBM developers, and some are prototypes of future LAN Server utilities and internal product features.

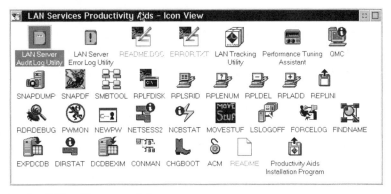

*Figure 12.1 **Productivity aids, or applets.***

Utilities for Migration and Backup

The migration and backup utilities can be used to back up and restore critical access control files, migrate from early versions of LAN Server and Microsoft's LAN Manager, migrate between the Entry and Advanced versions of LAN Server, and move access control profiles across different domains. A brief description of each of the utilities in this category follows. Use the references provided in the introduction to this section for details on syntax and usage.

BACKACC is used to back up the access control profiles for files and directories, the user and group accounts database (NET.ACC), and the audit log (NET.AUD) of a server. XCOPY alone will not back up access control profiles associated with the files and directories on a server; but used in conjunction with BACKACC and RESTACC, a full backup and restore of server directories can be performed. BACKACC can also be used on a specific directory or file to clone access control profiles across servers or domains. When used without specifying a file or directory, BACKACC will back up only the NET.ACC and NET.AUD files. A backup of the NET.ACC file is used to recover from problems in which the NET.ACC of an active server is corrupted and unable to be restored by FIXACC. If such a disaster occurs, the backed up NET.ACC will save you from having to re-create all of the group and user accounts on the affected server from scratch.

FIXACC is first aid for a damaged NET.ACC file; it should be attempted before resorting to restoring the NET.ACC from a backed-up copy. How does the NET.ACC get damaged, and how do you know when first aid is needed? A NET.ACC could be damaged by an improper shutdown or power outage during its update, or by an inadequate time interval set for NET.ACC updates on a large multiserver network. LAN Server sets an *in-use* flag when updating the NET.ACC and resets it when finished. If an attempt to update the NET.ACC encounters the in-use flag, LAN Server assumes a problem occurred during the last update to render the file invalid. If the problem is not too serious, running FIXACC will fix the problem and reset the in-use flag. FIXACC will also remove access control profiles for directories that don't exist any more. FIXACC logs errors and progress information to a file called FIXACC.LOG, which can be reviewed to help pinpoint where the original problem occurred.

HDCON migrates user's home directory aliases from a format used prior to LAN Server 2.0 to the current format and back again. This allows an administrator to move the location of personal storage of network users between different versions of LAN Server without disrupting users.

PREPACL is used to back up, remove, and restore HPFS386 access control files when a server is being reinstalled with a new version of OS/2. A backup of the entire server using PREPACL is usually not required; only those files on the HPFS partition that will be overwritten by an OS/2 installation need to be backed up. Many administrators set up a minimum of three partitions on each server: one for the operating system and nonshared applications, one for shared applications that do not require frequent backup, and one for data that does. Under this strategy, the use of PREPACL would be unnecessary, because the new operating system would have no chance of overwriting shared files.

RESTACC is used to restore the access control profile information that was backed up using BACKACC. An important note in the fine print of using BACKACC and RESTACC is that user accounts that have been deactivated by password expiration or an explicit action by the administrator are not backed up and restored. To be reactivated, these accounts might need to be re-created.

THIN386 creates a modified HPFS386 environment that allows OS/2 2.1 or later to access files that are protected by HPFS386 access control files when an Advanced version of LAN Server is being reinstalled. Another way to accomplish the preceding is to use PREPACL to back up and remove all access control profiles on the HPFS386 partition prior to the reinstall.

 ## Utilities for Fault Tolerance

The following utilities allow you to configure the mirroring and duplexing of LAN Server data transactions, monitor errors, and correct errors detected during server startup. DISKFT.SYS is the program that implements disk mirroring and duplexing. When fault tolerance is enabled, you will see *DEVICE = DISKFT.SYS* in the server's CONFIG.SYS file. If you must recover from a disk failure, the */READPRIM:[drive]* parameter can be added to this statement to force read requests to be satisfied from the unaffected (good) partition. Be sure to update your backup copy of the OS/2 Installation Diskette using the MAKEDISK utility with the /FT parameter whenever you enable, disable, or change the fault-tolerant configuration on your server.

FTADMIN displays the fault-tolerant error log and drive statistics on a selected server, and can be used to control error correction and disk verification. It uses the OS/2 graphical interface and can be run from any OS/2 Server or Requester workstation. The server must first have fault tolerance enabled via the FTSETUP utility before FTADMIN can be used to administer it.

FTMONIT compares fault-tolerance disks during system startup, logs errors, and alerts administrators when disk errors are detected. A line, *RUN=FTMONIT.EXE*, is added to CONFIG.SYS when FTSETUP is used to enable fault tolerance. This line causes FTMONIT to automatically start whenever the server is rebooted.

FTREMOTE is a command-line interface equivalent to FTSETUP and FTADMIN. It is useful for performing automated maintenance activities on the server, as FTREMOTE can be called from any batch or CID response file. It is also compact enough to be run from a bootable diskette and should be part of an administrator's traveling toolkit.

FTSETUP is one of two utilities that can be used to configure fault tolerance and mirror drives on a server. FTSETUP employs a graphical interface, whereas FTREMOTE uses the command-line interface.

 # Utilities for Remote IPL

Remote IPL utilities assist in all phases of setting up, migrating, and managing boot image servers and remote clients. Remote IPL, you may recall, allows a client workstation to boot off an image located on the server. This supports the use of medialess workstations for economy and added security (it is rather difficult to walk off with confidential files when there is no media to which to copy them). The following is an overview of the utilities available for remote IPL:

GETRPL migrates remote IPL files from previous versions of LAN Server to the current version. You must run GETRPL after installing or reinstalling LAN Server, and after using the RIPLINST utility; this must be done before the remote IPL service is started on the server.

MAKEIMG packages the system programs required for a DOS remote IPL requester into an image file. MAKEIMG is run from an OS/2 command line.

MKRDPM creates DOS remote IPL boot diskettes. MKRDPM is run from an OS/2 command line with a bootable diskette, formatted using /S inserted in the disk drive. The diskette can then be used to boot a remote workstation by initializing the network adapter and starting the remote IPL process.

RIPLINST is used to set up OS/2 to support remote IPL on a server. RIPLINST copies the entire OS/2 operating system from the OS/2 install diskettes onto your server, where it can be subsequently accessed by remote IPL workstations.

RPLDSABL disables the remote IPL service at a requester to allow it to boot from its own hard drive. RPLDSABL must be copied onto a bootable DOS diskette. The diskette is then used to boot the requester and run the utility. RPLDSABL returns control to the hard disk, allowing it to be accessed when the workstation is restarted.

RPLENABL enables the remote IPL service at a requester, causing it to boot from the operating system image on the server. RPLENABL is used in the same way as RPLDSABL, but with the opposite results.

RPLLSOBJ is used at an OS/2 command prompt at a remote IPL workstation to re-create the desktop icons for LAN Services, LAN Server Books, and User Profile Management.

RPLSETD upgrades existing remote IPL clients using 16-bit display drivers to allow use of the more efficient 32-bit display drivers available with OS/2 2.0 ServicePak and later releases.

Utilities for Multimedia

Multimedia presents a special challenge to operating systems and networks, because it requires large amounts of data to be processed smoothly over an extended period within the system or network. Smooth processing requires that each task be executed within a tight time constraint. The requirement for timeliness is known as *real-time* processing. We have all seen examples of systems that were not up to the task of processing multimedia real time: distorted audio and video reminiscent of vintage movies. The preemptive multitasking environment of OS/2 combined with the LAN Server's high-performance file system provides an exceptionally robust environment for multimedia. LAN Server's multimedia utilities further enhance this environment by organizing the hard disk to allow multimedia files to occupy large areas of contiguous diskspace, thereby improving the efficiency of the file input/output.

MMUTIL applies and removes the multimedia disk format without requiring the files to be backed up or restored. MMUTIL invokes the PRO-FILER utility to ensure that the files on the designated drive are optimally stored. If inadequate space exists to adequately defragment the drive, you can correct the problem by backing up one or more of the files, rerunning MMUTIL, and restoring the file on the newly processed drive. After using MMUTIL, you should create new copies of your HPFS386 boot diskettes using the MAKEDISK utility; because MMUTIL changes the version number of your HPFS file system, making it inaccessible to previous versions.

PROFILER analyzes files below the subdirectory specified in the path name, and depending on the selected options, displays and/or corrects any fragmentation problems.

Utilities for Administration and Performance Tuning

AT allows you to schedule LAN Server tasks to be run at a server without your intervention. For example, you could schedule a regular backup of data to occur every Friday night at 10 P.M., send a message out to all users to warn them that maintenance will be performed on a particular server, and set up all the necessary maintenance tasks to perform that maintenance while you are at home enjoying dinner. Sound good? The main caveat of using this utility is that any commands or programs you execute must be able to run without video input or output. Any program that runs within the OS/2 command-line interface can have its output redirected to a file, as in this example:

```
AT 22:00 /E:F "C:\OS2\CHKDSK.COM C:>C:\CHKDSK.OUT"
```

The preceding command tells the server that at 10 P.M. every Friday, it will run CHKDSK and redirect the results to CHKDSK.OUT. The double quotes are required when including special characters, such as the redirection symbol (>) in the command. If you are unsure about whether your program will be able to run with the AT command, you can find out by running a little test at the command line; type: **DETACH [command] <NUL > C:\OUTFILE 2> C:\OUTFILE**, where **command** is the command or program you want to be able to run with the AT utility. OUTFILE will contain any output, including errors, from the program you just attempted to run. If OUTFILE indicates the program ran successfully, you will be able to run it using the AT utility as well.

CHGSRVR is used to change the name of any domain controller or additional server, and update all references to the server name in the Domain Control Database. These references include the paths associated with alias definitions, home directories, logon authentication, and remote IPL images. CHGSRVR should be run on the domain controller when all users are logged off.

After the utility is run on the domain controller, you may want to do some additional cleanup: Server references in IBMLAN.INI and command files may need to be updated. All servers in the domain, including the domain controller, should be stopped and restarted after running CHGSVR, allowing time for replicating the new names out to the additional servers. References to the old server name are retained in the SERVERS group and user accounts when CHGSRVR is run; this should be removed using the Administrative GUI or NET USER command once you have successfully restarted the servers and accessed their resources under the new name.

CHKSTOR checks the home directory storage used against the maximum amount of storage defined for the user's home directory through the NET USER command, and can be used to send an alert to a list of administrators and to the users who exceed their storage limits. This utility is separate from the feature available on the Advanced Server, which enforces disk storage limits on HPFS partitions.

DSPDOMDF displays information from the domain controller on users, groups, aliases, and applications defined within the domain. The output can be redirected to a file for keeping track of the network configuration and resources.

LTU helps you manage LAN Server licenses by scanning and reporting all servers and requesters on your network. It allows you to designate which software is licensed, and saves the information in a file for later reference.

The _LAN Server Performance Tuning Assistant_ guides you in tuning your server configuration for optimum performance. The GUI of the utility displays key parameters, such as number of printers shared by the server. You provide the values that best correspond to your current or projected network configuration, then select Calculate. The Updated Files page displays the Performance Tuning Assistant's recommendations, with changes to the configuration files highlighted. Selecting Apply will update the configuration files to apply the changes when the server is rebooted. The old configuration files are copied to the \IBMLAN\BACKUP subdirectory and can be reinstated if needed. To keep your network in top condition, remember to rerun the Performance Tuning Assistant and apply changes when you make major changes to the number of users or shared resources, or make major changes to the network topology.

LSAUDIT invokes the audit utility, a GUI based tool that displays, sorts, prints, outputs to a file, and clears audit log entries. Use the NET START command with the /AUDITING parameter to select the events to be audited, then start the audit. The new selections will override any audit parameters in the IBMLAN.INI file until the server is stopped via a NET STOP or workstation shutdown. The Server section of the IBMLAN.INI file is used to specify events that will be audited automatically whenever the server is started. The default parameter in IBMLAN.INI is _AUDITING = NO._ The syntax for setting the auditing parameter in IBMLAN.INI is documented in the _Network_ _Administrator's Reference_, Volume 2. An example for setting the audit to capture all bad attempts to log on and use resources is:

AUDITING = BADNETLOGON; BADSESSLOGON; BADUSE

Notice that each audit parameter must be separated by a semicolon. The server must be shut down and rebooted for any changes in IBMLAN.INI to take effect. The CPU overhead for auditing all events is very large, so it is best to audit on specific events that suit your purposes. A good _starter kit_ for maintaining network security would be to audit for bad resource access attempts, as shown in the preceding example, plus any changes to user accounts (USERLIST parameter), access permissions (PERMISSIONS parameter), and starting and stopping of services on the server (SERVICE parameter).

LSERROR invokes the error log utility, a GUI-based tool that displays, sorts, prints, outputs to a file, and clears error log entries. LSERROR can also be used to temporarily change the maximum size of the error log; these changes will override the parameters within the IBMLAN.INI file and remain in effect until the server is stopped via NET STOP or a shutdown. Unlike auditing, error logging is automatically invoked when you start LAN Server. The default order in which the error and audit logs are displayed and printed are in chronological order in which the oldest record is displayed first. LSAUDIT and LSERROR can be used to display the logs in a more convenient reverse chronological order; subsequent output to files or printers will retain the last order selected.

MAKEDISK creates OS/2 operating system diskettes that you can use to boot up and access the HPFS386 file system of the Advanced Server. First, make a backup copy of all OS/2 diskettes. Then run MAKEDISK /BOOTDRIVE:A with a backup copy of the OS/2 Installation/Diskette 1 installed in the A drive (you may substitute drive B for drive A by changing the drive letter entered after the colon). A second parameter, /FT, can be used to update the diskette with changes to the fault-tolerance configuration. The HPFS386 file system cannot be accessed by booting up from a normal DOS or OS/2 diskette, so it is very important that these diskettes be created after installing the Advanced Server, and kept up to date with any changes made with the fault-tolerance setup programs. A separate copy of the OS/2 Installation/ Diskette 1 should be kept handy for each Advanced Server on the network.

PRIV is used to start a *privileged* program on an Advanced Server configured with local security. Privileged means the program and any process it calls are allowed to run locally on a server, and will continue to run even if the administrator logs off. The PRIV utility is used to kick off long running programs that may need to access numerous files on a locally secured server; for example, a sort or a file backup utility. An alternative to the use of PRIV lets you automatically start one or more privileged applications when the server boots: Simply add the name of the applications to the PRIVINIT.CMD file, and add RUNPRIV.EXE to the STARTUP.CMD file.

LAN Server Productivity Aids

Table 12.1 provides a summary of the productivity aids offered in LAN Server 3.x and 4.0. The sections that follow provide additional detail on their usage.

Table 12.1 **LAN Server Productivity Aids**

Category/Name	Releases	Description
Installation/Configuration		
AIDINST	v4.0	Productivity aid install utility
REPLINI	v3.0/4.0	Configuration toll for DCDB and data replicator
User Tools		
CONMAN	v3.0/4.0	Management of resource connections
NEWPW	v3.0/4.0	Password synchronization aid
REMOTEFS	v4.0	Mobile cache and remote file sync
Administration		
ACM	v4.0	GUI tool for managing access control profiles
DCDB2ASC	v4.0	Exports DCDB to an ASCII file
DCDBEXIM	v4.0	Scripting tool for DCDB export and import
DISCUSER	v4.0	Disconnects a user from the network
EXTALIAS	v4.0	Creates aliases for external resources
FORCELOG	v4.0	Pauses all services and disconnects all users
IMPACC	v4.0	Imports data from ASCII file to NET.ACC
IMPALIAS	v4.0	Import aliases from ASCII file to DCDB
IMPGROUP	v4.0	Imports user groups from ASCII file to DCDB
IMPGRPPM	v4.0	GUI tool to import groups from ASCII to DCDB
IMPUSER	v4.0	Imports user profiles from ASCII file to DCDB
LOGOFF	v4.0	Logs off all or selected users
LSRXUTIL	v4.0	REXX utilities for LAN Server
MOVESTUF	v4.0	Moves aliases and home directories
QMC	v3.0/4.0	Displays workstation hardware config
REMUSER	v4.0	Removes user's account, profiles, and directories

Table 12.1 (continued)

Category/Name	Releases	Description
Problem Determination		
DIRSTAT	v3.0/4.0	Displays network adapter status
FINDNAME	v4.0	Locates duplicate NetBIOS names
LSS	v4.0	LAN Server Problem Determination Specialist
NCBSTAT	v3.0/4.0	Displays NetBIOS statistics
NETSESS2	v3.0/4.0	Displays session statistics
RDRDEBUG	v4.0	Dumps internal data structures
SMBTOOL	v4.0	Tool to capture and view System Message Blocks
SNAPDF	v3.0/4.0	Tool to format and view SNAPDUMP data
SNAPDUMP	v3.0/4.0	Data collection tool
Remote IPL		
RPLADD	v3.0/4.0	Remote creation of RIPL definitions
RPLDEL	v3.0/4.0	Remote deletion of RIPL definitions
RPLENUM	v4.0	Remote enumeration of RIPL definitions
RPLSRID	v4.0	Remote enumeration of RIPL server record IDs
RPLFDISK	v4.0	Enable/disable remote IPL harddisk

Productivity Aids for Installation and Configuration

AIDINST is a PM-based applet install tool that allows a user to select the programs to install, and creates a tools folder containing the selected utilities. Typing AIDINST starts the program. It should be noted that AIDINST installs most but not all of the productivity aids. The use of AIDINST and the process for installing the remaining tools is covered in Chapter 6.

REPLINI is a replicator configuration program for setting up the domain control database (DCDB) and data replication services. Type REPLINI with no parameters at an OS/2 command prompt to view the main screen. Changes based on your entries to enable or disable the replication services are made to LAN Server's IBMLAN.INI file. You could make the changes directly to IBMLAN.INI using an ASCII editor, but the settings are interrelated and a bit tricky to configure. REPLINI makes this somewhat easier. Additional information on the parameter settings for the replication services can be found in the *LAN Server Network Administrator's Reference*, Volume 2.

 # Productivity Aids for the User

CONMAN (Connection Manager) displays the current state of all LAN connections while allowing an OS/2 user to connect, release, and reassign LAN resources. This tool complements the LAN Server public applications support by providing a means for OS/2 users to customize and automate their logon assignments. Resources can be displayed in list or graphical format for added usability. A full description for installing and using CONMAN is provided in the README file contained on the first of the Productivity Aids diskettes. CONMAN can be invoked from an OS/2 command line or a STARTUP.CMD file. The syntax is:

```
[path]CONMAN [/MIN|/MAX [/N=nickname] [/F=alias[@x:]]
[/P=alias[@LPTx:]] [/S=alias[@COMx:]]
```

where:

- path specifies the location of CONMAN.EXE. */MIN* displays CONMAN as an icon.
- */MAX* displays the CONMAN main screen.
- */N* connects a nicknamed resource that has been defined in the CONMAN.INI file.
- */F* specifies a file alias to attach.
- */P* specifies a printer alias to attach.
- */S* specifies a serial device alias to attach.
- *x:* specifies a logical drive for the file resource.
- *LPTx* specifies a logical port for the printer resource.
- *COMx:* specifies a logical serial port for a serial device.

You can run a local copy of CONMAN from your workstation, or alternatively, a remote copy from the server after logging on by using the universal naming convention of \\SERVERNAME. For example:

```
\\myserver\tools\CONMAN /MIN /N=public /F=mydat
/P=printer1 @ LPT2:
```

runs a copy of CONMAN located within the tools directory of a server called *myserver*. */MIN* displays the CONMAN icon on the desktop of your workstation. */N=public* connects you to all aliases specified by the public nickname defined in the CONMAN.INI file. */F=mydat* tells CONMAN to use the next available logical drive letter to attach the *mydat* file alias. */P* connects you to the printer called *print1* and attaches it to your LPT2 port.

CONMAN displays your logon status in the upper left-hand corner. Your current attached resources are displayed in the main window. Also displayed is a list of all available servers and all available resources to which you can attach.

The nickname entries are obtained from data files named CONMAN.INI. These files must be located in the same directory as CONMAN.EXE or a directory specified in the DPATH of your workstation's CONFIG.SYS. See the information in the README file of the LAN Server productivity aids for information on the format of CONMAN.INI files.

CONMAN function keys are:

ALT-A   Attaches resources.
ALT-F   Sets current device type to files.
ALT-G   Changes main window display to graphics mode.
ALT-L   Log on or off network.
ALT-M   Activates Move Resources window.
ALT-P   Sets current device type to print.
ALT-R   Activates Release window.
ALT-S   Sets current device type to serial.
ALT-T   Changes main window display to text mode.
ALT-V   Activates View Resources window.
ALT-2   Changes main window display to half-size graphics mode.
F1   Displays Help screen.
F3   Exits CONMAN.

NEWPW (Figure 12.2) helps users synchronize password changes across multiple domains. Invoke by selecting the icon or typing NEWPW at an OS/2 command line. The following fields are displayed:

Domains	Highlight one or more by selecting with a mouse or Enter key.
User ID	Enter your user ID here.
Old Password	Enter your old password here.
New Password	Enter your new password here.
New Password	Enter the new password again.
Check Password Age	Displays the password *age* on each domain.
Change Password	Changes the password on each domain.

REMOTEFW is a caching front end designed for mobile users. Users may disconnect from their file servers and continue to work on files that were cached on their laptops as though they were connected. When the users reconnect their laptops to the network, REMOTEFW will replay any changes that the users made while disconnected. During replay, checks are made to ensure that the changes being replayed do not conflict with changes made while the users were disconnected. If conflicts are detected, the user is notified and allowed to resolve the conflict using a GUI tool supplied with REMOTEFW. The README file on the LAN Server Productivity Aids

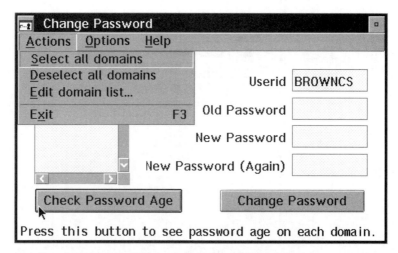

Figure 12.2 **Synchronize password changes across multiple domains.**

diskette provides instructions for installing REMOTEFW. Once installed, a separate README file on the installed directory provides additional instructions for its use.

Productivity Aids for Administration

ACM (Access Control Manager) (Figure 12.3) is a GUI-based productivity tool for managing access control profiles across the network. It allows administrators and users with the appropriate privilege levels to view, add, delete, change, copy, move, and selectively apply (propagate) access control profiles within and across multiple servers. Start ACM from an OS/2 command prompt with no parameters, or optionally, with the name of a single server

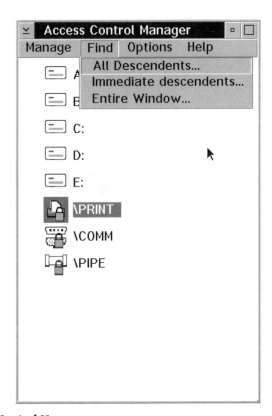

Figure 12.3 ***Access Control Manager.***

you want to administer. Select a server via the Options menu or via the Context menu that appears when you press the right mouse button. Scan a drive, directory, or device for profiles by selecting the drive, directory, or device you want to scan, selecting the Scan menu, then selecting the Descendent menu. Scan or edit a profile by selecting the profile's icon with a double click of the right mouse button. You can also edit the profile by displaying the Context menu for the profile icon and selecting the Edit menu item. The Find menu item allows you to search multiple access control lists for a specific set of profiles.

DCDB2ASC is an OS/2 command-line version of the EXPDCDB tool, which can be used in a command file to automate the backup and reporting process for DCDB data. DCDB2ASC writes the output from the specified domain's DCDB to your screen unless the output is redirected to a file. The syntax for doing this is:

```
DCDB2ASC [domainname] [> [path]\outputfile]
```

DCDBEXIM is a scripting program that can be used to put together custom utilities that use the import/export tools and other executable commands for DCDB backup and restore. The script created is called a *profile*. A sample profile (SAMPLE.PRO) is provided to help you get started.

DISCUSER forces a single user off the network by disabling the user account and disconnecting the user from all servers on the domain. The syntax is **DISCUSER [userid]**.

EXPDCDB is a graphical-based program that exports the Domain Control Database (DCDB) to an ASCII file containing all of the definitions (users, aliases, applications, and access control profiles) for all servers in a domain. The file can be employed as an effective backup and reporting mechanism. The file can also be used as a template, edited, and imported to a domain controller using the DCDB import utilities listed under IMPDCDB.

Two files, QDRIVE.EXE and PWDEXP.EXE, must be located in the \IBM-LAN\NETPROG subdirectory of the domain controller for these utilities to work. EXPDCDB is invoked with no parameters.

EXTALIAS migrates LAN Server 3.0 external aliases into LAN Server 4.0 format for more convenient access. The syntax is **EXTALIAS [external domain name] [/Y]**. The optional /Y parameter disables the confirmation prompts. Without /Y, the user is prompted to confirm each alias to be migrated.

FORCELOG pauses all services and disconnects all users from a single server. Except in an emergency, its use should be preceded with a warning message to all users to allow them time to save their work and log off the server.

IMPDCDB is actually a set of six tools that can be used to restore information from an EXPDCDB-generated ASCII file back into a Domain Control Database (DCDB). The import tools must be run in the following order to successfully restore the DCDB:

1. IMPGROUP or IMPGRPPM
2. IMPALIAS
3. IMPUSER
4. IMPACC

IMPGROUP imports all groups from the export file into the DCDB of the designated server. The syntax for invoking IMPGROUP from an OS/2 command line is **IMPGROUP [domain name] [export file name]**. IMPGRPPM is a GUI version of IMPGROUP.

IMPALIAS imports all aliases from the export file to one or more designated servers. In addition, IMPALIAS can be used to make alias changes for moving or consolidating resources on one or more servers. The syntax is **IMPALIAS [old server name] [[\\]new server name] [export file name]**. The old server name is used to determine if the aliased resources are being moved. If the old server name and the new server name are the same, the alias portion of the export file is imported into the DCDB of the new server unchanged. If the old server name is * (an asterisk), IMPALIAS assumes all server resources are being consolidated on the new server. It alters all of the access control definitions, such as alias locations, to point to an equivalent directory on the new server. If the old server name is ! (an exclamation point), copies of the access control definitions listed in the export file will be imported back to the old server names in addition to the domain controller designated by *new server name*.

IMPUSER imports all user definitions, public and private applications, and logon assignments from the export file to the DCDB of the designated server. The syntax is **IMPUSER [domain name] [export file name]**.

IMPACC imports access controls from the export file to one or more designated servers. The syntax is **IMPACC [old server name] [[\\]new server name] [export file name][/create]**. The command works in much the same way as IMPALIAS, where the old server name determines whether the access controls will be unaltered, consolidated on a single server, or copied back to other member servers. The optional /CREATE parameter tells

IMPACC to create the resource directories before restoring the access control profiles. Though IMPACC does not copy resource files, /CREATE is useful in setting up the resource directories and access controls on a newly installed server using a directory and access control template created from the old one.

LOGOFF allows administrators to force logoff of all or selected OS/2 requesters logged onto a particular domain. The program is a client/server application that requires that the server piece, LOGOFF, be installed on any OS/2 workstation used to force logoff; and that the client piece, CLNTLGFF, be installed on the workstations to be logged off. The server portion consists of a graphical and a command-line interface, and can be installed on multiple requesters, such as the administrator's workstation, as well as network servers for remote administration. The client piece runs in a detached (background) process that can be invoked by including the following command in the STARTUP.CMD file: **DETACH CLNTLGFF.EXE**.

If the server sends the domain and user ID that is currently logged onto the workstation, the user is logged off. If the server sends the correct domain and *ALL,* CLNTLGFF logs all requesters except the one running the server piece off the network. An error log, C:\LOGOFF.ERR, logs error messages and keeps track of successful user logoffs. Up to 100 users can be logged off at one time. LOGOFF is useful for ensuring users are logged off prior to data backups or other maintenance. It is always a good idea to broadcast a warning to all users on the domain a few minutes prior to logging them off.

MOVESTUF (Figure 12.4) is a GUI-based tool for moving and copying home directories and file aliases around the network. The program can move a resource within a server, between two servers in a domain, and from one domain to another. Three combo boxes represent the source server, resources to be moved, and the destination server. The combo boxes display the servers and resources present in your current domain and domains specified by the OTHDOMAINS parameter in your IBMLAN.INI file. You can select from these boxes or alternatively type in the name of an external server if it is not on the list. When typing the target directory, be careful to ensure that the directory exists. A bug in the version shipped with LAN Server that has since been fixed caused the files to be deleted if the specified target directory did not exist. A radio button is used to indicate whether the resource is a file set or a home directory, and to control the content of the list box. A check box allows you to copy the files and access control profiles between servers rather than move them. No parameters are used when invoking MOVESTUF from an OS/2 command line.

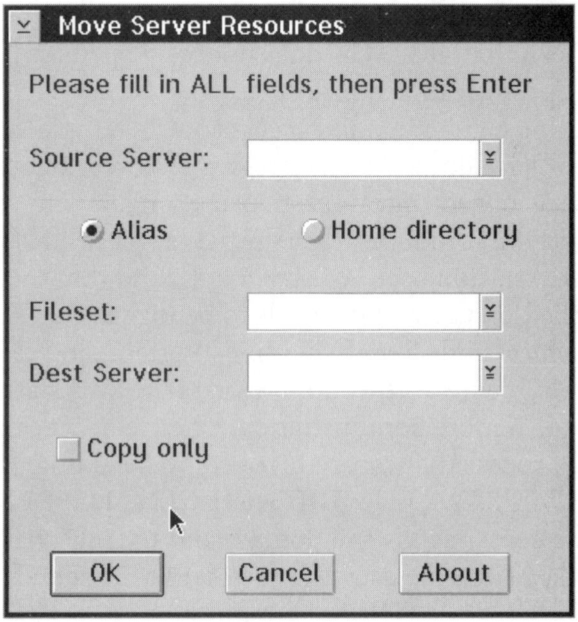

Figure 12.4 ***Move and copy home directories, using MOVESTUF.***

PWMON disables a user's account when a specified number of unsuccessful logon attempts has been detected. PWMON runs on the server and requires auditing to be enabled for BADNETLOGON and BADSESSION alerts (see LSAUDIT in the "Utility" section of this chapter). The syntax is **PWMON [limit] [LOG[=logfile]]**, where *limit* is the number of access attempts allowed, and *LOG* specifies the name and location of the **logfile** that records the names of all disabled accounts. If no limit is specified, the default allows three unsuccessful attempts. If *LOG* is specified without any additional parameters, the **logfile** will be called PWMON.LOG and it will be located in the current directory.

QMC displays the hardware configuration of the workstation on which it is run. The syntax of the QMC is:

```
QMC [/?] [/A] [/B] [/C] [/D] [/E] [/I] [/M] [/O[file]] [/P] [/Q]
[key="text"]
```

where:

/?   Displays syntax.

/A   Displays all Micro Channel adapters supported by QMC.

/B	Displays debug information.
/C	Displays additional detail on asynchronous ports.
/D	Displays a detailed listing of hardware.
/E	Displays current environment.
/I	Displays CONFIG.SYS, STARTUP.CMD, and AUTOEXEC.BAT files.
/M	Displays all machines supported by QMC.
/O	Redirects output to file QMC.OUT.
/Ofile	Redirects output to specified file name.
/P	Pauses the output between screens.
/Q	Does not display redirect message.
key=*text*	Defines key with text to be written to output.

As with other screen output, the output from QMC can be redirected to a file. This program is very useful for collecting information on the hardware configuration of workstations on your network.

REMUSER erases a user's account, logon profiles, and home directory. The syntax for running REMUSER on the server is **REMUSER [userid] [/Y]**. The */Y* parameter disables the confirmation prompt for each file to be deleted. The syntax for running REMUSER from a remote location is:

```
NET ADMIN\\[servername]/C "REMUSER [userid]/Y"
```

LSRXUTIL is an easy-to-use network extension for the OS/2 procedural language, REXX. LSRXUTIL provides access to more than 80 network commands previously accessible only through the LAN Server Application Programming Interface (API). Unlike the LAN Server API, LSRXUTIL procedures are run from command files and do not require a program compiler. LSRXUTIL is an excellent tool for automating routine administrative tasks, testing the LAN Server API, prototyping network applications, and writing sophisticated tools for customizing and automating the use of LAN Requester. Instructions for using the LSRXUTIL extensions are given in the LSRXUTIL.INF file that is viewable using the OS/2 View program. The following useful command files are provided as examples to get you started:

- ALIASES.CMD exports all alias definitions into a comma-delimited output file for easy import into a database, word processor, or spreadsheet.

- USERS.CMD exports all user definitions into a comma-delimited output file.
- HOMEDIR.CMD reestablishes a user's home directory connection in the event of a broken connection.

 # Productivity Aids for Remote IPL

The README file that comes with the LAN Server Productivity Aids provides full instructions for use of the remote IPL tools. Following is a synopsis of each tool's function.

RPLADD can be used to create remote IPL definitions from any OS/2 workstation within the same domain. The local workstation and the target remote server must both be running the same version of LAN Server. The local workstation must be logged on with administrator privilege. The target IPL server must have the Server service started, but does not require that the Remoteboot service be started. The RPLADD for LAN Server 3.0 and 4.0 are different and cannot be used interchangeably.

RPLDEL can be used to delete remote IPL definitions from any OS/2 workstation within the same domain. The local workstation and the target remote server must both be running the same version of LAN Server. The local workstation must be logged on with administrator privilege. The target IPL server must have the Server service started, but does not require that the Remoteboot service be started. The RPLDEL for LAN Server 3.0 and 4.0 are different and cannot be used interchangeably.

RPLENUM enumerates remote IPL definitions from any OS/2 workstation within the same domain. The local workstation and the target remote server must both be running the same version of LAN Server. The local workstation must be logged on with administrator privilege. The target IPL server must have the Server service started, but does not require that the Remoteboot service be started.

RPLFDISK enables and disables the hard disk on an OS/2 remote IPL machine. The remote IPL machine does not require any network services to be running. RPLFDISK can be executed from any OS/2 command prompt. The RPLFDISK.EXE file should be copied into a subdirectory under the \\[ripl_servername]\RPLFILES shared directory tree so that the OS/2 remote IPL workstations will have access to the file. If you are not certain where the

RPLFILES share is located on your remote IPL server, you can use the NET SHARE command on the remote IPL server to determine the subdirectory's location. The recommended target subdirectory is d:\IBMLAN\RPL\IBM-LAN\NETPROG, where *d:* is the remote IPL server drive letter where the IBMLAN\RPL directory tree was installed.

RPLSRID enumerates remote IPL server record identifiers from any OS/2 workstation within the same domain. The local workstation and the target remote server must both be running the same version of LANServer. The local workstation must be logged on with administrator privilege. The target IPL server must have the Server service started, but does not require that the Remoteboot service be started.

Productivity Aids for Problem Determination

DIRSTAT displays network adapter status information from the workstation on which it is run. DIRSTAT is invoked from an OS/2 command line with no parameters, and its output can be redirected to a file. The information supplied includes the burned-in universal adapter address, the assigned adapter address, the group address, the functional address, the maximum configured service access points (SAPS), the open SAPS, the maximum link stations, the open link stations, the adapter type, the amount of adapter shared RAM, the data rate, the microcode level, and the last ring status for each installed network adapter.

FINDNAME searches for duplicate NetBIOS names in your local name table. If no duplicates are found, the utility will prompt the user for a NET-BIOS name to search for duplicates across the network, returning the address(es) of workstations with that NetBIOS name. The tool is useful for locating workstations that may be causing a duplicate name conflict due to misconfiguring a computer name. FINDNAME is executed at the OS/2 command line without additional parameters.

LSS (LAN Server Specialist) is a problem determination tool that generates problem reports based on errors, messages, and alerts issued by the requesters and servers being monitored. LSS is composed of agents and a server. The agents are installed on each requester and server to be managed, and the server is installed on the domain controller. The LSS Server collects the information generated by the agents and supplies useful information, such as a listing of error messages resulting from a single initial cause, possible causes of the error(s), and recommended actions to fix the problem. Instructions for installing LSS is on the README file supplied with the Productivity Aids. The LSS.INF file on the Productivity Aids diskette provides details for using LSS; this file is viewed using the OS/2 View tool. This LAN Server 4.0 productivity aid can also run on LAN Server 3.0.

NCBSTAT (Figure 12.5) displays NetBIOS network statistics. The syntax is:

```
NCBSTAT [-A#]  "NAME "                * [-hxx]
```

where:

- −*A#* is the adapter number (1, 2, or 3); 0 is the default that indicates the first NIC is installed.
- *NAME* specifies the NetBIOS name, which must capitalized, padded to a total of 16 characters, and enclosed in quotes. The name parameter is necessary only if you are querying a remote PC. If you are working at the PC, use an * to specify the local workstation.
- −*hxx* appends the hex value xx to the remote name.

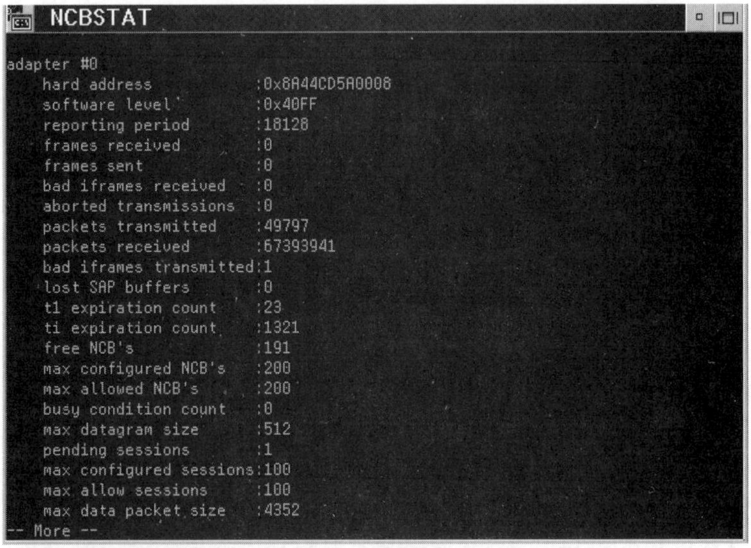

Figure 12.5 **NCBSTAT displays NetBIOS network statistics.**

NETSESS2 displays session statistics obtained from the local workstation's NIC. The syntax is:

NETSESS2 [-1#][session_name]

where:

- *-1#* is the adapter number (1, 2, or 3); 0 is the default, which indicates the first NIC.
- *session_name* prints only the statistics for sessions with that local name; otherwise, if this parameter is not specified, statistics are printed for all sessions.

The output, which can be redirected to a file, contains information on:

- The local session numbers that are assigned to each session by the NIC
- Session status
- Name used at the local NIC in the CALL or LISTEN command that established the session
- Name used at the remote NIC in the CALL or LISTEN command that established the session
- The number of outstanding RECEIVE, SEND, RECEIVE DATAGRAM, and RECEIVE ANY commands for this session

RDRDEBUG dumps internal OS/2 requester data structures. RDRDEBUG requires that the LAN Server requester service be started on the local workstation. It is executed at the OS/2 command line without additional parameters. Output appears on the screen but can be redirected to a file. This tool would be used to capture data for reporting a LAN Server redirector problem to IBM Customer Support. The output includes information on the system message blocks sent and received, commands executed, time-out values, buffer chaining, retries, machine ID, and the configuration of the server. The server configuration includes the server name, domain name, OS/2 version, LAN Server version, SMB protocol support, type of security enabled, buffer limits, and other configured parameters. There is also information on the file system type, logical drive, and remote UNC name of the shared resources being accessed. A sample output is included in the README file that comes with the LAN Server productivity aids.

SMBTOOL is used to capture and view various types of network traces. It provides extensive formatting and filtering features for analyzing SMB trace data for advanced problem determination. The utility takes no parameters and requires OS/2 2.1 or higher. SMBTOOL includes an online HELP function that provides additional information for its use.

SNAPDF provides a graphical interface useful for viewing and formatting the contents of a file containing data collected by SNAPDUMP. The formatting program provides views of the data in hexadecimal plus ASCII, ASCII only, or hexadecimal plus EBCDIC. SNAPDF also allows you to extract and view portions of a dump based on an entry title tag. The syntax for SNAPDF is **SNAPDF [dump filename]**, where *dump filename* specifies the name of the SNAPDUMP output file to be viewed. No parameter tells the SNAPDF program to view the default output file named SNAPDUMP.DMP. If no output file is found, SNAPDF displays an Open File window, from which you can select the name of the desired output file.

The Dump Formatter window displays the output file name, a dump segment identifier, the date/time/program, and data items. The dump segment identifier is a scrollable list of all of the data entries (segments) in the output file. You can select the segment(s) you want by highlighting them with the mouse button. The date/time/program field displays the date and time at which the dump file was created, and the program that created the dump file. The data items field is a scrollable list of data items for the selected segment. Select (highlight) the data item(s) you want. Pressing Enter at this time displays the selected data. The formatted data can be saved to a file for reports or later viewing.

SNAPDUMP is a set of tools that assist with problem determination in an OS/2 environment. SNAPDUMP provides the ability to capture a wide variety of system data into a single, easily transportable file. This data includes the contents of binary and ASCII files, named shared segments, system trace buffers, environmental information, and standard output and error from programs SNAPDUMP invokes. The collection of data is controlled by the contents of a tailorable flat ASCII file. The sample file included, SNAPDUMP. DAT, can be used as a template to customize the collection of data. The syntax for invoking SNAPDUMP from an OS/2 command line is **SNAPDUMP [input_filename][output_filename]**, where:

- *input_filename* is name of the flat ASCII file containing the list of files, data, and programs to be processed (default is SNAPDUMP.DAT).

- *output_filename* is the name of the file into which SNAPDUMP outputs all captured data (default is SNAPDUMP.DMP).

The first two characters encountered on each line of the SNAPDUMP input file indicate the type of data to collect:

- f/ indicates that a file is to be captured; that is, f/ config.sys.
- p/ indicates that a program is to be invoked; that is, p/c:\qmc.exe -d.
- m/ indicates that a named shared memory segment is to be captured; that is, m/\SHAREMEM\ACS\RAS_SEG.
- A line beginning with any other character is treated as a comment.

Selected files, the contents of shared segments, and the standard and error output of selected programs are appended onto the SNAPDUMP output file. Information presented within GUI-based programs cannot be captured. The names of the named shared memory files in the system may be obtained by issuing pstat /m at the OS/2 command prompt.

Summary

The LAN Server-supplied utilities and productivity aids provide an excellent base for managing your network. If your network is not very large, these may be all the tools you will need. With a little planning and experimentation, you can create a network environment that is reliable, easy to upgrade, and easy to use. Chapter 13 will explore some additional techniques for enhancing the usability of your network. Chapter 14 will describe the use of some of the problem determination tools for debugging problems on your network.

Advanced Topics

Being and nonbeing produce each other; difficult and easy complete each other;
Long and short contrast each other; high and low distinguish each other;
Sound and voice harmonize each other; front and back follow each other.

—*Lao Tzu,* Tao-te Ching

 ## Logon Assignments

Logon assignments are resources that are assigned to you automatically when you log on to the network. These resources may be directories, files, printers, or serial devices; or they may be a special category of resources known as *public* and *private* applications. Public and private applications are normal programs, such as editors, databases, spreadsheets, and graphics tools that reside on the server but that you can access and use over the network. The use of public and private applications makes a lot of *cents* (pun intended). It allows you to access a broad range of up-to-date software, while your company pays only for the number of software licenses that are actually used at a given time. Monitoring software usage for capacity planning and providing software upgrades become relatively easy tasks for the network administrator who is interested in keeping up with changing demands.

What distinguishes public applications from private applications is a matter of who assigns the users of the application. With public applications, the administrator specifies the users of the application. With private applications, the administrator sets up the applications to be shared, and the users select the ones they want to be assigned from this pool of shared applications. The icons for the applications are displayed in the network application folder of the graphical user interface immediately after logging on to the network. The applications can then be started by simply double-clicking the icon with mouse button 1.

Not all applications are designed for networks; some applications assume they are running locally on a stand-alone workstation. These applications can be stored on the server, but must be transferred across the network to run on the client workstation. Other applications may be run on the server, the client workstation, or a combination of client and server; you specify how and where you want the application to run. However you configure the application, it should look and feel just like an application installed on your local machine. *The LAN Server Network Administrator's Reference*, Volume 3 gives step-by-step instructions and some good examples for setting up public and private applications. A synopsis of the steps for configuring a public application using LAN Server 4.0 follows.

Configuring a Public Application

1. Install the application on the server.
2. Create aliases for the directory containing the application and any other resources needed by the application. For example, the application may access data from a separate working directory; this data directory will need its own alias. You create aliases via the Resource Definitions folder of the LAN Server 4.0 Administrative GUI by dragging the template for the type of resource you are using into an open area of the folder. The alias settings notebook is displayed (Figure 13.1). Enter the alias name, description of the resource, the server name, and the path to the aliased directory. The path name is the path on the server. For example, if you are sharing applications from a tools directory located on the C drive, you would fill in **C:\TOOLS**. While LAN Server gives you plenty of flexibility in determining when a resource is shared, in most cases you will want to share the resource at server startup. You can use the maximum concurrent connections to limit the number of concurrent users of an application to a level determined by your licensing agreement. Aliases can also be created from the command line or a command file using the NET ALIAS command.

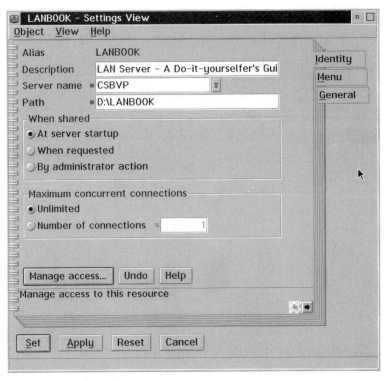

Figure 13.1 **Alias settings notebook.**

3. Assign an access control profile for each alias. The Administrative
    GUI will prompt you for this after you create the alias. You should
    assign R (Read) permission for the application itself, and RWCAD
    permissions for any read-write directories. See Chapter 8 for more
    information on access control.

4. Define the application via the Administrative GUI by opening the
    Public Applications Definitions folder (Figure 13.2) and dragging the
    OS/2 Template (if defining an OS/2 application) or the DOS template
    (if defining a DOS or Windows application) to an open area of the
    folder. This will display the Identity page of the Application Defi-
    nitions notebook (Figure 13.3). Required fields are identified with an
    asterisk (*). Remember, you can always select Help for information on
    specific data required for each field.

5. On the Identity page, fill in an Application Name by which you can
    identify the application, and a description of the resource (Figure

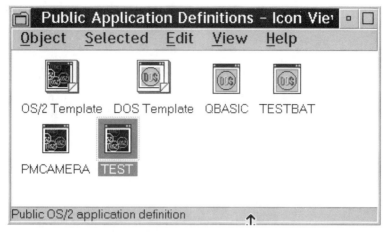

Figure 13.2 **Public Application Definitions folder.**

13.3). You might want to include the version number, for example, as part of the description.

6. On the Invocation page (Figure 13.4), type the command you would use at a command line to start the program. For example, if you wanted to set up Freelance Graphics for OS/2 as a public application,

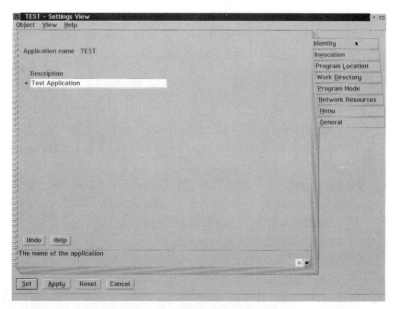

Figure 13.3 **Identity page of the Application Definitions notebook.**

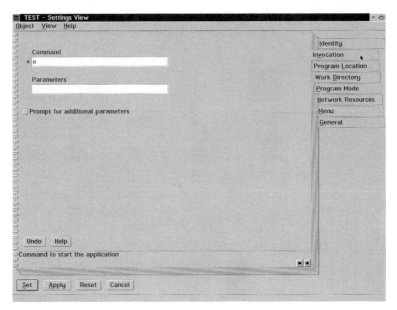

Figure 13.4 **Invocation page.**

you would type the command FLG. If the program uses parameters when invoked from a command line, these parameters should be entered in the Parameters field; otherwise, this field is left blank.

7. Check the Program Location page (Figure 13.5). After filling in the alias name, it should display the correct path to the resource. Unless your users or shared applications assume a specific drive letter for accessing the program, use Next Available as the Assigned Drive; this gives LAN Server maximum flexibility to reassign drives as needed.

8. Use the Work Directory page (Figure 13.6) to define where data and temporary files will be stored. If these files will be in the same directory as the program, the entries will be the same as were entered on the Program Location page.

9. Program Mode (Figure 13.7) specifies the environment in which the program will be run. For example, OS/2 GUI programs run in an OS/2 Presentation Manager (PM) mode. Other options are to run programs in Protected or VIO mode.

10. On the Network Resource page, select Assign. Within the Resource Type list, select the resource type you are sharing (for example, Directory). If not already filled in, complete the Alias and Device fields. Select OK. Select Create.

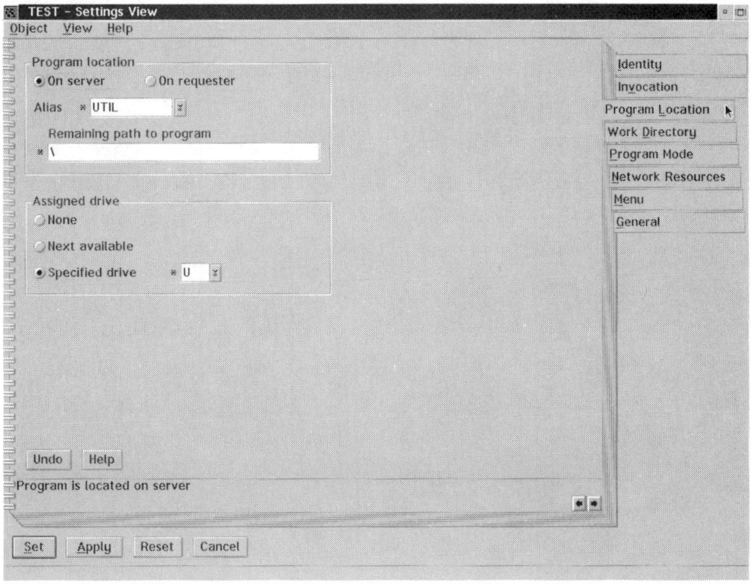

Figure 13.5 **Program Location page.**

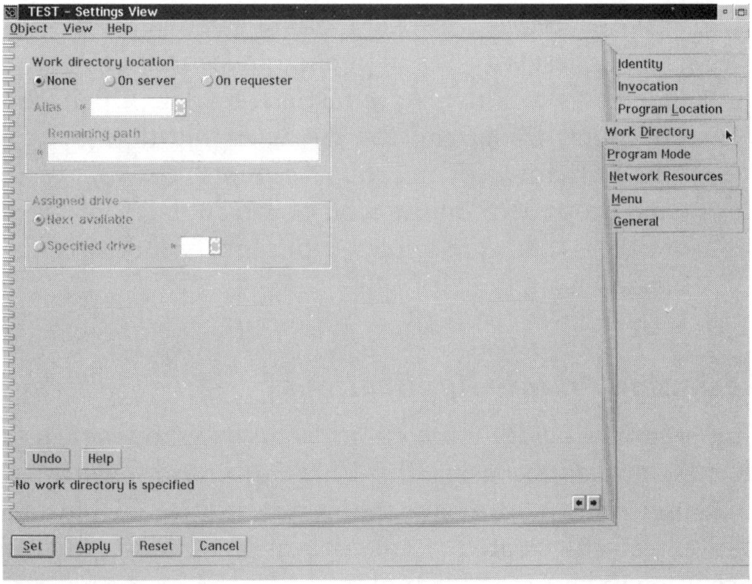

Figure 13.6 **Work Directory page.**

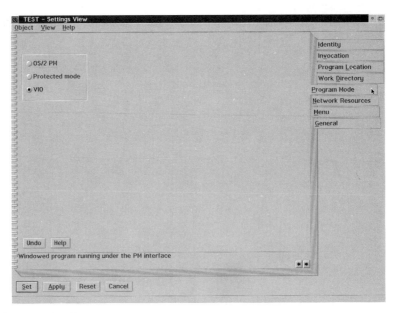

Figure 13.7 **Program mode.**

11. Congratulations! You have just created your first public application! Now, if you want to automatically assign the application to users when they log on to the network, proceed with Step 12. If you want your users to select their own private applications from the set you have shared, the instructions are given in the next section.

12. The easiest way to add public applications to your user's logon assignments is via the Administrative GUI. Open the User or Group Accounts folder and the Public Application Definitions folder. Drag the icons for User or Group Accounts you want to access the resource, and drop them on the icon of the Public Application you want them to access. An Add Public Application window is displayed. Select OK and you are done!

Assigning Private Applications

This section provides instructions for users who want to automate access to shared applications using the LAN Server Administrative GUI. OS/2 and DOS users who do not have the Administrative GUI installed on their workstations can still create private applications through the command line interface using the NET APP command.

1. Open LAN Services from the desktop.
2. Open LAN Server Administration.
3. Open the domain that provides the application you want to access.
4. Open User Accounts, select your account, and press mouse button 2 to display the pop-up menu.
5. Select the arrow to the right of Open, and select Private Applications to display the folder.
6. Drag the Private Applications Template to an open area of the folder. Fill in the required fields, indicated by an asterisk (*) on each of the settings pages. When you are finished, select Create.

To use the application, log off LAN Server and log back on. The application should appear in your Network Application folder.

Configuration Installation Distribution (CID)

Did you ever wonder why the workstation beeps at you when it needs a new diskette during installation? It does it to get the attention of those of us who are busy reading the install manual while pumping diskettes into the slot. CD-ROMs are a WONDERFUL invention, because you can put dozens of diskettes full of information on a single CD-ROM and save the time and elbow fatigue of feeding diskettes to your computer. As nice as CD-ROMs are, however, CID is even better. CID allows you to simultaneously install programs, including OS/2 and LAN Server, on network-attached workstations using a single master code copy located on the Server. Two diskettes containing the OS/2 Kernel and basic requester services are used to boot the workstations. A response file, which can be customized for each workstation, is used to respond to each product's installation questions—so you just start installation and go! A multiproduct installation can be handled automatically by writing a REXX procedure, which contains a series of chained commands to initiate the individual installation procedures. With CID, an installation that may have taken half a day can be accomplished in minutes!

Table 13.1 gives an example of a response file that would upgrade an OS/2 LAN Requester from a previous version. DELETEIBMLAN and UPDATEIBMLAN specify changes that are to be made to LAN Server's main configuration file, IBMLAN.INI. The next several statements that begin with

Table 13.1 **CID Response File for Upgrading LAN Requester**

```
DELETEIBMLAN = Networks<
net1b=

>

UPDATEIBMLAN = Peer<
security = Migrate

>

UPDATEIBMLAN = Requester<
useallmem = No

>

ConfigApplDumpPath = Migrate
ConfigApplMaxDumps = Migrate
ConfigAutoStartFFST = Migrate
ConfigAutoStartLS = Migrate
ConfigDisplayMSG = Migrate
ConfigMsgLogName = Migrate
ConfigRouteAlertsTo = Migrate
ConfigSourceDrive = C
ConfigSystemDumpPath = Migrate
ConfigSystemMaxDumps = Migrate
ConfigTargetDrive = Migrate
ConfigWsId = Migrate
ConfigWsSerial1 = Migrate
ConfigWsSerial2 = Migrate
ConfigWsType1 = Migrate
ConfigWsType2 = Migrate
InstallAPI = INSTALLIFREQUIRED
InstallClipBoard = INSTALLIFREQUIRED
InstallDeskTopIcons = INSTALLIFREQUIRED
InstallDosLanAPI = INSTALLIFREQUIRED
InstallFFST = INSTALLIFREQUIRED
InstallGUI = INSTALLIFREQUIRED
InstallInstallProgram = INSTALLIFREQUIRED
InstallMSGPopup = INSTALLIFREQUIRED
InstallPeerService = INSTALLIFREQUIRED
InstallRemoteFaultTolerance = INSTALLIFREQUIRED
InstallRequester = INSTALLIFREQUIRED
InstallUPM = INSTALLIFREQUIRED
```

Config specify the values to assign various LAN Server parameters. *Migrate* tells the LAN Server Installation and Configuration programs to keep the same values as were assigned when installing the previous version.

The last group of statements beginning with *Install* specifies which LAN Server features to install. *INSTALLIFREQUIRED* tells LAN Server to install the feature if this is the first time LAN Server is being installed. If LAN Server is being upgraded from a previous version, *INSTALLIFREQUIRED* will upgrade only the features that have been previously installed. CID gives you the flexibility to create a customized response file for each workstation or to allow specific values to be entered during the install process, such as a computer name or domain name. The latter is accomplished by simply not assigning a value to the parameter. You can also save a value requested from the user at the beginning of the install process to use during the install.

CID is part of the transport services supplied with LAN Server. Appendix I of the *LAN Server 4.0 Network Administrator's Reference*, Volume 1 gives a detailed description of all the key words used for configuring LAN Server. Additional information on CID can be found in the *LAN Server Configuration, Installation, and Distribution Utility Guide.*

REXX and REXX LAN Extensions

REXX is an *interpretive* language used for writing programs and interfacing to IBM software. Interpretive means that REXX programs work like an application macro; they do not have to be compiled to run. REXX programs do not run as fast as compiled programs but they are VERY useful for creating utilities to automate routine tasks and for creating software prototypes. REXX runs in DOS, OS/2, OS/400, and numerous other platforms. A REXX program file is an ASCII file with a .CMD file extension.

REXX program files can be distinguished from OS/2 command files by the first line of the program, which always contains a comment line beginning with /* and ending with */. REXX is readily expandable through the use of extension libraries, and is utilized by numerous applications other than OS/2 and LAN Server. The basic REXXUTIL library is provided with Warp, and the extensions for interfacing with LAN Server are contained on the LAN Server 4.0 Productivity Aid diskettes. Online references for using the LAN REXX Utilities are contained in a file called LSRXUTIL.INF. This file can be viewed by typing **VIEW LSRXUTIL** at an OS/2 command line.

Prior to the REXX LAN extensions provided in LAN Server Version 4.0, users who wanted to create tools and services that required more interoperability than could be obtained through the command line interface were forced to develop programs in C that used the LAN Server Application Programming Interface (API). The LAN Server API is very efficient and functionally very rich; it is still the interface of choice for commercial tool development and programs that are meant to be run on a large scale. A good example would be a utility for managing a large network. REXX is meant for people who are busy doing lots of things other than programming, but who are interested in making their networks work for them, rather than being slaves to their networks. REXX is also a programmer's playground. It lets you create routines quickly and easily, so you can try them out before implementing them in C.

LAN Server 4.0 provides 157 REXX call extensions organized into eight categories:

- Base Functions provide calls for copying, importing, and exporting DCDB information.
- NetAdd is used to add accounts, aliases, logon assignments, and other entries.
- NetDelete is used to delete accounts, aliases, logon assignments, and other entries.
- NetEnumerate is used to list aliases, installed devices, hard disk limits and usage, and other information on the network and LAN Server configuration.
- NetGetInfo is used to find addresses associated with a NetBIOS name, and obtain details on resources and configurations.
- NetMisc provides control over audit and error logging and other miscellaneous functions.
- NetSetInfo is used to change accounts, aliases, logon assignments, and other entries.
- RxSpl provides control over spooler and network print functions.

A good way to get a flavor for REXX is to start with one of the utilities provided with the LAN Server productivity aids and customize it for your own use. Warp has an online reference for using REXX, which is very useful. There are also several books available on the topic of REXX if you decide to pursue it further.

The LAN Server API

As described in the previous chapter, the LAN Server API is the interface of choice for C and C++ Language programmers to create large-scale software applications for the network. LAN Server uses OS/2 for its base set of operating system calls, and extends this set with calls to support network administration, security, auditing, and other LAN Server specific functions. The LAN Server API uses a common interface for both client and server, which allows programmers to reuse code for both sides of their transactions. The LAN Server calls are documented in the *LAN Server Programming Guide and Reference.*

 # Extending the Local Area Network

While LANs typically operate within a single building or site, many networks are interconnecting to form a worldwide web of communications. A number of terms such as *information superhighway* have sprung up in our vocabulary seemingly overnight. An example of the trend toward network communications is the Internet, which began life 25 years ago as a network for the scholarly exchange of scientific and business data, and today is a popular conduit for everything from finding out where your favorite musicians are playing to sending messages to the President of the United States (whose Internet e-mail address is *president@whitehouse.gov*).

Like LANs, these networks require hardware and media to connect the networks and workstations together, and an appropriate transport protocol through which to communicate. Increasingly, people are dialing into an Internet provider, such as the IBM Global Network and many others. This gives them direct access the the World-Wide Web, Internet e-mail, USENET newsgroups, FTP/Gopher servers, and other services. Most people use a standard switched telephone connection to access their businesses as well as these network service providers. When using a standard telephone service, a modem is required to convert the digital signals of the computer to the analog signals that are carried over the local telephone line. This can also be a suitable means for the occasional exchange of data between two or more business locations. For example, a chain of retail stores might use a modem to dial into the central office once a day to exchange information on sales, inventory, and price changes.

There are many reasons for tapping into these broader-based networks. The cheapest and most effective way to get connected depends on how you want to use the network. From simplest to more complex, uses include:

- Accessing global forums plus sending/receiving e-mail and files
- Accessing information from a single workstation via remote dial-in
- Accessing resources distributed across your business network
- Providing a casual (low-volume) long distance connection between two networks
- Providing a permanent (high-volume) long distance connection between two locations

Accessing global forums and sending and receiving e-mail require only a workstation, a modem, a service provider (such as the one of those listed earlier), and some rudimentary software for connecting to and using the service. The more popular of these software programs, such as WebExplorer, NewsReader/2, and Gopher, are included with Warp. Otherwise, the software is included as part of the package supplied by the service provider. Many computers now come preloaded with the programs needed to access these services and a free trial period to try the services out. Use this trial period to compare several services before committing to one. The services provided and the cost structure for the services vary. One service provider, for example, has specialized in providing entertainment for young people, with such things as *party lines*, where multiple people *chat* in real time over the network.

Other providers have tried to provide tools and services to capture the more serious business and financial markets. Some service providers offer unlimited access for a monthly fee, while others charge by the time and services you access. File transfer capabilities are not always supported with these services, or may be provided at an extra charge. File transfer is valuable if you think you will want access to *freeware* or software fixes available on the network. File transfer is also useful for sending and receiving electronically formatted programs and documents between individuals on the network.

To access information by dialing into another computer from your home computer, you must install a compatible modem and software on both machines. You have a few choices in the type of software you choose. You can use an emulator to run programs on the target machine and access data by remote control, or you can extend the client/server network to include a remote client. With an emulator, the commands you enter at your keyboard are sent over the switched network to be executed on the target machine. The screen output from executing the command is then sent back over the telephone lines and is displayed on your machine's monitor. DCAF, one of the complementary products listed in Chapter 3, uses this remote control technique.

The second technique is a natural extension of network operating systems' peer and client/server roles. The client and server, or two peers, are installed with modems but utilize the same software applications in the same way as they would on a LAN. The only change required is a program that allows the client to dial into the remote site and connect to the target server. The LAN Distance Remote Client (Figure 13.8), supplied with Warp Connect or purchased separately, can be installed on LAN Server and each remote Requester to provide this level of remote LAN access capability. More about how LAN Distance works will be described in a later section.

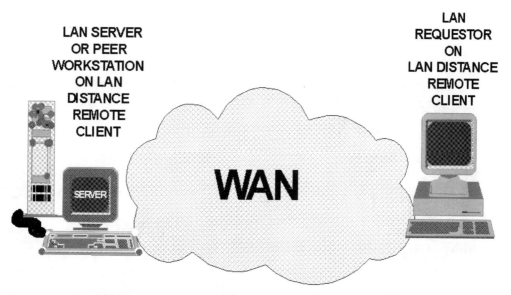

Figure 13.8 ***LAN Distance installed on LAN Server.***

To remotely access resources distributed across your business network, you must either install a modem and remote access software on each server, or provide a single entry point on the network that can connect the remote user and correctly route data and requests. The second approach is the most desirable, because it allows for more efficient use of modems and lets a remote user access multiple servers and peers without having to hang up and redial each new service. The single entry point also aids in providing secure access to the network, and reducing unnecessary traffic through the use of filters. This level of support is provided by the LAN Distance Connection Server (Figure 13.9), a companion product to the LAN Distance Remote Client.

The LAN Distance Connection Server not only allows remote clients to dial into a LAN, but it also allows LAN clients to dial out. Two remote networks can use the LAN Distance Connection Server to provide a casual (low-volume) long distance connection between the two sites (Figure 13.10). The connection is established when the first user dials the remote site. LAN Distance allows multiple users to share the same connection. The connection is terminated when the last person sharing the connection hangs up.

If two remote locations regularly exchange large volumes of data, the use of modems and standard telephone lines may not provide adequate data transfer rates or be the most cost-effective solution. Other options to consider are leasing a private nonswitched line from a communications provider, looking into the availability of Integrated Switched Digital Network (ISDN)

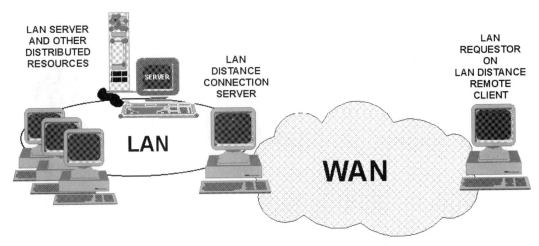

Figure 13.9 **LAN Distance Connection Server.**

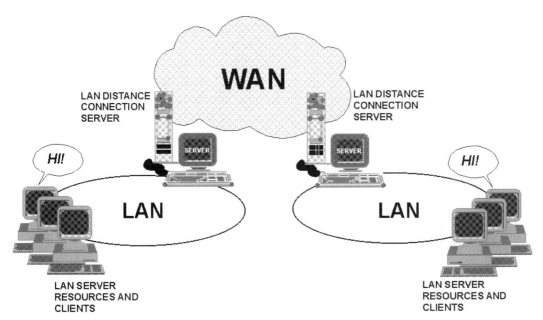

Figure 13.10 **Two separate remote networks using the LAN Connection Server.**

services in your area, or exploring the many communications bridge, router, and gateway products emerging on the market today. LAN Distance supports nonswitched and permanent as well as switched connections using asynchronous, synchronous, and isochronous communications. LAN Distance also includes support for ISDN, X.25, and wireless networks using such technologies as infrared and digital cellular.

After you have solved the question of hardware and a means to connect your remote sites, the next consideration is the protocol you will use to communicate. While NetBIOS has long been the protocol of choice for high-speed LANs, TCP/IP, included with LAN Server 4.0, is a popular protocol for transferring files and communicating between remote networks. TCP/IP supports several applications, such as File Transfer Protocol (FTP) and Telnet (a host emulation service). These applications are not included in the LAN Server 4.0 package, but are bundled with LAN Requester, LAN Distance, and all kinds of other great stuff in Warp Connect. The applications can also be acquired separately by purchasing the TCP/IP for OS/2 Applications Kit.

Since LAN Server uses NetBIOS as its transport interface, running LAN Server over a TCP/IP network requires NetBIOS over TCP/IP (called TCP-BEUI) to be configured on each participating client workstation. If you do not plan to use TCP/IP applications but simply want to run LAN Server over a TCP/IP, SNA, or IPX protocol network, another option is to use gateway hardware to provide the protocol mapping from NetBIOS to TCP/IP, SNA, or IPX. While extra hardware costs are associated with the gateways, the client workstations do not have to be configured with both NetBIOS and TCP/IP, and so, would require less memory and disk space to implement.

You may feel you are faced with a dizzying array of options when connecting across global networks! Just remember the principles are the same as discussed for connecting local area networks in Chapter two:

1. You must have a common connection between any two workstations that need to communicate.
2. The workstations must share common applications and protocols.

As discussed earlier, network providers such as CompuServe require use of special software that provides a set of matching client services. Likewise, using LAN Requester over a remote network requires LAN Server or a LAN Requester Peer to provide the resources on the other end of the connection. If you use TCP/IP applications, TCP/IP and the applications must be present on both workstations in order for the workstations to communicate.

 ## More about Using LAN Distance

As mentioned in the last section, you can think of remote LAN access as a natural extension of a network operating system to accommodate remote clients. Like people who use network service providers, remote clients typically dial directly into network servers via modem connected telephone lines. You install the network applications you wish to use, such as LAN Requester, Lotus Notes, Communication Manager, or TCP/IP, just as if you were planning to run them on the local area network. For example, even though Lotus Notes provides its own options for running it over a modem connection, you install Lotus Notes using the LAN options.

LAN Distance can be installed anytime after installing the network transports. LAN Distance provides a transport layer that maps the code controlling the modem or communications adapter to the code that expects to be talking to a NIC. Workstations using LAN Distance can be configured to connect via modem or via a NIC; a convenient *shuttle* feature lets you select which mode you want to use next before shutting down the application. LAN Distance requires you to supply a logical adapter address, which it uses to emulate a NIC when attaching to the network. This logical adapter address must be unique to the network to allow data to be correctly routed to your machine.

When connecting to a network, LAN Distance checks for any duplicate addresses on the network before allowing you to connect. The main panel of LAN Distance is a phone book that contains the phone numbers you have entered of frequently called services (Figure 13.11). You dial one of these numbers by selecting the phone entry and then selecting Dial. You can also type the number you want in the space provided. The status of your call and the amount of time you are connected is also displayed on this page. The optional security service prompts you for your User ID and Password before allowing you access to the network.

LAN Distance user accounts are configured using notebooks similar to those used within the LAN Server Administrative GUI (Figure 13.12). Once you have dialed into the network via another LAN Distance Client or

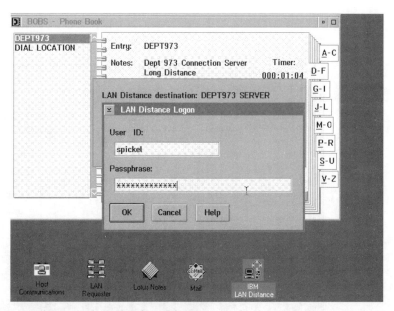

Figure 13.11 **LAN Distance phone book and logon.**

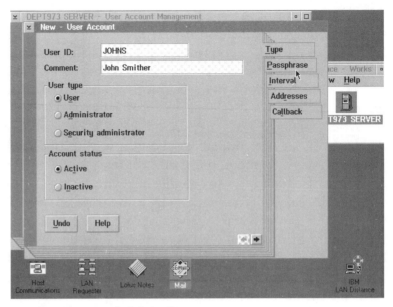

Figure 13.12 **LAN Distance user administration.**

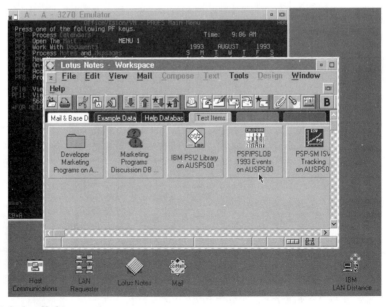

Figure 13.13 **Lotus Notes.**

Connection Manager, you can run all of your network applications, including graphics, just as if you were locally attached to the network (Figure 13.13).

The transmission speed of the network should be taken into consideration when choosing applications to run over a modem connection. In general, your best choice will be applications that either run on the server or a combination of client and server. Applications that have to be transmitted from the server to a client to run will take much longer to load over a 19.2-Kbps modem than it would over a 10- or 16-Mbps LAN.

Summary

This chapter has explored some of the ways you can use optional services and products to increase the usefulness of your network. Hopefully, this chapter and the chapters preceding it have given you all the background information you need to pursue these advanced topics as far as you want to take them. The next and final chapter will show you what to do when all does not go as smoothly as planned.

CHAPTER 14

Tips for Troubleshooting

*The significant problems we face cannot be
solved by the same level of thinking that created them.*

—*Albert Einstein*

 By far, the most difficult tasks of administering a network are installing and configuring it. The proliferation of independent network hardware and protocols have offset a serious effort on the part of software developers to find new ways to simplify the installation of their products. Chapter 6 focused on the LAN Server install process and provided some recommendations for an incremental approach for complex installations. This chapter will focus on isolating and debugging the problems that might occur after LAN Server has been up and successfully running.

Lessons from the Past

During each release of LAN Server, IBM performs a causal analysis of problems reported through IBM's many customer support channels. IBM uses this analysis to improve the quality of future products. An interesting statistic that emerged for LAN Server 3.0 was that over 70 percent of the problems found were reported by only 5 percent of LAN Server's customers! These customers had two factors in common:

- They were running networks of well over a thousand users.
- They were supporting a broad mix of communications hardware, software, and release levels.

The IBM test organization responded to these statistics by enlisting the help of developers across the IBM site to pool their workstations to form a giant test bed to run overnight at regular intervals. They also greatly increased the diversity of hardware and software in the test lab and, for the final exam, concocted a grueling stress test known as the *7 by 24*. The test is so called because to pass, the product must run this test at high load 24 hours a day for a solid week. There are two things you can glean from this experience: 1) IBM is VERY serious about providing the most reliable products possible; 2) you can improve the reliability of your own network by limiting the mix of hardware, software, and release levels you support.

Another thing you can do today to more easily solve problems tomorrow is to familiarize yourself with problem determination and recovery procedures, and have the necessary data and tools on hand. The first few chapters of this book discussed the importance of regular backups and keeping a log book. Configure at least two Administrator IDs so that if the first one is damaged or accidentally disabled, you will still have a second one to use. Print out

a copy of the *LAN Server Problem Determination Guide* (Figure 14.1) and system recovery procedures and keep them in a handy place along with a set of tools and backups.

A General Approach to Problem Determination

In *Zen and the Art of Motorcycle Maintenance*, Pirsig describes how the step-by-step approach to maintaining a motorcycle is, for him, the embodiment of rational thought. Many of the observations Pirsig makes about troubleshooting a motorcycle could also be applied to computers.

Step 1: Observe and Record

Observation is one of the most important tools you have for detecting and isolating problems (Figure 14.2). An equally important factor in observation is familiarity with how the network normally (or should) runs. A truly seri-

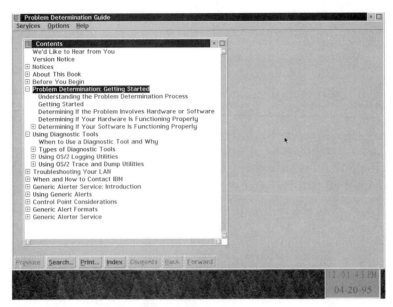

Figure 14.1 **The Problem Determination Guide.**

Figure 14.2 **Regularly monitor your network and log your observations.**

ous problem rarely happens all at once but is often a sequence of events that could be more easily corrected if detected early. Examples of these sorts of problems are running out of such resources as buffers, CPU capacity, memory, disk space, data transmission bandwidth; and some hard disk failures. Your best tool for detecting these sorts of problems before they turn into emergencies is to regularly monitor your network and compare the data for changes over time.

When a problem does occur, copy or print all error messages and alerts, noting the order and time in which they occurred. Check your log book and note any system and network configuration changes that might be related to the problem. What was being attempted at the time of the error? Who and how many people encountered the error? Is there anything unique about their system configurations? Is there anything unique about the circumstances in which the error was encountered? Can the circumstances causing the error be repeated?

Step 2: Gather Information on the Problem and Possible Solutions

 Chapters 6 and 12 presented much of the information and tools available for administering and better understanding LAN Server. The following are useful sources for help in problem determination:

- Error and Transaction Logs
- LAN Server Statistics
- Productivity Aids
- OS/2 Trace Facilities
- Documentation
- The IBM Technical Connection
- User Forums
- Network Management Tools and Protocol Analyzers

Error and Transaction Logs

Three logs that are particularly useful for debugging network errors are the LANTRAN.LOG located in the IBMCOM subdirectory (Table 14.1), LAN Server Error Log, and the OS/2 System Log. LANTRAN.LOG is an ASCII file that provides a wealth of information on your system's network software

Table 14.1 **Example of LANTRAN.LOG**

IBM OS/2 LANMSGDD [09/13/93] 2.01 is loaded and operational.

IBM OS/2 LAN Protocol Manager

IBM OS/2 NETBEUI 2.01

NETBEUI: Using a 32-bit data segment.

Installing NETWKSTA.200 version 3.0. IBM LAN Redirector (Jul 09, 1993)

IBM OS/2 NETBIOS 4.0

Adapter 0 has 90 NCBs, 108 sessions, and 18 names available to NETBIOS application

NETBIOS 4.0 is loaded and operational.

IBM OS/2 LANDD [09/13/93] 2.01.2

IBM OS/2 LANDLLDD 2.01

IBM OS/2 LANDLLDD is loaded and operational.

IBM - IBM Token-Ring Network Driver, Version V.2.02

IBM LANVDD is loaded and operational.

IBM OS/2 LAN Netbind

IBM Token-Ring adapter data rate is 4 mbps.

IBM LANDD is accessing IBM 802.5 LAN Interface.

Adapter 0 was initialized and opened successfully.

Adapter 0 is using node address 10005A8F9DEE.

IBM LANDD was successfully bound to MAC: IBMTOK_nif-> VECTOR.

Adapter 0 is using node address 10005A8F9DEE.

levels, the NICs installed and their addresses, and the network transmission rate. The LANTRAN.LOG also contains a record of the initializations or errors encountered when your network protocols and services are activated.

The LAN Server Error Log can be viewed by selecting the Error Log icon within the Administrative GUI, entering NET ERROR at the OS/2 command prompt, or using the LSERROR utility by entering **LSERROR \\<server-name>** at an OS/2 command prompt. A list of the errors is, by default, displayed in chronological order. You can reverse this display to view the most recent errors first by adding a /R parameter after the NET ERROR command, or via the LSERROR options menu.

The OS/2 System Log provides an OS/2 Error Log Formatter Window that allows you to open, print, or display log files and to start and stop system logging. This window can be displayed by entering **SYSLOG** at an OS/2 command prompt.

LAN Server Statistics

LAN Server keeps a statistics log that is accessed via the NET STATISTICS, or NET STATS command. NET STATS can be run on any workstation (requester, server, or peer) and provides statistics on the amount of data sent and received, the number of retransmissions, the number of network transmission errors, the number of disconnections, the number of failed sessions, and the number of times the buffers have been exhausted. Table 14.2 shows the output from a NET STATS run performed on an OS/2 Requester.

 ### LAN Server Productivity Aids

The following productivity aids were introduced in the "Problem Determination" section of Chapter 12:

DIRSTAT	Displays network adapter status.
FINDNAME	Locates duplicate NetBIOS names.
LSS	Monitors network errors, messages, and alerts, and provides problem determination support.
NCBSTAT	Displays NetBIOS statistics.
NETSESS2	Displays session statistics.
RDRDEBUG	Dumps LAN Server internal data structures.
SMBTOOL	Captures and views System Message Blocks.
SNAPDF	Formats and views SNAPDUMP data.
SNAPDUMP	Data collection tool.

LSS is a general-purpose network management tool. The rest of the productivity aids previously listed provide specific information on a single workstation. See Chapter 12 for more information on their use.

OS/2 Trace Facilities

OS/2 and the LAN transport provide system trace hooks in the code that, when invoked, can be useful in determining how the code is being imple-

Table 14.2 **Example of NET STATS REQ Output**

Requester Statistics for \\SCHERER	
Statistics since 04-24-95 02:58 pm	
Network I\O's performed	
Redirector	151284
Server	0
Application	66367
Total	217651
Network errors	
Redirector	0
Server	0
Application	0
Total	0
Kilobytes sent	
Redirector	42994
Server	0
Application	119
Total	43113
Kilobytes received	
Redirector	12632
Server	0
Application	8085
Total	20717
Sessions started	17
Sessions starts failed	0
Sessions disconnected	1
Sessions reconnected	0
Connections made	19
Connections failed	2
Times buffers exhausted	
Big buffers	1
Request buffers	0
The command completed successfully.	

mented. This is an advanced problem-solving technique that takes some practice. The results are not very helpful to a casual user, but they are very valuable to developers and system technicians familiar with OS/2 processes and architecture. Information on OS/2 Trace can be found in the *Problem Determination Guide* and by typing **HELP TRACE** at an OS/2 command line. The syntax of the trace facility has changed between OS/2 and Warp releases, so be sure to check these references before attempting a trace. To perform a trace on OS/2 Warp 3.0, you will need to do the following:

1. Add the statements TRACE=ON and TRACEBUF=64 to your CON-FIG.SYS file.
2. Shut down your system and reboot to activate the changes made to CONFIG.SYS.
3. When you are ready to trace, type **TRACE ON** followed by the events you wish to trace. If you enter TRACE ON with no events specified, you will trace all events. Tracing all events will create an enormous amount of data that will overrun your trace buffer in seconds! To get something useful, you must select only the events that can provide information on the problem you are trying to solve, and you must run the trace for no more than five seconds. Recommendations for network related events are:
   —04 (Interrupts)
   —18 (Process Dispatches)
   —36 (Virtual Memory)
   —48 (DOS Calls)
   —164 (LAN Transports)
   —169 (LAN Transports)
   So the entire OS/2 command should be: TRACE ON 04, 18, 36, 48, 164, 169
4. Trace the event.
5. Stop the trace by entering **TRACE OFF**.

It may take some practice to do all this in less than five seconds. One technique is to go through the process once for practice and then use the buffered commands by pressing the Up Arrow on your keyboard to reissue the command sequence. Remember to clear the trace before restarting a new one.

The resulting trace can then be viewed using the OS/2 Trace Formatter. The formatter is invoked by entering **TRACEFMT** at the OS/2 command line. The Formatter lets you view the raw events in the order in which they occurred, as well as summaries by Process ID and by Major Code. The raw format is generally more useful for tracing the events leading up to an error condition.

 ### LAN Server Documentation

Three sources of useful documentation for problem determination are *Up and Running!*, the *LAN Server Network Administrators' Reference*, Volume 2, and the *LAN Server Problem Determination Guide. Up and Running!* provides lots of help for new installations and a chapter listing a few problems and fixes. While the subtitle of the *LAN Server Network Administrators' Reference*, Volume 2 is "Performance Tuning," this is really a guide for understanding the inter-workings of LAN Server's primary configuration file, IBMLAN.INI. The main source for LAN Server problem determination is the *LAN Server Problem Determination Guide.* This reference contains important information on error messages, alerts, and procedures for system recovery.

The IBM Technical Connection

The IBM Technical Connection is a set of products and services for OS/2 and LAN Systems product users. An example of one of the products is an expert system-based problem determination software program called AskPSP, which is used to isolate a problem and provide advice for fixes. The program asks a series of questions and determines the problem and fix based on the answers provided. AskPSP is used extensively by IBM Customer Support personnel. Updates to the AskPSP database are provided at regular intervals to continuously expand and improve the level of problems that can be addressed. More information can be obtained by calling the OS/2 Support number provided in Appendix B.

 ### Electronic Forums and User Groups

Appendix B also lists some of the key electronic forums. Local forums and user groups can also be good sources of information. These can be found through searching the Internet, through computer trade journals, and by checking with local suppliers.

Network Management Tools and Protocol Analyzers

Network management tools and protocol analyzers are not necessary for small networks but they are very valuable for large complex installations and network software development groups. Basic network management tools monitor the network for alerts, help locate and identify problems, and provide tools for recovery and maintenance. LSS, included with LAN Server 4.0, is an example of a basic network management tool. More sophisticated tools automate many of the preceding processes, provide remote console access, and may provide additional features, such as performance monitoring, network security, and software licensing and distribution.

Protocol analyzers passively monitor data transmitted over a network. Triggers can be set to log information when a particular sequence of events occurs. For this reason, protocol analyzers can be valuable tools for catching infrequent or intermittent problems affecting transmissions over a network.

Step 3: Isolate the Problem

Isolating the cause of a problem on a network can be a big challenge. Unfortunately, if you have software and hardware from numerous sources, it may be necessary for you to do some detective work just in order to contact the right people to supply a fix. There are two basic approaches to problem isolation: direct and indirect. The direct approach involves looking for the source of the problem by checking error logs and looking for anomalies in the configuration, statistics, traces, and dumps. Sometimes problems leave no trail of evidence and require an indirect approach.

The indirect approach works through the process of elimination and involves methodically changing one factor at a time to either re-create or eliminate the problem. All data collected during the indirect approach is relevant and should be noted. Really tricky problems may be intermittent: Changing one factor may increase or decrease the frequency of the problem reoccurring.

 Other difficult problems to isolate are those triggered by a combination of parameters or events; these require research into how the parameters interrelate. You could approach these problems by blindly changing combinations of parameters, but more often than not, the random approach will take more time and be more likely to leave your system in an unrecoverable state. Be sure to back up and record the original configuration before attempting any changes.

 The Ten Least Wanted List— and Their Solutions

The following is a list of LAN Server 3.0 and 4.0 problems and recommended procedures supplied by the IBM Technical Connection team and IBM Customer Support:

Problem 1: NET2297 Error–A Duplicate Name Exists on the Local Area Network

This message may come up when using LAN Server 3.0 and indicates that multilogon is not enabled and that you or someone else has already logged on to the network with the same user ID. If you need to log on from more than one workstation, you can enable multilogon by changing the MULTI-LOGON parameter to YES within the IBMLAN.INI file. The other solution is to add a new user ID for your use to the domain.

Problem 2: Error During Boot–Cannot Connect to <network type> Network

This often indicates that your network cable has come loose from the back of your computer.

Problem 3: Error During Boot–A Problem Exists with the System Configuration. The domain specified could not be used.

The cable is not attached to the port, or a break has otherwise occurred in the physical connection between your workstation and the domain controller.

Problem 4: Message During Boot—The MESSENGER Service is Not Started

This indicates that your messenger service is not configured. This does not affect anything other than the ability to send and receive NET SEND messages over the network. If you want messages enabled, edit IBMLAN.INI to add MESSENGER to the *wrkservices* parameter, or use the LAN Server 4.0 Tailored Install path to set the messaging service to *on*.

Problem 5: MPTS Configuration Update Not Recognized by LAN Server

The MPTS icon is used for configuring protocol support for products other than LAN Server. If you are adding or deleting more than one adapter, you must use the LAN Server Install and Config icon, rather than configuring LAPS through the MPTS icon.

Problem 6: Unable to Logon to Domain after Installing OS/2 Peer Services

Most likely, installing the Peer Service changed your logon profile to be verified locally rather than through the domain. If you are using LAN Server 3.0, change the LOGONVERIFICATION parameter in IBMLAN.INI to DOMAIN. If using LAN Server 4.0, the change is made by setting WORKHEURISTIC #37 to 2 in the IBMLAN.INI. Be very careful in changing the workheuristic bits! Depending on the editor you are using, the bits may not line up with the template provided in the preceding. If using the OS/2-supplied editor, select the *system monospaced* option to get the numbers aligned correctly, or select a character-based editor to use for this purpose. It is a good idea to make a copy of the original workheuristics line before altering it (you can use a semi-colon to comment out the unused line).

Problem 7: DOS LAN Services Trap Using GUI Logoff

Request APAR fix IC08471 from IBM customer service.

Problem 8: DOS LAN Services General Protection Fault When Logoff from Windows

Request APAR fix IC09087 from IBM customer service.

Problem 9: DOS LAN Services with LAN Support Program Hang on NET START

Request APAR fix IC08586 from IBM customer service.

Problem 10: NET3062 Error on 2nd Server— The Server Service Could Not Be Started

This indicates that a problem occurred with synchronization of the internal passwords between an additional server and the domain controller. This may occur if the domain controller is stopped without stopping the additional server, the additional server is down for an extended period of time, or an old copy of NET.ACC was installed on the domain controller or additional server. Other error messages listed in the NET ERROR log that may indicate this problem are:

- NET3056—A system error has occurred. OS/2 error #5 has occurred. SYS0005: Access denied.
- NET3113—An initialization failed because the requested NETLOGON service could not be started.
- NET3210—This server failed to authenticate with *<machine name>*, the domain controller for domain *<domain name>*.

The following procedure attempts to resynchronize the internal passwords used between the domain controller and an additional server. The technique is to isolate the two servers by reconfiguring the Additional Server as Stand-alone, manually change portions of the account data to agree on both servers, and try to trigger a resynchronization by reintroducing the Additional server as a Member of the domain. If the differences between the NET.ACC files are not too extensive, the first few steps of this process will fix the problem. If NET.ACC is severely corrupted, you will need to replace it. More information on specific commands used in these procedures can be found in Chapter 11 and in the "LAN Server Commands and Utilities" online reference. Information on specific parameters within IBMLAN.INI is found in the *LAN Server Network Administrators' Reference*, Volume 2.

1. Make sure the NETLOGON service is running on the domain controller by entering **NET START NETLOGON** at the domain controller's OS/2 command prompt. If NETLOGON cannot be started, skip to section labeled "NETLOGON Does Not Start".

2. At the additional server, enter **NET START SERVER** at the OS/2 command prompt. If the server does not start, proceed to the next step.

3. Log on to the additional server and ensure that passwords are being verified locally by entering **LOGON <userid> /P:<password> /V:LOCAL** at the OS/2 command prompt. If you cannot log on, skip to section labeled "Cannot Logon to Domain."

4. Stop the server service, if running, by entering **NET STOP SERVER**.

5. Set the internal password of the Additional Server on the domain controller by entering **NET USER <AScomputername> <newpassword>**, where *AScomputername* is the computer name of the Additional Server (as defined in the IBMLAN.INI file), and *newpassword* is an arbitrary password for resynchronizing the servers.

6. Set the Additional Server's role to Stand-alone by entering **NET ACCOUNTS /ROLE:STANDALONE**.

7. Set the new password locally on the Additional Server by entering **NET USER <AScomputername> <newpassword>**, where *AScomputername* is the computer name of the Additional Server, and *newpassword* is the same as that entered previously.

8. Reset the Additional Server's role to Member by entering **NET ACCOUNTS /ROLE:MEMBER**.

9. Restart the server service by entering **NET START SERVER**.

NETLOGON Does Not Start

1. Stop all services on the Additional Server by entering **NET STOP REQ**.

2. Restart the Requester by entering **NET START REQ**.

3. Log on to the domain by entering **LOGON <userid> /P:<password>**.

4. Delete the Additional Server from the servers group by typing **NET GROUP SERVERS <AScomputername> /D**, where *AScomputer name* is the computer name of the additional server, as defined in the IBMLAN.INI file.

5. Delete the server machine ID by typing **NET USERS <AScomputer name> /D**.

6. Redefine the Additional Server by typing **NET USERS <AScomp utername> <newpassword> /ADD**.

7. Add the new Additional Server definition to the Servers Group by typing **NET GROUP SERVERS <AScomputername> /ADD**.

8. Restart the server service by typing **NET START SERVER**. If the NETLOGON service does not start, try repeating Steps 3 through 9 of the preceding section. If the NETLOGON service still does not start, replace the NET.ACC file. See the following section, "Replacing a Corrupted NET.ACC," for instructions.

Cannot Log On to Domain

1. If logon was not successful, log on to the Additional Server with a different administrator ID.

2. If the default user ID is configured, delete it by entering **NET USER USERID /D**.

3. Re-create the default user ID with administrator privilege by entering **NET USER USERID PASSWORD /ACTIVE:YES /ADD /PRIVI-LEGE:ADMIN**.

4. Redefine the additional server role to stand-alone by entering **NET ACCOUNTS /ROLE:STANDALONE**.

5. Delete the default user ID from the Additional Server, if present, by typing **NET USER USERID /D**.

6. Add the default user ID with administrative privilege to the Additional Server by entering **NET USER USERID PASSWORD /ACTIVE:YES /ADD /PRIVILEGE:ADMIN**.

7. Reset the server role of the Additional Server by entering **NET ACCOUNTS /ROLE:MEMBER**.

8. Return to Step 3 of the first section.

Replacing a Corrupted NET.ACC

The NET.ACC file is the user accounts database that is used to store user IDs, group IDs, and passwords for LAN Server. On the LAN Server Entry version,

NET.ACC is also used to store access control profiles for all resources except for access control profiles of files and directories stored on a LAN Server Advanced HPFS386 partition. A copy of NET.ACC resides on every server on the domain. These are copies made from a master kept on the domain controller. NET.ACC can become corrupted or lost due to a corrupted hard disk as well as through synchronization errors. Symptoms of a corrupted NET.ACC include those described in the previous sections, plus the following:

- User IDs, group definitions, or access control profiles cannot be created or changed.
- Logon assignments disappear.
- Users cannot access some or all of their aliases.
- Users cannot log on.
- NET2247 Error—The user accounts database file is damaged.
- NET3122 Error—Initialization failed because the NET.ACC file is either incorrect or not present.
- NET3055 Error—A problem exists with the system configuration. Either the server cannot access the user accounts database (NET.ACC) or the user accounts system is not configured correctly.

The process for restoring a NET.ACC file is as follows:

1. Run the CHKDSK utility on the affected Server.
2. If the problem is not corrected by CHKDSK, run FIXACC.
3. Shut down the workstation, restart, and log on to the server. FIXACC removes entries from the NET.ACC file that it cannot fix, so if you can successfully log on you will need to reverify the presence of all user IDs, groups, and access controls.
4. If FIXACC does not adequately rebuild the NET.ACC, you must restore the NET.ACC from a backup or default copy. If you do not have a backup copy, skip to Step 7.
5. Copy your backup copy of NET.ACC to the IBMLAN\ACCOUNTS subdirectory. Shut down the Server workstation.
6. Restart the Server and try logging on.
7. If all preceding steps fail, you must rebuild your accounts using a default copy of the NET.ACC file contained in the \IBMLAN\ INSTALL subdirectory. Use the OS/2 COPY command to copy this

file from the \IBMLAN\INSTALL subdirectory to \IBMLAN\ ACCOUNTS\.

8. Change the Server's role to primary by entering **NET ACCOUNTS /ROLE:PRIMARY**.

9. Add the SERVERS group account to the NET.ACC by entering **NET GROUP SERVERS /ADD**.

10. Add the server to the NET.ACC file as a user account by entering **NET USER <server name> /ADD /PRIV:USER /ACTIVE:NO /EXPIRES:NEVER /PASSWORDREQ:NO**.

11. If the Server is a domain controller, set the server's account password to null by entering **NET USER <server name> ""**, and add the GUEST ID to NET.ACC by entering **NET USER GUEST /ADD /PRIV:GUEST /PASSWORDREQ:NO**.

12. Add the Server to the SERVERS group by entering **NET GROUP SERVERS <server name> /ADD**.

13. If the Server is not a primary domain controller, change its role back to MEMBER or BACKUP by entering **NET ACCOUNTS /ROLE: <MEMBER or BACKUP>**.

 # Tips for Working with Customer Support

Some problems simply do not yield to simple solutions. If you work with computers, sooner or later you will find yourself calling customer support. By following the tips outlined in this section, you can improve the likelihood that your problem will be resolved quickly.

Be calm. Solving problems takes a cool head. The more relaxed you are, the more likely you will be able to work effectively with Customer Support to isolate your problem.

Do your homework. Take reasonable actions to solve the problem yourself before calling Customer Support and take notes on all factors pertaining to the problem. Look up the meaning of any error messages and check the documentation. If the problem has a simple solution, you will probably find it. If not, doing your homework will help you eliminate *dead ends* and provide valuable information to Customer Support for getting the problem fixed. Customer Support loves working with such people, because informed interaction helps them make more efficient strides toward improving the product.

Clearly communicate the problem, all related information, and your requirements and expectations for getting the problem resolved. Include any observations you made when trying to isolate the problem. How serious is the problem? What impact does the problem have on your business? Would you be satisfied with a work-around rather than waiting for a code fix?

Take notes. When you call Customer Support, record the name and telephone number of the person assisting you, and the date and time of the call. Write down any actions suggested to further isolate and fix the problem. If you are satisfied with the helpfulness of the person assisting you, you may want to contact this same person if any follow-up actions are necessary. If you do not feel this person understands your problem, you may want to ask to speak to a person specializing in an area related to your problem or to the supervisor. Ask if there is a problem report number associated with your call and reference it if you need to call again. If a solution to the problem is not readily available, request information on what actions need to be taken and when you can anticipate a response.

Parting Thoughts

In planning and writing this book, Charlie and I spent many hours discussing the most useful materials we could include for someone just starting out in building and administering a network. We have drawn heavily from our combined experience as software designer, technical lead, network administrator, facilities engineer, software performance analyst, and user. We have not always agreed on approaches and have debated the merits of some in an effort to provide a straightforward yet realistic view of the complex topic of networking. We have learned a tremendous amount about our subject in the process. We hope this book has been as much value to you as it has been to us.

Reading maketh a full man, conference a ready man, and writing an exact man. And therefore, if a man write little, he had need have a great memory; if he confer little, he had need have a present wit; and if he read little, he had need have much cunning, to seem to know what he doth not.

—*Sir Francis Bacon,* Essays or Counsels Civil and Moral

APPENDIX A

Comparison of Selected NOS and Peer Products

Name	LAN Server v4.0	Netware v4.1	Windows NT v3.5
Price for 16 users	$1,599 (Entry)	$1,495	$1,339
Additional client licenses required for multiple servers?	No	Yes	No
Clients supported	OS/2, DOS, MAC (add-on), UNIX (add-on), Windows 3.x, Windows for Workgroups, Windows NT	OS/2, DOS, MAC, UNIX, Windows 3.x, Windows for Workgroups, Windows NT	OS/2, DOS, MAC, UNIX, Windows 3.x, Windows for Workgroups, Windows NT
Server platforms	Intel (OS/2), RISC (AIX), AS/400, VM, MVS	Intel (proprietary & OS/2)	Intel, RISC, PPC & DEC Alpha
Shared application support	Yes	No	No
Peer client support	Yes	Yes	Yes
Primary driver type	NDIS	ODI	NDIS
Other protocols supported	ODI, NetBIOS, NetBEUI, TCP/IP, 802.2, AppleTalk (add-on)	NDIS, NetBIOS, TCP/IP, 802.2, IPX/SPX, AppleTalk	ODI, NetBIOS, NetBEUI, TCP/IP, 802.2, IPX/SPX, AppleTalk
Remote IPL	Yes—DOS and OS/2 clients	Yes—DOS and OS/2 clients	Yes—DOS clients only
Multiprocessing support	Yes	No	Yes

Name	LAN Server v4.0	Netware v4.1	Windows NT v3.5
User level security	Yes	Yes	Yes
Share level security	Yes (peer only)	No	Yes
Password encryption	Yes	Yes	Yes
Set account expiration	Yes	Yes	Yes
Restrict logon times	Yes	Yes	Yes
Autodisconnect after specified inactive time	Yes	No	Yes
Lock after set number of failed logon attempts	Yes	Yes	Yes
Security audit trail	Yes	Yes	Yes
Remote Administration	Yes	Yes	Yes
Remote Access	Yes, LAN Distance and DCAF (Warp Connect or add-on)	Yes	Yes
Global Resource Access	Yes	Yes	Yes
Single Logon to Multiple Domains	Yes	Yes	Yes
Server-to-server File Replication	Yes	Yes	Yes
Disk Mirroring	Yes	Yes	Yes
Disk Duplexing	Yes	Yes	Yes
RAID Level 5	No (third party)	No	Yes
Public Application Support	Yes	No	No
Support for aliases	Yes	Yes	No
Printable and searchable online documentation	Yes	Yes (limited)	No
UPS	Yes	Yes	Yes
Alerts	Yes	Yes	Yes
Network Mgmt Interfaces	Native, 802.2; SNMP and CMIP (add-on)	802.2, SNMP	802.2, SNMP

Name	LAN Server v4.0	Netware v4.1	Windows NT v3.5
Maximum number of Concurrent Connections	1,016	1,000	NA
Maximum Server Volume Size	64 GB	32 TB	17 TB
Maximum number of Volumes/Server	24	64	24
Maximum Printers/Server	24	16	NA
Server Required RAM	12 MB	14 MB	16 MB
Server Recommended RAM	16 MB	16 MB	32 MB
Nondedicated Server	Yes	Yes, using OS/2	Yes
Tracks user access time	Yes	Yes	Yes
Tracks average response time	Yes	No	Yes
Tracks user space usage	Yes	Yes	Yes
Cache statistics	Yes	Yes	Yes
Server CPU Utilization	Yes	Yes	Yes
Tracks number of bad packets	Yes	Yes	Yes
Procedural Language Support	Yes, REXX extension	No	Basic
API Support	Yes, same APIs for client and server	Yes, separate APIs for client and server	Yes, mostly same APIs for client and server

APPENDIX B

Where to Get Additional Information

References

IBM OS/2 LAN Server Version 4.0 Easy Start (S10H-9743).

IBM OS/2 LAN Server Version 4.0 Guide to LAN Server Books (S10H-9688).

IBM OS/2 LAN Server Version 4.0 Up and Running! (S10H-9679).

IBM OS/2 LAN Server Version 4.0 Network Administrator Reference, Volume 1: Planning, Installation, and Configuration (S10H-9680).

IBM OS/2 LAN Server Version 4.0 Network Administrator Reference, Volume 2: Performance Tuning (S10H-9681).

IBM OS/2 LAN Server Version 4.0 Network Administrator Reference, Volume 3: Administrator Tasks (S10H-9682).

IBM OS/2 LAN Server Version 4.0 Problem Determination Guide (S10H-9685).

IBM OS/2 LAN Server Version 4.0 OS/2 LAN Requester User's Guide (S10H-9683).

IBM OS/2 LAN Server Version 4.0 DOS LAN Services and Windows User's Guide (S10H-9684).

IBM OS/2 LAN Server Version 4.0 Commands and Utilities (S10H-9686).

IBM OS/2 LAN Server Version 4.0 LAN CID Utility Guide (S10H-9742).

IBM OS/2 LAN Server Version 4.0 MPTS Configuration Guide (S10H-9693).

IBM OS/2 LAN Server Version 4.0 MPTS Programmer's Reference (S10H-9694).

IBM OS/2 LAN Server Version 4.0 MPTS Error Messages and Problem Determination Guide (S10H-9695).

IBM OS/2 LAN Server Version 4.0 Programming Guide and Reference (S10H-9687).

IBM OS/2 LAN Server Version 4.0 DOS Client Access for TCP/IP: Setup (S10H-9384).

IBM OS/2 LAN Server Version 3.0 Network Administrator Reference, Volume 1: Planning and Installation (S96F-8428-00).

IBM OS/2 LAN Server Version 3.0 Network Administrator Reference, Volume 2: Performance Tuning (S96F-8429-00).

IBM OS/2 LAN Server Version 3.0 Network Administrator Reference, Volume 3: Network Administrator Tasks (S96F-8428-00).

IBM OS/2 LAN Server Version 3.0 Command Reference (S96F-8439-00).

IBM OS/2 LAN Server Version 3.0 Productivity Aids (S59G-4684-00).

IBM OS/2 LAN Server Version 3.0 Problem Determination Reference, Volume 1: Problem Determination Guide (S96F-8431-00).

IBM OS/2 LAN Server Version 3.0 Problem Determination Reference, Volume 2: LAN Alerts (S96F-8432-00).

IBM OS/2 LAN Server Version 3.0 Problem Determination Reference, Volume 3: LAN Error Messages (S96F-8433-00).

International Technical Support Centers. 1995. *OS/2 Warp Generation, Volume 2: Exploring LAN Connectivity* (GG24-4505).

International Technical Support Centers. 1995. *Migration from Microsoft LAN Manager to IBM OS/2 LAN Server* (GG24-4387).

International Technical Support Centers. 1995. *Migration from Netware to IBM OS/2 LAN Server* (GG24-4388).

International Technical Support Centers. 1995. *Understanding Performance Tuning Theory for IBM OS/2 LAN Server* (GG24-4430).

International Technical Support Centers. 1995. *Inside OS/2 LAN Server 4.0* (GG24-4428).

International Technical Support Centers. 1993. *Experiences with the IBM OS/2 LAN Server Version 3.0 New Functions* (GG24-3959-01).

International Technical Support Centers. 1993. *The IBM OS/2 LAN Server Version 3.0 System Recovery Considerations* (GG24-4043-00).

Multiple authors. 1995. *OS/2 LAN Server Certification Handbook,* Indianapolis: New Riders (SR28-5649-00)

Orfali, Robert, and Dan Harkey. 1994. *Client/Server Survival Guide with OS/2.* New York: Van Nostrand Reinhold.

Hunter, Philip. 1993. *Local Area Networks: Making the Right Choices.* Great Britain: Addison-Wesley.

Publications

OS/2 Developer   (800) 926-8672

OS/2 Magazine	(800) 765-1291
OS/2 Pointers (USA)	(800) 776-8484
Personal Systems	(800) 547-1283

Useful Phone Numbers

IBM Help Center	(800) 772-2227
IBM Switchboard	(800) 426-3333
IBM Support Family of Services	(800) 799-7765
IBM OS/2 Support	(800) 992-4777
IBM Multimedia Help Line	(800) 241-1620
IBM Part Number ID and Lookup	(303) 924-4015
IBM Publications	(800) 879-2755
IBM PC Technical Books	(800) 765-4426
IBM Fax Information Service	(800) IBM-4FAX
IBM Developer's Assistance	(407) 982-6408
IBM Developer's Connection	(800) 633-8266
OS/2 Device Driver Sourcekit	(800) 633-8266
IBM PSS Canada	(800) 765-4426
IBM Publications Canada	(416) 474-7000
IBM Information FREEway	(800) 992-4777

Online Information and Forums

CompuServe	(800) 848-8990
OS/2 Developers' Forums	GO OS2DF1, GO OS2DF2
OS/2 Users' Forums	GO OS2USER
OS/2 Support Forum	GO OS2SUP
OS2BBS	(800) 547-1283
Prodigy	(800) 776-3449
OS2 Club	JUMP OS2CLUB
Internet (World-Wide Web)	
IBM's main home page	http://www.ibm.com/
IBM's Personal Software Products	http://www.austin.ibm.com/pspinfo/index.html

Conferences

IBM Technical Interchange   (800) 636-6634

Professional Training

OS/2 and LAN Server Professional   (800) 959-EXAM
    Certification Program

IBM Education and Training   (800) IBM-TEAC

Partial List of Suppliers

IBM Direct   (800) 426-2468

IBM Authorized Dealer Listings   (800) 3IBM-OS2

Egghead   (800) SOFTWARE

Indelible Blue, Inc.   (800) 776-8284

APPENDIX C

EtherNet and Token-Ring Network Interface Cards Supported by LAN Server

The following tables provide information on the adapters that have been successfully tested with LAN Server at this time (March 1995).

For Tables 1 through 8, a mark in the "Also DOS" category indicates that the card can be used with a PC configured with DOS LAN Services. A mark under "Also v3.0" indicates that the card is also supported by LAN Server versions 3.0 and 3.01. The "Detect Card" column shows the cards that can be detected and automatically configured by LAN Server's installation program. The "OS/2 NIF File Name" column is filled in for cards that have drivers supplied with LAN Server 4.0. This is the name of the file that describes the card and its drivers. You can correlate this name with the NIF file name in Table 9. The cards that do not have a name in this column supply drivers with the network interface card.

Busmaster cards provide superior performance and reduce load on the CPU; these cards are highly recommended for servers that will be supporting large networks, or frequent large file transfers. The latter includes servers supporting remote IPL or multimedia. The last column includes the cards that were successfully tested in a symmetrical multiprocessing environment. LAN Server also supports several PC Network and emulation adapters.

Table 9 shows the network adapters with drivers shipped in LAN Server 4.0. The "Adapter Title" column is just as displayed by LAN Server 4.0's LAPS Configuration window. You can correlate this with actual adapter names and models by checking the NIF file name and looking it up in Tables 1 through 8.

Tables are organized by the following topics:

Table 1   Ethernet ISA NICs
Table 2   Ethernet EISA NICs
Table 3   Ethernet MCA (Microchannel) NICs
Table 4   Ethernet NICs—Other bus types
Table 5   Token Ring ISA NICs
Table 6   Token Ring EISA NICs
Table 7   Token Ring MCA (Microchannel) NICs
Table 8   Token Ring NICs—Other bus types
Table 9   OS/2 NIC drivers shipped with LAN Server 4.0

Additional information on supported adapters can be found in the *Network Administrator Reference, Volume 1: Planning, Installation, and Configuration* documentation that comes with the LAN Server package.

Table C.1 **EtherNet ISA NICs**

Adapter Title	Also DOS	Also v3.0	Detect Card?	OS/2 NIF File Name	Bus Master	SMP
3Com EtherLink II (3C503)	Y	Y	Y	ELNKII		
3Com EtherLink II-16 (3C503-16)	Y	Y	Y	ELNKII		Y
3Com EtherLink II-16-TP (3C503-16-TP)	Y		Y	ELNKII		
3Com EtherLink 16 (3C507)						
3Com EtherLink 16-TP (3C507-TP)						
3Com EtherLink III (3C509)		Y	Y	EL3IBMO2		Y
3Com EtherLink III-Combo (3C509-COMBO)	Y		Y	EL3IBMOS		
3Com EtherLink III-TP (3C509-TP)	Y		Y	EL3IBMO2		
3Com EtherLink III-TPO (3C509-TPO)	Y		Y	EL3IBMO2		
Accton EtherCombo-16			Y			
Accton EtherPair-16			Y			
Accton EtherCoax-16			Y			

Adapter Title	Also DOS	Also v3.0	Detect Card?	OS/2 NIF File Name	Bus Master	SMP
Artisoft NodeRunner/SI 2000/C			Y	AEXNDIS		
Artisoft NodeRunner/SI 2000/T	Y		Y	AEXNDIS		
Artisoft NodeRunner/SI 2000/A	Y			AEXNDIS		
Artisoft LANTastic NodeRunner/SI 2000/C	Y		Y	AEXNDIS		
Artisoft LANTastic NodeRunner/SI 2000/T			Y	AEXNDIS		
Artisoft LANTastic NodeRunner/SI 2000/A	Y		Y	AEXNDIS		
Asante EtherPaC 2000+3			Y			
Asante EtherPaC 2000+N			Y			
Asante EtherPaC 2000+T			Y			
Cabletron Ethernet DNI Adapter (E1112)		Y		E11		
Cabletron Ethernet DNI Adapter (E1119)				E11		
Cabletron Ethernet DNI Adapter (E2112)	Y	Y		E21		
Cabletron Ethernet DNI Adapter (E2119)	Y			E21		
Cray Communications ScaNet Network Interface Adapter-ISA		Y		PC04		
D-Link Ethernet Interface Card for the PC XT/AT (DE-220C)			Y			
D-Link Ethernet Interface Card for the PC XT/AT (DE-220CAT)			Y			
D-Link Ethernet Interface Card for the PC XT/AT (DE-220CT)	Y		Y			
D-Link Ethernet Interface Card for the PC XT/AT (DE-220T)	Y		Y			
Eagle NE2000				IBMNE200		

Table C.1 **(continued)**

Adapter Title	Also DOS	Also v3.0	Detect Card?	OS/2 NIF File Name	Bus Master	SMP
Eagle NE2000T	Y			IBMNE200		
Eagle NE2000plus	Y			IBMNE200		
Eagle NE2000Tplus	Y			IBMNE200		
Eagle NE2000plus-3	Y			IBMNE200		
Eagle EtherXpert EP2000plus	Y			IBMEP200		
Eagle EtherXpert EP2000Tplus	Y		Y	IEMEP200		
Hewlett-Packard 27247	Y					
IBM LAN Adapter for Ethernet	Y	Y		IBMENI		Y
IBM LAN Adapter for Ethernet CX		Y	Y	IBMENI		
IBM LAN Adapter for Ethernet TP		Y		IBMENI		
Intel EtherExpress 16C	Y	Y	Y	EXP16		Y
Intel EtherExpress FlashC	Y		Y	EXP16		
Intel EtherExpress 16	Y		Y	EXP16		
Intel EtherExpress Flash			Y	EXP16		
Intel EtherExpress 16TP	Y		Y	EXP16		
Intel EtherExpress FlashTP	Y		Y	EXP16		
NCR Corporation WaveLAN Adapter		Y	Y			
Racal InterLan EtherBlaster TP-8INT						
Racal InterLAN AT-TP						
Racal InterLan N15210-16						
SMC EtherCard PLUS (8003EB)		Y	Y	MACWDAT		
SMC EtherCard PLUS Elite (8003EP)			Y			
SMC EtherCard PLUS Elite 10T (8003WC)	Y					
SMC EtherCard PLUS Elite 16T (8013WC)	Y		Y			

Adapter Title	Also DOS	Also v3.0	Detect Card?	OS/2 NIF File Name	Bus Master	SMP
SMC EtherCard PLUS Elite 16 (8013EPC)			Y			
SMC EtherCard PLUS Elite 16 Combo (8013EWC)	Y		Y			
SMC EtherCard Elite 16 Ultra (8216)						
SMC EtherCard Elite 16C Ultra (8216C)		Y	Y			
SMC EtherCard Elite 16T Ultra (8216T)	Y		Y			
Ungermann-Bass NIUpc Adapter		Y	Y	UBNEIPC		

Table C.2 **Ethernet EISA NICs**

Adapter Title	Also DOS	Also v3.0	Detect Card?	OS/2 NIF File Name	Bus Master	SMP
3Comm EtherLink III-EISA (3C579)		Y	Y	ELNK3		Y
3Comm EtherLink III-EISA-TP (3C579-TP)			Y	ELNK3		
Accton EtherCombo-32			Y			
Compaq NetFlex-2 ENET-TR Controller		Y			Y	Y
D-Link Ethernet Card for EISA Bus PC	Y		Y			
Eagle NE3210	Y		Y	IBMNE321		
Eagle EtherXpert EP3210	Y		Y	IBMEP321		
Racal InterLan ES3210		Y				Y
Racal InterLan ES3210-TP			Y			
SMC EtherCard Elite32C Ultra		Y	Y		Y	

Table C.3 **Ethernet MCA (Micro Channel) NICs**

Adapter Title	Also DOS	Also v3.0	Detect Card?	OS/2 NIF File Name	Bus Master	SMP
3Comm EtherLink MC (3C523B)	Y	Y	Y	ELNKMC		
3Comm EtherLink MC-TP (3C523B-TP)	Y		Y	ELNKMC		
3Comm EtherLink MC-32 (3C527B)	Y		Y		Y	
3Comm EtherLink III-MCA (3C529)		Y	Y	EL3IBMO2		
3Comm EtherLink III-MCA-TP (3C529-TP)	Y		Y	FL3IBMO2		
Artisoft NodeRunner/SI 2000M/TC	Y		Y	AEXNDIS		
Artisoft LANTastic NodeRunner 2000M/TC	Y		Y			
Cabletron Ethernet DNI Adapter (E3112)	Y	Y	Y	E31		
Cabletron Ethernet DNI Adapter (E3119)	Y		Y	E31		
Cray Communications ScaNet Network Interface Adapter-MCA		Y	Y	PC04		
IBM Adapter/A for Ethernet Networks		Y	Y	MACETH		
IBM Adapter/A for Ethernet Twisted Pair Networks	Y	Y	Y	MACETH		
IBM LAN Adapter/A for Ethernet	Y	Y	Y	IBMENII		
IBM EtherStreamer MC 32 Adapter		Y	Y	IBMMPC	Y	
IBM Dual EtherStreamer MC 32 Adapter		Y	Y	IBMMPC	Y	
Intel EtherExpress MCA	Y		Y	EXP16		
Intel EtherExpress MCATP	Y		Y	EXP16		
Racal InterLan InterLan MCA			Y			
Racal InterLan InterLan MCA-TP	Y	Y				
SMC EtherCard PLUS/A	Y		Y	MACWDMC		

Table C.3 **(continued)**

Adapter Title	Also DOS	Also v3.0	Detect Card?	OS/2 NIF File Name	Bus Master	SMP
SMC EtherCard PLUS Elite/A			Y			
SMC EtherCard PLUS Elite 10T/A	Y		Y			
Ungermann-Bass NIUps Adapter		Y	Y	UBNEIPS		

Table C.4 **Ethernet NICs-Other bus types**

Adapter Title	Also DOS	Also v3.0	Detect Card?	OS/2 NIF File Name	Bus Master	SMP
D-Link Ethernet VESA Combo Card						
IBM Credit Card Adapter for Ethernet				PCMNICCS		
IBM Credit Card Adapter II for Ethernet				PCMNICCS		
Xircom CreditCard Ethernet Adapter						
Xircom PS-CreditCard Ethernet Adapter						
Xircom Pocket Ethernet Adapter III						

Table C.5 **Token Ring ISA NICs**

Adapter Title	Also DOS	Also v3.0	Detect Card?	OS/2 NIF File Name	Bus Master	SMP
3Com TokenLink III (3C619)		Y	Y	TLNKIli		
Cabletron Token-Ring DNI Adapter (T3015)	Y	Y		T30		
IBM Token-Ring Network Adapter		Y	Y	IBMTOK		
IBM Token-Ring Network Adapter II	Y	Y	Y	IBMTOK		
IBM Token-Ring Network 16/4 Adapter	Y	Y	Y	IBMTOK		Y
IBM Token-Ring Network 16/4 ISA-16 Adapter	Y	Y	Y	IBMTOK		Y
IBM Token-Ring Network 16/4 Adapter II		Y			Y	
IBM Auto 16/4 Token-Ring ISA Adapter	Y			IBMTOK		
Intel TokenExpress ISA/16S	Y	Y	Y	INTEL16		Y
Madge Smart 16/4 AT PLUS Ringnode	Y	Y				
Madge Straight Blue 16/4 ISA		Y	Y	IBMTOKC		Y
Madge Straight Blue ISA Plus Blue Box			Y	IBMTOKC		
Olicom ISA 16/4 Adapter	Y	Y	Y	IBMTOKC		
Proteon p1392plus ProNET - 4/16 Plus	Y					
Racal InterLan InterLan T/R 16/4 ISA	Y		Y			
Racore Token-Ring ISA	Y			RTR16NDS		
Texas Instruments TokenLite Token-Ring Adapter	Y			TR2KNDIS		
Thomas-Conrad Tropic 16/4 Token-Ring Adapter/AT	Y		Y	TCCTOK		
Thomas-Conrad 16/4 Token-Ring Adapter/AT	Y			TCCTOK		

Table C.6 **Token Ring EISA NICs**

Adapter Title	Also DOS	Also v3.0	Detect Card?	OS/2 NIF File Name	Bus Master	SMP
3Com TokenLink III EISA (3C679)	Y	Y	Y	TLNKIII		
Compaq NetFlex-2 ENET-TR Controller	Y			NETFLX		
DCA IRMAtrac EISA			Y			
IBM 16/4 Busmaster EISA Adapter		Y	Y	IBMEIOS2		
Intel TokenExpress 16/4 LAN Adapter for EISA	Y		Y	INTEL 16		Y
Intel Token Express EISA/32 LAN Adapter	Y	Y	Y	INTEL32		Y
Madge Smart 16/4 EISA Ringnode	Y		Y			Y
Olicom EISA 16/4 Adapter			Y			
Olicom EISA/32 Adapter	Y		Y			Y
Proteon p1990plus ProNET - 4/16 Plus	Y		Y			Y
SMC TokenCard Elite Master 32	Y		Y			

Table C.7 **Token Ring MCA (Micro Channel) NICs**

Adapter Title	Also DOS	Also v3.0	Detect Card?	OS/2 NIF File Name	Bus Master	SMP
3Com TokenLink III MCA		Y	Y	TLNKIII		
Cabletron Token-Ring DNI Adapter (T3015)		Y	Y	T30		
DCA ClassicBlue MC 4/16 Token-Ring Adapter			Y	IBMTOKC		
DCA IRMAtrac Token-Ring Adapter /Convertible-MCA		Y	Y			
IBM Token-Ring Network Adapter/A	Y	Y	Y	IBMTOK		
IBM Token-Ring Network 16/4 Adapter/A	Y	Y	Y	IBMTOK		
IBM 16/4 Busmaster Server Adapter/A		Y	Y	IBMTRBM	Y	
IBM LANStreamer MC 16 Adapter			Y	IBMTRDB	Y	
IBM LANStreamer MC 32 Adapter			Y	IBMTRDB	Y	
IBM Auto LANStreamer MC 32 Adapter		Y	Y	IBMMPC	Y	
IBM Dual LANStreamer MC 32 Adapter		Y	Y	IBMMPC	Y	
Madge Smart 16/4 MC Ringnode	Y		Y			
Madge Smart 16/4 MC32 Ringnode	Y	Y	Y			
Madge Straight Blue MC Blue Box			Y	IBMTOKC		
Olicom MCA 16/4 Adapter	Y		Y			
Proteon p1892plus ProNET - 4/16 Plus			Y			
Racal InterLan T/R 16/4 MCA	Y					
Racore Token-Ring MC		Y		RTR16NDS		
SMC TokenCard Elite/A	Y		Y			
Thomas-Conrad 16/4 Token-Ring Adapter/MC	Y	Y	Y	TCCTOK		

Table C.8 **Token Ring NICs - Other bus types**

Adapter Title	Also DOS	Also v3.0	Detect Card?	OS/2 NIF File Name	Bus Master	SMP
IBM Token-Ring 16/4 Credit Card Adapter				IBMTOKCS		
IBM Token-Ring 16/4 Credit Card Adapter II	Y			IBMTOKCS		
Olicom Token-Ring PCMCA Card						
Xircom Credit Card Token-Ring Adapter						
Olicom Pocket Token-Ring Adapter	Y					
Xircom External Token-Ring Adapter						
Xircom Pocket Token-Ring Adapter III	Y					

Table C.9 **Network Adapters with OS/2 Drivers Shipped in LAN Server 4.0**

Adapter Title	NIF file name	Driver file name	Driver name
3Com TokenLink III Network Adapters	TLNKIII.NIF	IBMTOK.OS2	IBMTOK$
3Com EtherLink III Family	EL3IBMO2.NIF	ELNK3.OS2	ELNK3$
3Com 3C503 EtherLink II Adapter	ELNKII.NIF	ELNKII.OS2	ELNKII$
3Com 3C523 EtherLink/MC Adapter	ELNKMC.NIF	ELNKMC.OS2	ELNKMC$
Artisoft NodeRunner & AE-X Ethernet Adapters	AEXNDIS.NIF	AEXNDIS.OS2	AEXNDS$
Cabletron E11 Ethernet Adapter	E11.NIF	E11ND.OS2	E11ND$
Cabletron E31 Ethernet Adapter	E31.NIF	E31ND.OS2	E31ND$
Cabletron T20 Tokenring Adapter	T20.NIF	T20ND.OS2	T20ND$
Cabletron T30 Tokenring Adapter	T30.NIF	T30ND.OS2	T30ND$
Cabletron E21 Ethernet Adapter	E21.NIF	E21ND.OS2	E21ND$
Dowty Network Systems PC/PS-x1x4/x5	PC04.NIF	PC04.OS2	PC04X$
Eagle Technology NE2000plus Ethernet Adapter	IBMNE200.NIF	NE2000.OS2	NE2000E$
Eagle Technology NE3210 EISA Ethernet Adapter	IBMNE321.NIF	NE3210.OS2	NE3210E$
Eagle Technology EtherXpert EP2000plus Adapter	IBMEP200.NIF	EP2000.OS2	EP2000E$
Eagle Technology EP3210 EtherXpert Adapter	IBMEP321.NIF	EP3210.OS2	EP3210E$
IBM Credit Card Adapter for Ethernet with NDIS support	PCMNICCS.NIF	PCMNICCS.OS2	PCM_CS$
IBM PC Network II/A and Baseband/A Adapters	IBMNETA.NIF	IBMNETA.OS2	IBMNETA$
IBM PC Network II and Baseband Adapters	IBMNET.NIF	IBMNET.OS2	IBMNET$
IBM Token Ring Network 16/4 Adapter II	IBM16OS2.NIF	IBM16TR.OS2	IBM16TR$
IBM 16/4 Busmaster EISA Adapter	IBMEIOS2.NIF	IBMEITR.OS2	IBMEITR$

Adapter Title	NIF file name	Driver file name	Driver name
IBM SMP Token-Ring Network Adapter	IBMTOKMP.NIF	IBMTOKMP.OS2	IBMTOK$
IBM PCMCIA Token-Ring Network Adapters	IBMTOKCS.NIF	IBMTOKCS.OS2	IBMTOK$
IBM Token-Ring Network Adapter	IBMTOK.NIF	IBMTOK.OS2	IBMTOK$
IBM Compatible Token-Ring Network Adapter	IBMTOKC.NIF	IBMTOK.OS2	IBMTOK$
IBM LAN Adapter for Ethernet	IBMENI.NIF	IBMENI.OS2	IBMENI$
IBM LAN Adapter/A for Ethernet	IBMENII.NIF	IBMENII.OS2	IBMENII$
IBM Token-Ring Network Busmaster Server Adapter	IBMTRBM.NIF	IBMTRBM.OS2	IBMTRBM$
IBM LANStreamer Adapter NDIS Device Driver	IBMTRDB.NIF	IBMTRDB.OS2	IBMTRDB$
IBM Streamer Family Adapter	IBMMPC.NIF	IBMMPC.OS2	IBMMPC$
IBM 3270 Adapter for 3174 Peer Communications	IBMXLN.NIF	IBMXLN.OS2	IBMXLN$
IBM PS/2 Adapter for Ethernet Networks	MACETH.NIF	MACETH.OS2, MACETH2.OS2	MACETH$
Intel EtherExpress 16 Family Adapter	EXP16.NIF	EXP16.OS2	EXP16$
Intel TokenExpress(tm) 16/4 Adapter	INTEL16.NIF	INTEL16.OS2	OLITOK$
Intel TokenExpress(tm) EISA/32 Adapter	INTEL32.NIF	INTEL32.OS2	OLISRV$
Olicom Token-Ring Network 16/4 Adapters	OLITOK.NIF	OLITOK16.OS2	OLITOK$
Racore 16/4 Token-Ring Adapter	RTR16NDS.NIF	RTR16NDS.OS2	RTRNDS$
Standard Microsystems EtherCard PLUS Software-Configured Adapters	MACWDAT.NIF	MACWD.OS2, MACWD2.OS2	MACWD$
Standard Microsystems EtherCard PLUS Micro Channel Adapters	MACWDMC.NIF	MACWD.OS2, MACWD2.OS2	MACWD$
Texas Instruments TokenLite Compatible Token-Ring Adapter	TR2KNDIS.NIF	TR2KNDIS.OS2	TR2NDS$
Thomas-Conrad Token Ring Adapter	TCCTOK.NIF	TCCTOK.OS2	TCCTOK$
Ungermann-Bass NIUpc adapters	UBNEIPC.NIF	UBNEI.OS2	UBNEI$
Ungermann-Bass NIUps adapters	UBNEIPS.NIF	UBNEI.OS2	UBNEI$

APPENDIX D

OS/2 Warp Version 3.0 Printer Support

AST TurboLaser

Agfa Matrix ChromaScript v51_8, Compugraphic 9400PS v49_3 and Compugraphic 400PS

Apple LaserWriter,II NT,II NTX,Plus, and Plus v42_2

Brother HJ-100i, HJ-400, HL-10PS/DPS, HL-10V, HK-10h, HL-10h(PS), and HL-1260

Brother HL-1260(PS), 4PS, 4V, 630, 631, 641, 645, 655M, 660, 6, 6V, and 8PS

Brother HS-1PS, HS-1PS2, M-1309, M-1324, M-1809, M-1809 Color, and M-1824L

Brother M-1824L Color, 1909, 1909 Color, 1924L, 1924L Color, and 4309

COMPAQ PAGEMARQ 15 and PAGEMARQ 20

Citizen PN48 Portable Printer

ColorMaster Plus 6603 v233_1, 6613 v233_1, and 6613XF v260_0

Colormate PS v51_9

Dataproducts LZR 1260 v47_0 and LZR-2665

Digital DECcolorwriter 1000 17 and 100039

Digital LN03R ScriptPrinter and LPS PrintServer 40

Epson AP-2250, 3250, 3260, 5000, and 5500

Epson ActionLaser 1000 in PCL4, 1000/1500, 1600, and 1600 in PCL5

Epson DFX-5000, DFX-8000, EPL-7000, EPL-7500 v52_3, and EPL-8000 PS Card 82605

Epson EPL-8000, EX-1000, EX-800, FX-1050, FX-1170, FX-286e, FX-850, FX-870, and JX

Epson LQ-1010, 1050 (N9), 1050, 1070, 1070 plus, 1170, 150, 2500 Color, and 2550 Color

Epson LQ-500, 510, 570, 850 (N9), 850, 860 Color, 870, and 950 (N9)

Epson LX-800, LX-810, and MX-80

Epson Stylus 300 Inkjet printer, 800 Inkjet printer, and Color Inkjet printer

Generic PostScript Printer

HP 7470A, 7475A, 7550A, 7580A, 7580B, 7585A, 7585B, and 7586B Plotters

HP Color LaserJet, Color LaserJet PS, and ColorPro

HP DesignJet 200, 220, 600, 650C v2013_109RV), and 650C

HP DeskJet, 1200C, 1200C (PS), 310, 320, 500, 500C, 510, 520, 540, 550C, and 560C

HP DeskJet Plus, DeskJet Portable; DraftMaster I, II, MX, RX, and SX; and DraftPro

HP LaserJet 2000, 4, 4 Plus, 4L, 4/4M PS v2011_110, 4/4M Plus PS 300, and 4/4M Plus PS 600

HP LaserJet 4M, 4M Plus, 4ML, 4ML PS v2013_103, 4MP, 4MP v2013_103, 4MV, and 4P

HP LaserJet 4Si, 4Si Mx, 4Si/4Si Mx PS v2011, 4V/4MV (PS), 4V, 500 Plus, and Classic

HP LaserJet IID, IID v52_2, III, III v52_2, III Cartridge Plus, IIID, and IIID Cartridge Plus

HP LaserJet IIID v52_2, IIIP, IIIP Cartridge Plus, IIIP PS v52_2, and HP LaserJet IIISi PS v52_3

HP LaserJet IIISi, IIP Plus, IIP v52_2, IIP, Plus, and Series II

HP PaintJet, XL, XL300, GL/2 Color Printer, and XL300 PS v2011_112

IBM 2380 PPS II, 2381 PPS II, 2390 PPS II, 2390 PS/1, 2391 PPS II, and 3816-01D

IBM 3816-01S, 4019 LaserPrinter, 4019 LaserPrinter E, 4019 v52_1, and 4029

IBM 4029 LaserPrinter 10, 10L, 10P, 5E, 6, and 6P

IBM 4037 5E, 4039 LaserPrinter, 4039 LaserPrinter 10R plus, and 4039 LaserPrinter 10R

IBM 4039 LaserPrinter 12L, 12L plus, 12R, 12R plus, 16L, 16L plus, and plus

IBM 4070 IJ, 4072 ExecJet, 4076 ExecJet II, and 4079 Color Jetprinter PS

IBM 4201 Proprinter, II, and III; 4202 Proprinter XL, II XL, and III XL

IBM 4207 Proprinter X24 and X24E; 4208 Proprinter XL24 and XL24E

IBM 4216-031 v51_4 SheetFeed, 4224-01, 02, E3, and C2

IBM 4226 Model 302, 5183 Portable Printer, 5201 Quietwriter II, and 5202 QuietWriter III

IBM 5204 QuickWriter

IBM 6180, 6182, 6184, 6186-1, 6186-2, 7371, 7372, 7374, 7375-1, and 7375-2 Plotters

IBM Personal Page Printer, II-30, and II-31

Kyocera F-1000, F-1000A, 1800, 1800A, 2000A, 2200S, 3000A, 3300, 5000, and 5000A

Kyocera F-800, F-800A, F-820, P-2000, and Q-8010

Kyocera FS-1500, 1500A, 1550, 1550A, 3500, 3500A, 400, 400A, 5500, 5500A, 850, and 850A

Lexmark 4047 5E, 4076 Color, and WinWriter 600

Linotronic 100 v38_0, 100 v42_5, 200 v47_1, 200 v49_3, 300 v47_0, and 300 v47_1

Linotronic 300 v49_3 and 500 v49_3

NEC Colormate PS/40 and PS/80, LC-890, and Silentwriter 1097 v2013_109

NEC Silentwriter 95 v2010_121, 95fv2011_111, 97 v2011_111, and S62P v2010_121

Oki OL830-PS v52_5, OL840-PS v51_8, OL850-PS v52_5, and OL870 v2013_108

Okidata ML-192, ML-193, ML-320, ML-321, ML-3410, ML-380, ML-390, ML-391, ML-393

Okidata ML-393 Color, ML-395 Color, ML-395B, ML-520, ML-521, ML-590, and ML-591

Olivetti LP 5000

Panasonic KX-P1123, P1124, P1124i, P1150, P1180, P1191, P1624, P1654, P1695, and P2023

Panasonic KX-P2123, P2124, P2130, P2135, P2180, P2624, P3123, P3124, P3624, and P4400

Panasonic KX-P4401, P4410, P4420, P4430, P4440, P4450, P4450i, P4451, and P4455 v51_4

Panasonic KX-P5400 v2013_112 and P5410 39

Phaser Card v1_1

QMS 1060 Level 2, 1660 Level 2, 1725 Print System, 2025 Print System, and 3225 Print System

QMS 420 Print System, 4525 Print System, 860 Print System, and 860+ Print System

QMS ColorScript 100, 100 Mod 10, 100 Mod 30, 100 Mod 30si, 210, 230, and Laser 1000

QMS IS X320T, magicolor Laser Printer, PS 1500, PS 1700, PS 2000, PS 2200, and PS 2210

QMS-PS 2220, PS 410, PS 800 Plus, PS 800, PS 810 Turbo, PS 810, PS 815 MR, and PS 815

QMS-PS 820 Turbo, PS 820, PS 825 MR, and PS 825

Qume ScripTEN

Seiko ColorPoint PS Model 04, PS Model 14, PSN Model 14, and PSN Model 4

Seiko ColorPoint2 PSF; Personal ColorPoint PS, PSv241, and PSE; Prof_ColorPoint PSH

Silentwriter LC 890XL v50_5; Silentwriter2 290 v52_0, and Model 90 v52_2

Star LS-5 EX, LS-5, LS-5TT, LS5 TT, NX-1001, NX-1040R, NX-1500, NX-2415, and NX-2430

Star NX-2420R, Starjet SJ-144, Starjet SJ-48, XB-2420, XB-2425, XR-1020, and XR-1520

TI 2115 v47_0, MicroWriter, OmniLaser 2108, Omnilaser 2115, and microLaser PS17 v_52_1

TI microLaser PS35 v_52_1, Pro 600 L2 PS, XL PS17 v_52_1, and XL PS35 v_52_1

TI microLaser16, microLaser6, and microLaser9 Turbo v2010_119

TI microMarc Color and microWriter PS v_52_1

Tektronix Phaser 200J, 200e, 200i v2011_108, 220J v2013_113, 220e, and 220i v2013_113

Tektronix Phaser 300J v2013_113, 300i v2013_113, 440, 480, 480J, II PX v2_02, and II PXe

Tektronix Phaser II PXi v2010, II PXiJ, III PXi v2010, III PXiJ, IISD v2011, and IISDJ

Tektronix Phaser IISDX, PX, and PXi

Varityper VT-600

Wang LCS15 FontPlus and LCS15

Glossary

Access Control. The means by which network administrators restrict access to network resources.

Access Control List (ACL). A list associated with a network resource, which identifies all the users or groups who can access the resource and specifies each user's access rights.

Additional Server. A server other than the domain controller or backup domain controller in a LAN Server domain.

Administrator. A person responsible for maintaining the network.

Administrator Privilege. Privilege level assigned to network administrators, which allows full access to all resources in the domain.

Alert. An error message or warning sent to LAN Server users specified in IBMLAN.INI.

Alias. A nickname for a resource, which allows users to use the resource without specifying its server name.

Anynet/2. The product name for MPTS.

Application Programming Interface (API). A defined set of programming calls, usually in C Language, supplied by the product.

Apply. 1) A menu function in the LAN Server GUI, which puts modified settings into effect; 2) terminology used in OS/2 LAN Server for propagating a copy of the access control profile to all subdirectories below the directory in which the profile was created.

Asymmetrical Multiprocessing. The use of more than one processor in a computer by programs that do not attempt to evenly distribute their workload across the processors, for example, LAN Server 3.0 could run on one processor and interoperate with applications running on another.

Asynchronous. Common mode of data transmission, in which each character has a defined beginning and end, allowing each character to be transmitted independently.

Authorized Program Analysis Report (APAR). A tracking report used by IBM for customer-reported problems and associated code or hardware fixes.

BACKACC Utility. A LAN Server utility used to back up access control profile information.

Backbone Network. A network typically interconnecting individual LANs within a building or site.

Backup Domain Controller. A server designated to validate logon requests if the domain controller is busy, and take over management of the domain if the domain controller is offline.

Bits Per Second (bps). A measure of the transmission rate over a network medium.

Boot. *See Initial Program Load.*

Bridge. A device for interconnecting LANs, which allows the network to function as one large LAN.

Broadcast. To send a message to all workstations on a network rather than to a specific location.

Buffer. Temporary storage used for collecting data that is being processed. *See also cache.*

Bulletin Board Service (BBS). An Internet or other public network server where information is posted.

Byte. A unit of digital information, such as a character, usually consisting of 8 bits. *See also kilobyte, megabyte, and gigabyte.*

Cache. Memory that is allocated to provide faster access to data. Data can be accessed much faster from cache than from disk storage, so data accessed from storage is copied into a cache in case it is needed again.

Capacity. Peak workload that can be sustained by a computer, network, device, or individual component.

Carrier Sense Multiple Access with Collision Detection (CSMA/CD). The method used in Ethernet for controlling access for transmission over the network.

Central Processing Unit (CPU). The computer chips and board that provide the ability to process instructions.

Cheapernet. *See 10Base-2.*

Client. A computer that accesses shared network resources made available by other computers running as servers or peers; requester.

Client/Server Computing. The division of an application into two parts, where one is processed on a shared server and the other on client workstations.

Coaxial Cable. A cable consisting of a central wire surrounded by plastic insulation and then a second jacket of fine wire screening.

Code Server. A server that contains the source files for installation and maintenance of network clients.

Command Line Interface. The DOS or OS/2 command prompt at which commands are entered.

CONFIG.SYS. A file located in the root directory of OS/2 workstations, which is used to initialize device drivers and set the program environment when the workstation is started.

Configuration/Installation/Distribution (CID). A set of programs included with the LAN Server transport, which allows workstations to be installed from a code server.

Controlled Access Unit (CAU). An improved version of a media access unit that can attach up to 80 devices on a Token-Ring network to form a hub.

CPU Utilization. The percentage of total CPU capacity (or work capability) being used over a given period of time.

Cybernet. Another popular term for the global network.

Dedicated Server. On a network, a workstation that functions only as a server, not as both a requester and a server.

Device Driver. Code that controls input and output from a device, such as a NIC or printer.

Device Queue. An ordered list of device requests routed one at a time to a serial device or device pool.

Direct Access Storage Device (DASD). Hard disk or hard disk space.

Disk Duplexing. A fault-tolerant feature in which data is duplicated across two hard disks controlled by separate disk controllers.

Disk Mirroring. A fault-tolerant feature in which data is duplicated across two hard disks.

Distributed Computing Environment (DCE). An architecture that provides common services, such as directory, security, printer support, file system, interprocess control, and time synchronization for large heterogenous networks.

Domain. A group of servers that interoperate to provide resources as a single pool for requesters.

Domain Controller (DC). A server on the domain, defined as the primary server, which is designated to manage the domain.

Domain Control Database (DCDB). A LAN Server database that resides on the domain controller and contains information on shared resources, accounts, and logon assignments within the domain.

DOS LAN Requester (DLR). LAN Server 3.0 Requester provided for DOS and Windows.

DOS LAN Services (DLS). LAN Server 4.0 Requester provided for DOS and Windows.

Electronic Mail (E-Mail). Transmission and reception of text-based information between computers or other electronic devices.

Ethernet. A common type of LAN that operates at 10 Mbps and transmits signals via broadcasts.

Extended Memory Block (EMB). A section of memory mapped above the 640KB base memory line in DOS systems.

File Allocation Table (FAT). A file system used by DOS and OS/2.

File Server. A computer attached to a LAN, usually running a network operating system that allows clients access to shared files.

File System. The collection of files and file management structures on a physical or logical mass storage device, such as a hard disk.

First Failure Support Technology/2 (FFST/2). The LAN Server component that LAN Server and other applications use for problem determination and reporting.

Gigabyte (Gbyte or GB). 2^{30} or 1,073,741,824 bytes.

Graphical User Interface (GUI). Method of supporting user interaction with a computer using windows, icons, menus, and pointers rather than keyboard commands.

Group Account. A LAN Server account created for multiple users with an associated set of resources and privileges.

High-Performance File System (HPFS). An installable file system supplied by OS/2 Warp.

High-Performance File System 386 (HPFS386). An installable file system supplied by the Advanced version of LAN Server that replaces the Warp-supplied HPFS and provides faster access to shared files.

Hub. The device at the center of a star-shaped network, which provides functions for repeating signals and managing the medium.

IBMLAN.INI. The LAN Server initialization file that contains network parameters for configuring an OS/2 requester or server.

IEEE 802.2. A standard interface for logical link control defined by the Institute for Electronics and Electrical Engineers.

Initial Program Load (IPL). The initialization procedure that starts an operating system; boot.

Integrated Services Digital Network (ISDN). Digital successor to the analog public telephone network; capable of handling digital data without requiring a modem.

Internet. A worldwide public network containing tens of thousands of computers in government, business, and education.

Kernel. The base services portion of the OS/2 Warp operating system.

Kilobits (Kbit or Kb). 1,000 bits; often used as a unit in data transmission rates.

Kilobyte (Kbyte or KB). 1,024 bytes.

Local Area Network (LAN). A network of computers governed by strict rules over distance, control of access, and structure; which enables resources, data, and applications to be shared between multiple end users.

LAN Adapter and Protocol Support (LAPS). The transport code first provided in LAN Server 2.0 that is a subset of NTS/2 and MPTS.

LAN Distance. A remote LAN access product developed and marketed by IBM.

LAN Manager. A network operating system for OS/2 developed but no longer supported by Microsoft.

LAN Support Program (LSP). DOS transport software used to provide an interface between DOS LAN Requester and the network hardware.

LANtastic. A peer-to-peer network operating system for small networks from Artisoft.

Local Security. The LAN Server Advanced feature that protects files on the server from unauthorized local access.

Logical. Something that emulates a behavior that may or may not reflect its physical dimensions or appearance. An example is a logical drive letter that is used to access a resource on the network, not a physical hard disk on the local machine.

Logical Drive. A drive letter assigned to a shared resource on another workstation that allows the resource to be accessed as if it were on another local drive.

Log On. To enter a user name and password at a requester to enable access to the network.

Logon Assignments. Resources that are preassigned to be automatically accessed immediately following logon.

Loopback Driver. A LAN Server component that enables a server to emulate network operations without being connected to the network; used for test purposes.

Low Memory. First 640 Kbytes of addressable memory.

Media Access Control (MAC). The bottom half of OSI layer 2, the datalink layer, which controls access to the physical medium.

Megabyte (Mbyte or MB). 2^{20} or 1,048,576 bytes.

Messenger Service. A LAN Server service that allows users to send and receive messages.

Modem (Modulator/Demodulator). Device used by computers to transmit digital data over analog telephone lines.

Multiprotocol Transport Support (MPTS). The transport provided by LAN Server 4.0, which includes TCP/IP sockets and NetBIOS over TCP/IP support.

Multistation Access Unit (MAU). A wiring concentrator for Token Ring LANs supporting attachment of up to eight workstations in a star-shape cluster. Multiple MAUs can be connected together to support additional workstations in a single LAN segment.

Multitasking. Capability of operating system to run multiple tasks simultaneously. Preemptive multitasking implies dynamically scheduling tasks to allow those with highest priority at a given time to run.

NET.ACC. The LAN Server file that contains the user accounts database.

NetBEUI. An extension of NetBIOS that provides added efficiency and performance.

NetBIOS (Network Binary Input Output System). The most widely used transport for LANs.

Netlogon Service. The LAN Server service that allows servers on the domain to receive updates to the NET.ACC, which is maintained by the domain controller.

NetName. The name used in conjunction with the server name to identify a resource on the network when it is shared.

NetPopUp Service. A LAN Server Version 3.0 OS/2 LAN Requester service that causes messages to be displayed on the screen when they are received.

NetRun Service. The LAN Server service that allows applications to be shared by running a program on behalf of another workstation.

NetWare. A family of Network Operating Systems from Novell.

Network Adapter. *See Network Interface Card.*

Network-Aware. Applications and devices that support name and address extensions to allow their use over the network.

Network Driver Interface Specification (NDIS). An API that allows DOS and OS/2 systems to support multiple network interface cards and protocol stacks.

Network Interface Card (NIC). The card that fits into the expansion slot of a workstation or other device to provide a connection to the network.

Network Operating System (NOS). The software that controls operation of the server and administers all functions of the network.

Network Transport Services/2 (NTS/2). The transport service provided with LAN Server 3.0.

Operator. An assistant designated by a LAN Server administrator and set up with a specific Operator privilege level to manage user accounts or LAN Server resources.

OS/2. A 32-bit preemptive multitasking operating system currently marketed by IBM as OS/2 Warp.

OS/2 Peer. An OS/2 LAN Requester-based product packaged with Warp Connect, which allows OS/2 workstations to share resources and access shared resources on other OS/2 Peer and LAN Server workstations.

Parameter. A variable that can be adjusted to control the way a software or hardware product works. Parameters are used to customize configurations and tune performance to a specific environment.

Partition. A subdivision of a hard disk that is created with the FDISK utility.

Password. In LAN Server, a sequence of 14 or fewer characters known only to the user, which is authenticated with the user ID as a security measure to protect against unauthorized access to the network.

Peer Network. A network where resources and communications are exchanged directly between user workstations, rather than accessed from a server.

Peer Service. Service provided on LAN Server DOS and OS/2 Requesters for sharing resources with a single remote user.

Permission. The setting associated with users and shared resources that determines who can use the resource and how the resource can be used.

Pop-Up Menu. A menu within the graphical user interface, which appears when an item is selected using mouse button 2.

Primary Partition. The partition on a hard disk that contains the operating system and is active when the computer is started.

Printer Queue. An ordered list of print jobs waiting to access a printer.

Private Application. A shared application that is added to a user's logon assignments by the user.

Privilege. The right or authority to perform certain administrative functions.

Protocol. Rules governing the form that data takes when transmitted across a network, and how the data is interpreted by the receiver.

Public Application. A shared application that is added to a user's logon assignments by an administrator.

Random Access Memory (RAM). Volatile memory installed in the computer, which allows programs and information to be loaded and cached.

Remote Initial Program Load (RIPL). The ability to start a requester using an operating system, applications, and network services supplied by a server; also known as *remote boot*.

Remote IPL Service. The LAN Server service that supports remote IPL for DOS and OS/2 workstations; also known as *remote boot service*.

Remote LAN Access. The ability for a client to access a network operating system's server via a dial-up telephone link or other remote connection.

Remote Program Execution. The process of running a program on a server but initiating the program from a requester.

Repeater. A device that increases either the span of a LAN or the distance between devices attached to a LAN by reconstructing the signal.

Replicator Service. The LAN Server service that maintains identical copies of selected directories and files on multiple workstations.

Requester. *See Client.*

Requester Service. The LAN Server service that allows a workstation to access shared resources.

Resource. Files, applications, and access to printers, modems, and other serial devices.

Ring 0. Within the Intel processor architecture, Ring 0 is a service level used by the OS/2 kernel and device drivers.

Ring 3. Within the Intel processor architecture, Ring 3 is a protected service level used by applications.

Server. A computer that provides and controls access to resources on a network.

Server Message Block (SMB). The data format used by LAN Server to send and receive network commands.

Server Service. The LAN Server service that allows a workstation to share its resources with other workstations across the network.

Shielded Twisted Pair. Twisted-pair cable shielded from electrical interference by a wire gauze mesh.

Single System Image. The appearance to a user that all network resources and applications are being accessed from the user's own workstation; also described as *network transparency*.

Software Licensing. The practice of purchasing licenses to legally use software provided on an application server, instead of purchasing multiple copies of the software package.

Spooler (Simultaneous Peripheral Operation Online). The code that processes a print job and queues it for printing.

Symmetrical Multiprocessing. The use of more than one processor in a computer by programs that attempt to evenly distribute their workload across the processors.

Synchronous Transmission. Communication of data in blocks without the use of individual start and stop bits for synchronizing the beginning and end of each byte.

System. A term to describe any entity or group of entities that interoperate as one.

TCP/IP. A suite of protocols originally developed by the US Department of Defense, which has since gained increasing popularity as a wide area network transport.

Token Ring. A LAN type in which use of the network for transmitting data is controlled by possession of a token that is continuously passed around a logical ring from workstation to workstation.

Topology. Term to describe the structure of a network and how data flows within it; for example, ring, bus, or star.

Trace. A record of data that provides a history of events that occurred in a system.

Transport. The fourth layer of the OSI model; more loosely defined as the code that routes information between applications and the network.

Twisted Pair. Cable in which pairs of copper wire are twisted together to reduce electrical interference.

Uninterruptible Power Supply (UPS). A battery that sits between the main power supply and one or more computing devices that provide backup power in case of an outage.

Universal Address (UA). An address provided on a network interface card, which is guaranteed to be unique by the card manufacturer.

Universal Naming Convention (UNC). A syntax for names on a network, which allows the location of resources to be specified by a user or administrator.

Unshielded Twisted Pair. Twisted-pair cabling without any form of shielding.

User Accounts Database. The database contained in the NET.ACC file, which stores information about LAN Server users, what resources they are allowed to access, and what permissions they have been granted.

User ID. An ID, unique to the network, that is used to identify a LAN Server user.

User Profile Management (UPM). A LAN Server component that provides logon and user management facilities as well as support for single logon across multiple servers and domains.

Virtual. Something, like beauty, that exists only in the eye of the beholder; an illusion.

Wide Area Network (WAN). A network capable of spanning a greater distance than a LAN by use of telephone or other services.

10Base-2. An inexpensive version of Ethernet using thin coaxial cable.

10Base-5. A version of Ethernet using thick coaxial cable.

10Base-T. A version of Ethernet using unshielded twisted-pair cabling.

INDEX